1980

The
Developing
Child

HARPER & ROW, PUBLISHERS
New York, Hagerstown, San Francisco, London

The Developing Child SECOND EDITION

Helen Bee

University of Washington

For George, Rex and Arwen

Sponsoring Editor: George A. Middendorf
Project Editor: Cynthia Hausdorff
Designer: Emily Harste
Production Supervisor: Kewal K. Sharma
Photo Researcher: Myra Schachne
Compositor: Progressive Typographers, Inc.
Printer and Binder: The Murray Printing Company
Art Studio: Eric G. Heiber Associates Inc.
Illustrator: Stephen Laughlin

THE DEVELOPING CHILD
Second Edition

Library of Congress Cataloging in Publication Data

Bee, Helen L   Date—
    The developing child.

    Includes bibliographies and index.
    1. Child development.   I. Title.
RJ131.B36 1978   155.4   77-22042
ISBN 0-06-040583-X

Contents

15.54
B412

Preface xi

90237

vi

PHOTO CREDITS

Preface

Someone told me recently that the second edition of a textbook is always the best; certainly writing it has been a great deal more *fun* than writing the first. People using the book—both professors and students—have reacted in all sorts of ways to what I wrote the first time, and I have had a chance to respond to these reactions in this second edition. It is also a treat to go back to read some passage written three or four years ago and discover that it is not only still true, but that I wrote it rather well! Such literary M&Ms are counterbalanced, of course, by all those other passages that make me wince on rereading or that have become outdated by new material. The searching for new material, too, has its pleasures. At least with a second edition one doesn't have to go back to the beginning of time, but can read instead only the most recent research and theory, some of which is extremely fascinating. Research in developmental psychology over the past three years has become enormously sophisticated methodologically, but also much more intriguing theoretically. So there has been much to explore and muse about, and quite a lot of factual updating has been necessary. The whole process has been enjoyable, and I am convinced that this edition is an improvement.

The major change—other than the extensive revision and updating of factual content—has been to include the material on sex differences and social class differences in each chapter, rather than covering these topics in separate chapters at the end. Many users of the book reported that it was disjointed to have this material in separate chapters, and on rereading I agreed with them. So the material is interlaced. The chapter on aging has also been omitted, not because I do not think this is an important topic, but because I felt I could not really do justice to it in a single chapter. Otherwise, the basic content and organization are similar.

My major purposes are also the same. This edition, like the first, is informal in style and written in the first person. I have always disliked the formal, academic style of writing, with its heavy use of the passive voice and the royal "we." I wanted you to feel as if this book is really me speaking to you, so I have not only used the first person, I have also used personal examples and shared my biases and thinking with you as well. I have tried at the same time to keep the material brief enough so that the book could be a *starting point* for a course, and not an encyclopedia. I have assumed that some students will want more detail and have suggested some good sources for next steps at the end of each chapter. The projects have also been retained, since I am still convinced that it is important for students to see and work with some real children in the course of reading this book or taking a course in developmental psychology.

Some other comments on the use of language in this edition are in order. Over the past several years I have become increasingly conscious about the way language is used and misused. I worry about the loss of the noble adverb in our common speech. And I worry about the hidden—and sometimes not so hidden—messages in the words we choose. I know how to avoid the more obvious forms of sexism, but how is one to avoid *some* kind of "sexism" in the language in this or any other book? In the English language, unless you are willing to call all children "it," the standard child must be either a he or a she. I experimented at one point with alternating back and forth, but this proved confusing to the reader. My solution, which I admit is unorthodox, has been to use the feminine pronouns throughout in place of the customary male pronouns. So the standard child in this book is a she, not a he. Some of the readers of the first edition (including some women) accused me of reverse sexism; most readers found they forgot about the usage after a few pages. My point in doing this is simply to even the score a bit. Since every other book I know of (including my own first book) uses male pronouns, I thought it was time to balance the scale. See what you think.

I have experimented with other new versions of words as well, sometimes successfully, sometimes not. I have used the word *caregiver* rather than *caretaker* throughout the book, since I think caregiver is a better descriptive term. I have tried to use the word *parent* instead of *mother* when either parent is or could be involved, although I suspect I have slipped up a few times on that one. Part of the problem is that most research on parent-child interaction involves the study of only the mother, so in describing such research, inevitably I have used the word *mother* rather than *parent*. Finally, I tried my best to avoid using that truly dreadful word, *interpersonal*, but as you will see in the table of contents, I have failed. I found that there were no good synonyms that were not just as "jargon-y," and avoiding the word altogether led me into such tortured sentences that I finally gave up. My apologies.

My thanks to my several anonymous reviewers who have been so diligent and helpful at every stage of this revision. Thanks, too, to the students and faculty members using the book who sent in unsolicited comments and suggestions. I think that this edition is greatly improved because of them.

But again, as before, my greatest thanks go to my husband, George, and to my children, who managed not only to stay out of my hair while I was working, but to be supportive and helpful throughout.

H. B.

1

**Basic
Processes**

Several years ago while I was out working in the yard, my then-4-year-old daughter wanted to race me—she on her tricycle and I pushing a full wheelbarrow. When we arrived at the compost pile at the end of the race, she announced in an excited voice, "I beated you! I beated you!" Surely this was a perfectly ordinary encounter with a child. But there's at least one fascinating puzzle involved. Why did she say "beated" instead of "beat"? Was this a simple error that she had picked up from someone around her? It couldn't be. No one I know says "beated." And this was not the only such "mistake" she made then: she also said "winned," "sing-ed," and "boughted." So she was doing something consistently that she couldn't have learned from listening to anyone. As it turns out, most children learning English make the same "error," at least for a period of time. Where does this consistent error come from? Why do so many children make the same kind of error? How does a child learn to talk, anyway? The simple and obvious answer is that she hears other people talking and "imitates" them. But that can't be the answer, or at least not all of it, for my daughter never heard anyone say "beated." Listen to a 2-year-old some time and you'll encounter sentences like, "Me like," "Johnny up," and "Allgone sticky." *I* don't say things like that, and I presume you don't. So where do they come from? And why do all children apparently construct the same kinds of "mistakes"?

Let me give you another puzzle. The Russian poet Kornei Chukofsky has collected a whole book full of really delightful conversations with children and children's questions and sayings. One child asked, "Daddy, when you were little, were you a boy or a girl?" My own daughter, at about age 4, asked if she would be a boy when she grew up. We're so used to thinking of children as being boys or girls, and we understand so clearly that we are stuck with the sex we are born with, that it seems incredible that the child doesn't recognize this fact of life. But until about age 3 or 4 most children have *not* figured out their own sex, or if they have a label for it, they haven't figured out that they stay the same sex forever. But by age 6 or 7 the child has a very firm notion of her own gender and the constancy of it. When I recently asked my daughter (now 8) if she could be a boy when she grew up, her reply was a disgusted "Oh Mother!" But what brings about this change, and what are the implications of the child's understanding of her own gender?

There is an almost unlimited number of other questions, equally fascinating, about children and about the process of development. Why do so many children, quite suddenly at about 10 months of age, begin to be afraid of strangers? Why are children who grow faster also somewhat brighter? Why are some infants (and some children and adults) placid and easy to relate to, while others are fussy and active and difficult to have around? There are questions with important social implications as well. What is the effect of day care or other separation of the child from the mother in the early years? Should mothers of young children work, or is it important that they stay at home in the early years? How does aggression on television affect children's aggressiveness with each other or toward adults? What is the effect on a child of growing up with only a single parent?

Obviously, I could go on endlessly giving you examples of puzzles and questions about children and their development. In fact, this entire book is full of questions—many of which we don't yet have answers to. But perhaps the few I have given here will suggest the flavor of the book. I want, in this book, to share with you my own enthusiasm for and fascination with those amazing creatures, human children. How do they develop? Why do they turn out as they do? How are they all alike and how do they differ from one another? Where do these differences come from? How do they learn? *What* do they learn? I don't know the answers to all of these questions, but I will ask them, tell you about what we do know, and puzzle with you over those questions to which the answers are incomplete. If, after completing the book, you have become a more skillful "child watcher," I will have succeeded in one of my goals.

At the same time I want to sensitize you a bit to the social and political issues that are embedded in all of the information about children's development. Legislators and other policy makers have begun to ask developmental psychologists some tough questions about programs for children, and we have rarely had good answers. But in the past five years or so, there has been a marked increase in interest on the part of psychologists in the problems of applying research information to social policy problems. I will try to highlight some of the issues throughout the book.

Finally, I would like you to come away from reading this book with the information and analytic skills that will permit you to tackle new problems and puzzles that you may encounter long after you finish this course or this book. In doing that, I'll be posing two very broad questions about each topic we take up.

1. The "What" Question. What does the child do? What can we observe her doing? What can she be taught to do? For example, when I discuss newborn babies, I will begin by asking what the infant can do. Can she talk? No. Can she see? Yes, but how much? Can she tell the difference between her mother's face and someone else's? Nearly any mother will insist that her baby "knows" her practically from the beginning. But, in fact, the baby probably can't make this discrimination for several months.

The first task, then, is always one of description. The better the description, the more likely we are to be able to understand why the child behaves as she does.

2. The "Why" Question. Once we have described the behavior of children, we still have to explain *why* they behave as they do. To go back to my original example, I not only want to know *that* children say "boughted" and "beated," I want to know *why*.[1]

In answering the "why" question, we will nearly always be trying to decide whether the behavior we see in the child happens or comes about because of something in the environment (some experience or specific training the child has had), because of something inside the child (physical growth, unique genetic makeup, thinking), or because of some combinations or interaction of internal and environmental forces. For the sake of convenience, let me divide the vast array of possible explanations so that we can look at them individually:

Internal Factors
heredity: the child's individual inheritance from her parents
maturation: the unfolding of unlearned patterns of development that
    are the same for all children

External Factors
general environmental influences: for example, diet or "enrichment"
specific learning: for example, acquisition of vocabulary words and
    learning to eat with silverware

Interactions
between internal and external factors

Let me discuss each of these factors in turn.

INTERNAL INFLUENCES
Heredity

Barring genetic anomalies, each child receives 23 chromosomes from her mother and 23 from her father. At the moment of conception these 46 chromosomes combine to form 23 pairs, which are then duplicated in each new cell as development takes place.

One pair of chromosomes is responsible for determining the sex of the child. In the normal female each of the chromosomes in this pair is large and under a microscope bears some resemblance to an X; in the male there is only one X chromosome and one smaller Y chromosome. Unlike other body cells, each of which contains all 23 *pairs* of chromosomes, the sperm cells and ova contain only 23 chromosomes, one from each chromosome pair. The ova will always contain an X chro-

---

[1] I should point out that there is some risk in phrasing my questions with the word "why." It is easy to use "why" questions to get far beyond the rather simple level of explanation I am after here. One can ask, for example, "why does language exist at all?" This sort of "why" question takes us well beyond psychology, into the realms of religion and philosophy, where I do not want to go (at least not in this book.) But I do want to ask why in a narrower sense. Why does a child begin to talk at age 1 and not before? Why do children all over the world show similar patterns in their early language development? You may find similar questions phrased with "how" rather than "why," such as: "how do children learn to talk?" I will use the word "how" in this way at various places in the book. The point to keep in mind, regardless of the word that is used, is that beyond the level of description, there is still the problem of explanation, and we will have to address that problem throughout the book.

mosome, since the mother has only X chromosomes, but the sperm may carry either an X or a Y, depending on which half of the sex-chromosome pair occurred in that particular sperm. If the sperm that fertilizes the ovum carries an X chromosome, then the child receives X from the mother and from the father and will be a girl (XX). If the sperm fertilizing the ovum carries a Y chromosome, then the combination is XY, and the infant will be a boy.

GENES

Each chromosome is made up of thousands of *genes,* each of which contains part of the "information" that makes up the genetic blueprint for growth and development. The genes themselves are composed of a chemical called *deoxyribonucleic acid*—the famous DNA. In the late 1940s and early 1950s, there was considerable ferment among biolo-

FIGURE 1
Schematic diagram of the double helix; the hypothesized structure of the DNA molecule. (Source: G. E. McClearn. Genetic influences on behavior and development. In P. H. Mussen (Ed.), *Carmichael's manual of child psychology* **(Vol. 1, 3rd ed.). New York: Wiley, 1970, p. 57.)**

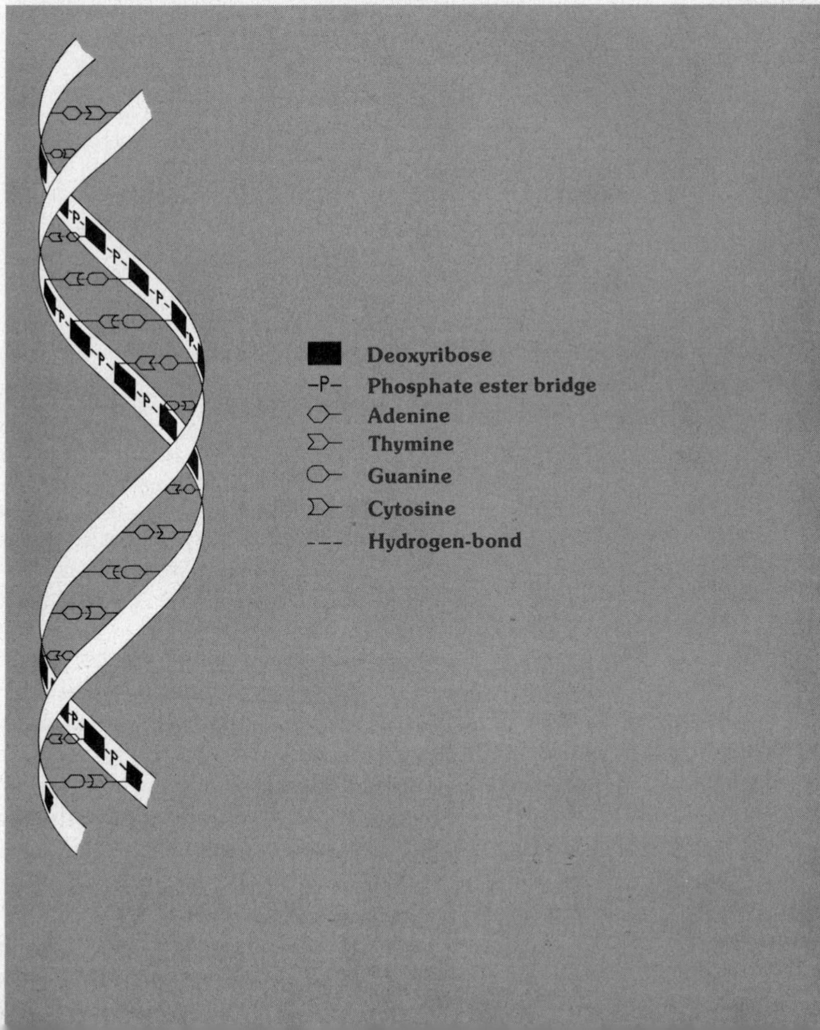

■ Deoxyribose
–P– Phosphate ester bridge
◯– Adenine
▷– Thymine
◯– Guanine
▷– Cytosine
--- Hydrogen-bond

BOX 1
Some Common Questions and
Misconceptions About Heredity

Why Aren't All Children Born to a Particular Set of Parents the Same? If you get 23 chromosomes from your mother and 23 from your father, why don't you look just like your sister or brother? The answer, of course, is that you don't get the *same* 23 chromosomes from your mother and the same 23 chromosomes from your father as does your sibling. Each ova or sperm cell contains a different combination of 23 chromosomes, so each of your brothers and sisters will receive from your parents a unique combination. Because the number of possible combinations is *very* large, it is not only possible, it is virtually inevitable that two children in the same family will have different inheritances.

What About Twins? The exception to this "rule" is in the case of identical twins, who come from the *same* fertilized ovum. In such cases the ovum for some reason divides into two distinct entities *after* it has been fertilized by the sperm; each of the two developing organisms then has the *same* genetic material in the same combination, and the two children should turn out to be alike in all those areas influenced by the genetic codes. Fraternal twins, on the other hand, are genetically just like any pair of brothers or sisters. Each develops from a separate ovum, fertilized by a separate sperm. Since some women ovulate more than once in a given month (particularly if the woman has been taking some kinds of fertility drugs), more than one ovum is available for fertilization, and more than one child may thus be conceived. The difference in the origin of identical and fraternal twins has been used by researchers as a way of exploring genetic influences. Identical twins, since they share a common genetic makeup, should be more similar to one another than are fraternal twins on all characteristics affected by heredity. So if you want to see if some behavior or trait is partially influenced by genetics, one way to go about it is to compare the amount of similarity between identical and fraternal twins. If the identical twins are more like each other than are the fraternal twins, then there is a very good chance that you are dealing with a characteristic that has been influenced by the genetic code.

Why Are There Some Physical Characteristics That Seem to Run in Families? I have made quite a point of the fact that brothers and sisters—except for identical twins—do not share exactly the same heritage. But if this is true why is it often the case that a particular facial feature, a distinctive nose, a particular eye or hair color, or some other characteristic occurs in all or many of the children in a given family? The answer lies in the "pecking order" among genes. Imagine that you receive a chromosome that contains a gene for blue eyes from your mother and one that contains a gene for brown eyes from your father. Who wins? What color do you have? Muddy blue? No. In this case you would have brown eyes, because brown is *dominant*. It turns out that in many gene pairs there is a clear hierarchy. Some genes always dominate over others, which are called *recessive*. A recessive trait simply will not occur unless both controlling genes—that is, from the mother and from the father—carry it. Since blue eyes are determined by a recessive gene, the only way you can have them is to receive one blue-eyed gene from your father and one from your mother. So, if either mother or father has a distinctive feature that is carried on a dominant gene, then each child who receives that gene will show that trait.

gists and chemists who were trying to discover the molecular composition of DNA. The scientists were convinced that if they could understand the makeup of these molecules, they would be much closer to understanding the process of genetic transmission. The model proposed in 1953 by Watson and Crick has served that function admirably.

Watson and Crick suggested that the DNA molecule was in the shape of a double helix—a kind of twisted ladder, as shown in Figure 1.

Identical and fraternal twins. Identical twins, having the same genetic patterning, look alike; fraternal twins are no more alike than any pair of brothers or sisters.

The outer portions of the ladder (the uprights) are made up of sugars and phosphates, while the rungs of the ladder are made up of four different chemicals called *bases*. Each rung consists of a pair of the bases. But not all possible combinations of the four bases occur; only two types of pairs occur, with *adenine* always occuring with *thymine,* and *guanine* always appearing with *cytosine.* But although the number of combinations of bases on the rungs is restricted, the number of different orders in which the rungs may occur is virtually unlimited, and it is apparently in this way that the genetic information is carried.

One of the great advantages of this model is that it helps to explain how the genetic information is passed from one cell to another in the process of growth. Because the bases always occur in the same pairings, the whole ladder can "unzip" in the middle and then duplicate itself. In this way each new cell contains precisely the same information as did the original cell.

WHAT DO GENES INFLUENCE?

I have talked about the genes as containing information, or a code. But what kind of information is contained? What sorts of behaviors, processes, or skills are mapped out in some way in the genes?

Genes affect the ways in which we are both like and unlike one another. A very large percentage of genes carry information that is the same from one human being to another. It is this set of instructions that makes us distinctively human, as opposed to, say, anthropoid or feline. We all have genetic instructions for prenatal developmental sequences and patterns, and for many bodily processes and changes over the life span. We all have genetic instructions for eyes and nose and ears, and for the development and formation of the nervous system.

But a smaller set of genes contains information that varies from one of us to the next, and these differences are one of the sources of the enormous variability among human beings. While all of us share genetic instructions for the sequence and form of body growth, we differ in instructions about such things as how tall we will be, and what eye color, hair color, facial features, or balding patterns we will have. A host of other physical characteristics are affected quite directly by genes as well.

Beyond these obvious physical differences, there is less agreement among psychologists about the behaviors or skills affected by genetic differences. There is good evidence that some aspects of intellectual skill are affected in some way by hereditary differences. I'll be discussing this evidence in some detail in Chapter 10, so I don't want to repeat myself here. But I do want to emphasize that no psychologist, and certainly no geneticist, has suggested that one inherits in any direct sense the ability to answer specific questions on tests. But we undoubtedly *do* inherit a collection of tendencies, which influence such things as the speed with which our nervous system carries messages or the rate of body or brain growth, and these in turn may affect the child's rate of learning. Geneticists estimate that the number of separate genes likely involved in the intellectual skills is on the order of 20 or 30, so the process is obviously a complex one.

There is less agreement about genetic influences on personality characteristics, although this has been an area in which there has been a good deal of interest lately. To take just one example—to give you a feeling for the sort of research and thinking in the area—let me look briefly at the work on inheritance of schizophrenia (a particular sort of mental illness). A number of researchers have found that identical twins—those who have the same genetic inheritance—are much more likely either to be *both* schizophrenic or *neither* schizophrenic than is true for fraternal twins. That is, if one identical twin is schizophrenic, the other is fairly likely to be also, while for fraternal twins, knowing that one is schizophrenic doesn't help you very much in predicting whether the other will be as well. (Incidentally, this does *not* mean that individuals who are identical twins are more likely to be schizophrenic; only that the pair tend to be *like* one another in mental health.) Irving Gottesman has suggested that what may be inherited is some *threshold* for responding to stress or tension with some kind of emotional disturbance. Identical twins would thus inherit the same threshold, and if they experienced similar above-threshold life stresses, they both would be likely to develop schizophrenia (or some other illness). But if one twin experienced a much higher level of stress or tension or other "triggering" experience than the other, then only that twin would be likely to develop the illness.

The notion that we may inherit not absolute traits or responses, but thresholds of various kinds, has opened a whole new series of doors in our understanding of potential genetic influences. We may well inherit a whole series of tendencies, which remain latent unless or until some particular sort of experience or cumulation of experiences triggers the behavior.

Bear in mind that the whole question of potential genetic influences on behaviors other than physical characteristics and intellectual skills is still very much in debate. But the breakthroughs in the chemistry and biology of genetic transmission, and in our thinking about the ways in which genes might influence behavior, may lead to far greater insights in this entire field over the next decades.

Maturation

The word *maturation* refers to those internally determined patterns of change in such things as body size, shape, and skill that begin at conception and continue until death. The "instructions" for the unfolding sequences of development are presumably part of the genetic code. So, in a sense I am talking here about a subset of genetic influences. But by convention, the term *heredity* is usually used when we are talking about those genetic characteristics on which we *differ* from one another (eye color, height, body build, intelligence, and so forth), while *maturation* refers to those genetic blueprints that produce similar patterns of growth and change in all of us.

Maturationally determined development, in its pure form, occurs regardless of practice or training. For example, as you will see in Chapter 3, most of the growth of the fetus in the womb is governed by maturation: Changes in body shape, the development of the organs, and so on all occur without intervention (other than nourishment) from the outside. But maturationally governed development does not stop at birth. The development of skills in crawling, walking, running, and climbing are also acquired in a *sequence* and appear to be at least partially the result of internal, physiological changes.

I want to emphasize, however, that there are very few cases of pure maturation in which practice or experience makes *no* difference. The maturational developments that lead to an infant's ability to crawl can be enormously slowed down by an unstimulating or improperly stimulating environment. In one famous study of orphanages in Iran by Wayne Dennis, children who spent their infancy lying on their backs, and who rarely had the opportunity to lie on their stomachs and thus practice the movements that come before crawling, were extremely slow in learning to crawl. They did crawl eventually, but the maturational timetable was apparently slowed by environmental forces.

But even though there are few cases of pure maturational influence, it is still important for you to understand that not all changes in behavior you may see in a child necessarily result from outside influence. The child's behavior may also change because of some internal alteration in her nervous system, muscles, heart, or other organs. Such internal changes may occur in a particular sequence according to a code contained in the genes.

There is one other possible point of confusion about the term maturation that I should touch on. The word maturation is often used as a synonym for the word *growth*, but they do not mean exactly the same thing. Growth refers to some kind of step-by-step change in quantity, as in size. We speak of the growth of the child's vocabulary or the growth of her body. Such changes in quantity *may* result from maturation, but not necessarily. A child's body may increase in size because her diet has changed, which would be an external influence, or because of a change in the size or makeup of her bones and muscles, which is likely to be an internal, maturationally governed change. Or the growth could be a product of both internal and external influences operating simultaneously.

The child's unique genetic makeup and the genetic map or timetable we see as maturational change create a kind of framework, but the details that fill in that framework are functions of experience, not of inheritance.

EXTERNAL INFLUENCES How can we make some sense out of the vast numbers of experiences encountered by a child from the moment of conception? It is reasonably straightforward to deal with internal factors, especially since some of the mysteries of the genetic system are now beginning to be understood. But understanding or describing the ways in which the environment influences a child is a great deal harder. Psychologists have gone about dealing with this problem in a variety of ways. One

10

strategy has been to ask just what kinds of environmental variations make a difference. In a sense this approach simply calls for further description—it is like asking other "what" questions. For example, what is the effect of poverty on a child? What is the effect of being in an institution such as an orphanage? What is the effect of being reared without a father or without a mother? What is the effect of insufficient protein in the diet? In each case we are comparing children from one kind of environment with children from another kind and asking whether they turn out the same or differently and, if differently, in what ways. Research based on such questions has given us an enormous amount of useful information about the kinds of major environmental forces that will have an effect on a child. We even know something about the kinds of effects we are likely to see—that a child who gets too little protein is likely to do poorly in school and be shorter; that a child raised in an unstimulating orphanage environment is likely to be slow in talking, slow in walking, and generally retarded in development; and so on. We are only just beginning in this line of research to go on to the "why" questions. Why does orphanage rearing have the effects that it does? Why do children with poor diets do poorly in school? Why do children raised in poverty environments have school difficulties as well? Simple answers do not emerge instantly (or even over the long haul) from questions of this kind, but as we collect and combine results, we will have a better and better picture of the mechanisms by which the environment influences the child's development.

A second, altogether different strategy has been used by a great many American developmental psychologists who have addressed the question of environmental influence. They begin by asking a different kind of "why" question: Why does the child's behavior change at all? We see that a 2-year-old can form single two-word sentences (such as, "Sarah up" or "I going"). Why does she change? Why does she go on to form three-, four-, and five-word sentences? The 2-year-old may eat with her fingers. Why does she change and use a spoon or fork, as pictured in Figure 2?

I have already discussed one of the possible answers to this question: maturation. Perhaps the child's behavior changes because of some internal changes. Perhaps there have been changes in the nervous system, or her muscles are more mature, or she is better able to coordinate them.

The alternative is to suggest that the child's behavior changes because she *learns* new behaviors as a result of specific experiences. The parent places a spoon in the child's hand, moves it toward the bowl, and then toward the child's mouth. The parent says "Good!" when the child manages to aim well enough to get the chocolate pudding into her mouth instead of her ear or all over her face, and the child is also rewarded by getting to eat the food.

FIGURE 2

Child in transition from eating with fingers to eating with a spoon. Does this change occur because of reinforcement? imitation? maturation?

But how does learning occur? How is the child influenced by the environment so that her behavior is changed? Three different kinds of learning have been identified, each of which plays a role in the child's development.

Classical Conditioning

Pavlov was the first to identify the process we call *classical conditioning*, a process by which reflexive responses can come to be triggered by new cues. Let me give you an example of this in an infant.

If you touch a baby on the cheek, she will turn toward the touch and begin to suck. In the technical terminology of classical conditioning the touch on the cheek is the *unconditioned stimulus,* and the turning and sucking are unconditioned responses. In the infant's normal experience the touches on the cheek are usually accompanied by a whole series of sounds and other touches: the mother's footsteps approaching, the feeling of being picked up, perhaps hearing the mother's voice, cuddling against the mother's breast, and so on. If any or all of these stimuli are paired often enough with the unconditioned stimulus of the touch on the cheek, they can become *conditioned stimuli;* that is, the sound of the mother's voice, or the sensations of being picked up can trigger the response of turning and sucking. The child may begin to show some kind of "nipple seeking" before being touched on the cheek. Eventually, the child may begin sucking movements at the *sight* of breast or bottle, thus appearing to show anticipation.

The same kind of process can explain the development of some

12

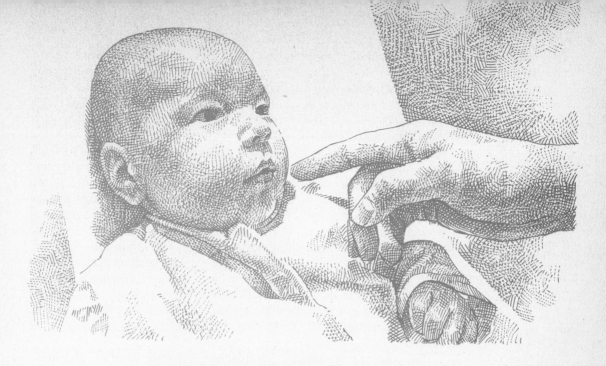

kinds of fears in children (or in adults for that matter). The classic example comes from an experiment by Watson, who showed that a child (named Albert) who had originally been unafraid of furry objects—such as rabbits, dogs, a fur coat, a white rat—could be taught to fear such things through classical conditioning. The child was shown a white rat, and the moment he reached for it Watson sounded a very loud noise behind the child's head. The child jumped (startled, which is a reflexive reaction) and began to cry. After a few such trials all Watson had to do was show Albert the white rat, and Albert would startle and begin to cry. Albert had learned to be afraid of white rats. But he had also learned to be afraid of other furry things, which illustrates the process of *generalization.* The more similar an object was to a white rat, the more fear Albert showed. So, he had generalized the newly learned reaction to a whole range of other objects.

There are many other examples I could give you—no doubt you can think of many yourself—to illustrate the role of classical conditioning in the child's early development. But although this type of learning does explain some of the changes we observe in children, it is clear that classical conditioning will not help to account for the majority of changes that occur. Most importantly, you should understand that classical conditioning does not involve the learning of any new *response.* The child doesn't suck any better than she did before; she merely sucks in response to a different cue. So, if we want to account for changes in the child's responses, improvements in her skills, and development of new skills or responses, we have to look to a different kind of learning.

Operant Conditioning

Classical conditioning involves learning to make an old response to a new cue. *Operant conditioning* (also called instrumental conditioning or just plain learning) generally involves learning to make a new response to an old cue. A child sitting in her high chair and eating with her fingers has a well-developed system: She associates all the cues about the high chair, the table, and the food with eating with her fingers. What you as a parent or as a psychologist want to do is to teach her a new behavior, a new response (in this case eating with a spoon), so that the whole complex of cues comes to be associated with spoon eating. This goal can be accomplished by a process of rewarding the child for approximations of the behavior that you want. You might, for example, put the spoon on the tray of the high chair or even in the child's hand. When the child manages to get the spoon into the food, you immediately provide some kind of reward, such as praise ("Good girl!"), or you put some food into the child's mouth. Gradually, you require the child to do a better and better job herself before you provide the reward, and over a period of time the child's spoon eating gets better and better until it becomes completely dominant over finger eating.

The essence of operant conditioning is that if, after making a response, there is some pleasant consequence, the child is more likely to make the same response again in the same situation. If having you say "Good girl!" is pleasant, then saying it when the child manages to eat with a spoon will increase the likelihood that she will pick up the spoon the next time you put her in her high chair.

In the language of operant conditioning, the "Good girl" is a *positive reinforcer.* Any consequence that tends to increase the likelihood of a response is a positive reinforcer, and for most children, praise, food, money, and attention function in this way. But some consequences have a strengthening effect on responses through their *removal,* and these are called *negative reinforcers.* Let me give you an example. If, when you are spanking your child she says, "Oh you're hurting me," you then stop spanking, the cessation of spanking serves to reinforce the child's saying, "You're hurting me." So you have increased the likelihood of the same comment the next time.

The potential confusion in this terminology is that negative reinforcement is *not* the same thing as punishment. The word punishment is ordinarily used (both by psychologists and by laypersons) to refer to consequences *thought to be unpleasant* to the child or to whoever is being punished. The term punishment used in this sense involves an inference about what the recipient of the punishment is likely to find unpleasant. Many psychologists who have focused their attention on operant conditioning are uncomfortable about such inferences and have tried to make the phrase negative reinforcement more precise. Some punishments *may* serve as negative reinforcers, but not quite in the same way that most parents suppose. For example, frowning at a

child may be negatively reinforcing; that is, whatever response the child makes that *removes* the frown will tend to become stronger or more likely. A child may stop hitting her brother when you frown at her. If you stop frowning then nonhitting has been reinforced. But think about other common sequences: The child hits her brother, the parent intervenes by picking her up, swatting her on her behind, and sending her to her room. During the entire interchange, the child cries. The cessation of spanking in this instance is reinforcing *crying*, not nonhitting.

The critical point I want you to remember here is that punishment, as the term is loosely used by most of us, does *not* automatically have the result of weakening or reducing the likelihood of the unpleasant behaviors that were punished. So it does not operate as the opposite to reward.

Parents use the principles of operant conditioning constantly, whether they label it that or not. In particular, parents praise a child when she does something they like, and they are likely to "punish" her when she does something they don't like. At the same time parents often unintentionally misuse operant conditioning. That is, they

BOX 2
Schedules of Reinforcement

In normal home environments it is extremely unlikely that any behavior will be reinforced every time it occurs. Parents are not always around at the crucial moment, and they may not be completely consistent in their own reactions. For example, when there is no hurry, or when the parent is feeling calm and patient, he or she may be quite willing to encourage a young child to try to tie her own shoe. But the same parent may scold the child for taking too long on another occasion. What is the result of this kind of inconsistency or of only intermittent reinforcement?

Extensive research with animals, as well as work with human subjects, shows that behaviors, once established, may be maintained for very long periods of time with only occasional reinforcement. In fact, such infrequently reinforced responses persist *longer* after reinforcement has been completely stopped than do responses that have been reinforced every time. In the more technical language of learning theory, the partially reinforced response is more *resistant to extinction.*

There are many possible patterns of partial reinforcement, each of which has slightly different effects on performance. If a subject is reinforced every ten minutes, or at some other specified time interval, this is called a *fixed-interval schedule.* Such a schedule brings about a sharp increase in behavior just before the next reinforcement is due. For example, if a rat is given a food pellet every ten minutes for pressing a bar, the rat will press the bar fre-

achieve results other than what they intend. For example, many parents find that attention-demanding, clinging behavior is fine in a 1½-year-old, but is annoying in a 3-year-old. When the 3-year-old comes into the kitchen while her mother is getting dinner and says "Mommy" repeatedly, the mother may not answer the first few times. After three or four demands for attention, the mother may with irritation say something like, "Well, all right! What do you want!?" Although her voice may (probably does) have an unpleasant tone, she has paid attention to the child, and if such attention is a positive event for the child, then repeated demanding is what has been reinforced. The mother may be convinced that she is *not* paying as much attention to the child, that she is trying to *extinguish* (to eliminate) the attention-demanding behavior, but in fact she is strengthening it.

I caught myself falling into such a sequence about a week ago. My daughter was having one of her low moments and was feeling "bored." The boredom was accompanied by a long series of heavy sighs, whimpers and whining noises, which I studiously and teeth-clenchingly ignored. This lasted for perhaps half an hour, at which point she burst into torrents of tears. My determination to ignore the behavior broke down totally, and I deposited her bodily in her room. But I *had* paid attention to her. So what I had undoubtedly done was to reinforce the whole sequence.

There are two lessons to be drawn here. First, there is abundant research evidence that the principles of reinforcement are valid. The probability of various behaviors can be increased in quite systematic

quently right around the time of reinforcement, then the rate of pressing will slow down greatly until just before the ten-minute period is up, when the rate will increase again. The same kind of effect may be seen in a child who is accustomed to having a snack after school each day. If at other times of the day request for food between meals meet with no success, but the child is given a snack each day after school, eventually, asking for food at other times should cease and only the after-school request will persist.

A more common schedule of partial reinforcement, at least in family situations, is the variable-interval schedule, in which the parent grants a particular request once in a while but not on a predictable basis. A schedule of this kind, with its unpredictability, tends to generate continuously persistent behavior. Nagging or whining on the part of a child, for example, may be maintained by just such a schedule. Most of the time the parents resist the nagging, but every now and then when they just can't stand it any longer, they relent and give the child what she has nagged for, thus reinforcing and perpetuating the nagging behavior.

The importance of the effect of partial reinforcement lies not only in the fact that partial schedules are so common in natural situations, but also in the fact that they help to explain how behaviors may persist for long periods without much apparent reinforcement.

ways by using these principles. But second, the application of sound reinforcement principles is less obvious in many cases than many of us suppose, and it is fairly easy to fall into patterns of interaction that result in an effect exactly the opposite of what is intended. (A more detailed discussion of some of the principles and consequences of reinforcement schedules appears in Box 2.)

One final point must be made about operant conditioning at this early stage. There is some risk that I have given you the impression that operant conditioning always requires some outside agent, such as a parent or a teacher, to reinforce the child. In fact, of course, that's not necessary. There are both positive and negative reinforcements that the child creates on her own and that have the same effects on behavior. A child may take off a shoe that is full of pebbles, and by easing the discomfort, reinforces the taking off of the shoes. Or if the child takes a toy away from a friend, the taking away is reinforced by the pleasure she gets out of playing with the new toy. Parents and educators *can* control some reinforcements, and by doing so systematically they can alter the child's behavior in many ways, but not all reinforcements are under the control of adults.

Observational Learning

Learning through operant conditioning involves some kind of reinforcement. The child is more likely to perform acts that have been followed by some kind of pleasant consequence. But not all learning requires this sort of reinforcement. Alternatively, a child may learn a whole host of new behaviors simply by observing someone else performing them. For instance, a child may learn to use a spoon simply by seeing other people eating with spoons; she may learn aggressive responses by watching aggression on television or by seeing her parents be aggressive when spanking her or another child. Whether or not the child will actually *perform* the response she's seen will depend heavily on the pattern of reinforcement she encounters. But the original learning can and does occur simply through observation.

INTERACTION EFFECTS

The word *interaction* has a number of different meanings that must be distinguished. In everyday language *interaction* usually means simply relationship. If I am having an interaction with you, I am relating to you in some way. The child naturally interacts with people and with the environment in this sense of the word. She relates to the people and to the objects in the world around her.

But in the following sentence the word interaction has a different meaning. "The child's behavior resulted from the interaction of biological and environmental forces." Here the word does not refer to any kind of relationship with people or with the world. Rather, it refers to a combination of influences, so that the outcome we observe can be attributed to several, rather than to a single, cause.

Internal and external forces are at work in every aspect of the child's developing behavior; there are no cases I can think of in which a behavior is entirely internally or entirely externally determined. The more interesting question is the nature of the relationship between internal and external influences. One possible relationship would be an additive one. The effects of internal forces, such as heredity and maturation, may simply be added to the effects of the environment. We might think, for example, of a child's diet as adding to the effects of the child's heredity, so that good intellectual heredity plus good diet would produce the brightest children. Either good diet and bad heredity, or good heredity and bad diet, would then result in children of medium brightness, and poor diet and poor heredity would result in the least gifted children. It would simplify the life of psychologists if it worked that way, but it doesn't. The actual relationships among the variables are nearly always much more complex than that. For example, some children may inherit genes that make them less vulnerable to various kinds of environmental events, including poor diet. Some children may be able to tolerate bad diet or insufficient early stimulation better than others. The outcome is the result of both the child's internal characteristics and the environmental influences, but the relationship is not a matter of adding the two together. The same environment may have different effects on children who come into the world with different beginning characteristics, or an environment may have different effects on a child at different points in time, when the child has developed different skills.

18

Let me see if I can make this point somewhat clearer with an example from some real research. Howard Moss was interested in knowing how the very early relationships between mothers and infants developed. Were such relationships determined entirely by the child's temperament or health? Were they determined by the mother's attitudes or skills or by some combination—some interaction—between the two? To get at this question, he observed 3-week-old infants with their mothers in their homes. An observer sat in a corner of each home for hours at a time, noting down each thing the baby did and the mother's response to it, as well as the behavior that the mother initiated. He found, among many other things, that 3-week-old infant girls slept more, fussed less, and were less irritable than were the baby boys. The mothers held the boys more often and generally responded more to them, perhaps because they were awake more and demanded more attention. But when a baby girl did fuss, the mother was quicker about responding with some kind of help. Two quite distinct patterns of relationship between mother and infant seem to be developing here. Moss observed a group of more placid and less fussy girls. When they did fuss, they were easier to soothe, so when the mother picked up the infant, the infant stopped crying, which made the mother feel effective and helpful. The boy infants in Moss's sample were fussier and awake more; they required more attention but were harder to soothe. The mother may have tried all sorts of things to soothe the baby, but wasn't completely successful, so she may not have felt as effective with the boy.

We would expect, if such a pattern were to continue over time, that eventually the mother of a particularly fussy and hard-to-soothe child would stop responding to the child's cries: If she feels there is nothing she can do to help anyway, why try? In Moss's study this expectation was confirmed. When he went back and observed the same families again when the babies were 3 months old, he noticed that the babies who received the least attention were the fussiest boys.

In the developing relationship between the mother and the infant, each has brought something. The baby brings his or her tendencies toward "soothability," fussiness, or crying, and the mother brings her expectations about what a "good mother" should be able to do and about how a "normal baby" should react. The mother may also bring her own expectations about sex differences to this encounter. But by 3 months of age, the child's behavior and the amount of attention she receives are a result of the *interaction* of these forces, not the sum of them.

Other researchers have *not* consistently found that boys are fussier or harder to soothe as infants, but the basic conclusion from Moss's research is still valid. The relationship between the mother and the infant is a complex product of forces internal to the child, the mother's expectations and behavior, and other external forces in the home.

It is important to keep the notion of interaction in mind when I talk about the impact of the environment throughout this book. It's so very easy to fall into the trap of thinking that somehow the environment "happens" to the child, that the child is somehow like a blotter for experience. But, of course, she is not, and the effects of varying kinds of environment will be different for different children, or for the same child at different points in her development.

ALTERNATIVE THEORETICAL VIEWS

In the chapters that follow I will be asking both what and why about each of the aspects of development: What is the nature of language development, and why does it occur in that way? What are the characteristics of physical, perceptual, or emotional development, and what are the factors that influence the patterns we see? But there is, and will be, another dimension to the discussions as well. For many psychologists the important task is not just the explanation of individual aspects of development, but the construction of a theory—an overall explanation—that will account for development in its entirety. A theory not only helps account for things that have been observed, but it allows us to go beyond what we have observed and make predictions about what *ought* to be true. A good theory thus guides our research, focuses our attention on different aspects of the total problem, and suggests new solutions or new relationships.

In developmental psychology there is no single theory that satisfactorily encompasses all aspects of development, but there are at least four major theoretical approaches, each of which places emphasis on a different type of explanation and each of which asks a somewhat different pattern of questions about development. Some theorists—most notably Jean Piaget—have focused their attention primarily on explaining the development of thinking; others, such as Sigmund Freud and his followers, have focused most of their efforts on explanations of personality development and changes in affective relationships. There are also differences among the several theorists in the type of questions they have asked. Piaget and Gesell have both been very much struck by the very great similarities in the patterns of development among children, while many of the learning theorists have found the differences among children more notable than their similarities. Obviously, a theorist who tries to devise a theory that will predict and explain individual variations is going to develop a quite different theory from one who is primarily interested in explaining how children come to be so alike. But all four theories share the assumption that it is possible to explain the ways in which children develop by using a fairly small set of explanatory principles.

Since I will be returning often to these same four theories and to the explanations that emerge from them, let me give you a brief taste of each now.

Psychoanalytic Theory

Sigmund Freud was the originator of the psychoanalytic approach, and both he and a number of his followers, including Erik Erikson (see Figure 3), Melanie Klein, Peter Wolff, Anna Freud and others, have proposed theories of development.

It is important to understand that Freud began by studying *abnormal* functioning in adults. His interest in development arose from his interest in explaining the origins of deviant behavior among adults. The adult disorders Freud observed were largely personality disorders of one type or another, so his interest was in the process of development of personality. In his theory personality is the centerpiece; the development of perception, language, and cognition were side issues for Freud.

Freud saw personality as emerging from important biological roots. As the body developed, there were changes in the type of stimulation that the infant and child was most sensitive to, and these changing sensitivities affected the child's relationship with the mother and other adults. But while the biological (maturational) underpinnings are important in Freudian theory, he places the greatest emphasis on the nature of the child's relationship with adults, particularly with the mother. At each stage the child's relationship with the mother (and later with the father) was seen as critical in determining whether the child achieved a healthy adult personality or a personality with serious conflicts and disturbances. Whether the mother is indulgent or strict, permissive or punitive, will have an effect on the child's developing personality. Particularly critical in Freud's view was the period approximately between ages 3 to 6, when the *Oedipal crisis* was thought to occur. During this period the child works through a series of very strong feelings about the mother and the father, resulting (at least in normal development) in an *identification* with the parent of the same

FIGURE 3
Sigmund Freud and Erik Erikson.

sex. If this crisis was not successfully resolved, Freud thought, it would have major implications for all later personality development.

Erikson, beginning from a similar set of assumptions, has extended and modified Freudian theory. He has suggested eight stages of development from birth to old age. In each of these developmental periods, Erikson sees the child or adult as facing a central dilemma or task. The successful or unsuccessful resolution of these dilemmas and tasks determines the overall health of the personality. For example, in the first stage the fundamental issue as Erikson sees it is whether the child will develop a sense of basic trust or basic mistrust. Whether trust or mistrust develops is a function of the kind of relationship the child has with her mother and other adults, of the predictability of the child's world, and of the warmth and affection lavished on her. Erikson suggests that the resolution of this original conflict affects, in turn, the resolution of each of the dilemmas yet to come.

All of the psychoanalytic explanations of development share an emphasis on the relatively greater importance of relationships with people rather than relationships with things and on the sequential development of personality through several stages or levels. Little is said in most psychoanalytic theories about the development of cognition, which is thought to be in some sense subsidiary to the process of personality development.

Cognitive Theory

Cognitive theorists reverse this order of dominance and place greatest emphasis on the development of thinking. The development of personality, when it is discussed at all by cognitive theorists, is seen as influenced by or subsidiary to the development of cognitive processes. The central figure in cognitive-developmental theory is Jean Piaget, although there are many other theorists, including Heinz Werner, Lev Vygotsky, Jerome Bruner, Barbel Inhelder, John Flavell, and Jerome Kagan, who have made significant contributions to this body of thought.

Piaget, like other cognitive theorists, has been struck by the very great regularities about the development of children, particularly children's thinking. He saw that children appeared to go through the same kind of sequential discoveries about their world, make the same kinds of mistakes (such as saying "winned," as I mentioned on the opening page of this book), and arrive at the same kinds of solutions. Piaget assumes that this process of discovery and growth occurs primarily through a process of the child's involvement with and action on her environment. In Piaget's view the child is not a passive recipient of environmental events, but rather, she seeks out experiences and uses the environment. He does not reject maturation as a fundamental process, but he does not believe that all of the regularities we see in development are merely the result of basic biological unfolding. The child's explorations may be limited by her physical growth, but those

22

FIGURE 4
Jean Piaget

explorations lead to new discoveries, which in turn lead to new explorations in a nearly endless pyramiding of cognitive accomplishments.

Piaget has focused almost all his attention on the child's mental growth. He has had little to say about emotional or personality development and almost nothing at all to say about the ways in which children differ from one another; however, he has noted that since the child's development results from explorations of and interactions with the environment, a rich and varied environment supplies more material to work with and may thus help the child to develop more rapidly. American cognitive theorists have been much more interested in environmental variations and in the possibility of training children to use specific cognitive skills. There has also been some recent attempt to develop a cognitive-developmental theory that encompasses emotional development as well. But these are variations on the basic theme set by Piaget.

Cognitive developmental theory, in one variation or another, has come to be a dominant theoretical force within developmental psychology in the United States. But this is a relatively new status for this theoretical approach. Prior to about 1960, despite the fact that he had been writing prolifically about child development since the 1920s, Piaget's views had had very little impact. Then, rather rapidly in the middle and late sixties, cognitive theory became a central force. There were probably many reasons for the shift in theoretical emphasis. I don't pretend to be an intellectual historian, so there were undoubtedly forces at work that I did not and do not perceive. But looking at it from rather a mole's eye view, one factor seems to be particularly important. In the fifties and early sixties, learning approaches were clearly dominant in the training and thinking of developmental psychologists. There was a large body of research on learning in children of various ages during this period. Researchers explored the learning of transitivity, or seriation, or other concepts in preschoolers, kindergartners, and older children. It began to be clear from this sort of research that there were differences in the ways in which children of different ages approached the learning tasks. It wasn't just that older children learned faster (although that was usually true, too), but that they approached the problem in a different way than did the younger children. Piaget's theory became influential when it did, I think, because he offered a framework by which we could begin to understand such age-related changes in strategy or approach. The introduction of this new (for many of us) way of looking at children produced a very rich theoretical ferment, which is still going on.

Learning Theories

The several theorists from the learning tradition who have focused their attention on children's development—including Robert Sears, Sidney Bijou and his colleague Donald Baer, Albert Bandura and his associates, and others—have, like the psychoanalytic and cognitive theorists, made some assumptions about how children are like one another. They assume that the behavior of *all* human beings (as well as of other animals) is governed by laws of learning, and that application of such laws to the study of children will show that development, too, follows the laws of learning. Bijou and Baer have relied primarily on an operant conditioning model. They have argued that children's behavior is under the control of environmental reinforcements, and that it can be modified by controlling the reinforcement patterns. In a large number of experiments Bijou and Baer and others with a similar theoretical viewpoint have shown that specific behaviors *can* be modified in predictable and lawful ways through control of reinforcements.

Bandura and his several associates and followers have focused primarily on observational learning rather than operant conditioning. Bandura argues that reinforcement patterns may be vital in some aspects of behavior, but that the learning of *new* behaviors is not well handled by an operant conditioning theory. He sees the learning of new behaviors as coming primarily through observation.

Sears has combined some concepts from psychoanalytic theory (such as the concept of identification) and principles of reinforcement in an effort to account for some aspects of child development. Sears has been particularly interested in the development of aggression and dependency in children.

Several elements tie these rather different theories together. First, they all use well-established principles of learning in accounting for children's behavior. Second, although they all assume that the laws of

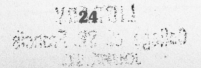

learning are the same for all children, the focus of their interest has often been on the use of learning principles to explain *differences* among children. For example, children clearly differ in their level of aggression or dependency. The task for the learning theorists is to explain how such differences might come about as a result of different patterns of reinforcement or observational learning in the child's history. Many studies of the relationship between child-rearing practices of parents and children's behavior have emerged from this sort of theoretical tradition.

A third similarity among the several learning approaches is that (unlike Freud or Piaget) on the whole such theorists have placed little emphasis on *sequences* of development. Learning theory proponents have argued that the laws of learning remain the same throughout the life span and that, although behavior does change, there are no fixed sequences in those changes. Piaget and Freud, on the other hand, have both suggested that new strategies for dealing with the environment develop in a fixed sequence as a result of the child's interaction with the environment. The older child, using different strategies, will thus approach tasks in a different way than does the younger child. Since this disagreement among the several theories is a fairly fundamental one, it will reappear in various forms throughout the book. Are there fixed, shared, sequences of development? If so, where do they come from? How much are they influenced by specific experience? These are important questions and will become familiar ones before we are through.

Maturational Theory

A fourth theoretical approach that is not particularly influential in the United States today deserves mention because it played an important role in developmental psychology some decades ago and may do so again.

Arnold Gesell was the major exponent of a theory of development that placed greatest emphasis on the role of maturation. Like Piaget, Gesell was struck by the enormous similarities among children in their developmental patterns. But unlike Piaget, Gesell concluded that such similarities must have biological origins. We are the same, he believed, because our genetic code makes us so. He coined the word *maturation* to describe the sequential unfolding which he thought was based on genetic instructions. Gesell acknowledged that the child did have to acquire specific knowledge (vocabulary words, concepts, manners, and so on) through direct experience, but he argued that the basic underpinnings of all development lie in biological change.

Note that both Piaget and Gesell, as well as the psychoanalytic theorists, emphasize *sequences* of development. For this reason, they are often labeled *stage theories*. In Gesell's theory the sequence of observable behavior is thought to come about because of biological changes, which occur in a fixed order. Piaget conceives of the observed sequences as resulting not only from maturation, but from a logical ordering. You have to learn to walk before you can run, but you also have to learn to add before you can multiply. So, Piaget suggests that in the child's discoveries about the world, the rules or strategies she constructs to make sense out of her experiences change in predictable, sequential ways. In most psychoanalytic theories the sequence emerges from a combination of maturational and experiential factors.

Gesell's theory provoked a great deal of so-called *normative* research during the 1930s and 1940s. Groups of children were observed and assessed through the first years of life, and the "normal" rate and sequence of development were charted. Much of our knowledge of the sequence of development of early motor skills, for example, comes from research spurred by Gesellian theory. More recently there has been a partial revival of interest in biological or maturational explanations of development, particularly in the area of language development.

Minitheories

In addition to these four major theoretical perspectives there have been and continue to be a great many less ambitious attempts to develop theory in developmental psychology. Many researchers, without any pretense of offering a comprehensive theory of development, have nonetheless attempted to devise theories that might account for a segment of what we observe in development. For example, Jerome Kagan has devised a theory about the development of attention in the young infant and child; Sheldon White has developed a minitheory about the changes in cognitive functioning that occur between the ages of 5 and 7; several minitheories have been proposed by Walter Mischel and Lawrence Kohlberg, among others, in the area of sex role development. Eleanor Maccoby and Carol Jacklin have also recently attempted a synthesis of theory in this area. In each of these and many other minitheories threads from one or several of the four main theoretical approaches may appear, but in each the researcher is attempting to develop an explanation of a narrower range of events. The hope, of course, is that over time these minitheories may somehow coalesce into a more comprehensive, synthesized conception of development than is presently offered by any of the four major approaches I have already described.

MY THEORETICAL BIASES

In describing each of the four central theoretical approaches, I have attempted to suggest that there are worthwhile concepts and strengths in each theory. At the same time, I do not want to give you the impression that I am completely unbiased in my own theoretical approach. I am not unbiased, as I am sure will become obvious as you read the book. But, rather than make you guess what my biases are, let me tell you now my assumptions about children and about the nature of their

26

development. You can then take those assumptions and biases into account as you go along.

1. First, like Piaget, I cannot accept the notion that the child is a passive recipient of events. The child, as I see her, is an extremely active participant in the whole process. She explores, examines, and compares each new experience. From these experiences she begins to construct her own notions about the way the world is organized—both the physical world and the world of people. Essentially, I see the process of development as a process of discovery and construction on the part of the child.

2. At the same time, I see the specific characteristics of the environment as extremely important. The child has to have something to discover—some objects, toys, people, events to explore and manipulate. If her environment is not rich with possibilities, and if the people around her do not respond to her overtures and explorations in a supportive way, then there is less for her to work with, and her development will be slowed in some ways. If I give you less to eat each day than your brother, you will grow less rapidly; and so it is with "food for thought." Within limits, I believe that the more there is, the more rapid the development. Of course, there *are* limits. A child can grow only so quickly, no matter how well she is fed, either physically or mentally. And there may well be the potential for overstimulation (perhaps we should call this mental obesity?), but within those limits, I think the richness and variety of the environment do matter.

3. I am also persuaded that there are broad sequences of development underlying many (but not all) of the changes we see. Some of these sequences are determined by the physical growth of the child, but other sequences, such as those Piaget discusses, represent a logical ordering. The infant has to be able to tell the difference between one person and another before she can form an attachment. She has to learn that objects have constancy and permanence before she can discover that their weights don't change when the shapes are changed. I am not suggesting that there is no individuality in experience or difference in heredity, but I do think that the individual variations are superimposed on underlying sequences of development.

4. One final bias is that in my view cognitive development plays a particularly central role in the child's overall development. I have always been more interested in mental development than in personality, social, or emotional development, so perhaps this bias arises because we are all tempted to consider the things that interest us as the most important. But I think there is more to it than that. It seems to me that in many instances the child's level of cognitive development sets limits of some kind on the sort of personal relationships she is able to have. Take the development of attachment again as an example. In order for a child to develop an attachment to her mother (or to her primary caregiver, whoever that may be), there are several requirements.

First, she must be able to discriminate the parent's face from other faces; second, she must recognize that the mother who comes to change her diapers today is the *same* mother who changed her diapers yesterday. Both of these recognitions are *cognitive* (or perceptual) accomplishments, not emotional ones. Emotional attachment can come only after these cognitive accomplishments have occurred. So, although the cognitive development does not *cause* the attachment in any direct sense, it sets the stage for it.

It is my suspicion that we will find many other similar links between the child's emotional and social development and her cognitive skills. As I see it, the child's interactions with others are in some sense limited by her cognitive abilities at that given moment. As her cognitive skills change, so may her social and emotional interactions with others.

Obviously, I am closer in my thinking to Piaget than to any other theorist. But I trust that my commitment to a cognitive-developmental view does not blind me—and through me, blind you—to the advantages of the other theoretical approaches.

SUMMARY

1. In studying the process of development in the child, two broad questions may be asked: *What* happens, and *why* does it happen?
2. The "why" questions may be further broken down into those dealing with internal influences and those dealing with external influences.
3. Among important internal influences are heredity and maturation; among the important external influences are the processes of learning and the effects of such broad environmental variations as poverty or diet.
4. Also needed is an analysis of the *interaction* between internal and external influences. How does the same environment affect different children? How do the child's charac-

teristics affect the way in which she is treated? And so on.

5. Four major theoretical approaches to answering such "why" questions have been proposed: psychoanalytic, cognitive developmental, learning, and biological (or maturational) approaches.
6. The several theories differ in the sort of questions on which they focus and in the assumptions that they make about the process of development.
7. My own bias is toward the cognitive-developmental approach, although I recognize that each of the others has important strengths.

REFERENCES[2]

Suggested Additional Readings

Baldwin, A. L. *Theories of child development.* New York: Wiley, 1967.
An advanced textbook, now slightly out of date, but containing a good basic description of the several theoretical views I have discussed in this chapter. Difficult reading, but

[2] References listed under Other Sources Cited are those technical papers or specific research reports to which I have referred in the chapter but which seem to me to be of less specific interest than the items listed under the subheading, "Suggested Additional Readings."

a good next step for those of you interested in development theory.

Bijou, S. W., & Baer, D. M. *Child development.* (Vol. 1). New York: Appleton, 1961.
A small pocketbook, easy to read and quite clear, that presents a cohesive learning theory explanation of child development.

Chukofsky, K. *From two to five.* Berkeley: University of California Press, 1963.
An absolutely delightful book by a Russian poet about his observations of children, the kinds of language they use, the concepts they have, and the poetry of their speech; entirely nontechnical, it may turn you on to children if you aren't already.

Erikson, E. H. *Childhood and society.* New York: Norton, 1950.
The basic early presentation of Erikson's theory of development, not too difficult to read, though rather long; you may find Chapter 7 of special interest.

Gesell, A., & Thompson, H. *The psychology of early growth.* New York: Macmillan, 1938.
The basic presentation of some of Gesell's concepts.

Ginsburg, H., & Opper, S. *Piaget's theory of intellectual development: An introduction.* Englewood Cliffs, N.J.: Prentice-Hall, 1969.
If you cannot manage to read Piaget's own writing, or if you are looking for a good, complete introduction to his theory, this is the best source I know. If you are interested in theory, read the introductory chapter now and save the rest until you get to Chapter 9 in this book.

Piaget, J. Development and learning. In R. Ripple & V. Rockcastle (Eds.), *Piaget rediscovered.* Ithaca, N.Y.: Cornell University Press, 1964, pp. 7–19. Also reprinted in C. S. Lavatelli & F. Stendler (Eds.), *Readings in child behavior and development* (3rd ed.). New York: Harcourt Brace Jovanovich, 1972.
In this short paper Piaget assumes that you have some familiarity with his theory, which may make it slightly difficult at this stage, but this is by far the least technical, most "chatty," and clear of his writings in my opinion.

Other Sources Cited

Dennis, W. Causes of retardation among institutional children: Iran. *Journal of Genetic Psychology,* 1969, *96,* 47–59.

Gottesman, I. I. Beyond the fringe—Personality and psychopathology. In D. C. Glass (Ed.), *Genetics.* New York: The Rockefeller University Press and Russell Sage Foundation, 1968, pp. 59–68.

Moss, H. A. Sex, age and state as determinants of mother-infant interaction. *Merrill-Palmer Quarterly,* 1967, *13,* 19–36.

Watson, J. D., & Crick, F. H. C. Molecular structure of nucleic acids: A structure for deoxyribose nucleic acid. *Nature,* 1958, *171,* 737–738.

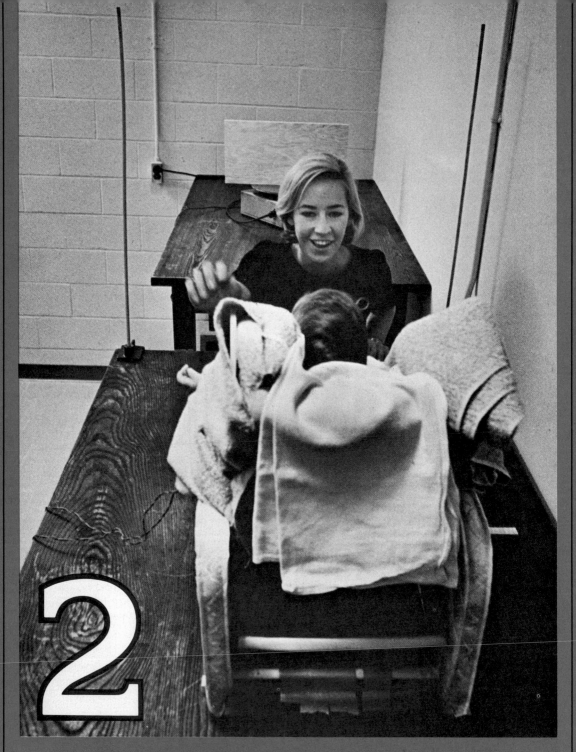

2

Methods
of Study

HOW DO YOU ANSWER ALL THOSE QUESTIONS, ANYWAY?

In the chapter you have just read I have asked hundreds of "what" and "why" questions. But how does one go about answering them? How do we obtain good information about what the child does or about the impact of the environment on her behavior? How do we pin down the roles of heredity or maturation in explaining the behaviors we observe? And if good information can be obtained, what do we do with it when we have it?

On only a few occasions in this book will I describe specific research in great detail, so there is little need for a lengthy or subtle discussion of methods. But for a variety of reasons it is important for you to know something about the basic types of research in developmental psychology. More importantly, you should have some understanding of the kind of logic used in interpreting the results of such research.

First, you will need to have some skill in judging the usefulness or value of psychological research findings. Even if you never read another book or take another course in the field, you will frequently encounter findings from various kinds of social science research in the public media. You may hear on television that "research has shown that" brand X is better than brand Y, or you may read in a news magazine about the latest research findings in psychology, all couched in very general terms. Basic knowledge about research methods and interpretation may help to shield you from some misinformation given under the rubric of "research," and it may put you in a better position to evaluate broadly stated findings from research studies. I cannot give you any real research sophistication in this chapter, but I can at least sensitize you to some important issues and help you to see through some common misuses.

Second, research findings will be discussed throughout the book, and issues associated with interpreting those findings will crop up often. You need to know why it is so often important to be cautious about drawing sweeping conclusions, even from the best research findings. Students are often frustrated by psychologists' common use of qualifying expressions such as "often," "probably," "likely," and "it seems most reasonable." But these expressions are not just the quibbles of academicians. Statements of probability are usually as far as we may legitimately go in drawing conclusions from the research findings that we have. Occasionally clear, unqualified statements can be made, as in the area of physical growth and development. More often, the best that can be offered is a strong probability or an opinion well backed up by research findings. So bear with the qualifiers, and try always to see why the qualification is necessary.

HOW TO OBTAIN INFORMATION

Three general strategies (and subvarieties of each) are used to obtain information about what the child does or is capable of, and why she does it.

Observation   The simple and obvious place to begin is to observe a child in her natural environment, or in a specially created environment, interacting with other people or reacting to objects that have been provided. In the most unstructured type of observation a child may be observed in her "natural habitat" for days, weeks, or months, with no intervention of any kind by the observer, who simply keeps a detailed running record of all the child's activities. The most outspoken advocates of observation of this type (often called *specimen description*) are Barker and Wright, who emphasize that the observer in the less structured procedures must be deliberately unselective in what he watches and writes down; he must attempt to capture the entire situation in which the child exists—her activities and the responses of people or other aspects of her environment to her.

This kind of observation offers the possibility of learning something about the "ecology" of a child's life—the total set of circumstances in which she lives. Such information is badly needed in many areas. For example, one widely replicated finding is that children raised in poverty environments do less well in school and on standardized tests than do children from more affluent family backgrounds. Some psychologists have argued that poor children are just as capable of solving problems in their own environments as are middle-class children in their environments. Since school is a middle-class environment, the middle-class child copes with it better. One way to approach this question is to do some lengthy specimen description observations of children in their "natural habitats" and in school situations. Such observations may show instances of real competence in the poor child in her own environment.

Another very broad kind of observational technique is to keep a "diary," with periodic notes on behavior, newly developed skills, and interactional patterns in an individual child over time. You may, for example, observe a child once a month in school over a period of years, each time noting anything that particularly strikes you about the child's behavior or summarizing your observations at the end. This kind of observation, more than specimen description, is a genuinely developmental technique because it permits some statements about changes and continuities over time.

Obviously, though, with either of these very general or unfocused types of observation, the problem of objectivity is very great indeed. In a diary or periodic summary system the observer notes only what seems especially interesting or remarkable, which is clearly a judgmental process. In the specimen record an effort is made to maintain objectivity by writing everything down, but complete detail is physically impossible, so some selection and judgment inevitably take place. (In the project at the end of this chapter you will have an opportunity to try out a short specimen record and will see for yourself some of the difficulties.) In addition, of course, the very presence of the ob-

server changes the behavior of the child. If I decide that I want to know how black ghetto children interact with one another and solve problems when they are in their own environment, I am unlikely to find out much by taking my white face and middle-class manners into the heart of the ghetto and standing around on street corners making specimen records. It is, of course, possible to reduce the impact of the observer by having him present over a long period of time before the actual observations are taken, but the problem of impact cannot be eliminated entirely.

Because of the very large problems of judgment that enter into most general kinds of observation, many researchers have preferred to use more structured procedures. Most commonly, the observer will watch for one or more specific, well-defined behaviors and will simply count how often they occur. Suppose, for example, that you want to know if girls of nursery school age receive more attention from teachers than boys do. You might begin by defining very carefully what you mean by "attention from the teacher" and by classifying kinds of "attention": for example, "attention after injury," "praise of the child's accomplishments," and so on. You would then go to one or more nursery schools (preferably quite a few) and observe many different teachers interacting with the children, counting each instance of a teacher's attention to a child and noting whether that attention is directed at a boy or a girl.

Detailed counts of specific behaviors in natural settings may also be used to measure the "base line" of a child's behavior before some change is introduced. Teachers and researchers using operant conditioning techniques invariably observe in detail throughout their behavior modification procedures. For example, one of the problems that faces many nursery school or day-care teachers is the withdrawn child who sits or plays alone and does not often interact with other children. Before beginning any kind of behavior modification program it is necessary to have a good measure of just how often the child in fact does interact with her peers. To do this, you may observe the child over several days, counting each instance of contact with others. Then a reinforcement schedule is introduced. Some form of positive reinforcement (perhaps smiles or attention from the adult) is provided each time the child moves toward or joins another child; she is ignored each time she plays alone. All during this phase the observer continues to note the frequency of contact with other children. Figure 5 shows the sort of cumulative observational record that can emerge from such studies. Observations of this kind can be highly reliable; the more precisely the behavior is defined, the more reliable the observation becomes.

But even these more definite and precise techniques can involve difficulties of judgment and interpretation. Suppose, for example, that you are interested in aggressiveness in children. Perhaps you want to know if there are any sex differences in aggression or whether or not parents who use a lot of physical punishment at home have children who are more aggressive at school. Whatever the specific nature of your interest, the one common denominator is the need for a good observational count of aggressive acts by each of several children. But how should aggressive behavior be defined?

If a child accidentally knocks over another child's block tower as she is racing by, is that aggression? Robert Sears, who has done several studies of this kind, thinks it is not. He has defined aggression as an action in which the child intends to injure someone or something. So accidentally knocking over someone's block tower is not aggression. But how do you see intentions? How do you know what the child intends simply by watching her play with other children? Maybe she knocked over the block tower on purpose. You can't tell just by watching her. You can guess about what she intends, according to what you see, but you cannot observe intention directly, so you can't really observe her aggression directly, at least not if you accept Sears's definition of aggression.

Despite all the difficulties and other technical problems discussed in Box 3, observation plays an important part in the study of children

34

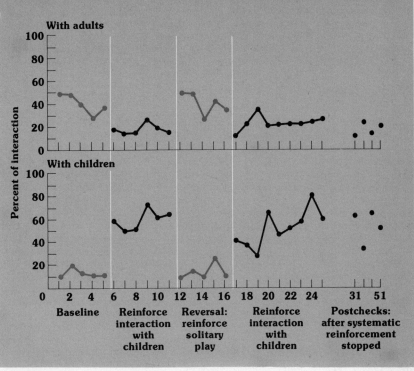

FIGURE 5
An example of the results of an observational record of a withdrawn child, studied in a behavior modification experiment. Behavioral counts were converted to a percentage of activity for each day; the graph shows the changes in the child's observed behavior throughout the experiment. (Source: F. R. Harris, M. M. Wolf, & D. M. Baer. Effects of adult social reinforcement on child behavior. *Young Children.* Reprinted by permission from *Young Children*, Vol. xx, No. 1. © 1964, National Association for the Education of Young Children, 1834 Connecticut Avenue, N.W., Washington, DC 20009.)

and their development, partly because there are some questions we can answer only by observing children in their natural surroundings. In Moss's study of mothers and infants, which I described briefly earlier, the only way he could find out what he wanted to know about the developing patterns of interaction was by being in the home to watch the normal situation. Observation also provides us with important information about the effects of different kinds of environmental variables. If you want to know whether children in a first-grade classroom with a teacher's aide in addition to the regular teacher receive more individual attention than do children in a classroom with only a teacher, the piece of information you need is the number of individual adult contacts that each child has in each of these classrooms. The only way to obtain that information is to go into the classrooms and watch.

BOX 3
Problems and Types of Observations

Researchers using observation as their major source of information about children and their environments face a difficult set of practical problems. No observer can write down everything that happens in any detail, so some kind of summary statement or some sampling of behavior is what we have to settle for. But even summaries or samples pose problems. If categories are used, with the observer noting each time behavior of a particular kind occurs, there are at least two difficulties. First, the observer cannot watch all the time; it takes some time to look down at the paper and note the proper category, so some behavior will be missed. Second, category counts do not tell the researcher anything about the *sequence* of behavior. If you as a researcher want to know about the child's behavior and about the *consequences* of such behavior (for example, whether it is praised or criticized, successful or unsuccessful), then a simple behavioral count will not give you the information you need.

One solution to the first problem has been a technique called *time sampling*. The observer watches for some period of time—perhaps 15 or 20 seconds—and then during an interval records each occurrence. The observer may note simply which categories of behavior occurred, or the behavior and the consequence, or some combination of the two. The basic quality of time sampling is that it is *not* continuous recording, but a sampling of behavior across discrete time intervals. Obviously, this has practical advantages. In addition to easing the problem of continuous watching, it makes it quite simple to switch from observation of one child to another in the same setting if you are collecting data about a number of children. But time sampling

Clinical Method

A close cousin of observation is the clinical method. Perhaps the most famous user of the clinical method is Jean Piaget. He has not been content merely to observe (although he was and is a superb observer). Instead, when he sees or hears something that he doesn't understand or can't interpret, he wants to explore it right then, so he invents small "tests" to see if he can figure out what the child is doing or how she is thinking. For example, suppose that he is observing a baby lying on her back in her crib, with a mobile hanging above her. He sees the baby moving her right arm in the direction of the toy, but as the mobile is out of reach, he can't tell whether she would grasp it if she could. So he moves the toy closer to see what she will do.

The essence of the clinical method is a kind of systematic exploration with one child at a time, tailoring the probing to the individual child. With an older child Piaget presents a task of some kind or asks a question, then continues with questions or new tasks until he is satisfied that he understands what the child can do or how she reasons. Let me give you one example from Piaget's studies of "moral development." In this conversation he was discussing lies with a 6-year-old boy named Clai:

Piaget: Do you know what a lie is?
Clai: It's when you say what isn't true.
Piaget: Is 2 + 2 = 5 a lie?
Clai: Yes, it's a lie.

36

makes the problem of detecting long chains or consequences of behavior even worse, since you are recording only short bursts of behavior.

Solutions to the continuity problem are hard to come by. Some researchers have tried to deal with this problem by having two observers, each speaking into tape recorders. One notes specific behaviors of the target subject, while the other notes general background characteristics of the environment or the responses of adults or others to the target individual. The two records can be coordinated by having a "bleep" every so many seconds on each tape. The problem with this technique, as I am sure you can see, is that the task of synthesizing the two sets of information is monumental.

The best current overall solution involves direct hookup to a computer. The observer uses a small keyboard, similar to a pocket calculator. Each key or combination of keys represents a behavior or consequence of interest to the researcher. The observer simply "types" on these keys as behavior occurs, and the resulting record is punched immediately into computer tape (Sackett, Stephenson, & Ruppenthal, 1973). The observation and recording is continuous and can capture chains of behavior over time. Since a key is depressed only when a particular behavior occurs, the computer tape shows the events in "real time," and the researcher can go back and analyze the amount of silence or nonresponse in the pattern as well as the rate of occurrence of the behavior of interest. Such equipment is obviously expensive, and not all settings will be appropriate for its use, but the existence of such technically advanced systems has made detailed and far more accurate observation much more feasible in many settings.

Piaget:	Why?
Clai:	Because it isn't right.
Piaget:	Did the boy who said that $2 + 2 = 5$ know it wasn't right or did he make a mistake?
Clai:	He made a mistake.
Piaget:	Then if he made a mistake, did he tell a lie or not?
Clai:	Yes, he told a lie.
Piaget:	A naughty one?
Clai:	Not very.
Piaget:	You see this gentleman (a student)?
Clai:	Yes.
Piaget:	How old do you think he is?
Clai:	Thirty.
Piaget:	I would say 28. (The student says he is really 36.)
Piaget:	Have we both told a lie?
Clai:	Yes, both lies.
Piaget:	Naughty ones?
Clai:	Not so very naughty.
Piaget:	Which is the naughtiest, yours or mine, or are they both the same?
Clai:	Yours is the naughtiest because the difference is biggest.
Piaget:	Is it a lie, or did we just make a mistake?
Clai:	We made a mistake.
Piaget:	Is it a lie all the same, or not?
Clai:	Yes, it's a lie! (J. Piaget. *The moral judgement of the child*. New York: Macmillan, 1932, p. 143)

37 Methods of Study

Piaget pushed this child as far as he could by continuing to ask questions until he was satisfied that he understood that, for Clai, any untrue statement, regardless of the intent of the person making it, is a lie. Please notice that Piaget did not stop after the first answer that Clai gave. "It's when you say what isn't true." Most of us would have stopped there and assumed that Clai understood the concept of lying in the same way that an adult does. But Piaget continued, and, as a result of his probing, he discovered that Clai's concept of lying is not the same as that of an adult.

A kind of clinical method is also used in giving standardized tests, except that in this case the probing questions are the same for each child tested. Individual intelligence tests, such as the Stanford-Binet, are of this type, as are many tests of the child's personality, fears, or anxieties. The obvious advantage of having the same set of probing questions for each child is that it makes it possible to talk about the answers given by groups of children and to compare one child with another. But what you lose when you use the same questions and probes for each child is the flexibility that permits you to explore each new avenue with the specific child. Which style of clinical method you choose will depend on the kind of information you hope to get.

The more flexible styles of clinical method, as used by Piaget and others, have their drawbacks, not unlike some of those associated with broad observations. The observer-interrogator is very much involved in

the process of interpreting what the child does and possibly in suggesting answers to the child as well. Because of this problem many researchers are unwilling to use individualized clinical methods alone, although they often use them in the early stages of research on a particular question in order to "get a feeling" for children's behavior or to generate hypotheses. Such exploration with the clinical method is then followed up with more rigorous experimentation or observation.

Experimental Procedures

In moving from "pure" observation to the clinical method, the major change is in the intervention of the observer-experimenter. In the clinical method, the situation itself is not left entirely to chance; rather, the investigator intervenes in some fashion, asking specific questions or introducing special objects or tests. In an experiment proper one step farther is taken toward control of the situation. Ideally, in an experiment the experimenter seeks to "hold constant" all factors except the one that he wants information about. Take the example of children's aggression again. Suppose you want to know whether or not reinforcement for aggression will lead to an increase in aggressiveness. One way to go about solving this problem would be to determine how often each of a series of children is reinforced for aggression at home, either by observing directly in a series of homes or by questioning the parents. Then the children would be observed, either at home or in a school setting. This procedure seems reasonable for many purposes, as it involves natural settings and may tell you something about child-rearing practices and their effects, but there are many uncontrolled variables. For example, you do not control what happens to the child in the school setting. Some children may be permitted to show quite a lot of aggression before the teacher steps in. Others may receive a reprimand from the teacher after only slight aggression. And there is equally little control over the amount of reinforcement or punishment at home, over the type of reinforcement, or over the consistency with which reinforcement or punishment is given for a particular behavior. Surely there is inconsistency in "real life," and if we want to study what happens in "real life," the less structured observational procedures will be the method of choice. But observing the full details of the total situation is so enormously complex that it will be difficult, if not impossible, to sort out the real "causes" of aggression. The alternative is to set up an experiment.

Suppose one of your hypotheses about the differences among children in aggression—drawn from learning theory—is that children who are rewarded for aggression will be more aggressive than children who are not rewarded. You want to look at this question under conditions in which you have control over the rewards given to the child. So you take one group of children, usually one at a time, into a separate room with some toys that might invite aggression, such as a punching bag, a gun, a hammer, and the like. The child is encouraged to play freely, and each time she shows any aggressive behavior with the toys you say something like "Good" or "That's the right way to play." With another group of children the same procedure is followed, except that nothing at all is said to the child about her play. This second group is usually called the control group. It is designed to tell something about how children behave if there is no intervention at all, so that the behavior of the "experimental group" can be compared with the behavior of the control group. You can probably think of several other variations that might be included: a group to which the experimenter said "Good" in response to nonaggressive play, a group in which each child is given candy or money instead of praise for behaving aggressively, and so on. There are lots of possible comparison groups.

The next step is to devise some sort of test that will tell whether the treatment of the children has had any effect or not. One way to do so would be to observe children in the nursery school to see whether or not those who had been rewarded for aggression in the experiment showed more aggression in the natural setting than did children in the control group. But there are obvious problems with this approach. For example, different children will encounter very different experiences in nursery school. A better strategy for a good experiment would be to set up a standard test situation that all the children would undergo. One way would be to have each child, immediately after her original play with the toys, go into a room with another child (usually a child who has not participated at all) and ask the two to play some specific game together. In one experiment, somewhat similar to the imaginary one I'm describing, the children played a game called "cover the X." An X had been painted on the floor, and the two children were to compete to see who would be covering the X with her body at the end of a two-minute period. During the play period, the experimenter kept track of the amount of kicking, scratching, biting, and the like, to see whether or not children who had been rewarded for aggressive play were more aggressive with their play partners than were children from the control group. If it turns out that the experimental group is more aggressive than the control group, then we can conclude that reward for aggression has at least something to do with the levels of aggression that we see.

The crucial features of an experiment of this kind are (1) that the experimenter has control over the critical or relevant aspects of the situation, (2) that normally only one variable is changed at a time, and (3) that children are assigned randomly to the two (or more) groups. A variation of random assignment of children to separate groups is to have the subjects serve as their "own controls" by having each child tested or observed in both the experimental and control conditions.

Experiments of this kind obviously have distinct advantages over observation or the clinical method, for they permit us to sort out the various forces working on the child (or adult) and to look at them one at a time. The disadvantage is that the experimental situation is always artificial, so that there is a problem of generalizing from the experiment to real life.

With each of the three methods I have described there are clear advantages and equally clear disadvantages. Fortunately, we ordinarily do not have to make a final choice among them. Combinations of methods may be used, and the conclusions from research of several types may be combined. Hypotheses generated from observation or clinical methods may be tested in experimental situations or the reverse. Experimental manipulations can be introduced into real-life settings, so that a broader range of reactions or responses may be observed. Most researchers move back and forth between unstructured or semistructured observation and experimental procedures. Combining the methods in this way allows researchers to maximize the advantages of each.

SPECIAL PROBLEMS IN DEVELOP-MENTAL RESEARCH

All three of the techniques I have described—observation, clinical method, and experimental procedure—are used by investigators in studying adults, too. In fact, all that I have said so far is equally applicable to any research area in psychology, although my examples have all been drawn from developmental psychology. But there are some problems unique to research on child development that deserve mention.

First, in very young children there is a severe restriction on the range of possible responses. A baby or a toddler cannot talk to you, cannot tell you in words whether or not she can see, hear, or understand something. The experimenter who wishes to explore the world of the very young infant must be ingenious in discovering alternative ways in which the child can respond informatively.

A second and extremely difficult problem has to do with the whole issue of studying development at all. By definition, to be interested in development is to be interested in change. What developmental psychologists want to study is change, both visible change—for instance, increases in height or weight—and internal change, such as the acquisition of such complex concepts about the world as spatial relations, time, number systems, and morality. In the case of physical changes, the same yardstick may be used throughout the age span: You can always measure height with a ruler. But in the case of changes in personality or cognitive skills, there are no equivalent rulers. If we assume that a common path is being traveled by all children, then the task is to find some measuring tool that will tell us how far along that path each child is at a particular time. Some developmental processes, particularly in cognitive development, may work that way. But some may not, and in any case, aside from those for physical changes, there are no very good measurement tools that span the entire age range. The IQ

BOX 4
Longitudinal and Cross-Sectional Research

In studying children and their development, we are often interested in seeing what happens over time. How is a 4-year-old different from a 2-year-old? What can the older child do that the younger child cannot? How much consistency in behavior is there from 2 to 4 (or between any other two ages)? Is the child who is most aggressive at age 2 the one who is most aggressive at age 4? If not, when do consistent individual patterns emerge? There are dozens of such questions, all of which involve comparing children through long age spans.

Two techniques have been used to get at questions of this kind. The first is the *longitudinal* study, in which the same group of children is studied over time. Many longitudinal studies begin with children at birth and follow them, through observations and tests each year or so, as they grow up. There are several famous studies of this kind. One, carried out at the Fels Research Institute in Ohio, began with a group of infants born between about 1930 and 1940

(Kagan & Moss, 1962). The children were observed and tested several times a year until they were 12 years old and then again when they were in their middle twenties. A similar study was conducted in Berkeley, although in that study the children were not followed into adulthood (Macfarlane, Allen, & Honzik, 1954). Occasionally, a longitudinal study is directed at a particular group that is of special interest. Louis Terman and his associates at Stanford University, for example, selected a group of mentally gifted children in California during the 1920s and followed them into middle life (Terman, 1925; Terman & Oden, 1947).

Longitudinal studies of this kind, as well as shorter-term studies in which groups of children are observed and tested over several months or years, are necessary if we are to answer any questions about consistency of behavior over time; there is simply no other way to study consistency adequately. Longitudinal research also permits us to see what kinds of environmental

test is an admirable attempt to devise such a tool, but it too presents difficulties (see Chapter 10).

A related problem arises when we seek to study continuity over time. In Chapter 4 there is some discussion about differences in temperament among babies from birth. Some babies seem placid, even sluggish; others are quicker or more restless. Do these temperamental differences persist throughout life? It is an interesting question, and one that has drawn some attention from researchers, but the measurement problem is extremely complex. I may measure the passive-active dimension in an infant by watching the amount of bodily movement. But is that an appropriate measure for an older child or an adolescent? It is entirely possible that there is an underlying consistency in the temperamental trait, but that the trait manifests itself in different ways as the child grows older. Physical agitation may be replaced, for example, by mental quickness or impulsive behavior. If we measure physical restlessness throughout the age span and find that there is no tendency for restless babies to grow up into restless teenagers, can we conclude that there is no consistency of temperament? We can only conclude that there is no consistency in physical restlessness and speculate about the other forms that the original trait may take at later points.

events alter the child's behavior. For example, if we start out with a group of equally healthy children at birth and follow them over the first several years, we will find that some will turn out to have emotional or mental disorders, which may be traceable to particular experiences during the years that we studied them.

But longitudinal studies obviously take a great deal of time. We have to wait until the children grow before we can make the next observation or take the next measurement, so it is often a long time before we get answers to questions that interest us. Such studies are also extremely expensive and very difficult to do, if only because the subjects move away or drop out and we are left with only a self-selected subgroup of the original sample. So unless the questions we are asking absolutely require a longitudinal study—and some do—we are more likely to find a kind of study called *cross sectional*, in which a different group of children of each age is studied. If you want to know how 2-

and 4-year-olds differ and how they are the same, it's usually sufficient to take a group (preferably a large group) of each and to compare them on standard tests or under experimental conditions. There is an enormous amount of research of this kind in the child-development literature. Children of different ages are all given the same tasks or observed in the same settings and their behavior compared. But bear in mind that a cross-sectional study is thus not an experiment. The subjects are not assigned randomly to groups. Rather, the groups are picked because of a difference that already exists between them. At the completion of such a study, you may have a good description of the difference, but you will not have explained why 2- and 4-year-olds are different. It takes good theory along with good experimentation to bridge that gap.

These problems are not insoluble. Research designs have been devised to get at some of the issues (see Box 4 for a discussion of several design alternatives), and some theoretical advances have suggested new answers to the problems of measurement over time. But any developmental psychologist needs to be aware of and sensitive to these problems.

INTERPRETING INFORMATION

Once you have performed your experiment, made your observations, or examined a child using the clinical method, you have some information. Now what do you do with it? What conclusions can you legitimately draw from it?

If all you want to do is to describe what children do in particular situations, any of these methods will be helpful. That is, if you want to answer the "what" question, you may use any of the three. If you observe in a natural setting, you may be able to say something about what the child does in a free situation. If you use the clinical method, you may be able to say something more about the child's ideas and concepts or what she is capable of doing. If you have used an experiment, you may be able to say something about the conditions under which a child will or will not be able to perform some task.

But what about the "why" question? Immediately we are into the area of causal relationships. We would like to be able to say that a child's behavior is caused by something, and here the various alternative techniques are not equally useful.

From observational and clinical method studies, the best we can usually do is to talk about relationships among things. We may be able to say, for example, that children who are highly aggressive are more likely to have parents who are permissive toward aggression. But that is not the same as saying that permissiveness toward aggression causes aggression. All we know is that the two things occur together; we don't know whether one causes the other, nor can we ever draw a causal statement from such an observation alone. The statistic you will see in studies and textbooks describing such a relationship is a correlation. It is simply a number, which can range from 0.00 to ±1.00, that describes the strength of a relationship between two variables. A correlation of 0.00 indicates that there is no relationship between the variables. You might expect, for example, to find a zero or near-zero correlation between the length of big toes and IQ; that is, you could not predict a person's IQ by knowing the length of her big toe or vice versa. A correlation of 1.00 (either + 1.00 or − 1.00) indicates that the two variables are totally predictable, one from the other.

Of course, correlations of 1.00 are not found in the real world, but correlations of 0.80 or 0.90 are found and suggest very strong relationships. For example, the correlation between IQ test scores of identical twins is in this range. Knowing one twin's IQ, you can predict the other's IQ with considerable accuracy. A negative correlation occurs when the two variables are inversely related, so that a high score on one variable goes with a low score on the other. For example, there is a small negative correlation between the number of children in a family and the IQ score of the last child: low IQ scores tend to go with high numbers of children in the family. Overall, the closer the correlation is to 1.00, the stronger is the relationship between the two variables. Correlations of 0.50 or 0.60, which are fairly common in psychological research, suggest moderate degrees of relationship, but with many variations or exceptions.

It is important to remember that correlations as descriptions of relationships, though interesting and suggestive of causes, cannot prove causes in themselves.

Let me give a fairly silly example. It is a fact that there is a correlation between the number of refrigerators sold each year since 1900 and the number of deaths from lung cancer. The more refrigerators sold, the more lung cancer. But neither you nor I would ever draw the conclusion from this correlation that the sale of refrigerators causes lung cancer. Rather, we would suspect that other factors in our environment have changed along with the increase in refrigerators, and that one or more of these factors is probably the cause of increased lung cancer.

The refrigerator example is an easy one, because it is so clearly not a causal relationship, but watch out for other situations where you may well be tempted to conclude that there is a causal relationship. It is a fact that women who smoke are more likely to have premature babies than women who do not smoke. That is, there is a correlation between smoking and prematurity. It is terribly tempting to say, "Aha! Smoking causes prematurity, so if all women would stop smoking, we'd have fewer premature infants." It may be a causal relationship, but we cannot conclude that from this simple piece of information. We have to have a variety of other facts before we can draw any kind of causal conclusions. For example, why do some women smoke and some not in the first place? Maybe some women smoke because they are more nervous, and it's the nervousness that causes prematurity. The only way to settle the question properly would be an experiment in which you took some of the women from a group that did not smoke and assigned them to a "smoking group." But, of course, we can't do that, for it is not ethical to ask someone to do something in an experiment that we know may be harmful to her or him. One alternative would be to take a group of women who already smoke and have half of them stop smoking during the pregnancy, but for various practical reasons (including the difficulty of persuading people to stop smoking), this particular experiment has not been performed. Instead, we must rely on information from research with animals (in which case we have the problem of generalizing the findings from animals to man) and on detailed correlational explorations of the relationships involved. For example, if we suspect that nervousness may be the causal factor, we may devise a separate measure of nervousness and find out whether or not nonsmoking women who are highly nervous are more likely to have premature babies than are less nervous nonsmoking women. Causal relationships can be approached through this sort of digging, but they cannot be fully demonstrated through correlational techniques alone.

An experimental procedure, on the other hand, can permit us to make some kinds of causal statements. If we hold everything constant except the one element that we manipulate, and if we see differences in behavior, we can be quite sure that the cause of the differences in behavior was our treatment. If children who have been rewarded for aggression are more aggressive in play with their partners than are children who have not been rewarded for aggression, we can be quite sure that in this experimental situation previous rewards for aggression were the cause of the increase in aggressive play. Of course, that doesn't mean that all aggression is caused by a history of reinforcement. All the experiment tells us is that rewarding aggression may increase it under some conditions. But there may be many other factors that increase aggression as well.

The point of all of this discussion is to emphasize that drawing conclusions from any variety of research is difficult. If you stick with the natural situation, you are unlikely to be able to disentangle cause and effect; if you opt for more controlled experimentation, you will have difficulty saying how the behavior you observe in the experiment relates to what may happen in the natural situation. The best is to combine the several techniques, as I have already suggested. A combination of experimental and correlational methods may permit some fairly clear conclusions about causes, as in the research on diet to be discussed in Chapter 3. Drawing conclusions from research, in fact, is nearly always a process of adding up findings from several studies done with several methods. If the same conclusion seems to hold up among different researchers and across research strategies, then our confidence in that conclusion is increased.

A WORD ON GOOD AND BAD RESEARCH

I hope that what I have said so far about styles of research will give you some clues on how to evaluate any research you read about. But perhaps it is worthwhile for me to spell out some more specific guidelines.

1. The type of research technique, whether primarily observational, clinical, or experimental, does not in itself determine whether the research is good or bad. Which of these techniques is helpful and good will depend on the questions you are asking and the kind of conclusions you want to draw from the research. So don't let anyone persuade you that observation or the clinical method is bad because it is "unscientific"!

2. If experimental research is done, it is crucial that the experimenter really does control the situation and has not made some major technical error. To give you an example from another field, in an agricultural study I once read, the experimenter wanted to know whether potatoes would grow better if hay were placed around them while they were growing, or whether they'd do better with black plastic around them. Fine so far. But then, instead of using the same variety of potatoes for each treatment, he also varied the type of potato, so that one variety was growing under hay and another was growing under black plastic. When he was all done, he couldn't tell whether differences in yield under the two conditions were the result of the variety of potato or the treatment he'd given. This example may sound silly, but it's from a real study. Equally badly designed research is to be found in the child-development literature as well, so just because a piece of work is described as an "experiment," its "results" are not necessarily gospel.

3. Equally, just because a piece of research is new does not make it more worthwhile than old research on the same question. There was a lot of marvelous research done from the 1920s to the 1960s; it's easy to fall into the habit of putting greater value on the newer work, and that's not always appropriate.

46

4. The number of children studied or observed is an important factor. There are some kinds of studies in which it makes sense to include only very small numbers of children for observation or clinical investigation. In many studies of the effects of operant conditioning, for example, there is only one subject. A single child is observed before treatment, her reinforcement pattern is changed, and her behavior is observed afterward to see if it has changed. What this observation tells us is that operant-conditioning principles hold for this child and this particular behavior. In other circumstances, however, you should watch out for studies using very small numbers of subjects. We simply cannot generalize as well from a piece of research involving 6 children as from research involving 60 or 600 children.

You should also note that I am really saying something here about your own personal experience as well. If you have children of your own or have been around children a good deal, it is terribly tempting to take your own experience as "the truth" and to ignore the findings from carefully controlled experiments or observations on larger numbers of children when they don't agree with your own experience. Your experience may be helpful and valid, but it is based on a small sample of children under uncontrolled conditions, with your own biases influencing your observations. Don't toss out your own observations, hunches, or conclusions. Use them as sources of hypotheses, and see how they fit with existing theory and observation. But don't ignore good research either simply because it disagrees with your own observations. If there is a disagreement between your "intuition," observations, and the conclusions from research, think about the possible biases in your own observations. Consider the quality and generalizability of the research, and see if some kind of synthesis is possible.

For myself, I use several major criteria in evaluating any individual piece of research.

1. Is it clear? Can I understand what was done and what was found?
2. Is it an important finding, or is it trivial? There is a lot of technically very good research on very small and not very interesting problems. Obviously, I prefer to have technically good research on important problems, but even technically defective research on important questions may be of value in the long run.
3. Does the research provoke new ideas, new insights, new theoretical proposals? Again, research that may have technical flaws may also have this quality of provoking new thought on a particular problem. Obviously, in such a case the new insights or ideas need then to be followed up with further, better designed research.
4. Is the finding from a particular study consistent with other findings in the same area? Inconsistency with other findings should not lead you to throw out a finding, as new hypotheses may be generated by an inconsistent finding. But if there are ten studies

that show one result and there is one study that suggests another conclusion, you should look at the method in that one study very carefully.

5. Are the findings replicable? That is, if the same piece of research were done over again, would the same results be obtained? Replication is perhaps a criterion used by professional researchers more than by laypersons, but it is an important one nonetheless.

6. Finally, are the conclusions drawn by the researchers consistent with the data and appropriate to the methods? For example, are causal statements being made on the basis of correlational data?

SUMMARY

1. Some knowledge of research methods and of the logic of research analysis is necessary both to avoid being misled by bad research and to help in interpreting findings presented in this and other books.

2. Three main strategies are used by researchers to obtain information about children's behavior.
   a. Observation, of which there are several types;
   b. Clinical method, in which there is more judgment and intervention by the researcher;
   c. Experiment, in which the researcher controls all but the one or two variables he is particularly interested in, so that he can observe behavior in a less complex setting and see more clearly the effects of possibly important independent variables.

3. Each variety of research has particular advantages, and most investigators use a combination of the several methods.

4. In interpreting information from research of the several varieties, answers to the "what" questions can be obtained from any method: Observation, clinical method, and experiments all can yield factual, descriptive information.

5. Explaining the causes of behavior is more complex. Hypotheses about causes may be generated from observation or from the clinical method, but experimental approaches are needed at some point to provide clear indications of causation.

6. We must be particularly careful about interpreting the results from research of a correlational nature; drawing causal conclusions is often tempting and must be guarded against.

7. Decisions about whether a given piece of research is good or bad should be made on the basis of several criteria, including clarity of the research, whether the finding is important or trivial, whether or not the research provokes new ideas, whether or not the findings are consistent with other findings, and whether or not the conclusions drawn are consistent with the method used.

REFERENCES

Suggested Additional Readings

Barker, R. G., & Wright, H. F. *One boy's day: A specimen record of behavior.* New York: Harper & Row, 1951.
A particularly excellent example of the use of detailed observation.

Gollin, E. S. A developmental approach to learning and cognition. In L. P. Lipsitt &
C. C. Spiker (Eds.), *Advances in child development and behavior* (Vol. 2). New York: Academic Press, 1965.
One of the clearest presentations of the set of difficulties associated with doing developmental research. Gollin suggests one solution to some of the difficulties. The paper

was written for professionals, not for students or laypersons, and assumes quite a lot of technical knowledge; recommended only to those who are really interested in the problems of doing developmental research.

Jones, R. R., Reid, J. B., & Patterson, G. R. Naturalistic observation in clinical assessment. In P. McReynolds (Ed.), *Advances in psychological assessment.* San Francisco: Jossey-Bass, 1975, pp. 42–95.
A good recent discussion of some of the difficulties involved in setting up efficient and helpful observational techniques.

Kagan, J. *Change and continuity in infancy.* New York: Wiley, 1971.
Contains an excellent brief discussion of the problem of studying continuity in development (particularly on pages 12–22). The language is moderately technical but clear.

Mussen, P. H. (Ed.). *Handbook of research methods in child development.* New York: Wiley, 1960.
A comprehensive discussion of all aspects of research methods with separate chapters, by different authors, covering different facets of the problem. All the chapters are quite technical, but you might find Bijou and Baer's chapter on "The laboratory-experimental study of child behavior," and one by Wright on "observational child study," helpful.

Wright, H. F. *Recording and analyzing child behavior.* New York: Harper & Row, 1967.
An excellent introductory discussion of specimen or "ecological" observational techniques. A very good place to start; more recent than the Barker and Wright book listed above.

Other Sources Cited

Kagan, J., & Moss, H. A. *Birth to maturity.* New York: Wiley, 1962.

Macfarlane, J. W., Allen, L., & Honzik, M. P. *A developmental study of the behavior problems of normal children between twenty-two months and fourteen years* (University of California Publications in Child Development, Vol. 2). Berkeley: University of California Press, 1954.

Sackett, C. P., Stephenson, E., & Ruppenthal, G. C. Digital data acquisition systems for observing behavior in laboratory and field settings. Behavior research methods and instrumentation, 1973, 5, 344–348.

Terman, L. M. *Genetic studies of genius* (Vol. 1). Stanford: Stanford University Press, 1925.

Terman, L. M., & Oden, M. H. *The gifted child grows up.* Stanford: Stanford University Press, 1947.

Because what follows is the first in a series of projects that are suggested at the end of many of the chapters in this book, some general comment seems in order. You may undertake these projects on your own or under the direction of a teacher. You may do your own thinking and musing about the conclusions from the study, or you may share your efforts with others. My purpose in devising the projects is to suggest ways in which you can experience some of the material discussed in the chapters more directly. You have read about observation; here is a chance to try it out to see for yourself what some of the difficulties are. In later chapters there will be suggestions for projects involving listening to and recording the language of a young child or the conversations between a young child and her mother, and for administering simple standardized tests to older children. In each case I have given detailed instructions, which should be followed as closely as possible.

PROJECT 1
OBSERVATION OF A CHILD

I have several purposes in suggesting this project. First, many of you reading this book will have had relatively little contact with young children and need to spend some time simply observing a child. Such an observation will help to make other sections of the book more meaningful. Second, I think it is important that you begin to get some sense of the difficulties involved in observing and studying children. So I am suggesting here, as a preliminary step, that you keep a straightforward observational record, noting down each thing that the child does or says. You will find, I think, that the task is less straightforward than it seems, but this is the simplest place I know of to begin.

Step 1. Locate a child between 18 months and 6 years of age; age 2, 3, or 4 would be best.

Step 2. Obtain permission from the child's parents for observation. Tell them that it is for a course assignment, that you will not be testing the child in any way, but merely want to observe a normal child in her normal situation.

Step 3. Arrange a time when you can observe the child in her "natural habitat" for about one hour. If the child is in nursery school, it's all right to observe her there. If not, the observation should be done at home or in some situation familiar to the child. You must not baby-sit during the observation. You must be free to be in the background and cannot be responsible for the child during the observation. So someone else has to be there, either in the house to be called upon if needed, or in the nursery school.

Step 4. When the time for the observation arrives, place yourself in as unobtrusive a place as possible. Take a small stool with you if you can, so that you can move around as the child moves around. If you are in a nursery school setting, you will probably not have to make any explanation to the child. If you are in the child's home she will probably ask what you are doing. Say that you are doing something for school and will be writing things down for a while. Do not invite any kind of contact with the child, don't meet her eyes, don't smile, and don't talk except when the child talks directly to you. If the child talks to you, say that you are busy and will play a little later.

Step 5. Begin your observation. For one hour write down everything the child does insofar as possible. Write down the child's speech word for word. If the child is talking to someone else, write down the other person's replies, too, if you can. Describe the child's movements and play behavior. Throughout, keep your description as free of evaluation and intent as you possibly can. Do not write, "Sarah went into the kitchen in order to get a cookie." You don't know why she went originally. What you saw was that she stopped what she had been doing, got up, and walked into the kitchen. There you see her getting a cookie. Describe the behavior that way, rather than drawing conclusions or making assumptions about what is happening in the child's head. Avoid words like "try," "angrily," "pleaded," "wanted," and so on. Describe only what you see and hear.

Step 6. When you have completed the observation and have had a chance to think a little about your experience, go back and reread what you did, and consider the following questions: Did you manage to keep all description of intent out of your record? Were you able to remain objective? Were you able to write down all that the child did? If not, what sorts of things were left out? Did you find that as it became more difficult to record everything you began to summarize the child's behavior more? How do such summaries affect your ability to use the information? What kind of information about this child do you think could be extracted from your record? Could anyone get a measure of the child's level of activity from your record or count the number of times the child asked for attention? What else could you draw from your record? What changes in the method of observation would you have to introduce to obtain other sorts of information? What was the effect, do you think, of your presence on the child's behavior?

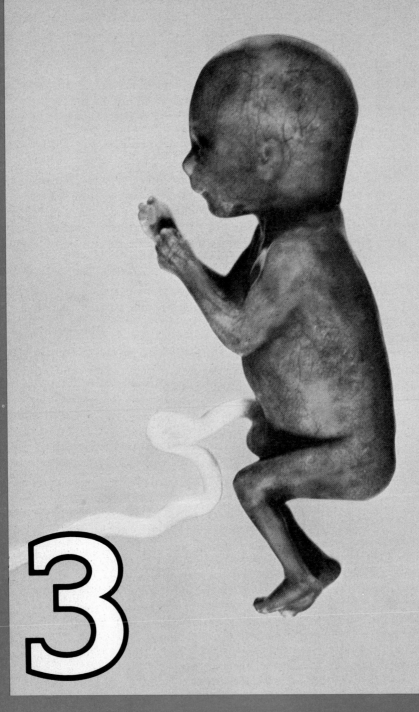

3

Prenatal Development and Birth

No doubt most of us naively think a child's life begins at birth. We all know that there are nine months before that, but except for the mother, who feels the baby moving inside her, a child doesn't have much reality for the rest of us until she is born. Because of this bias and because until fairly recently we didn't know as much about what happens to a child during the time spent *in utero*, we tended to overlook the importance of those first nine months.

But the prenatal period—the development of the child before birth—is vitally important because it lays the groundwork for everything that follows. The fact that development during the prenatal period is completely normal for most infants doesn't reduce the importance of the period at all. There are many things that can go wrong, and when something goes wrong prenatally, it is usually serious and often permanent.

Let us begin, as usual, with description. Just what is the normal course of development for the newly conceived child?

CONCEPTION AND EMBRYONIC DEVELOPMENT

The first step in the development of a single human being is obviously conception—that moment when a single sperm cell from the male pierces the wall of the ovum from the female. Of course, conception cannot occur at just any old time. The ovum must be in a position where it can be reached by the sperm, and that only occurs for a brief period during each menstrual cycle. Although some women, either naturally or because of fertility drugs, produce more than one ovum a month and thus may conceive more than one child at a time, ordinarily a woman produces one ovum per month from one of the two ovaries. The ovum travels from the ovaries down the fallopian tube into the uterus. If the woman has had intercourse recently, a sperm cell may reach the ovum during its journey and pierce the outer cell wall: A child is conceived. (See Figure 6 for a sketch of the relevant parts of the body.) If conception does not occur the ovum disintegrates in the uterus within a few days' time, after which there can be no possibility of conception until the next ovulation.

If conception has occurred the 23 chromosomes from the sperm cell and the 23 chromosomes from the ovum combine to produce the 23 pairs of chromosomes that will map the development of the individual child.

Some time during the first 24 to 36 hours after conception, the single cell splits in two (a process called *mitosis*); the DNA making up the genes "unzips" (as I described in Chapter 1), so that each of the new cells contains the full 23 pairs of chromosomes. Mitosis continues so that within several days there are several dozen cells, and the whole mass is about the size of a pinhead. Within about two weeks the fertilized ovum (called the *zygote*), still continuing to subdivide, has traveled down the fallopian tube, reached the uterus, and implanted itself

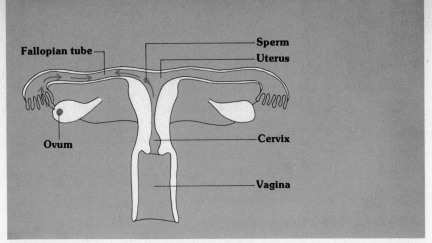

FIGURE 6
Schematic diagram of the female reproductive system showing how conception occurs. (Source: P. H. Mussen, J. J. Conger, & J. Kagan. *Child Development and Personality* (3rd ed). New York: Harper & Row, Publishers, Inc., 1969, p. 65.)

in the uterine wall. In order to attach itself to the wall of the uterus, the developing group of cells has to achieve its first division of labor—the first clear differentiation of cells into separate types. The total group of cells divides into two groups, one of which forms a sort of sphere around the inner group of cells. The sphere then develops tendrils, which attach themselves to the wall of the uterus.

From the time of implantation into the uterus until about eight weeks after conception, the developing organism is called an *embryo*. During the embryonic period rapid differentiation takes place. A series of membranes develop around the embryo, within which there is a liquid substance (technically the *liquor amnii*). The *placenta* also develops during the early embryonic phase. It is a critical organ that separates the infant's bloodstream from that of the mother and through which nourishment passes to the embryo and later the fetus. The relationship among these several structures, when fully developed, is shown in Figure 7. As you can see in the diagram, the embryo is attached to the placenta by means of the umbilical cord. The umbilical cord contains two arteries and a vein, which carry blood to and from the embryo via the placenta. The mother's bloodstream opens into the placenta, but between the mother's blood and the embryo there are membranes that serve as screening devices, preventing the passage of many potentially harmful substances, such as viruses. Such important components of the mother's blood as proteins, sugars, and vitamins pass through the membranes to the child's bloodstream, as do some drugs (including alcohol and nicotine).

Growth during the embryonic period is extremely swift, with rapid cell division and differentiation of function occurring among the devel-

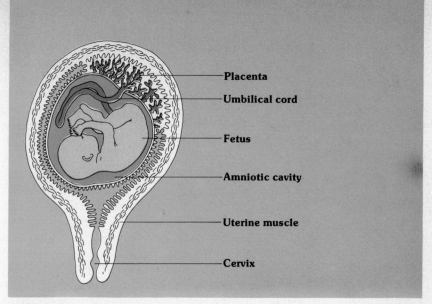

FIGURE 7

The fetus during the early part of the fourth month of pregnancy, showing the placenta, the umbilical cord, and the amniotic cavity. (Source: E. L. Potter. *Fundamentals of human reproduction.* New York: McGraw-Hill, 1948.)

oped cells. As you can see from pictures of embryos, the head is the largest part of the developing body at this stage, but other parts of the body, including various organs, also develop during the embryonic period. By 8 weeks of age the embryo, now about 1¼ inches in length, has all of the following:

eyes
ears (although set lower on the head than they will be eventually)
a mouth that already opens and closes
a nose
a liver that already secretes bile
a heart (with a rudimentary heartbeat) and circulation system
arms with elbows and legs with knees
fingers and toes (although webbed, rather like a duck's foot)
a tail (which grows smaller after this stage. The tail bone at the end
    of your spine is the remnant of this tail)
a spinal cord
bones

THE FETAL PERIOD

Beginning in about the third month of pregnancy, the embryo becomes the fetus and remains the fetus for the remainder of the prenatal period. During the embryonic period virtually all major organ systems appeared, along with all the other major parts of the body and the rudimentary muscles and nerves. The remaining seven months involve primarily a process of refining and improving what has already been developed. It's a bit like the process of building a house. You first put up the floor and then the framework for the walls and roof. This skeleton of the house has the full shape of the final house; you can see where the windows and doors will go, what shape the rooms will be, how the roof will look. This stage is reached quickly, but after that, there is a very long process of finishing the house, which consists of filling in around the skeleton already established. So it is with the embryo and the fetus. At the end of the embryonic period, the main parts are all there, at least in some basic form; the next seven months are for the finishing process. The main exception to this developmental pattern is the nervous system, which is present in only very rudimentary form at the age of 8 weeks. At that point only a small part of the brain and only the suggestion of a spinal cord have developed. The major development of the brain and the nervous system does not occur until the last three months or so of pregnancy and continues for the first six months to a year after the baby is born.

To give you some idea of the kinds of development that occur during the seven months of the fetal stage, let me sketch some of the more important ones.

By the end of 12 weeks the fetus is about 3 inches long and has developed eyelids. Muscles are developing more extensively, and the sex organs are well enough developed so that the sex of the child can be readily determined.

By the end of 16 weeks the mother can usually feel the first fetal movements, the fetus is about 4½ inches long. Lips are well formed and can be moved, the mouth can be opened and closed, and the fetus even shows some swallowing activity. The hands

FIGURE 8
Fetus at approximately 4 months of gestational age, sucking its thumb.

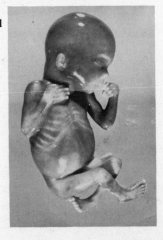

FIGURE 9

A fetus at approximately 6 months of gestational age.

can be opened and closed, and the thumb can be curled under. A fetus of about this age is shown in Figure 8.

The fetus is about 10 inches long by the end of 20 weeks. It is much more human looking and may begin to grow hair. During this period some fetuses apparently—accidentally or otherwise—get one thumb into the mouth and show thumb sucking.

By the end of 24 weeks fingernails have developed, eyes are completely formed, and the fetus has sweat glands and taste buds. Fetuses at this age occasionally survive if born prematurely, for they are now capable of breathing. Still, survival is rare for infants born this young. Figure 9 shows a fetus of about this level of development.

The end of 28 weeks marks the line between likely survival and nonsurvival. The nervous, blood, and breathing systems are all well enough developed to support life should the child be born prematurely, although there are still great difficulties, and children born this early do not have a very high survival rate. Premature infants born at this stage still have very poorly developed waking and sleeping cycles, and their breathing is not very regular.

From 28 to 40 weeks there is gradual improvement and organization of the infant's skills and systems. The nervous system (brain and nerves) continues to develop during this period, as do the sensory systems.

57 **Prenatal Development and Birth**

The sex of the child is determined at the moment of conception by the code contained in the combined maternal and paternal chromosomes. As I pointed out in Chapter 1, if the child receives an X chromosome from both the mother and the father, the child will be a girl; but if a Y chromosome is received from the father, the child will be a boy.

This initial genetic patterning, however, does not *guarantee* the later sexual development of the infant. Recent work with animals has led to the discovery that during the gestation period of a male organism there is a particular point when an infusion of *androgen* (the male hormone) occurs. The hormone is apparently produced in the child's own developing body and not by the mother. It is this infusion of androgen that is critical for the later development of male genitals, and it may also affect such later "male" behavior as rough-and-tumble play and aggression as well. If the hormone is *not* present at the appropriate time, the developing fetus develops as a *female* even though it is genetically XY. The reverse is also true. A genetically female fetus, if exposed to the male hormone at the appropriate time, will develop some features of male genitals and will show more normally male patterns of behavior as well.

Although most of the research on the effects of hormones on early sexual differentiation has been done on primates and other animals, there is enough evidence from studies of human subjects that is consistent with the animal research to make me fairly confident about the generality of the conclusions. The conclusions to be drawn are several: (1) The "basic" form appears to be female, not male! A developing embryo, without the addition of appropriate hormones, will develop sexually as a female. (2) For the development of a male *two* genetically controlled signals are necessary. First there has to be the appropriate genetic code (XY), but second, somewhere in the maturational process there must be a signal to secrete appropriate levels of androgen. Unless both of these conditions occur, a sexual male does not develop. (3) In a girl the process will develop normally with only the single signal of the XX genetic pattern, but the process can be interfered with from the outside if the mother takes drugs that are chemically similar to androgen, or if for some reason inappropriate hormones are secreted by the fetus during development.

**THE
IMPORTANCE
OF SEQUENCE**

One of the most important points about the child's prenatal development is how remarkably regular and predictable it is. The various changes occur in what is apparently a fixed order, in a fixed time period. To be sure, things can go wrong, as I'll explain more fully, but for the vast majority of children the entire process runs off in a predictable, fixed pattern.

We don't have to look far for an explanation. Whenever there is that much regularity in a fixed sequence, maturation seems the obvious answer. The fetus doesn't learn how to grow fingernails. She doesn't have to be stimulated from outside to grow them. Rather, the fingernails, along with all the other parts of the complex system, are apparently controlled by the developmental code contained in the genes.

The sequence of development, which is controlled and regulated by the genetic information, is not impervious to outside influence or modification, but it takes a fairly sizable intervention to make very much difference. And whether any outside influence will have any negative effect on the developmental pattern seems to be heavily dependent on the *timing* of the intervention or outside influence. Developing systems are most vulnerable at the point of most rapid development. Since most organ systems are developing most rapidly during the earliest months of gestation, the potential impact of external influences is likely to be largest at this time as well.

GENETIC ABNORMALITIES

Although the genetic code governing the major features of prenatal development is ordinarily the same for all children, the genetic information itself can be abnormal in some cases, and when that occurs a series of abnormalities may emerge. The most common anomalies are those that come about because of a failure of proper chromosome division. For example, in *Down's syndrome* (also called mongolism), the 21st chromosome does not separate during the "unzipping" process I described in Chapter 1. One of the resulting cells ends up with two number 21 chromosomes, while the other has none. The cell with too few chromosomes ordinarily does not survive, but the cell with an extra one may. If this is an ova, then on fertilization the zygote will have three number 21 chromosomes (one from the father and two from the mother), and the child will have Down's syndrome. Such a child is usually (although not always) quite severely retarded and often has a variety of physical anomalies, including characteristic eye folds, a flattened face, and occasionally heart defects or other internal disorders.

Other sorts of genetic anomalies may occur if there is incomplete or incorrect division of the sex chromosome. Some individuals have only one X and no Y chromosome (called *Turner's syndrome*). Such a child looks like a girl, but is usually short, frequently mentally retarded, and sterile. Other individuals may have two X chromosomes and one Y (*Klinefelter's syndrome*), or an XYY pattern, in which the child looks like a male, and is unusually tall.

Any of the genetic anomalies can be diagnosed during the first three months of pregnancy through a process called *amniocentesis*. A sample of the amniotic fluid is taken and a chromosomal analysis of the cells is done. If there is some anomaly present, the mother may—if such an action is consistent with her own moral judgment—choose to abort the fetus at this stage. Eventually, as researchers come to understand the causes of genetic mutations, it may become possible to prevent the occurrence of these syndromes entirely.

ENVIRONMENTAL INFLUENCES ON PRENATAL DEVELOPMENT

I have emphasized the universality of the developmental sequence and that this sequence is difficult to disrupt. But while the process of prenatal development is robust, it is also intricate, and like most intricate things, it can break down or be affected by outside influences. It is important to have some sense of its sweep and robustness, but it is equally important to know something about the sorts of influences that *will* disrupt the normal maturational process.

You should note as you go through the discussion of diseases, diet, and other influences that in many cases the potential adverse effects can be averted by reasonable preventive or precautionary measures. I have tried to point out, in each case, the sort of preventive measures or other solutions that have been found to be effective. In addition, you will find that recent evidence paints a far less gloomy picture about the *long-term* consequences of various kinds of prenatal and birth complications. So, while a number of things can and do go wrong in prenatal development, many potential hazards can be avoided, and many deviant outcomes can be ameliorated with later interventions. If you keep these two hopeful points in mind as you read through the long list of potential disasters, it may help to keep the information in perspective.

Diseases of the Mother

Most diseases cannot be passed through the placental membranes to the child, but there a few exceptions in which the disease agent is small enough to pass into the child's bloodstream.

RUBELLA

This disease (also called *german measles*) can be one of the most dangerous for a pregnant woman to contract, although it is ordinarily risky to the fetus only if the mother contracts it during the first three or four months of the pregnancy. Although the mother herself may be only slightly ill, the disease organism passes through the placenta, infects the child, and may interfere with the organs and systems that are developing at that time. The most common abnormality among "rubella babies" is deafness, and they sometimes have heart defects or cataracts as well. These abnormalities are sometimes accompanied by mental retardation, although it is very difficult in most cases to determine whether the retardation is a direct result of the rubella or an indirect effect of the deafness. I want to emphasize here, and in the discussions of other environmental effects, that the relationship between the specific environmental event—in this case rubella—and the effect on the child is *not* invariable. *Most* infants whose mothers had rubella during the early months of the pregnancy do *not* show any abnormality. In one study by Sheridan of 200 children whose mothers had had rubella during the first 16 weeks of pregnancy, only 13 had significant hearing loss, and by ages 8 to 10 the children as a group had average IQs. Obviously, in this case, as in most others, we are a long way from understanding the relationship between the environmental stress or disorder and the effect on the child. It may be that the range of times during which rubella has negative effects on the developing embryo-fetus is very narrow, or it may be that some fetuses, for one reason or another, are more vulnerable to stresses of this kind.

In any case rubella *is* preventable. Vaccination is available and should be given to all children as part of a regular immunization program. Adult women who were not vaccinated as children can be vaccinated later, but it must be done at least three months before a pregnancy to provide complete immunity. (Those women among you who are not sure whether or not you have ever had german measles or who have not been vaccinated for rubella should be checked for immunity. If you are not immune, you should be vaccinated, but only if you are absolutely sure you are not pregnant at the time of vaccination! A vaccination for rubella during the first three months of a pregnancy has the same effect on the embryo-fetus as does the disease itself.)

SYPHILIS

Mothers with syphilis may pass the disease onto their children, although they do not invariably do so. Research suggests that the fetus is infected in about 25 percent of cases in which the mother is infected. Often such syphilitic fetuses are miscarried; if they are born, they have a high incidence of mental subnormality and physical deformities. Again, there is a possible preventive measure. If the syphilitic mother receives treatment and the disease is cleared up within the first 18 weeks of pregnancy, the fetus is unlikely to be infected.

OTHER DISEASES

A few other diseases, most notably diphtheria, influenza, and typhoid, may be passed to the fetus through the placenta, although in these cases the effects on the infant do not appear to be as severe.

Drugs Taken by the Mother

Ours is a drug-taking culture. We pop aspirin into our mouths at the slightest sign of pain, decongestants at the sign of a cold, tranquilizers when we are nervous, sleeping pills when we cannot sleep, and so on. Pregnant women are no exception. In fact, in an effort to maintain physical comfort, they are perhaps more likely to take medication during pregnancy than at other times, either on their own decision or by prescription of a physician. What are the consequences of this? Do any of the drugs have harmful effects on the embryo or fetus? What about smoking, alcohol, barbiturates, or heroin?

World attention was focused on the problem of drugs during pregnancy when, in the early 1960s, large numbers of babies were born (particularly in Germany and England) without arms, sometimes without legs, with limbs arrested in very early stages of embryonic development and thus foreshortened, or with hands attached directly to the shoulder. After some medical detective work, it was discovered that the culprit was a new tranquilizing drug called *thalidomide,* which had been taken by many pregnant women during the first three months of pregnancy. Apparently the drug not only passed through the placental barrier but also had a direct effect on development of the infants' limbs. The children seemed normal in other respects. In this case the timing of the taking of the drug was crucial: If the mother had taken the drug during the period when the limbs were developing, there was a very strong likelihood of an abnormally formed infant. But the same drug taken later did not have the negative effect. Again, it is the timing of the environmental event that appears to be crucial in determining whether or not there will be any effect and, if so, what kind.

The impact of smoking is more complex. For some years it has been clear that women who smoke are quite a lot more likely to have low birthweight infants. And since low birthweight is associated with a variety of other difficulties, a great many physicians recommended that pregnant women not smoke. The difficulty, as I pointed out in Chapter 2, is that a causal conclusion is being drawn from fundamentally correlational data. The repeatedly observed fact is that there is a correlation between the child's birthweight and the mother's smoking. But does the mother's smoking *cause* low birthweight in the infant? Or, instead, could the cause be the smok*er* rather than the smok*ing*? Might women who smoke be different in some respects than those who do not, so that it is the personality of the smoker that is at issue? Yerushalmy, who did the best study on this question, developed some new hypotheses. Again, this is correlational research, but he found that women who did not smoke during the pregnancy but began smoking *after* the birth of the child were just as likely to have low birthweight infants as those who had smoked during the pregnancy. In addition, women who smoked during pregnancy but were able to quit afterward did *not* have more low birthweight infants. These findings make it look very much as if it is something about the personality or other behavior of women who smoke that is different from those who do not, or from those who smoke but are able to quit. In this case it appears not to be the nicotine or other drug in the cigarettes that affects the child.

In the case of alcohol there is some new evidence that points to a more direct effect of the drug. A *fetal alcoholism syndrome* has been identified among infants born to alcoholic mothers. Such infants are usually mentally retarded and often have a series of minor physical deformities. They are underweight at birth and slow to develop throughout infancy. Thus far, this syndrome has been linked only to very extreme forms of alcoholism. Research now underway may show whether milder levels of alcohol intake may have smaller or less frequent effects.

I should point out that in many cases the effects of alcoholism are compounded by malnutrition, for many alcoholics eat little, and what they do eat does not constitute a well-balanced diet. But the characteristics of the infants with fetal alcoholism syndrome are not typical of children born to other malnourished mothers, which suggests that there is some additional effect from the alcohol.

Other potentially addicting drugs, such as heroin and barbiturates, seem to have fairly clear effects. Excessive use of barbiturates during pregnancy may cause damage to the developing brain, apparently as a result of loss of oxygen in the blood. Heroin, too, has an effect. Mothers addicted to heroin may pass on this addiction to their infants. In one study infants born to heroin-addicted mothers showed signs of withdrawal symptoms immediately after birth; the babies were irritable, vomited often, and trembled. After several days these immediate symptoms wore off, but there were signs of possibly permanent brain damage. The infants did not have the same regular sleep cycles as do normal babies, and their heart rates varied a good deal.

The Mother's Diet

When I first wrote this section three years ago, it was one area in which I felt most confident about my ability to offer firm conclusions. It seemed to me then that a number of lines of research evidence were pointing clearly to the conclusion that malnutrition during the prenatal period and during infancy had major effects on the child's brain development, and consequently on later intellectual development.

Now I am not so sure, although it is still possible that at least part of my earlier conclusion is correct. There are at least three questions to be dealt with. First, what are the effects of malnutrition on physical development? Second, what are the implications of such effects for the child's behavior and intellectual development? And three, does the timing of the malnutrition make a difference? Because I think these questions are both practically and theoretically important, and because new data are not entirely consistent with the earlier conclusions, I am going to give more detail and more specific research evidence than I usually do. I hope in the process that I can give you some sense of the kind of problems facing psychologists in their efforts to understand developmental processes. At the very least you might want to think of this section as a kind of detective story.

First, then, what do we know about the effects of malnutrition on physical development? Here the information seems the clearest. For obvious reasons most of the good experimental research has been done with animals who have been deprived of sufficient calories or protein during various stages of gestation or after birth. The conclusion from this research is that one major effect of malnutrition in the pregnant mother is a reduction in the number of brain cells in the offspring.

(Lewin's paper, listed in the References at the end of the chapter, includes a review of research on this question.) In addition, malnutrition seems to have an effect on the development of the interconnecting links between individual nerve cells, so that a malnourished animal has a brain that has fewer linkages. What little information is available from postmortem examinations of children who have suffered malnutrition suggests that parallel processes occur in humans.

Do these detrimental effects on brain growth have an impact on behavior? It certainly seems logical that they should, since the brain is involved in virtually all aspects of learning as well as perception, movement, and other functions. The results here are somewhat mixed. The animal research, on the whole, points to slower learning among offspring deprived of proper nutrition either *in utero*, after birth, or both. To give you just one example, Vore and Ottinger fed some pregnant female rats a normal diet, and others only half as much. In order to make sure that any eventual lowered learning rate could be associated with malnutrition alone and not with some lesser mothering ability on the part of the malnourished mothers, Vore and Ottinger "cross-fostered" the offspring after the pups were born. That is, half of the pups born to malnourished mothers were raised by well-nourished mothers, and half of the pups born to well-nourished mothers were raised by malnourished mothers. The reduced food intake to the mother, who had been malnourished during pregnancy, was continued until the pups were weaned, after which all the animals had a normal diet. Some time later, all the animals were tested on several learning and problem-solving tasks. The animals who had been malnourished *in utero*, after birth, or both were slower to learn or to solve mazes than were the well-nourished animals.

Obviously, the same kind of research cannot be done with children. Studies of malnutrition in humans have been of three types. First, it is possible to explore this question by giving nutritional *supplements* to women who are thought to be experiencing malnutrition of some kind because of poverty. There is not a great deal of research of this kind, but what little there is seems to point to a positive effect of such supplements on the child (see, for example, the paper by Ebbs and his colleagues). Ramey and his associates have also shown that dietary supplements to infants directly after birth may also have a beneficial effect on the child's measured IQ, at least in the short run.

A second research strategy involves correlational techniques. The most famous studies of this kind are a series of investigations carried out in Aberdeen, Scotland, and including most of the infants born in that city from 1947 to the present (Baird, 1946). The first finding of these researchers was that women who had had histories of poor nourishment during their own childhoods were likely to be significantly shorter than were women who had had adequate nourishment as infants and girls. Because of this finding, the Aberdeen researchers have used height as a rough index of nutritional history. They are not suggesting that height is uninfluenced by genetics, but only that if you look at large groups of women, shorter ones are more likely to have been malnourished.

Their further investigations showed that shorter women were more likely to have abnormal pelvic shapes (and thus more difficulty in delivery) and were more than twice as likely to have stillborn infants or premature deliveries. It is important to bear in mind that these are correlational findings; we cannot draw any kind of firm causal conclusions from them, but it is notable that these results are consistent with what has been found in experiments with animals. The Aberdeen studies also suggest one additional hypothesis: The effect of malnutrition on infant growth and development may last over several generations. If increased complications during pregnancy are the result not only of the mother's diet during the pregnancy itself but also malnourishment during her own growth, then it may take at least two generations to eliminate the effects entirely.

By far the best way of approaching the problem of understanding the effects of malnutrition is by selecting children who have experienced this *in utero* or in early infancy, and following them as they grow or assessing them at a single time. Ideally, the researcher would want to compare such malnourished children with others from similar environments who had not been malnourished. This is extremely difficult research to do, because so many factors tend to go along with malnutrition. Malnourished children usually come from very poor families and may suffer other disadvantages as well. But there are a few good studies of this kind, and the results from them are simply not consistent. Several studies of malnutrition in infants and young children show slower learning or poorer discrimination ability among malnourished children compared to well-nourished children. (See, for example, Brockman & Ricciuti, 1971.) In particular, a number of researchers have recently suggested that is is especially on tasks requiring focused attention that the malnourished infants and children do least well.

A major study done in Jamaica by Stephen Richardson and his colleagues is consistent with this same kind of conclusion. They studied a group of boys who had been severely malnourished during their first two years of life, comparing them to their own brothers who had not been malnourished (or not so severely) and to children from other families from the same areas and social class level. When the boys were school age (7 to 10) those who had been malnourished were doing significantly less well in school and less well on standard tests of reading and arithmetic and on standard IQ tests. Richardson tried to determine if these results were occurring only because the malnourished boys were from homes that offered less stimulation in other ways. Obviously, studying the siblings of the malnourished children is one way to get around this problem. Additionally, Richardson tried to evaluate the amount of intellectual stimulation available in each home, and then combined this information with what he knew about the child's malnutrition. The children who were best off in cognitive development were well nourished and from relatively enriched homes. Children who were malnourished but living in pretty stimulating environments were in the middle and about equal to children from impoverished environments who had *not* been malnourished. The least well off were those children who had had *both* malnutrition and an unstimulating environment. So malnutrition alone has some impact, but the impact is far greater if it is combined with poverty of environment.

All of the research I have discussed so far seems to point to a fairly clear conclusion, and by now you may be wondering why I am being so cautious. But I have saved the counterevidence for last.

The single major study with results inconsistent with the overall picture I have been painting is one by Zena Stein and her several associates. Ordinarily, a single inconsistent study would not weigh very heavily in the balance against all the other findings in this area. But the Stein study is an extraordinarily good one from a technical standpoint. Because of the researchers' care in trying to explore the alternative explanations, we simply must take this study seriously.

The study was made possible by an accident of history. In the fall of 1944, as a reprisal against the Dutch and against the Allied armies, the German army cut off all civilian transport to and within Holland. Farming areas of the country managed to survive fairly well, but in the industrial and western part of the country severe food shortages began by about October or November (see Figure 10). The famine continued until early May of 1945 when the Allied forces took control of the famine area. The food shortage was *severe.* At the height of the famine the official food ration was as low as 500 to 600 calories a day, although most people managed to scrounge somewhat more than that, and there were some public soup kitchens and the like which provided supplements. Apparently, most infants and young children were given preference, so they did not suffer from severe malnutrition. But pregnant women were not given any official preference, so there was apparently fairly severe malnutrition experienced *in utero* by children born during or after the famine.

What Stein and her colleagues did was to compare 18-year-old men who had been born in the famine area during the critical times with other men who had been born at the same time, but in parts of Holland not affected by the famine. In Holland all men must report for military induction at age 18, and the induction procedures include extensive physical and mental testing. The researchers also examined the records of hospitals in the famine and nonfamine areas so that they could see what the immediate effects on infants might have been. The results are surprising.

66

FIGURE 10

The famine and nonfamine areas of Holland, studied by Stein and her associates in their research on malnutrition. (Source: Modified from *Famine and Human Development: The Dutch Hunger Winter of 1944–1945* by Zena Stein, Mervyn Susser, Gerhart Saenger, and Francis Marolla. Copyright © 1975 by Oxford University Press, Inc. Reprinted by permission.)

They found first of all that malnutrition, particularly during the last three months of the pregnancy, was associated with lower birthweight in the infants and with heightened rates of infant death during the first three months after birth. Fertility also dropped way down during the famine, so that far fewer children were conceived then. So there were clear short-term effects. But they could detect *no* long-term effects at all. The young men who had been born during or immediately after the famine were equivalent on all the cognitive measures used at age 18 to those who had not experienced this prenatal malnutrition. And there was no increase in the rate of mild or severe retardation among the famine group either.

How are we to make sense of these findings, particularly in light of all the other research I have mentioned? My only hunch at the moment—which is consistent with what Stein et al. also finally conclude—is that what is at issue here is the *timing* and *duration* of the malnutrition. In the Dutch study only prenatal malnutrition occurred; infants received adequate nourishment. But in virtually all the other studies I have mentioned, the malnutrition has occurred both prenatally and postnatally, and it may be the combination of these effects that is detrimental to the child's later learning. This hypothesis is consistent with what we are coming to know about the maturational timetable for the brain. While a good deal of brain cell development occurs prenatally, most of the development of the interconnecting tissue between nerve cells occurs *after* birth. So we might reasonably suppose that postnatal malnutrition would have a particularly severe effect.

The Dutch study points to the robustness of the human organism. Although Stein et al. believe that some cell depletion probably did occur in the children who experienced the famine prenatally, they are struck by the fact that this reduction in brain cells didn't have any noticeable effect on their ability to function as children or adults. Perhaps there is some redundancy, some excess of brain cells, so that a 10 or 20 percent depletion has little effect on behavior; longer-term malnutrition might "use up" the reserve, so that effects on behavior could be detected.

I hope that this rather lengthy discussion of the current facts and speculation about the effects of dietary deficiency on prenatal development has given you some feeling for the enormous complexity of research on such seemingly simple problems. It seems clear that malnutrition has *some* effect on brain development and on later learning, but we now need to take a much closer look at the question of the timing and duration of the deprivation before we can draw much firmer conclusions.

What is a good diet? For many years pregnant women have been advised to limit strictly the amount of weight that they gain. One rule of thumb was 2 pounds a month, which would result in a maximum total weight gain of 18 pounds during the whole pregnancy. Of course, doctors cautioned that the diet must be balanced, but in order to avoid gaining more than 2 pounds a month, many women had to count calories rigorously, running the risk of unbalanced diets. There were several reasons for this advice, which seemed reasonable at the time. First, many women were concerned about regaining their youthful figures after the birth of their baby and wanted to gain as little as possible so that there would be as little as possible to lose later. Second, doctors thought that there was a smaller risk of some diseases of pregnancy, such as toxemia, if the mother gained less. Third, some doctors suggested that keeping weight gain to a minimum would result in a smaller baby, which would be easier to deliver.

As it happens, most of these assumptions are not true. There is no evidence that the risk of toxemia is lower in a mother who gains less weight. Mothers who gain very little do on the average have smaller babies, but that's probably something to worry about, not to be proud of. Small babies—even those that are carried for the full nine months—have more difficulty immediately during and after birth, and may have greater difficulty later on as well. In fact, doctors, who for many years had thought that the gestational age of the baby (the number of weeks since conception) was the crucial factor in the infant's survival and development, are now beginning to realize that the infant's weight is the much more important factor. Small babies just have more trouble, and small babies often result from inadequate diet during pregnancy.

Despite all this research, we don't yet know as much as we need to know about specific dietary requirements during pregnancy, so it's not possible to write a very precise prescription for a pregnant woman. This much is clear: Both sufficient calories and sufficient protein are essential. A normally adequate weight gain during pregnancy is now thought to be about 24 pounds (though more than that is not disastrous), and the mother, in order to maintain herself and the growing fetus, needs to take in about 1000 calories a day more than she would normally eat. Of this caloric intake, protein seems to be the most crucial part. Under conditions of stress, which would include pregnancy, the protein requirement goes up, not just as a function of increasing body weight but also because of extra strain on the body. As a rough index, the protein need for a pregnant woman is about one-third more than her normal requirement for her body weight.

Obviously, other things beside protein and calories make a difference, although we have less information about the effects of other deficiencies. We do know that iodine deficiency in the pregnant mother increases the risk of mental subnormality and such physical impairments as blindness and deafness in the infant. Research with animals also suggests the importance of a sufficiency of zinc; rats with insufficient zinc in their diets had offspring who were almost always physically deformed in some way. Iron deficiency also is of particular concern because iron deficiency anemia is so common in the United States, as are vitamin C and vitamin A deficiencies. But we don't yet have the kind of evidence that we need to determine the effects of these deficiencies on the developing child, except that it is certainly reasonably to assume that the unborn child needs optimal amounts of all vitamins and minerals for proper growth.

X-rays and Other Radiation Large doses of X-rays, such as those used for the treatment of some kinds of cancer in the mother, may increase the risk of miscarriage and may also produce physical deformities in the child, depending on the timing of the X-ray treatment. There has been some concern about the effects of less massive doses, such as X-rays to detect tuberculosis or ulcers, but there is presently no evidence that such single, brief doses of X-rays are harmful to the fetus.

The Mother's Emotional Stress

So far, I've talked about the effects of definable and measurable factors like disease, drugs, radiation, and diet. But what about the mother's state of mind? What if she is nervous? What if she doesn't want the child and feels upset throughout her whole pregnancy? What if she receives some kind of emotional shock during pregnancy? Can all these psychological states affect the unborn child? Evidence suggests that they can, apparently by altering the mother's physical state, which in turn affects the infant's physical state. You know the feeling of "arousal" when you are angry or afraid: Your heart beats faster, your breathing changes, and you may feel tingly all over. These effects are produced by a flooding of your system with a substance called *adrenalin*, which prepares you for "fight or flight." Adrenalin can pass through the placental barrier to the fetus and can arouse it in a similar way, as can other substances produced by the mother's body as a result of her emotional state. So, although the mother's nervous system and that of her infant are not interlocked, her feelings can have some effect.

There are some reasonable conclusions that emerge from studies of emotional stress during pregnancy.

1. During the time that a mother undergoes high degrees of stress or upset, the fetal activity rate is greatly increased. If she remains upset or distressed over a long period of time, the baby's rate of activity may stay high during the whole period of stress.

2. Mothers who are tense and anxious during their pregnancy (because they don't want their babies, are afraid of delivery, are concerned about their ability to handle the babies after birth, or who experience other forms of tension or stress) have more difficult deliveries. The babies are more irritable, cry more immediately after birth, and also seem more likely to be "colicky". (It doesn't seem quite fair that the most nervous mothers, the ones who worry the most about being able to cope, wind up with the hardest babies to handle; but that's the way it often works!) Mothers with *severe* psychiatric disturbances, such as schizophrenia, are also likely to have more complications during pregnancy and delivery.

3. Mothers who experience some stress during pregnancy may have infants who, although they are not physically deformed, are prone to various kinds of illnesses and physical problems throughout life.

The Mother's Age

One woman I know, who was having her first baby at the age of 36, was quite startled to find on her chart in the hospital the phrase "elderly primipara." She figured that 36 wasn't all that elderly! But for having a first infant (which is what primipara means) 36 is comparatively old. For women over 35 having a first baby or for women over 40 having a second or later baby, there are a variety of additional risks. Labor is usually longer, and the risk of a stillborn infant is greater, as is the chance of having a Down's syndrome child. For mothers between the ages of 20 and 30, the chance of having a Down's baby is about 1 in 1000; for mothers between 40 and 45, it is 1 in about 100; and for mothers over 45, it is about 1 in 45. But all these increased risks, except for the chance of a Down's syndrome child, are more likely in mothers from poverty environments, which suggests that age itself is not the only factor. Rather, the mother's overall physical health is crucial, and older mothers, particularly if they live in poverty, are likely to be less healthy.

Very young mothers also face some additional risks, including an increased risk of having Down's children. Some increased risk of prematurity, birth difficulties, and the like occurs for any mother under about 20, but, the younger the mother, the greater all these risks become. And in the United States we have many very young mothers. Each year there are something on the order of 30,000 babies born to mothers who are 15 years old or younger. In these cases the mother herself has not finished growing and has extra nutritional needs of her own. When the strain of carrying an infant is added to her other body stresses, decided hazards to both the mother and the child are created.

One other group that is "at risk," in addition to older mothers and very young mothers, are women who have had more than four pregnancies, particularly if the pregnancies have occurred very close together. Babies born within a year of the next oldest brother or sister are likely to be smaller at birth, to have lower IQs at age 4, and to have slower motor development. The fifth or later child in any family, no matter how widely spaced the preceding pregnancies, is also likely to have a lower IQ, possibly because of the cumulative strain on the mother's body.

THE BIRTH PROCESS

Like the prenatal period, the birth process for most infants is normal and without complications. The mother's labor proceeds steadily, the infant's heartbeat remains strong, the infant is born normally (that is, vaginally, rather than by Caesarian section) without much pulling and tugging, the baby breathes soon after birth, and all is well. Doctors have a system of rating infants at birth, called the *Apgar score*, which is a combination of ratings of the amount of time before breathing, the infant's color, and so on. The score can range from zero to 10; a score of 10 indicates a perfect, healthy-looking infant. The vast majority of infants are given scores of 8, 9, or 10 at birth. They look and act normal. But, as in the prenatal period, there are some things that can go wrong at birth.

Lack of Oxygen
One of the most common risks is that the infant will not breathe immediately and thus will be deprived of oxygen, particularly oxygen to the brain. A lack of oxygen (anoxia) can result in the kind of motor problems that we call *cerebral palsy*, in which there are tremors or uncontrolled muscular spasms. Cerebral palsied children often have great difficulty later in learning to walk and to speak clearly. But it takes quite a long period of oxygen deprivation for this serious effect to be observed. More recently, there has been great interest in the possible effects of much shorter times of oxygen deprivation, as when the infant does not breathe for 30 to 60 seconds or longer after birth. The research evidence we have now suggests that infants who have suffered this kind of anoxia are slower to develop, both in motor and in early mental development, but that they catch up to their peers in most areas by about age 7.

Prematurity
Two kinds of newborn baby used to be called premature—those clearly born before the full nine months of pregnancy had been completed, and those who were very light in weight at birth. Obviously the two events are correlated, for a baby born too early is likely to be very small. But many babies who have gone through a normal, or nearly normal, prenatal period are also very small, and these children too have come to be a cause for concern. The most common term now used by professionals for a baby who weighs less than 2000 grams (about $4\frac{1}{2}$ pounds) is *low-birthweight* infant. Babies born after short prenatal periods are called *short-gestation-period* infants, and those who are unusually

small for the length of gestation, however long gestation may have been, are called *small-for-date* babies. Whether or not these three groups of babies have different kinds or amounts of difficulty later on is not yet known, for research on prematurity has tended to lump all three types together. What is clear is that an infant born before she is ready—either because it is too early or because she is too small—has a variety of difficulties. Breathing is more difficult, and sleep patterns are not well established. The short-gestation-period baby in particular has not yet developed the normal layer of fat just below the skin, so that she has to be kept warm. In fact, all early and underdeveloped babies cannot survive long without the special womb-like care of an incubator. They are often sad-looking little creatures, with mottled skin, irregular breathing, and a great deal of apparently random movement.

After a month or two in an incubator, most early or small babies are ready to go home and to be cared for in the usual way. The crucial question is whether or not there is any long-term effect of early birth or lower birthweight. Most of the research on these questions has used birthweight as the single index of prematurity. That research indicates that premature babies are likely to suffer long-term retardation if they grow up in poverty or less stimulating environments, but they may eventually become completely normal if they grow up in middle-class or more stimulating environments. The premature child does start out at a disadvantage, both physically and mentally, but this disadvantage can be overcome if she is exposed to sufficient stimulation, encouraged to be independent, and given the kind of educational opportunities more common to the middle class. The disadvantage is not so likely to be overcome if the child is reared in less affluent surroundings, perhaps because her diet is likely to be less good or because there is less intellectual stimulation and encouragement for development. The evidence for this dual conclusion about the effects of prematurity comes from several sources (see the Drillian and Werner references at the end of the chapter). The most encouraging aspect of these findings is their suggestion that prematurity does not *necessarily* lead to all sorts of problems later on except when it is accompanied by other sorts of complications, such as physical abnormalities, brain damage, and so on. A premature baby can be completely normal by school age. What we need now is to sort out the factors that produce this curative effect in the middle-class child, but fail to do so in the premature child reared in conditions of poverty.

SEX DIFFERENCES IN PRENATAL DEVELOPMENT

The subject of sex differences in development has recently been receiving a great deal of attention from researchers, theoreticians, and from nonpsychologists who have strong feelings about what they believe are "real" or "unreal" sex differences. This ferment has brought forth some good research on sex differences, but the research has raised as many questions as it has answered, so most of the issues are by no means settled. Because this is an area of substantial interest—both practically and theoretically—I will include a section on sex differences at the end of each chapter. For similar reasons, I have also included a section on social class differences.

Since nearly all prenatal development is controlled by genetic information, which is the same for all members of our species, there are relatively few sex differences in pattern or rate of development during this period. But there are a few differences worth noting.

1. As I pointed out earlier in this chapter, there are differences in the hormones secreted prenatally. The early infusion of androgen not only serves to trigger the development of male genitals, but also appears to "program" the brain in some way, so that appropriate hormones will be secreted at adolescence. The specific pattern of fetal hormones is critical, then, not only in prenatal sexual differentiation, but in later growth patterns.

2. There is some evidence that girls may be a little faster in development prenatally. We know that at birth girls are about 4 weeks ahead in the process of bone hardening, but it is not clear whether girls are also somewhat faster in neurological development as well.

3. Girls are, on the average, somewhat smaller at birth.

4. There is a fair amount of evidence that male fetuses are more vulnerable to a variety of stresses and abnormalities. Complications of pregnancy and delivery are more common for male fetuses, and more males are born with deformities or disorders of various kinds. Precisely *why* this should be the case is not at all obvious. But the fact remains that the male fetus (and the male child after birth) is quite a lot more likely to show deviant development in one form or another.

SOCIAL CLASS DIFFERENCES IN PRENATAL DEVELOPMENT

Virtually all the disorders of pregnancy and birth I have described in this chapter are more common among the poor or minority groups than among the more affluent majority. This is true in the United States as much as in exceptionally poor countries. For example, infant mortality rates are about twice as high among blacks in the United States as among whites, and they are higher among the poor than among the middle class. Prematurity and other birth complications are also more common among the poor—about three times as common among minority group poor and about twice as common among white poor as among the white middle class. The Scottish studies of malnutrition, which I mentioned earlier, also show that very short women are much more often found among the poor. These women are the most likely to experience some kind of disorder of pregnancy or delivery, and their children are most likely to suffer deformities, prematurity, or other prenatal stress.

There are several possible explanations of these social class and ethnic differences. First, it may well be that there are important dietary deficiencies among the several groups. The Dutch study of famine showed that higher rates of prematurity (low birthweight) and infant mortality occurred for mothers malnourished during the last trimester of pregnancy. If poor mothers in our country experience significant malnutrition during pregnancy, this could help account for the higher rates of both infant mortality and prematurity. I am sure that differences in nutrition are contributing factors to the social class differences we observe, but few pregnant women in this country, even among the poor, experience the severe levels of malnutrition common in Holland during the famine. We know very little about the impact of chronic *sub*nutrition on the development of the fetus or on infant mortality or other indices of difficulties. So diet is probably not the only answer.

A second difference between the poor and the affluent in our society is the amount and quality of prenatal care available. There is good evidence linking prenatal care with later outcomes of pregnancy. Women who have had little or no prenatal care are far more likely to experience difficulties in birth, and the infant mortality rate is far higher in such pregnancies as well. (See the paper by Birch, given in the References section, for a good review of this evidence.) We know, in addition, that poor and minority group women are much less likely to have adequate prenatal care. These findings demonstrate that there is a link of some kind between prenatal care and complications of pregnancy or infant mortality, but you should notice that these are essentially correlational findings. We cannot conclude that lack of prenatal care *causes* complications, only that the two tend to go together. We *can* conclude from other research in this area, however, that provision of good prenatal care can prevent or reduce the likelihood of disorders. When poverty level women who would otherwise be unlikely to receive good prenatal care are given such care, the rate of disorders and complications drops.

What sort of social policy might we design that would help to eliminate, or narrow, the social class differences in prenatal complications? A few years ago, when I was more confident about the role of prenatal nutrition in later development, the simplest social policy seemed to me to be some kind of dietary supplement policy. Such a policy still makes sense as an aid in the prevention of prematurity and infant death, but the long-term gains from *pre*natal dietary supplements may be less than we had thought or hoped. Improvement in prenatal care among the poor or among ethnic groups not habitually encountering health delivery systems also seems like a high priority item for national or local social policy.

75 **Prenatal Development and Birth**

OVERVIEW   To me, one of the most amazing aspects of the whole story of prenatal development and birth is how often it goes well. With such a long list of things that can go wrong, it is easy to find yourself thinking that no child can be "normal" and that something is bound to go wrong. But, of course, in most cases it doesn't. The maturational system is extremely powerful. An adequate environment is required within which the maturational pattern can be fully realized, but if there is no serious outside interference, the embryo and fetus grow and develop with regularity and predictability, and the birth process is normal. It takes fairly major interference to cause anything very serious to go wrong, although there appear to be definite critical periods during which quite small interferences can have very large bad effects.

The risks—and there are risks for the developing child and the mother—are more and more defined and predictable, and many of them can be avoided with proper diagnosis and good prenatal medical treatment. Unfortunately, the very women who are most prone to difficulties—the poor, the poorly nourished—are those who are least likely to receive good medical treatment, often because they can't afford it but sometimes because they do not see the need for it. Whether "better education" alone is enough to close this gap is not at all obvious. But there is a need for some serious thought about social policies in this area.

SUMMARY

1. At the moment of conception, when the sperm cell pierces the wall of the ovum, 23 chromosomes from the mother combine with 23 from the father to provide the complete genetic map for that individual child.

2. During the early weeks of gestation, the cells of the embryo multiply and differentiate their functions, developing eventually the several protective membranes around the embryo.

3. The embryo is attached by the umbilical cord to an organ called the placenta, through which the mother's blood passes to the child. Membranes in the placenta act as filters for most potentially disruptive substances, but nourishment passes through to the child.

4. At approximately two months of gestational age the developing organism, now called the fetus, has a heartbeat, rudimentary limbs, and other features.

5. By 7 months of gestational age, when the child can live if born early, most organ systems are quite well developed, with the notable exception of the nervous system, which has a major portion of development still to be completed.

6. The sex of the developing child is determined by the XY (male) or XX (female) patterning in the chromosomes, but the actual genital sex, and some aspects of later behavior, are determined as well by the amounts or timing of hormone infusions for the developing male. Male fetuses not receiving appropriate hormones at the right time do not develop male sexual characteristics.

7. Some genetic anomalies can occur if the division of the chromosomes is not completed fully during cell division. Down's syndrome is the result of one such anomaly.

8. Although gestation and delivery are normal for the vast majority of infants, there are environmental influences that can have an impact during this prenatal phase:

a. Diseases in the mother, such as rubella, syphilis, and typhoid.

b. Drugs taken by the mother. Some drugs, like thalidomide, have specific effects on the development of particular organs while others may have more diffuse effects. Smoking *may* be linked to greater likelihood of prematurity, but the connection seems not to be a direct one.

c. Malnutrition in the mother may result in a depletion of brain cells in the fetus and a greater likelihood of premature birth or infant mortality. Long-term effects of prenatal malnutrition are still debated.

d. X-rays and other radiation.

e. The mother's emotional state, including pervasive anxiety, or brief or prolonged shock.

f. The mother's age: very young and older mothers incur higher risks of several kinds.

9. The majority of the environmental effects are most marked during particular limited periods of embryonic or fetal development. A given environmental influence may have a marked effect at one stage of development and little or no effect earlier or later.

10. A great many of the possible hazards of the prenatal period may be prevented or treated if the pregnant mother receives adequate prenatal care.

11. During birth there are additional possible risks from lack of oxygen or prematurity, but there are only slight signs of long-term negative effects from such conditions.

12. There are relatively few sex differences in prenatal development, except that the hormone patterning is different for the two sexes and that girls develop skeletally at a somewhat faster rate.

13. The risk of virtually all prenatal problems is greater among the poor than among the affluent; there is particular need for improved prenatal care and education among women in poverty environments.

REFERENCES

Suggested Additional Readings

Birch, H. G. Health and the education of socially disadvantaged children. *Developmental Medicine and Child Neurology*, 1968, *10*, 580–599.
A technical paper in a somewhat forbidding-sounding professional journal; however, a highly readable paper on malnutrition and the medical care available (or not available) to the poor.

Lewin, R. Starved brains. *Psychology Today*, September 1975, pp. 29–33.
A general discussion of malnutrition and its possible effects. A good starting place if you are interested in this topic.

Rugh, R., & Shettles, L. *From conception to birth: The drama of life's beginnings*. New York: Harper & Row, 1971.
The best book for beautiful pictures of the embryo and fetus at various stages of development.

Sameroff, A. J., & Chandler, M. J. Reproductive risk and the continuum of caretaking casualty. In F. D. Horowitz (Ed.), *Review of child development research* (Vol. 4). Chicago: University of Chicago Press, 1975, pp. 187–244.
A marvelous paper on the long-term outcome for infants with various types of prenatal and birth difficulties. A very good starting place for other references if you are interested in this topic.

Stein, Z., Susser, M., Saenger, G., & Marolla, F. *Famine and human development. The Dutch hunger winter of 1944–45*. New York: Oxford University Press, 1975.
This book about the Dutch famine, which I have discussed in some detail in the chapter, is quite technical, but would be a good source if you are interested in the problems of malnutrition. Read Birch first and perhaps the Lewin paper for an alternate view.

Other Sources Cited

Baird, D. The epidemiology of prematurity. *Journal of Pediatrics,* 1964, *65*, 909–924.

Brockman, L. M., & Ricciuti, H. N. Severe protein-calorie malnutrition and cognitive development in infancy and early childhood. *Developmental Psychology,* 1971, *4*, 312–319.

Drillian, C. M. *The growth and development of the prematurely born infant.* Baltimore: Williams and Wilkins, 1964.

Ebbs, J. H., Brown, A., Tisdall, F. F., Moyle, W. J., & Bell, M. The influence of improved prenatal nutrition upon the infant. *Canadian Medical Association Journal,* 1942, 608.

Ramey, C. T., Starr, R. H., Pallus, J., Whitten, C. F., & Reed, V. Nutrition, response-contingent stimulation, and the maternal deprivation syndrome: Results of an early intervention program. *Merrill-Palmer Quarterly,* 1975, *21*, 45–54.

Richardson, S. A., Birch, H. G., Grabie, E., & Yoder, K. The behavior of children in school who were severely malnourished in the first two years of life. *Journal of Health and Social Behavior,* 1972, *13*, 276–284.

Richardson, S. A., Birch, H. G., & Hertzig, M. E. School performance of children who were severely malnourished in infancy. *American Journal of Mental Deficiency,* 1973, *77*, 623–632.

Sheridan, M. D. Final report of a prospective study of children whose mothers had rubella in early pregnancy. *British Medical Journal,* 1964, *2*, 536–539.

Vore, D. A., & Ottinger, D. R. Maternal food restriction: Effects of offspring development, learning, and a program of therapy. *Developmental Psychology,* 1970, *3*, 337–342.

Werner, E., Simonian, K., Bierman, J. M., & French, F. F. Cumulative effects of perinatal complications and deprived environment on physical, intellectual, and social development of preschool children. *Pediatrics,* 1967, *39*, 408–505.

Yerushalmy, J. Infants with low birth weight born before their mothers started to smoke cigarettes. *American Journal of Obstetrics and Gynecology,* 1972, *112*, 277–284.

eral ways. For example, she may move or her heartbeat may accelerate. The fact that the child shows some reaction indicates that she heard the sound in some fashion, although it does not tell us whether or not she can tell the difference among various sounds. Other researchers have attempted to discover how loud a sound has to be before the baby will react. The most representative conclusion from this body of literature is that there is little reaction on the part of the newborn to sounds softer than about the level of the normal speaking voice (about 50 to 60 decibels). There is some response to softer sounds, but the likelihood that the baby will react is greatly increased when the sound is just below the 60-decibel level. There is some further hint that newborns may also be especially sensitive to sounds within the pitch range of the human voice. The baby responds less to very high and to very low sounds than to the middle-pitch range.

It is far less clear that the newborn can tell the location of sounds. You and I can tell the location of a sound because we are highly sensitive to very small differences in the amount of time it takes a sound to get to one ear versus the other. The ability to locate sounds is present in 6-month-old babies—they will turn their head and eyes toward a sound (see Chun, Pawsat, & Forster, for example), but in younger infants the issue is undecided. Some researchers have reported that infants as young as 1 day old turn head and eyes in the direction of a sound, but more recent findings indicate that the position of the child's head before testing begins makes a big difference in the child's localization ability. This question will have to remain open until more sophisticated techniques for measuring the very young infant's reactions to sounds can be developed.

A final interesting finding about the very young infant's response to sound is that she seems particularly sensitive to rhythmic sounds, which appear to have a generally soothing quality. One suggestion has been that because the baby has just spent nine months listening to the rhythmic sound of her mother's heartbeat, any sound with the same rhythmic qualities will be a kind of reminder of the soothing atmosphere of the womb. Mothers through the ages have intuitively taken advantage of their baby's tendency to quiet down with rhythmic activity. The creak of the rocking chair, rhythmic cooing, repetitive lullabies all will soothe the baby. (See Brackbill et al. for a systematic exploration of this question.)

SEEING

In order for the infant to be able to use her eyes effectively, she needs a number of skills. She must be able to focus both eyes on the same point, move them to follow a moving object, discriminate among colors, and respond appropriately to different brightness levels by contracting her pupils in bright light and expanding them in dimmer light.

After the first few days of life the newborn baby appears to have all these skills in at least rudimentary form. The ability to move both eyes in the same direction is apparently present at birth but improves over the first weeks. The pupillary response to brightness differences is also present immediately, although it becomes somewhat more efficient during the first days of life. The ability to discriminate colors is more difficult to establish in the newborn. In W. P. Chase's classic study of this problem children 15 days old were found to be able to make discriminations among a range of colors; it is unclear whether or not younger babies can. (The major difficulty in studying color discrimination is to make sure that the baby is really responding to color and not brightness, for colors vary in brightness as well as hue.)

The ability to focus both eyes on the same point and to move the focus to closer and farther objects or to moving objects is probably somewhat slower to develop. The usual conclusion is that the infant's best focus is on a point about 8 inches from her head (see Haynes, White, & Held). As changing the focus to nearer or farther objects is not skillful in the early weeks, many objects within the child's field of vision will be blurry during this period. As an aside, it is interesting that during nursing, the average distance between the infant's face and the mother's face is about 8 to 10 inches, which is just about the optimal range for the infant's focus. So the mother's face may be more often in focus than are other regular elements in the child's environment.

Tracking objects is also only rudimentarily developed at first; the baby attempts to move her eyes in the direction of the moving object, but she is not very skillful.

SMELLING

Newborn babies do react, sometimes quite violently, to intensely bad smells, so we know that they can smell. But we don't know how subtle their sense of smell is. Can they smell differences among the fragrances of flowers, for example? Can they tell the difference between different kinds of foods on the basis of smell? We don't know as much as we'd like to about this problem partly because it's extremely difficult to study. If the baby reacts in the same way to all the different smells, how can we know if she can tell the difference?

Several research strategies are open to an investigator who might wish to explore the development of the sense of smell. The first alternative is a learning experiment in which the infant is trained over a series of trials to make one response in the presence of a particular odor and some other response (or no response) to the presentation of another odor. This strategy would require a very complex procedure. For example, following the general design used by Lewis Lipsitt and his associates, we might present an odor to the baby, and then stroke her cheek to cause her head to turn. If the baby turns her head, a nipple is presented and she is allowed to suck on it. With another smell the same procedure could be followed, except that there would be no nipple to suck after head turning. If, after a series of trials, the baby showed more

FIGURE 11
A young infant showing visual fixation on objects above her head.

head turning to the smell associated with the opportunity to suck, then the ability to discriminate between the two smells would be demonstrated. The whole procedure would have to be repeated with new pairs of smells.

A much simpler alternative research strategy is to demonstrate that a baby makes different responses to two or more smells. Some early researchers attempted to use the baby's facial expressions as a guide to reactions to different smells, but making judgments about grimaces and smiles in the newborn is more difficult than you might imagine. Lipsitt and his associates (Engen, Lipsitt, & Kaye, 1963) approached the problem more precisely, using measures of change in activity rate and breathing in the baby. Using such a procedure, they found that babies breathed faster and moved more in response to some odors than to others, suggesting that not all strong odors are equal for the infant.

Because they are the two major logical options, these same two research strategies—learning experiments and studies of preference or differential reaction—have been widely used to study a whole range of developing perceptual skills in the newborn, and not only for studies of the development of the sense of smell.

TASTE

Although taste sensitivity in the newborn has not often been studied, the sum of the research evidence indicates that the newborn can tell the difference between the four basic tastes—sweet, salt, sour, and bitter. The classic study on this subject is by Kai Jensen.

TOUCH

Babies are very sensitive to touch, particularly around the mouth and on the hands. Most of the earliest reflexes are triggered off by touches at different parts of the body. When the infant is touched on the cheek or lips, for example, she turns her head toward the stimulus.

SUMMARY OF NEWBORN'S PERCEPTUAL SKILLS

Let me add up this rather long catalogue of newborn skills. The newborn infant can hear individual sounds and make some simple discriminations among them; she can focus her eyes somewhat, track moving objects somewhat, and *perhaps* make color discriminations; she responds to smell and taste differences. We do not yet know whether newborn infants can locate sounds accurately or just what range of visual, auditory, tactual, or olfactory discriminations they can make, but it is clear that they can make *some* discriminations. Generally speaking, the more we have studied the newborn and the more sophisticated the research techniques have become, the more skillful we discover the newborn infant to be.

What the Infant Can Do

We know that the infant can't yet walk or talk, add or subtract. She can't even hold up her head at first. She does have perceptual skills, as I have just described, but what about bodily movements? What is she capable of during the first weeks and months of life? To answer that, I must divide the baby's responses into reflexive and nonreflexive actions.

REFLEXES

I mentioned reflexes when describing classical conditioning in Chapter 1. A reflex is a response that is automatic and is triggered involuntarily by some specific stimulus. Adults retain quite a collection of such reflexes, including the reaction of the pupil to light and dark, the blink when a puff of air hits the eye, the knee jerk, and so on. In the newborn there are dozens of reflexes, only a few of which are of any particular interest to the psychologist. Of these reflexes, the most important are those that have to do with eating.

First, the infant comes equipped with a *rooting reflex,* If you touch her on the cheek, anywhere near the mouth, she will turn her head and root around to put her mouth on the object that touched her. This reflex is extremely sensible, if you think of the position in which a baby is held to be fed, particularly for breast feeding. If the baby's head is facing upward initially, the nipple will touch her on the cheek; her reflexive turning in the direction of the touch and her searching behavior will eventually get her mouth around the nipple.

Next in the sequence is the *sucking reflex.* The baby will automatically make sucking movements if touched on the lips or if something is inserted in her mouth. Finally, there is the *swallowing reflex.* At this early stage the baby hasn't learned that you have to stop breathing in order to swallow, at least if you want to avoid swallowing a lot of air, so the baby doesn't alternate these well. She swallows air and then has to burp it up again. But swallowing does occur reflexively from the very earliest days of life.

A second group of reflexes—although not as essential to the infant's survival as are the various feeding reflexes—is interesting because they seem to be controlled by the part of the brain that develops first: the midbrain. As the more advanced—cortical—parts of the brain develop and come to dominate during the first year or so of life, these primitive reflexes drop out. (Some of these primitive reflexes are used to diagnose certain kinds of brain damage in older children and adults; if the primitive reflex is still present later on, it indicates that something has gone wrong with the development of the more mature parts of the brain or that there has been some damage.)

The *moro reflex* is one of these primitive reflexes. If a loud sound is made near the baby, if the baby's position is changed suddenly, or if there is some similar major change, the baby will throw both arms outward and then bring them back. This response disappears at about 3 months of age, except in babies who have certain kinds of brain damage. Another of the primitive reflexes is the *Babinski.* If you stroke a baby on the bottom of her foot, she'll first splay out her toes, and then

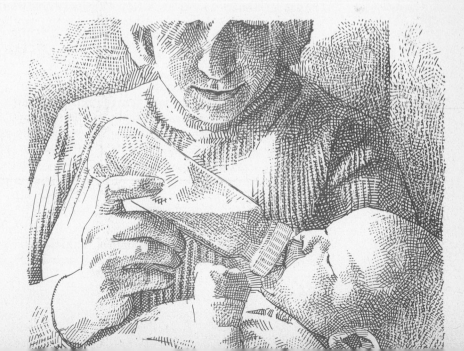

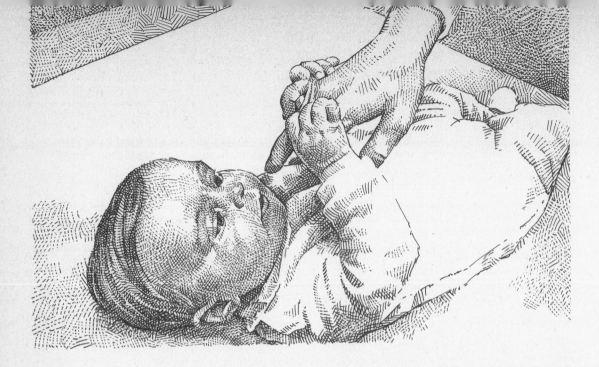

curl them in. In an adult or an older baby, only the curling in occurs. This response would be totally uninteresting except for the fact that when it occurs in an adult, it's a sign of abnormality in the neurological system.

A further, perhaps more interesting, primitive reaction is the *grasp reflex*. If you touch a baby across the palm of her hand, her fingers will close tightly around the object touching her. Her grip is so strong, in fact, that a baby grasping a rod with both hands can often be lifted completely off the ground. Some psychologists have suggested that this reflex is a remnant of our evolutionary past, when we needed to be able to hang onto tree branches or onto part of the mother while she was moving. The reflex disappears by about 6 months of age, when the more mature parts of the brain have developed more fully.

NONREFLEXIVE BEHAVIOR

If you watch a newborn baby for any length of time, you will notice a great many activities other than the reflexes I have listed. The baby looks around her, moves her body in various ways, opens and closes her hands and mouth, cries, sleeps, and so on. We can't conclude from such an observation that the baby intends to explore her world, although that is one possibility. It is equally possible that most or all of her early behavior is guided by quite specific stimulus-response connections.

For example, there is good evidence that from the very earliest days, babies examine objects or sights visually in a nonrandom way. Newborn babies will look longer at figures that have sharp contours than at those that do not, and within any figure their eyes tend to focus on the

BOX 5
The Newborn's Perception of Form

I have said in the main part of the text that the baby, preferring to look at contours, will apparently look at the edges of objects rather than at their middles. The evidence comes from a whole series of studies by William Kessen and Philip Salapatek and their associates, who developed an apparatus for taking pictures of an infant's eyes while she is looking at a figure such as a triangle. The researchers can tell from the pictures exactly where the baby is looking. The accompanying figure shows some of the results. Kessen has said, "For the large majority of newborns, the eyes were directed toward an angle. Thus, the newborn can select and maintain a focused scan on a relatively circumscribed feature of a visual pattern." (Kessen et al., 1970, p. 359)

Kessen and Salapatek's work is really the first to have shown the systematic quality of the newborn's visual exploration, although their work doesn't really tell us yet what "rule" the baby is using. We don't know whether it's the contour of the figure, the contrast between the darkness of the figure and the lightness of the background, or some other feature that attracts the baby's attention. All we know is that some features do attract the infant's attention, and that her scanning, once she is attending, is focused.

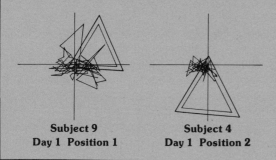

Subject 9
Day 1 Position 1

Subject 4
Day 1 Position 2

The scanning pattern of the newborn baby looking at triangles above her head. The infant was 1 day old when these patterns were observed. Note the focus on the corners and edges of the figure. (*Source:* Salapatek, P., & Kessen, W. Visual scanning of triangles by the human newborn. *Journal of Experimental Child Psychology*, 1966, 3, 163.)

contours of the figure or the places where there is sharp contrast (see Box 5). Does the infant do so intentionally, or is she merely "programmed" to scan in this way? Most likely there are built-in programming strategies from the beginning, such as a rule of "look at the edges first," but these strategies very probably function automatically without any intention or purposeful exploration on the part of the child. The scanning strategies do change with age, as do the infant's preferences among pictures. For example, by about 6 months of age, the baby has developed some preference for pictures or objects of moderate complexity. Very complex and very simple figures are less often chosen by infants of this age. Whether the change in visual preferences results merely from changes in the automatic "rules," or whether the visual preferences also change as a result of the child's experience in looking, touching, and exploring can't be determined by the current state of the art. The important discovery, however, is the nonrandom quality of even the very earliest visual explorations.

The same sort of puzzle arises in studying body activity in the newborn. There is quite a lot of such activity, most of it quite global during the earliest weeks. What we don't know is why the child moves. Is it some attempt at intentional exploration within the limits of the child's physical development? Or are there internal stimuli that touch off the movement, much as a touch on the cheek touches off the rooting reflex? Most observers agree that during the first month of life, the child's movements, like its visual explorations, are probably neither entirely random nor entirely purposive. But by about 2 months, at least according to Piaget, Kagan, and others, there is a shift toward more purposive behavior. But whether we believe that the child's activities are guided by some intent or merely by routine reflex-like strategies, it is perfectly clear that the child gradually gains motor control during the first 6 months. By 1 month a baby can hold her chin up; by 2 months she can lift her chest off the mattress or floor and can look around a little. Some ability to reach and grasp things develops at the same time. The baby begins at about 2 months to swipe with her hand at objects near her (for instance, at a mobile hanging above the crib). By about 5 months, she is reaching for the object, directing her aim with her eyes.

From the very earliest days the baby explores her world with the tools that are available to her, and that exploration is apparently governed by some kinds of rules, such as the contour-scanning rule for looking. In the first weeks the explorations are mostly visual, for she has greater control over her eyes than over other parts of her body. As motor control gets better other kinds of exploration become more possible.

Learning and Habituation

Two other aspects of the infant's response to the environment must be touched on: *learning* and *habituation*. Can the newborn baby learn? Obviously, the child's behavior changes during the early months. But is this change just maturation or is the child responding to specific experience? Does classical or operant conditioning occur in the newborn? Does the baby respond to reinforcement in the way that an older child would? There has been a surge of interest in this series of problems during the past 15 years or so, and research has yielded some quite clear conclusions.

Newborn infants can be conditioned classically, although it is somewhat difficult to do so. In particular the sucking response seems to be conditionable during the earliest days of life. An experiment by Lipsitt and Kaye is fairly typical. Using the sucking reflex as the unconditioned response, they put a nipple into the child's mouth while sounding a loud tone. The nipple is thus the unconditioned stimulus, and the tone is the conditioned stimulus. After a number of pairings of the nipple and the tone, the 4-day-old subjects were tested by having only the tone sounded. Classical conditioning would be shown if the infants showed increased rates of sucking to the tone alone, which is precisely what happened. Control subjects, who heard the tone and had the nipple inserted in their mouths at separate times showed no increase in sucking to the tone alone.

These results show that newborn infants *can* be classically conditioned, although many researchers have found it more difficult than did Lipsitt and Kaye to establish clear conditioned responses in infants this young. By 3 to 4 weeks of age, however, classically conditioned responses are quite easy to establish.

Operant conditioning is also possible in newborns. Again, a study by Lipsitt is a good illustration. He and his colleagues taught newborn babies to suck vigorously on a rubber tube by reinforcing them with sugar water through the tube. Initially, the babies had shown a strong preference for sucking on a nipple instead of a tube. In the operant conditioning experiments, a group of infants was first given a series of sucking experiences with the rubber tube without any sugar water coming through. Under such conditions, they did not suck long. During the main experimental trials, sugar water was given through the tube after the infants had sucked for 10 seconds, and the babies then increased their sucking time significantly. When sugar water was no longer given, the sucking dropped off markedly. What this and other studies demonstrate is that the newborn possesses all the necessary neurological wiring to make connections between events. It's not easy to teach the newborn infant something because the baby is so seldom alert and unhungry, but it can be done, suggesting that the baby can and probably does learn such connections on her own.

A second skill that the baby comes equipped with goes by the rather forbidding name of *habituation*, and is a bit harder to describe. Let me see if I can make it clear with an example from your own experience.

Have you ever tape-recorded a lecture, a piece of music, or your own voice in an ordinary room? Suppose it is a lecture that you are taping. While you are doing the taping, you can hear the lecturer clearly, so you have no concern about the tape being clear. When you get home and listen to the tape, however, you discover that the sound of airplanes overhead periodically drowns out the sound of the lecturer's voice, and that the street traffic makes a steady loud noise, so that sometimes you can't make out individual words. But you didn't hear all those things when you were in the lecture room. Why not? The answer is habituation. You block out the sound, but the tape recorder doesn't. If I sound a loud bell right next to your ear, the first time you may jump; at the least you will certainly hear a loud bell. But if I keep doing it every 30 seconds, eventually you will not only stop reacting, you will actually not hear the bell as loudly. You will have habituated, that is, you will have reached the stage of not responding to a stimulus and, in fact, of not hearing it. The same thing happens with airplane and street noises. Over the years you have simply learned to filter them out because your ear and brain are so constructed that you can do that. But the tape recorder can't habituate, so it picks everything up.

I hope you can see that being able to habituate is one of the skills that makes living possible in our complex world—or even in a simpler one. If you were to react to each sound, sight, and touch as if it were new, you would spend all your time reacting and would have no time to note things that are really new. In order to make any kind of progress you have to be able to learn about something and then be able to stop responding to it.

I've given you this rather lengthy example because I think it's important for you to recognize how crucial it is that the newborn baby be able to habituate too. In the beginning, of course, everything is new to the baby. But starting from the very earliest hours of life, the baby is able to cut down by means of the process of habituation the number of stimuli that have to be attended to. The process is not voluntary; rather, it results more or less automatically from repeated exposure to the same stimuli. But the fact that the newborn is equipped very early with the ability to habituate makes it possible for her to have some attention left over for the genuinely novel things that do happen all the time.

Daily Cycles   Thus far I have described what an infant can experience and what she can do. But a more important issue for many parents, day-care workers, or others caring for an infant day to day is what she does with her time. How is the infant's day organized? What sort of natural rhythms occur in the daily cycles? And how can a caregiver blend in with, or accommodate to, the child's cycles?

Newborn infants spend more time sleeping than doing anything else. In the newborn something on the order of 16 hours per day are spent sleeping, and this reduces to about 14 hours by 3 months of age. (See Roffwarg, Muzio, & Dement in the References section for some sample findings.) Sleeping may seem to be a totally uninteresting phenomenon, but there are several intriguing aspects to it. First, there is the question of cycles and patterns in the child's sleep. Parents are anxious that the child establish some kind of regular or predictable sleep pattern, since this makes caregiving that much simpler. The *absence* of clear cycles of sleeping and waking in the young infant may also be taken by physicians and others as potential evidence of some kind of disorder. You may remember that I mentioned in Chapter 2 that one of the characteristics of babies born to drug-addicted mothers is that they seem unable to establish a pattern of sleeping and waking. Brain damaged infants have the same kind of difficulties in many cases, so any failure to establish some clear sleep-wake regularity *may* be a sign of trouble.

The other interesting thing about sleep in newborns is that they show all the same external signs of dreaming as do older children or adults. In adults the outward sign of a dream is a fluttering of the eyeballs under the closed lids (called *rapid eye movement sleep*, or REM sleep). You don't dream all night, but only at certain points in your own sleeping-waking cycle. If I were to wake you during REM sleep, you would usually report that you had been dreaming. Newborn infants also show REMs and even premature babies as young as 32 weeks of gestational age show REM sleep. In fact, in the newborn a larger percentage of sleep time is REM sleep than at any later age. Roffwarg and his associates have found that newborns spend about half of their sleep time in REM sleep, while in young adults, by contrast, only about two hours of the sleep time is REM sleep. Of course, we do not know whether the infant "dreams" in our sense of the word; probably she does not. But we do know that during the infant's REM sleep there is a kind of intense stimulation of the central nervous system. So the sleep time of the newborn is not empty—it is full of internal activity of some kind.

What about the rest of the day when the infant is *not* sleeping? From the perspective of the parent (or the researcher for that matter), the most interesting awake time is the time the infant is apparently alert. She is looking around, not crying, not drowsy, and not hungry. In the newborn such an alert state occurs only about a third of the time she is awake, but by the end of the first month, alert awakeness is about 50 to 60 percent of the awake time.

Crying occurs most often just before feedings, with the most alert times usually occurring shortly after. So the typical newborn cycle is sleep, wake up, fuss and cry, eat, be alert, become drowsy, sleep, and on around again. This cycle then changes as the periods of sleep change in length, so that by approximately 1 to 2 months of age, most children have one long sleeping period during the night and several shorter sleeping periods during the day.

These several daily cycles can be seen clearly in the diaries kept by mothers in an ongoing study by Kathryn Barnard and her associates. The mothers were asked to note when the infant was asleep; when she woke; when she cried, ate, had a change of diapers; and when she was alert. The records for two different 1-month-old infants are given in Figure 12. One of these infants has a very regular daily cycle, the other a more irregular cycle.

INDIVIDUAL DIFFERENCES AMONG BABIES

So far I have been talking as if all babies were alike, and of course in most ways they are. Barring some kind of physical damage, all babies have similar sensory equipment at birth and can experience the same kinds of happenings around them. But they do differ quite markedly in temperament and in some kinds of sensory sensitivities. The evidence that we have suggests that there are differences among infants on a number of dimensions.

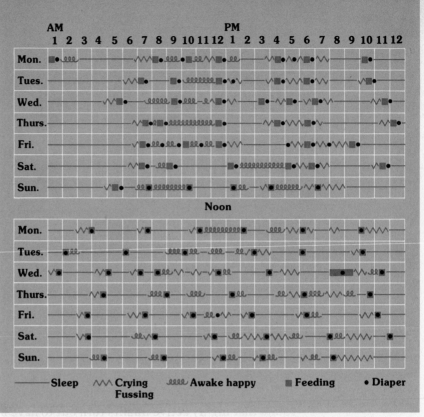

FIGURE 12
The daily cycles of two infants at 1-month of age, as recorded by their mothers. (Source: Barnard, K. Unpublished data from the Nursing Child Assessment Project, University of Washington, 1976.)

1. Vigor of Responding. Some babies react strongly to stimuli, either by crying or by active movement, and they tend to respond vigorously to a wide range of stimuli, both pleasurable and surprising. Other babies are slower to respond; it takes a stronger stimulus to evoke any response.

2. General Activity Rate. Some babies are more active in general. From the very beginning they move their bodies more, move their hands toward their mouths more, turn their heads more, and so on. Other babies don't move around nearly as much, although they may look at things around them.

3. Restlessness During Sleep. Some babies sleep "soundly," with little movement; others are restless during most of their sleep time.

4. Irritability. Some babies cry a great deal, fuss with little apparent provocation, and are difficult to soothe. Others are more placid.

5. Rate of Habituation. From birth, or shortly afterward, some babies seem to habituate more rapidly than do others. If this difference is really consistent and pervasive, it could obviously have profound implications for the child's rate of perceptual and cognitive development.

6. Cuddliness. Some babies don't like to be picked up and held. They don't adjust their bodies much to the bodies of those holding them, even when they are tired, ill, or unhappy. Other babies react positively to being held and cuddled by adjusting their bodies to the adults', do not struggle to get away, and show other signs of pleasure.

That babies differ in their responses from the earliest days is of great interest for at least two reasons. First, we want to know whether or not the early differences continue to show up consistently throughout the child's life. Does a placid baby remain placid? Does she turn out to be a quiet, inactive preschooler and a shy teenager? Does the active baby continue to be active and responsive to the environment throughout her lifetime? Such questions about the consistency of early differences in temperament or style have been asked by many researchers during the past ten years, and some tentative answers are emerging. Schaffer and Emerson, for example, have found that cuddliness persists at least through the first 18 months of life (which is as long as they studied the children). Furthermore, they found that babies and toddlers who were not cuddly were more active and restless in general and intolerant of physical restraint. Perhaps because they spent more time exploring and moving about, these children were quicker in overall perceptual and motor development than were the cuddly babies. Escalona has also found that highly active infants turn out to have better gross motor development than do the more placid infants. The active infants in Escalona's study also showed somewhat faster cognitive development in some areas, although their language was not accelerated.

The best known studies of temperamental differences in infancy have been done by Chess and Thomas and their associates. They have followed a group of subjects from earliest infancy through the early elementary school years. Their findings suggest that one of the most consistent temperamental characteristics is the child's degree of reactivity to stimulation. Babies who are quick to respond to new stimuli continue to show that characteristic throughout their childhood.

Chess and Thomas have also found clusters of early temperamental differences that tend to hold together over the early childhood years. They describe three types of children. The "easy child" approaches new events positively (for example, tries new foods without much fuss), is regular in biological functioning (has a good sleep cycle, eats at regular intervals, and so on), is usually happy, adapts to change easily, and in general is moderately responsive to stimulation. The "difficult child," in contrast, is less regular in body functioning and is slow to develop regular sleeping and eating cycles, shows negative reactions to new things and to change, cries and is often irritable, and is highly responsive to stimuli. This child reacts to many more things and often reacts negatively. Chess and Thomas point out, however, that the difficult child, once she has adapted to something new, is often quite happy about it, but the adaptation process itself is very difficult. Finally, they describe the "slow-to-warm-up child," who is not as negative in responding to new things or new people but shows a kind of passive resistance. Instead of spitting out new food violently and crying, as a difficult child might do, the hard-to-warm-up child may just let the food drool out and may resist mildly any attempt to feed her more of the same. These children show few intense reactions, either positive or negative, to anything. Once they have adapted to a new person or a new experience, however, their adaptation is generally positive.

A second, equally important reason for interest in the earliest differences among babies is that such information may shed some light on the earliest development of parent-infant relationships. Infants with different temperamental characteristics demand different kinds of caregiving and evoke different feelings and responses in the caregiver. An infant who is difficult to soothe may initially receive a great deal of attention from the parents as they try out their entire repertoire of potentially soothing activities. But there is little reinforcement for the parent for all those efforts if the child continues to be unsootheable, and the parent may show less and less soothing and attention to the infant. You may recall that Moss found something rather like this in his short-term longitudinal study of mother-infant relationships. The fussiest infants received a lot of attention at 1 month and relatively little attention at 4 months. An infant with poor rhythmicity—one who does not establish good, predictable daily schedules—is also a difficult child to deal with, and will evoke different kinds of feelings and responses on the part of parents. There may also be problems of mismatch between the infant's temperament and what the parents wanted or expected. Many parents assume that infants are cuddly. If such a parent has a wiggly, active, uncuddly infant, this discrepancy may well affect the parents' response toward the child. The parent may feel "rejected" because the infant does not cuddle or soothe, and such a feeling may in turn affect later reactions of the parent to that child. Most infants, of course, fall within some broad normal range of behavior, and most parents are able to adapt to their own children's signals and temperament. But the pattern of interaction between parent and child may be significantly influenced by the child's temperamental qualities and the parents' expectations.

THE INFANT'S RELATION TO THE ENVIRONMENT

The baby comes into the world with a repertoire of skills and some important individual temperamental characteristics. But the environment she is born into matters enormously as well. She can respond only to stimuli that are available to her; if there's nothing there, she can't respond and can't learn how to respond to new things later. Her diet matters as well, just as it did during the prenatal period. And her relationship with her parents or caretakers is of great importance.

Effects of Impoverished Environments

A great deal of interest in the effects of generally impoverished environments upon infants grew out of concern for children who had been raised in orphanages from their earliest days of life. In many orphanages around the world—and in this country until recently—babies are given very little individual attention, are not held or cuddled, are often placed on their backs in their cribs with nothing to look at or play with. In this kind of world babies do not thrive. They often become unresponsive to any kind of stimulation. They are retarded in language development, in motor development, and in development of normal attachments to others. As you might imagine, there is substantial disagreement among those doing research on this question about the crucial variables. Some have argued that it is the lack of a single mother figure that produces difficulties for the child. Others have emphasized the lack of sufficient visual and motor stimulation, whereas still others emphasize not the absence of a single mother figure but the lack of affectionate contact with adults in general.

Most of the research on the effects of impoverished environments, for obvious ethical reasons, has been done with animals. Researchers have deprived animals of specific kinds of stimulation over particular periods of time and have been able to see short- and long-term effects of such deprivation. Harlow's research on social isolation in rhesus monkeys is by far the most famous of the animal work in this area. Harlow raised infant rhesus monkeys in a number of settings: with other infant monkeys but with no adults, in total isolation, and in isolation but with a "cloth surrogate"—an imitation mother monkey made of wire and with a soft cloth covering. Infant monkeys raised in total isolation for eighty days had difficulty later relating to peers, but they did eventually adjust. Those who had been isolated for six months or longer were apparently quite permanently socially disabled. The isolation apparently did not have any effect on the monkey's later learning ability, however. Raising monkeys with cloth surrogate mothers didn't seem to help much in the long run. Such monkeys do have something to cuddle up to, and they spend a large amount of their time clinging to the surrogate mother (as you can see in Figure 13), but as adults they show essentially no normal social or sexual behavior. Other monkeys raised with peers, or with opportunity to play with peers, showed largely normal social development, even if the only mothering they had access to was a cloth surrogate. These several findings appear to show that normal social development is dependent on having contact of some kind with peers, with parents, or with both. Harlow thinks that contact with peers is the fundamental need, since animals raised with only peer contact turn out to have pretty normal adult social behavior. Whether this conclusion can be generalized to

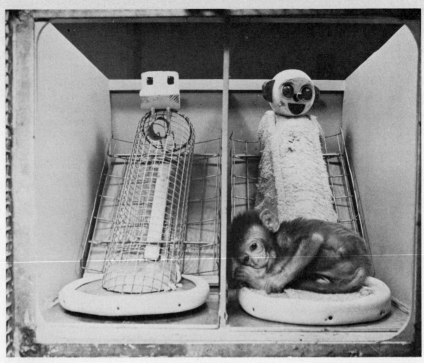

FIGURE 13
Infant monkeys with cloth and wire surrogate mothers. Monkeys in this situation invariably prefer the cloth surrogate and spend quite a lot of time clinging to it. (Source: Harlow, H. F., & Zimmerman, R. R. Affectional responses of the infant monkey. *Science*, 1959, *130*, 422.)

human infants is not completely clear. It is true that in many orphanages and other institutional rearing situations there is little contact among the infants, and such reduced peer contact may be one of the sources of the social and emotional difficulties noted in such children later. But it is also true that human babies, if placed together, have relatively little contact with one another, in part because of their very limited mobility. Monkey infants have nearly full mobility from a very early age, so for them peer contact may be more critical or helpful in the early months than it is for human infants.

Other animal research, done largely with rats, dogs, and other subprimate species, suggests that *perceptual* deprivation in infancy also affects the animal's later learning and perceptual skills. Some of the studies of orphanage reared children confirm this general conclusion. For example, Wayne Dennis's study of three separate institutions in Iran (to which I have referred in earlier chapters) showed that in two institutions where children were seriously deprived of opportunities for movement, play, and perceptual stimulation of various kinds, the children were severely retarded in all aspects of early development. In a third institution, in which there were greater opportunities for experience—play with other children as well as motor practice and perceptual enrichment—there was little if any retardation in the development of such skills as crawling and walking.

Taken together, the deprivation studies point to the importance of several varieties of stimulation. Interesting objects to look at and opportunities for movement and play are important and appear to affect perceptual and motor development. For normal language development the infant needs to be around people who talk, and for normal social development the infant needs to have reciprocal interaction with adults and peers.

Another way to study the problem of the effects of impoverishment is to ask what happens when you specifically provide a richer environment for the child. Burton White, in a classic study of this kind, provided every kind of stimulation he could think of for one group of orphanage babies: mobiles hanging above the crib, bumpers around the crib with pictures on them, sheets with pictures on them, and objects sticking out from the side of the crib so that the babies could reach them with hands or mouths. In addition, the babies were picked up and cuddled for extra periods each day. When these babies were compared to babies who had experienced the usual institutional regime, they were clearly advanced in reaching and looking. There is a difficulty, however, in predicting what would happen to such richly stimulated infants if the same degree of richness were provided over long periods of time. There is some hint in White's findings that it is possible to overstimulate an infant so that she becomes more fussy and distressed than a slightly less stimulated baby might be. Other researchers (like Wachs, Uzgiris, & Hunt) have found similar indications that there is such a thing as too much stimulation. Undoubtedly, the amount of stimulation an infant can tolerate is partly a function of her own approach to new experiences and to stimulation in general, but for each baby there is probably some threshold above which more experience, more novelty, and more stimulation are uncomfortable rather than interesting. The possibility of overstimulation is worth emphasis, for the easy conclusion from research on institutionalized infants is that more stimulation is always a good thing. That may well not be the case. Rather, some moderate amount of stimulation is probably optimal, although the Chess and Thomas research and other work on temperamental differences in infants underline the fact that what is "moderate" may be different for each infant.

The other very difficult theoretical and factual puzzle in the study of early deprivation is the problem of the single mother figure versus multiple mothering. It is obvious that a baby needs handling, cuddling, and individualized attention from caregivers of some kind, but it is not obvious that it has to be from the same person at all times. There are cultures in which multiple caregiving is the rule rather than the exception, as on kibbutzim in Israel. Children reared in such environments show no detectable long-term disabilities. On the other hand many psychologists (both Erikson and Ribble, for example) have been impressed by the importance of the earliest bond of trust and mutual attachment that develops between the baby and a single mother figure. Most likely, the total amount of affectionate interaction between a baby and all her caregivers, the ways in which affection and emotional support are offered, and the timing of separation from the single mother figure all make a difference. Research on the development of attachments (which I will discuss in some detail in Chapter 11) indicates that for the first four or five months of life the child's attachments are very diffuse, narrowing down to a single attachment only at about 6 months of age. Then, by 8 months or 1 year of age the child begins to have attachments to several people at once. Such findings suggest that perhaps the presence of a single figure, or at least of a primary caregiver, may be more important during the period from 4 to 8 months than either earlier or later. Similarly, research on the effects of maternal employment on children's development indicates that if the alternative care provided to the child is stable, there is little or no observable detrimental effect, but that if the child is shifted from one caregiver to another with little constancy, there is greater risk of emotional disturbance in the child.

Thus, as is often the case, posing the problem as a choice between a single mother figure and multiple mothering is probably much too simplistic. Many other variables are important. The new resurgence of interest in the development of attachments in infancy may yield the information necessary to define the problem still further and to provide more conclusive answers.

Variations in Normal Home Environments

Just as babies differ in temperament, so do mothers, fathers, and other caregivers. Parents expect different things from their babies, and they have different patterns of interaction with them as well. Some parents quite naturally talk to the baby from the very first day of her life; each interaction is punctuated not only by cooing and other loving sounds but also by "conversation." Some infants are handled a lot, whereas others are handled primarily when they are diapered, fed, and bathed. Some infants are given a lot of visual stimulation, such as mobiles above the crib and varied, colorful things to play with. Other babies are given fewer such stimulating items. Some parents like babies; some do not, nor do they feel confident or comfortable about taking care of their infants. The research findings on differences in maternal styles suggest that ordinarily better educated mothers talk to their infants more than do mothers with less education, and that mothers talk to first babies more than to later ones.

Such differences in maternal or paternal style of interaction with the infant have an impact on the child's behavior during infancy and in some instances over the long term as well. For example, there is evidence that babies who are talked to a lot during their early months vocalize more themselves. They make more cooing and babbling noises than do babies who have heard less language around them. Such children may also begin talking somewhat earlier. In addition, Annelise Korner and her co-workers have found that a baby who is held at her mother's shoulder, rather than being cradled in her arms, is more alert visually. Both these findings suggest that some quite specific aspects of early handling may have equally specific outcomes in the child.

Other researchers (Rubenstein, 1967; Yarrow, Rubenstein, Pedersen, & Jankowski, 1972) have found that infants who receive a high amount of social stimulation (including being held, being talked to, being looked at, and being played with) are more likely to be advanced in some aspects of early cognitive development. Yarrow and his associates also found that the richness and variety of inanimate stimulation (such as the number and variety of toys, textures to feel, things to look at) make a difference in the child's early cognitive development. Babies of 5 months who had received a rich variety of stimulation showed somewhat faster motor and perceptual development, more reaching and grasping, and more exploration of the environment.

Another facet of the mother's behavior, other than the pattern of stimulation that she provides for the baby, is her own feeling of competence or emotional well being. Elsie Broussard and Miriam Hartner have done one of the most comprehensive studies of the effects of the mother's emotional state on her interaction with her infant. They have found that mothers who are depressed and irritable after the birth of their babies are more likely to think that their babies are below average in development. They are also more likely to be bothered by the infants and by the demands that infant care makes on them. Of course, we can't tell from this kind of correlational evidence just which way the causation may run. It may be that these mothers are realistically depressed; they may have babies who are fussier, harder to soothe, more colicky, and generally difficult. But it could also be that a mother's own personality characteristics—her inclination to depression and irritability—makes her see a perfectly ordinary, normally fussy baby as a great burden and drain.

Broussard and Hartner also found that the babies who at 1 month of age were considered by their mothers to be below average in development and functioning turned out to have more problems when they were 4 years old, when they were more likely to require some kind of therapy. Again, it may be that the mothers were simply good judges of their babies at 1 month. More likely, if a mother were herself depressed and overwhelmed by the demands made on her by an apparently normally difficult baby, there would develop between the two of them a pattern that resulted in later emotional difficulties for the child. In either case the finding is intriguing and should be followed up, so that we can begin to untangle the causal relationships.

Effects of Poor Diet

I have discussed the problems of sorting out the effects of malnutrition at some length in Chapter 3, so I needn't go into enormous detail here. But I do want to emphasize, again, that since some important neural structures develop entirely after birth, the effects of *postnatal* malnutrition may be greater than those of prenatal malnutrition. The research literature suggests that the first six months after birth may be the most critical for brain cell growth and for the growth of the interconnections among brain cells, so this period may be one in which adequate nutrition for the infant is particularly important. Malnutrition *both* prenatally and postnatally seems to have a cumulative negative effect. For the poor child it is precisely this sort of chronic malnutrition or subnutrition that is most likely to occur. Research with animals points to the *permanence* of the effects of malnutrition after birth; those missing cells and connective tissues aren't grown later if the diet improves. So the impact on the child's learning skills may also be permanent. But bear in mind that these are as yet only tentative conclusions, based largely on research with animals. The findings from the Dutch famine study have made me more cautious in drawing too-sweeping conclusions at this stage about the long-term effects of malnutrition, although the evidence seems to point to permanent and detrimental effects of malnutrition after birth.

SEX DIFFERENCES IN INFANCY

I have already pointed out some of the dimensions on which infants differ from one another. Do male and female infants differ on these same or other dimensions? In attempting to account for observed sex differences in the skills or behavior of older children or adults, it is of considerable interest to know just what kind of differences do and do not exist at birth. Those theorists who have taken an essentially environmental position in explaining observed sex differences emphasize that males and females have different experiences, different reinforcement patterns, and that these differences account for the variations in behavior between the two sexes. Others have argued that there may be hormonal or other biological differences as well, and that these initial differences form the base on which later experience is built. The results of studies of early sex differences provide some support for both sides of this argument. Let me summarize the findings briefly:

1. At birth girls are physically more mature than boys. Girl babies are, on the average, smaller and lighter than are newborn boys, but they are a month or six weeks ahead in overall bodily development. Myelinization of the nerves (the development of the nerve sheath), for example, is farther advanced in the girl at birth than in the boy.

2. From birth a large proportion of the boy's body weight is devoted to muscle tissue. The muscle tissue in the girl's body is more fully developed, but it represents a smaller amount of her total weight than is true for the boy.

3. Girls show greater reactivity to some kinds of stimulation, particularly touch and pain stimuli; this difference is observable as early as the first days of life.

4. Girls are less vulnerable to virtually all varieties of physical stress after birth as they were prenatally. For example, more boys have low Apgar scores at birth, more physical abnormalities are present in males at birth, and approximately 33 percent more boys die during the first year of life. (As an aside, it is conceivable that this greater vulnerability of males is related in some way to the fact, discussed in Chapter 3, that the female form seems to be the "basic" form; for a male to develop, some additional elements must be included. So, since the developmental pattern for the male is more complex in some ways, perhaps more can go wrong.)

Contrary to many popular beliefs, however, there are no systematic differences between boys and girls in activity rate in the early days or months of life. There is some reason to suppose that infants who have suffered some birth trauma are more likely to show high levels of activity. Because boys are more likely to have experienced difficulties before or during the birth process, there may be differences in observed activity levels. But such differences are an artifact and cannot be attributed directly to the sex of the child. When only babies with no delivery complications are studied, no differences in activity rate between males and females are found.

In sum, there are sex differences at birth, and they cannot and should not be ignored. Girls are on a slightly faster developmental timetable, which may in turn affect the way in which they interact with their parents. The larger size and greater weight of boys may also have some effects on their later experiences. But it is equally important to note that on the majority of dimensions on which all infants differ, there are no observable sex differences. Girls are not generally more cuddly, boys do not cry more, and so on. Chess and Thomas's work suggests that the differences in temperament, not the variables on which the sexes differ, are the more important factors in the enduring patterns of behavior, at least during the early years of life.

SOCIAL CLASS DIFFERENCES

As I mentioned in Chapter 3, there are higher rates of several sorts of prenatal and birth difficulties among poor women, particularly poor minority group women. This is reflected in substantially higher rates of premature births, lower Apgar scores, and other indices. It seems logical to assume that these higher levels of risk to the child would result in slower development during infancy among children born into poverty level families. But that does not appear to be the case.

Using standardized measures of early perceptual and motor development, most researchers find *no* evidence of overall social class differences in rate of development in the early months of life. (See, for example, the paper by Nancy Bayley in the References.) Clear social class differences in test scores emerge among children 2 to 3 years of age, but ordinarily not earlier. Such findings are frequently interpreted as meaning that very early perceptual and motor development is an extraordinarily robust process, requiring only minimal outside stimulation. Through the first years of life, as the skills and abilities acquired by the child become more complex, the child's need for environmental richness may increase. I am of several minds about this sort of interpretation. On the one hand, it fits the social class difference data fairly well. On the other hand, there is some good research by Yarrow and others, which I mentioned earlier in this chapter, showing that quite specific features of the environment of young infants will affect the rate of perceptual, motor, and cognitive skills. So I am not persuaded that for the young infant the environment somehow matters less. But it does seem clear that on the environmental dimensions that *do* matter at this age, middle-class and poor families probably do not differ systematically.

SUMMARY

1. Research during the past 10 to 15 years has shown that newborn infants have a great many more perceptual skills than we had previously thought.
2. The newborn can hear sounds of moderate loudness and medium pitch—the loudness and pitch ranges of the human voice. Babies also respond positively to rhythmic sounds.
3. At birth the infant can move both eyes in the same direction, has a developed pupillary response to brightness, and may be able to see some colors. Babies can focus both eyes on one point, but not at a point very near to or very far from the body.
4. The senses of smell and taste are both developed, at least in rudimentary form, at birth. The sense of touch is also developed and is particularly sensitive in the mouth and hands.
5. The newborn has a collection of reflexes, the most important having to do with feeding; they include the rooting reflex, the sucking reflex, and the swallowing reflex.

Other "primitive" reflexes, such as the moro reflex or the Babinsky, are present at birth but disappear during the first six months of life.

6. Other activities in the newborn, such as body movement and looking at objects or touching things, may be her intentional attempts to explore her environment, or they may be automatic reactions to stimulation of certain kinds. Newborns do have specific patterns of responses to objects, such as looking more at the contours than at the middles of pictures, and these strategies for exploring may be "built in."
7. Newborns can and do learn, both through classical conditioning and operant conditioning. Equally important, they show some ability to habituate from the earliest days.
8. Young infants spend the majority of their day sleeping and are in an awake and alert state only a fraction of the time. Rhythms and daily cycles of sleep, waking, crying, and eating are established early.

9. Babies differ from one another on several dimensions, including vigor of response, general activity rate, restlessness, irritability, speed of habituation, and cuddliness. There is some evidence that such temperamental differences may persist throughout life.
10. Although much of this early development is controlled by maturation, a minimum environment is needed for normal development. Severely impoverished environments retard development in a number of ways. More specific aspects of early stimulation, such as the way the baby is held and the amount that she is talked to, may also have a long-term impact on her development of motor, perceptual, language, and cognitive skills.
11. Good diet appears to be particularly vital in the early months since neurological development is continuing and requires appropriate nourishment.
12. Male and female babies differ at birth on a number of dimensions; girls are more mature physically, are more reactive to several types of stimulation, and are less vulnerable to stresses of many kinds. No sex differences are observed, however, on such dimensions as activity, cuddliness, or sootheability.
13. No consistent differences between middle-class and poor infants are found on standarized tests of early infant development.

REFERENCES

Suggested Additional Readings

Birch, H. G. Malnutrition, learning and intelligence. *American Journal of Public Health,* 1972, *62,* 773–784.
One of the best and most complete discussions of the role of malnutrition in subsequent development, dealing with malnutrition both before and after birth and discussing some of the known and guessed consequences; moderately difficult paper, but well worth reading.

Bower, T. G. R. *Development in infancy.* San Francisco: H. W. Freeman, 1974.
A very good and generally quite readable discussion of a range of issues about infancy. Particularly good if you are interested in early perceptual skills.

Harlow, H. F. Early social deprivation and later behavior in the monkey. In A. Abrahams, H. H. Garner, & J. E. P. Thoman (Eds.), *Unfinished tasks in the behavioral sciences.* Baltimore: Williams & Wilkins, 1964, pp. 154–173.
This paper is also reprinted in a more accessible place, in L. J. Stone, H. T. Smith, & L. B. Murphy (Eds.), *The competent infant.* New York: Basic Books, 1973, pp. 824–831. Harlow has written many papers, and they are nearly all very easy to read and often funny. This is a good summary of a lot of his earlier work and might be a good place to start.

Kessen, W., Haith, M. M., & Salapatek, P. H. Infancy. In P. H. Mussen (Ed.), *Carmichael's manual of child psychology* (Vol. 1, 3rd ed.). New York: Wiley, 1970.
An encyclopedic description of the initial abilities of infants and their early development, with an exhaustive bibliography, but written for professional psychologists in highly technical terminology; a good general reference, but not for reading through on a cold winter night.

Korner, A. F. Individual differences at birth. Implications for early experience and later development. *American Journal of Orthopsychiatry,* 1971, *41,* 608–619.
An excellent paper, clearly written and not too technical, reviewing a large number of studies on early differences in infants, with particular attention to the effect of those differences on the mother's response to the baby.

Lipsitt, L. P. Learning processes in human newborns. *Merrill-Palmer Quarterly,* 1966, *12,* 45–71.
An excellent paper describing in more gen-

eral terms than usual the several research strategies available for studying learning in very tiny infants.

Ribble, M. A. *The rights of infants*. New York: Columbia University Press, 1943.
A classic book written during the period when there was great concern about the consequences of institutionalization on children and emphasizing the importance of a single mother figure in the child's development.

Streissguth, A. P., & Bee, H. L. Mother-child interactions and cognitive development in children. In W. W. Hartup (Ed.), *The young child* (Vol. 2). Washington, D.C.: National Association for the Education of Young Children 1972.
Includes a review of several studies on the effects of maternal stimulation upon the child's development; intended to be read by a semiprofessional audience; not too technical.

Westman, J. C. (Ed.). *Individual differences in children*. New York: Wiley, 1973.
An excellent book containing a series of papers on individual differences, including a paper by Arganian on sex differences in early development and a good summary paper by Chess and Thomas. A very good first place to look if you are interested in this topic.

Yarrow, L. J. Separation from parents during early childhood. In M. L. Hoffman & L. W. Hoffman (Eds.), *Review of child development research* (Vol. 1). New York: Russell Sage, 1964.
An excellent review of all the literature touching on effects of institutionalization and other forms of separation of the child from her parents, including a discussion of multiple mothering, though the information in that section is somewhat out of date.

Other Sources Cited

Arganian, M. Sex differences in early development. In J. C. Westman (Ed.), *Individual differences in children*. New York: Wiley, 1973.

Bayley, N. Comparisons of mental and motor test scores for ages 1–15 months by sex, birth order, race, geographical location, and education of parents. *Child Development*, 1965, *36*, 379–412.

Brackbill, Y., Adams, G., Crowell, D. H., & Gran, M. L. Arousal level in neonates and preschool children under continuous auditory stimulation. *Journal of Experimental Child Psychology*, 1966, *4*, 178–188.

Broussard, E. R., & Hartner, M. S. Further considerations regarding maternal perception of the first born. In J. Hellmuth (Ed.), *Exceptional infant: Studies in abnormalities* (Vol.2). New York: Brunner/Mazel, 1971.

Chase, W. P. Color vision in infants. *Journal of Experimental Psychology*, 1937, *20*, 203–222.

Chess, S., & Thomas, A. Temperament in the normal infant. In J. C. Westman (Ed.), *Individual differences in children*. New York, Wiley, 1973.

Chun, R. W. M., Pawsat, R., & Forster, F. M. Sound localization in infancy. *Journal of Nervous and Mental Diseases*, 1960, *130*, 472–476.

Engen, T., Lipsitt, L. P., & Kaye, H. Decrement and recovery of responses to olfactory stimuli in the human neonate. *Journal of Comparative and Physiological Psychology*, 1963, *56*, 73–77.

Erikson, E. H. *Childhood and Society*. New York: Norton, 1950

Escalona, S. K. The differential impact of environmental conditions as a function of different reactions patterns in infancy. In J. C. Westman (Ed.), *Individual differences in children*. New York: Wiley, 1973, pp. 145–157.

Haynes, H., White, B. L., & Held, R. Visual accommodation in human infants. *Science*, 1965, *148*, 528–530.

James, W. *The principles of psychology* (2 vols.). New York: Holt, 1890.

Jensen, K. Differential reactions to taste and temperature stimuli in newborn infants. *Genetic Psychology Monographs*, 1932, *12*, 361–479.

Kagan, J. Change and continuity in infancy. New York: Wiley, 1971.

Kessen, W. Sucking and looking: Two organized congenital patterns of behavior in the human newborn. In H. W. Stevenson, E. H. Hess, & H. L. Rheingold (Eds.), *Early behavior.* New York: Wiley, 1967.

Korner, A. F., & Grobstein, R. Visual alertness as related to soothing in neonates: Implications for maternal stimulation and early deprivation. *Child Development,* 1966, *37,* 867–876.

Lipsitt, L. P., & Kaye, H. Conditioned sucking in the human newborn. *Psychonomic Science,* 1964, *1,* 29–30.

Moss, H. A. Sex, age and state as determinants of mother-infant interaction. *Merrill-Palmer Quarterly,* 1967, *13,* 19–36.

Roffwarg, H. P., Muzio, J. N., & Dement, W. C. Ontogenetic development of the human sleep-dream cycle. *Science,* 1966, *152,* 604–619.

Rubenstein, J. Maternal attentiveness and sub- sequent exploratory behavior in the infant. *Child Development,* 1967, *38,* 1089–1100.

Schaffer, H., & Emerson, P. Patterns of response to physical contact in early human development. *Journal of Child Psychology and Psychiatry,* 1964, *5,* 1–13.

Wachs, T. D., Uzgiris, I. C., & Hunt, J. McV. Cognitive development in infants of different age levels and from different environmental backgrounds: An explanatory investigation. *Merrill-Palmer Quarterly,* 1971, *17,* 283–317.

White, B. L. An experimental approach to the effects of experience on early human behavior. In J. P. Hill (Ed.), *Minnesota Symposia on Child Psychology* (Vol. 1). Minneapolis: The University of Minnesota Press, 1967.

Yarrow, L. J., Rubenstein, J. L., Pedersen, F. A., & Jankowski, J. J. Dimensions of early stimulation and their differential effects on infant development. *Merrill-Palmer Quarterly,* 1972, *18,* 205–218.

5

Physical Growth
and Development

The topic of physical growth is not often one that students look forward to with delight. To many of you it may seem dull or even unimportant, a view I shared until recently. Having been trained as an environmentalist and thus having believed firmly that most of what was important in a child's development was triggered from outside, I considered the study of the child's body and its physical changes not only uninteresting but also largely irrelevant to the questions that intrigued me. I have since changed my mind completely on this point, and I hope that in this chapter I can persuade you that the study of physical growth and development is vital to understanding the child's overall development.

Even the most confirmed environmentalist has to agree that not only does the environment act on individual children, but that each child comes to that interchange having some physical skills and lacking others. So, in the very simplest sense, the child's physical abilities—whether or not she can crawl, walk, or talk; whether or not she can pick things up with her thumb and forefinger; whether or not she can ride a bike or play baseball well—set a kind of limit on the influence of the environment. The child who is not yet able to crawl can only explore and manipulate objects that are placed right beside her or that she can reach from a stable position. Things have to be brought to her. But when she learns to crawl, she experiences the world very differently—she can now go toward things and can explore them on her own. Not only does this physical change massively expand the range of experiences that the child can have, but it also greatly changes the child's interactions with her parents (or other caregivers). The parent who has been used to the relatively immobile baby must now adjust to a child who gets into absolutely everything, who has to be chased all over the house and have her movements restricted in some way. It used to be said that toilet training was the first major disciplinary encounter between parent and child, but for most parents the first such major task is to teach the child what she can and cannot do when she starts to crawl around.

The child's physical growth sets other limits as well. Take toilet training as an example. In the United States, until quite recently, it was common to see mothers attempting to begin toilet training with babies 10 months or 1 year old. I can certainly understand why mothers might want to have the child toilet trained at that age. For most people changing dirty diapers is not one of the joys of life. But the attempt is doomed to failure at this age for the very simple reason that the muscles needed for voluntary control over elimination simply have not yet developed. Mothers of 10-month-old children who tell you that their babies are toilet trained are simply kidding themselves. In fact, it is the mother who is trained. She has learned the signals—grunts or other noises or body movements—that the child makes just before elimination, and she pops her on the pot at the right moment. But that's not voluntary control by the child.

The child's physical growth and development thus set limits not only on what the child can experience but also to some extent on what she can learn. A second enormously important aspect of the child's physical development is the effect that growth and change have on her own self-image and on her relationships with others. The experiences and interactions of unusually small children, or those who develop very slowly, may be quite different from those of bigger, faster-growing children. This difference becomes especially important during adolescence, when the early developers often have quite different social experiences from those of the later developers. The psychological impact can be considerable and can last well into adulthood, even past the point at which the later-developing boy or girl has caught up completely in both height and growth of various secondary sex characteristics. In this case it's not just the actual physical growth that influences the child's interactions, but also the child's reactions to her own growth or lack of it, and her feelings about how other people are reacting to her growth or nongrowth.[1]

Obviously, society's stereotypes about desirable physical characteristics for children and adults enter into this process, for the child is comparing her own self-image with the ideal in her head. Her actual physical characteristics in this kind of situation may be less important than her perceptions or feelings about them.

I hope that by now I've persuaded you that it's worth your while to read the rest of this chapter. Let me begin, as usual, by describing some of the facts of physical growth and development and then come back to some of the psychological issues relating to growth and development.

HEIGHT AND WEIGHT

Difficult as it is to believe, the newborn baby is already about one-third of her final height, and by age 18 months for girls and 2 years for boys, the toddler is about half as tall as she will be when completely grown. (Most of us think of babies and toddlers as so tiny that it may take a real effort to accept the fact that they already have so much of their final height.) Figure 14 shows the growth curves for a "typical" boy and girl quite clearly. You can see that there is very rapid growth during the first two or three years, after which there is a long stretch from about ages 3 to 11 when growth is steady and regular, followed by the so-called adolescent growth spurt. You can also see from Figure 14 that

[1] I'm sure you can think of examples from your own experience; I certainly can from my own. I was and am unusually tall for a woman. That has certain advantages, of course. It is possible to reach the top shelves in kitchens and laboratories, to see over people at movies and baseball games, and so forth. But it was never the positive parts of height that I paid attention to as an adolescent. The thing that I thought important then was that my being taller than virtually everyone made me look odd.

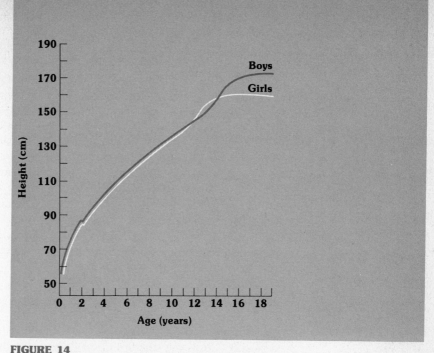

FIGURE 14

Typical individual height curves for boys and girls. (Source: J. M. Tanner, R. H. Whitehouse, & M. Takaishi. Standards from birth to maturity for height, weight, height velocity and weight velocity: British Children, 1965. *Archives of Disease in Children*, 1966, 41, 467.

the adolescent growth spurt comes somewhat earlier for girls, lasts for a shorter time, and results in lower average height than for boys.

One of the reasons why it is difficult to visualize the baby or toddler as a third or half her final height is that she is proportioned differently. She is not yet a miniature adult (although in some medieval paintings children are drawn as if they were). The baby's head is enormously large in proportion to the rest of her body. At birth it is one-quarter the total length of the body, and by the age of 2 it is about one-fifth the length. Compare this proportion to that of the adult; only about one-tenth of the adult body length is in the head.

By adolescence the child's proportions are very close to those of an adult, although there is still quite a lot of height and weight to be gained. Somewhere between ages 10½ and 15 the adolescent spurt occurs, with a growth rate of about 3 to 4 inches a year for several years. There is a great deal of individual variability in both the timing of the growth spurt and in the rate growth during that period, but the two are not correlated. That is, children who begin to grow earlier don't, on the average, wind up taller than those who begin later (with the exception of some comparatively rare cases in which the growth spurt doesn't occur at all). The period of rapid adolescent growth is often a bane to parents, who struggle to keep the child in clothes and to feed her enough to maintain her rapidly growing body. And, of course, it can also be a bane to the developing child, because her body is changing so rapidly that it is often difficult to keep up with all the changes. Different parts of her body grow at different rates. The hands and feet grow fastest, followed by the arms and legs. The trunk is the slowest part to grow, so there is a period during which the hands, feet, arms, and legs are all much longer or larger in proportion to the rest of the body, which gives the appearance of "legginess" and may create a feeling of awkwardness in the child. Having gotten used to a particular shape of body, the pubescent child must now adapt very rapidly to changes in proportions, and there may be periods when she is not always sure where her arms, legs, hands, and feet are at any given moment.[2] But, of course, rapid growth doesn't last forever; ordinarily it lasts for only two years or so, after which the height gradually increases to full adult height.

MUSCLES AND BONES

At birth most of the baby's bones are still soft; they haven't yet hardened (ossified) into the sort of material that you and I think of as bone. In fact, some parts of the body have no bone at all at birth. The fontanelles are a good example. These fontanelles are the "soft spots" on the baby's head, where the skull has not yet completely covered the brain. Gradually during the first two years, these spots disappear as bone grows to cover the gaps.

The bones harden at different rates, those in the hand and wrist being among the first to stiffen completely. The ossification of bones in the hand and wrist is an important development from the point of view of the child, for it is then easier for her to grasp objects, pick them up, and move them around with her wrist and hand.

Muscles too, although all present at birth, change enormously during the growth years, with especially major changes occurring during adolescence. The baby does have at birth all the muscle fibers that she will ever have. But they change in length and thickness, so that the total mass of muscle increases greatly over the first 14 to 15 years of life. During the adolescent growth period, there is a sharp increase in muscle tissue—particularly in boys—and an accompanying decrease in fat. One of the consequences of this shift is, of course, a marked increase in strength at adolescence, again particularly among boys. For example, between the ages of 13 and about 17, a boy's arm strength just about doubles.

[2] I cannot resist one further example from my own experience, because it illustrates this point so well. Once, when I was about 13, I was sitting at the dinner table holding forth on some subject. To illustrate some important point, I made a grand gesture, swept my hand through the butter, and hit my mother in the face with both hand and butter. I was astonished to discover that my arm was that long!

MOTOR DEVELOPMENT

From the parents' point of view one of the most striking things about the first year or two of life is the baby's growing ability to control her muscles and to move around her world independently. Parents are turned on by the first smile and first word, but the first step is surely as big a moment as any during the early months. I recall a meeting that I attended several years ago at which a mother with a baby of about 8 months was present. The baby crawled around, attracting lots of attention from everyone, and then, quite suddenly, flexed his legs and stood up without any help. The entire meeting stopped while we oh'ed and ah'ed about his accomplishment. So it isn't only parents who are tuned in to changes in motor skills. Later developments in motor skills are noticed, too. The moment when the preschooler can first catch and throw a ball is important, as is her first successful bike ride, and so on.

Figures 15, 16, and 17 show some of the sequences. Figure 15 shows the transition in reaching and grasping, from whole hand grasping to thumb-forefinger opposition. In Figure 16 you can see the transition from sitting to standing to walking, while Figure 17 shows the sequence in an older child of catching a ball. In each case you can see the progression in coordination of the large and small muscles of the body. The timing of these several accomplishments varies quite a bit from one child to another, but some average ages at which the several skills are acquired are given in Table 1.

Obviously, the child's motor ability—her developing skills in moving around the world, grasping and manipulating with hands and feet, and so forth—is directly linked to the development of bones and

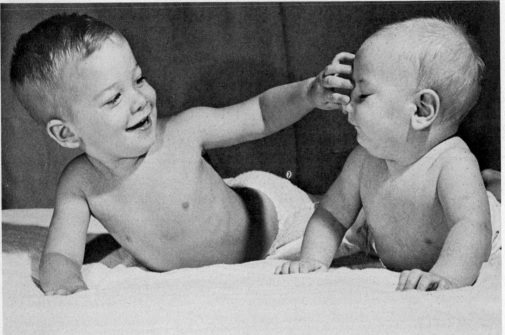

FIGURE 15
The development of grasping skill. Note the shift from an all-hand grasp to thumb-forefinger opposition.

muscles. Until the muscles of the neck and back have developed to some extent, the baby can't hold up her head; until the bones in the hands have developed and the muscles have grown, the child is unable to grasp objects. This fundamental maturational component in the development of motor skills is really beyond dispute. As the body grows, motor ability improves.

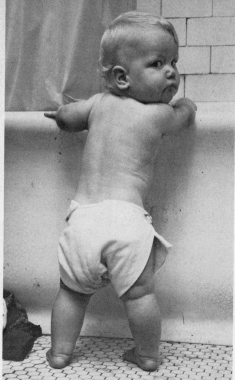

FIGURE 16
The development of motor skill from sitting to walking.

FIGURE 17
More advanced motor skills: catching and throwing a ball.

TABLE 1
Milestones in Motor Development

Average age when skill appears	Motor skill
1 month	Lifts chin up while lying on stomach
2 months	Lifts chest, as well as chin
4.8 months	Manages to roll over for the first time (does so easily by about 6 months)
7 months	Picks up objects using the palm without thumb and fingers
8 months	Tries to stand by hanging onto furniture
8.3 months	Sits up easily
8.3 months	Stands independently for the first time
12 months	Takes first few steps without holding on
13–14 months	Grasps with thumb and forefinger
18 months	Walks well alone
2 years	Walks up and down stairs alone but still with both feet on each step
2 years	Runs well
30 months	Walks on tiptoe
3 years	Rides tricycle
4 years	Walks down stairs, one foot to a step
4 years	Throws ball overhand
4 years, 8 months	Hops on one foot

But what about practice? If a child were completely immobilized and given no opportunity to practice crawling, walking, or grasping, would those skills develop anyway? Is the underlying growth of muscles and bones all that is needed, or does the baby have to have a chance to try out the coordination of muscles, bones, and senses?

There's still a good deal of disagreement about the answers to these questions. On one hand, there is quite a lot of evidence that practice plays only a small role in the development of such skills as walking and climbing stairs. Several older studies of pairs of twins were focused on this question directly (see Gesell & Thompson and McGraw). In each case one twin of the pair was given a lot of early practice on the particular skill. Later, the second twin was given a brief period of practice, and then the two twins were tested. In general, if the "untrained twin" had been given even the briefest practice, the two children performed almost equally well on the task. For at least these early motor skills, then, a little bit of practice later is as good as a lot of practice earlier, presumably because in the intervening time physical changes have taken place in the body. Another example of the need for only

BOX 6
Ethnic Differences in Rate of Motor Development

A number of different researchers have reported that black infants have more rapid motor development during the first year of life than do infants of other ethnic groups. Mary Ainsworth observed this in her studies of mother-infant attachment among families in Uganda (Ainsworth, 1967), and Bayley found a similar acceleration of motor development among black infants in her very large national study of early mental and motor development (Bayley, 1965). Ainsworth also cites a study by Geber, who studied infants in Uganda ten years before she did and who noted the same thing.

How are these differences to be explained? Conceivably, there could be some genetic difference accounting for the faster rate of development among black infants. If rate of motor development during these early months is primarily controlled by some kind of genetic map or timetable, that timetable quite simply may be faster among blacks. It seems to be faster for girls in some respects, so it is entirely logical that it might be faster for some other subsets as well. But as reasonable and attractive as that hypothesis may be, it is probably not correct.

A number of pieces of evidence point to an environmental explanation. First, Geber reported that when she tested a group of Ugandan children whose families had adopted more western ways, these children were *slower* in motor development than were village children. They developed motorically at about the same rate as did children from Caucasian western families. These black children from westernized families were kept in their cribs more and were carried less, whereas in the villages the infants are handled a great deal, are held in a standing position, or sit facing away from the mother, and generally

limited practice comes from studies of Hopi Indian children, who are commonly carried around on their mother's back during their first year or so, strapped down firmly to a flat board so that only their head and eyes can move. Such children develop walking normally when they are removed from the backboard. Some practice is available to these children, however, for in the evenings the baby is taken off the backboard, played with, and allowed to move about on the ground.

These findings and others of a similar nature suggest that extra practice cannot speed up the maturational process; the infant cannot learn a physical skill before the muscles, bones, and nervous system have developed to an appropriate point. But once that particular point is reached, at least some opportunity to exercise the muscles and to practice the particular activity is probably required.

But the importance of practice cannot be completely deemphasized either. In the twin and the Hopi lifestyle studies, the babies had at least some opportunity for normal physical exploration and body movement. The untrained twin was not kept completely immobile; she could practice parts of the acts of walking or crawling, even if special practice was not given. Hopi infants have a chance to exercise their muscles and to try out movements. When such opportunities for exercise and movement are greatly restricted, there is some retardation in motor development. Dennis's study of children raised in orphanages in Iran is a case in point. Babies whose opportunities to move or to play

seem to receive a great deal of both visual and vestibular stimulation.

An older study by Williams and Scott (1953) of black families in Washington, D.C., yielded some very similar results. They found that infants from poor families showed *faster* motor development than did black infants from middle-class families. The infants in the poor families were less often physically restricted and were given more free rein in a number of ways than were the infants in the middle-class families. Regardless of the family's economic situation, families that were more permissive toward the child's motor explorations and other expressions had children who showed more rapid motor development.

Finally, a study by Brazelton, Robey, and Collier of Zinacanteco Indian infants in southern Mexico shows that restricted opportunities for motor activity may be associated with slowed motor development. Infants in this culture are heavily swaddled and usually have their faces covered. The infant is carried on the mother's back a good part of the time, but in a way that restricts both movement and visual experience. These infants are slower in motor development than western children.

There is no indication that the Zinacanteco children are *permanently* retarded in motor development, nor that Ugandan children are permanently accelerated; all the groups studied eventually achieve the major motor milestones. But the rates of development do differ and seem to be quite markedly influenced by rather specific aspects of treatment and rearing.

had been severely restricted were slowed down as much as a year in development of walking and were equally retarded in a whole host of other areas of motor developments, such as grasping. Research with animals also shows that lack of opportunity to practice coordination of limb and eye movements will result in substantial retardation of development of this skill.

What at first appeared to be a simple maturational process is clearly more complex than this. Motor development is affected by opportunity for practice and by environmental variations such as those discussed in Box 6. The maturational process undoubtedly sets some kind of limits on the rate of physical growth and motor development that is possible, but the rate may clearly be retarded or delayed by the absence of appropriate practice or experience.

GROWTH OF THE NERVOUS SYSTEM

Growth in height or weight involves changes that you can see. But there are a great many changes in the child's body that can't be seen. There are changes in hormones, which I'll take up in the next section, and, most important, there are changes in the child's nervous system.

The most important point about the growth of the nervous system is that the brain and the nervous system are not "finished" at birth. Most other organ systems are at least operative, even though they undergo further maturation after birth. For example, the baby has a heart and a circulatory system that are much like the adult system, and her lungs work from the beginning. The brain at birth is developed in the sense that it is nearer in size to its final form than are some organ systems. But the functioning of the nervous system is in only rudimentary form at birth and changes rapidly during the first two to four years. The growth that occurs during those early years is of several kinds.

At birth the parts of the brain that are most fully developed are those contained in what is usually called the *midbrain*. They are in the lower part of the skull, just above where the neck and head connect, and include the systems that regulate such things as attention, sleeping, waking, elimination, and so forth. They are also the parts of the human brain that are most like the brains of lower animals. The part of the human brain in which we differ most from lower animals is the *cortex*, the convoluted gray matter that most of us think of when we visualize the brain. The cortex is present at birth but is considerably less developed than it will be later. During the first few months and years of life, some new cortical cells are added, the cells become bigger, and the existing cells build up more connections among them. The brain becomes heavier. You can see the general locations of these different parts of the brain in Figure 18.

You can recall from the discussion of reflexes in Chapter 4 that the primitive reflexes seem to be under the control of the midbrain and that they drop out at about 6 months when the cortex begins to dominate. Cortical development is about half complete by 6 months, about

FIGURE 18

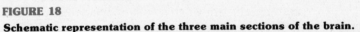

Schematic representation of the three main sections of the brain.

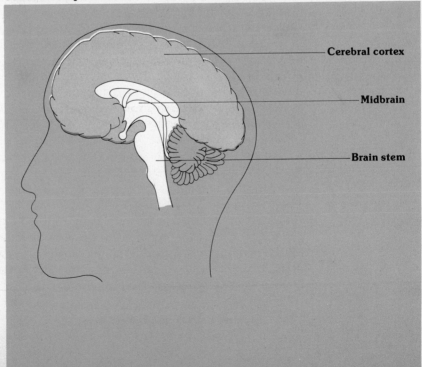

75 percent complete by age 2, and almost entirely completed by age 4.

But the cortex does not develop all at once or all at the same rate. Some parts of it develop right away, other parts not until much later. Up to about 6 months of age, the parts of the cortex that govern such senses as hearing and seeing are already developed, and the motor areas are partly developed, particularly those controlling the hands, arms, and upper trunk. The motor area of the brain that governs leg movements is the last of the motor areas to develop and isn't really fully developed until well into the second year. This sequence of brain development is obviously related to the sequence of motor development and sensory skills. The first things that the baby can do are see and hear. She has very little voluntary muscle control, and when voluntary muscle control does begin it begins in the arms, hands, and head, rather than in the legs. So the rate of development of the different parts of the cortex obviously sets some kinds of limits on, or perhaps guides, the development of the child's motor and perceptual skills.

A second important process is the development of sheaths around individual nerves, which insulate them from one another and make it easier for messages to pass down the nerves. This sheath is called *myelin*, and the process of developing the sheath is called *myelinization*. At birth, for example, the spinal cord is not fully myelinized, and without this sheathing the child has little ability to "communicate" with the bottom half of her body. (The infant can feel touch or other sensations in the lower part of the body, but has little muscle control.) The process of myelinization occurs during the early months and years and is almost complete by the time the child is 2 years old, following much the same pattern as the growth of nerve cells in the brain.

Both the growth pattern of the brain and the myelinization of the outgoing and incoming nerves are important because they tell us something about the limits on the baby's earliest skills and motor development, and because they suggest an area of the child's development that would be vulnerable to deprivation. During the prenatal period each organ system is most vulnerable to outside influence during the period when it is developing; once it is developed in its more or less final form, diseases, malnutrition, and other "insults" from outside have comparatively little effect. If the same is true of neurological development, then the period after birth up to about 2 years of age should be a time of special vulnerability for brain and nerve development.

HORMONES AND THEIR EFFECTS

Most of us, I suspect, are used to thinking of hormones as important during adolescence; after all, puberty is triggered by hormone changes, as I shall describe shortly. But hormones of various kinds are important before adolescence as well.

TABLE 2
Pubertal Development in Boys

Characteristic	Average age of onset	Normal range of onset ages	Average age at completion	Range
Height spurt	$12\frac{1}{2}$	$10\frac{1}{2}$–16	16	13–$17\frac{1}{2}$
Accelerated growth of penis	$12\frac{1}{2}$	$10\frac{1}{2}$–$14\frac{1}{2}$	$14\frac{1}{2}$	$12\frac{1}{2}$–$16\frac{1}{2}$
Accelerated growth of testes	$11\frac{1}{2}$	$9\frac{1}{2}$–$13\frac{1}{2}$	15	$13\frac{1}{2}$–17

Source: Adapted from Tanner, J. M. Growth and endocrinology of the adolescent. In L. J. Gardner (Ed.), *Endocrine and Genetic Diseases of Childhood* (2nd ed.). Philadelphia: Saunders, 1975.

Prenatal Period

I have already discussed in Chapter 3 the prenatal role of the hormone androgen in determining the child's external sexual characteristics. Shortly after birth, however, males and females are essentially equivalent in the amount of so-called sex hormones in the blood (or at least our instruments are not good enough to detect consistent differences).

Other growth hormones that have little to do with the development of sexual organs and behavior are also crucial both before and after birth. The pituitary gland, for example, secretes hormones, as do the thyroid and adrenal glands, and the pancreas. The various glands that secrete growth hormones develop during the prenatal period, and their secretions govern the child's growth throughout her development.

Between Birth and Adolescence

We know that there are hormones in the blood from the beginning, but we don't know yet precisely which ones control the different facets of the child's growth or what determines the fact that some children will grow rapidly and that others will grow more slowly. We do know that the secretions of the thyroid gland have something to do with physical growth, because children who have too little thyroid are delayed in the growth of their bones, teeth, and brain. In normal growth patterns the secretions of the thyroid gland decrease after about age 2 and then remain steady until about adolescence, which certainly fits what we know about the patterns of most rapid growth in the child.

Adolescence

Study of the role of hormones in puberty is incredibly complex. Let me say merely that very rapid physical growth and the accompanying development of reproductive systems and secondary sex characteristics that occur during adolescence all seem to be triggered and main-

TABLE 3
Pubertal Development in Girls

Characteristic	Average age of onset	Normal range of onset ages	Average age at completion
Height spurt	$10\frac{1}{2}$	$9\frac{1}{2}$–$14\frac{1}{2}$	14
Menarche (first menstruation)	13	10–$15\frac{1}{2}$	—
Breast development, beginning with the first buds	$10\frac{3}{4}$	8–13	$14\frac{3}{4}$

Source: Adapted from Tanner, J. M. Growth and endocrinology of the adolescent. In L. J. Gardner (Ed.), *Endocrine and Genetic Diseases of Childhood* (2nd ed.). Philadelphia: Saunders, 1975.

tained by rather sharp increases in particular hormone levels. In girls estrogen (the female sex hormone) increases rather sharply and becomes cyclic, producing the menstrual cycle. In boys there is a sharp increase in the production of testosterone (the male sex hormone), leading to the development of the reproductive system in boys.

Increases in the sex hormones are themselves triggered by activating hormones released in larger quantities by the pituitary gland. These activating hormones stimulate production of the whole range of growth-related hormones in the body. Researchers have not yet been able to trace the process back past the role of the pituitary gland, however. We do not know why the pituitary gland increases its output of activating hormones at adolescence, although presumably the signal to do so is contained in the maturational code in the genes.

The normal sequence of puberty for boys and girls is given in Tables 2 and 3. In order to underline the enormous variability in the timing and duration of the pubertal changes, I have given both the average age at which each of several changes is seen and the normal range of ages. The range of ages is in every case quite large, but it is important to realize that any age within that range is considered to be within the limits of normal development. So a boy who does not begin the major growth spurt until age 16 is still within the normal range.

To underline still further the variability in timing of the various pubertal changes, look at Figure 19, which shows children of the same ages who are vastly different in pubertal changes.

IMPLICATIONS AND EXPLANATIONS

As usual, in attempting to account for the growth patterns, we look to both internal and external explanations.

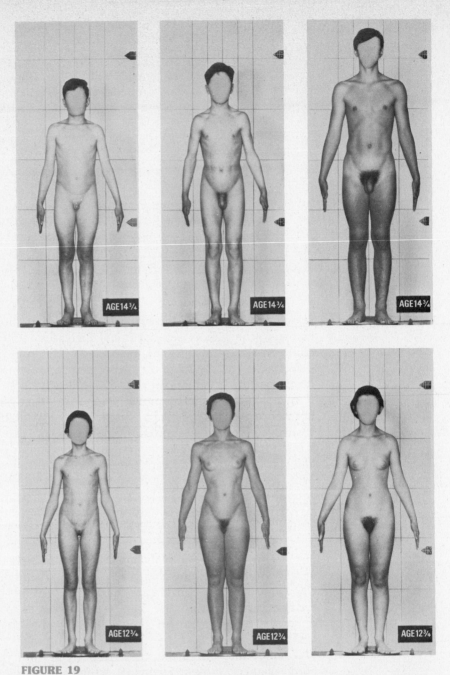

FIGURE 19
Variations among children in timing and speed of pubertal changes. (Source: J. M. Tanner. Growth and endocrinology of the adolescent. In L. J. Gardner (Ed.), *Endocrine and genetic diseases of childhood*. Philadelphia: Saunders, 1969, p. 32.

Maturation

It seems clear that some set of internal signals governs most of the growth patterns I have described. (See Box 7 for a more detailed discussion of Gesell's view of these processes.) The sequences of physical growth are the same for all but the most unusual children, although the rate varies considerably. And although practice seems to make some difference in the development of some motor skills, most physical changes simply happen; they are not under voluntary control and do not require practice. You don't have to tell your nervous system to myelinate, you don't have to tell your bones to grow in particular ways, and you don't have to practice menstruating.

Just what internal signals do promote such growth are not yet understood. The point to remember for now is that most physical growth and development is controlled by internal maturational processes.

Heredity

When I use the term maturation, as I've pointed out several times, I am referring to inherited processes that are shared by all humans. But our genetic heritage is individual as well as racial, and we each inherit some different growth tendencies. Obviously, height is one inherited factor. Tall parents tend to have tall children, and short parents tend to have short children. Rate of growth, as well as final height, is also affected by specific inheritance. Identical twin girls, for example, will begin to menstruate, on the average, within 2 months of each other, whereas sisters who are not identical twins may begin menstruating at ages differing, on the average, by about 10 months. Sisters and mother-daughter pairs are in turn more like one another in age of onset of menarche than are random pairs of girls. The same set of relationships holds as well for overall rate of growth, rate of bone solidification, timing of eruption of teeth, and so on (see Tanner, 1970, for a more detailed discussion). All of these physical growth rates are clearly influenced by specific inheritance.

Environmental Effects

But, as usual, nothing is ever completely one-sided. Although physical development is probably the aspect of growth and development that is least affected by environmental factors, it is affected in some important ways. The most important single external influence on the child's physical development is her diet. Poorly nourished children not only grow more slowly—with all maturational processes apparently slowed down—but, more important, they don't grow in quite the same way. As nearly as we can tell on the basis of current research, the major impact during the early months and years is on the growth of the nervous system. The cortex does not develop as many interconnecting tissues and does not become as heavy as in well-nourished children. In addition, the development of both muscles and bones is affected, which in turn affects the child's strength, eventual height, and coordination.

I should emphasize again that the effects of early malnutrition appear irreversible; you can't make up for the loss of brain weight and in-

BOX 7
Gesell's Maturational Concepts

I have mentioned Arnold Gesell before and have touched on his notion of maturation. Gesell went farther, though, than simply defining the term *maturation*. He also attempted to specify some of the principles inherent in maturational processes, drawing most of his examples from prenatal development and early motor development. Some of these principles are as follows.

The Principle of Directionality. Gesell suggested that we would always find that development governed by maturation—as opposed to environmental forces—has a clear directionality. In the case of fetal development and motor development there are two clear directions:

Development proceeds from the head downward (cephalocaudal) and from the trunk outward (proximodistal). Thus, the head and trunk develop first, but the arms and hands develop before the feet because they are closer to the head.

The Principle of Functional Asymmetry. In addition to the fundamental directions of development, and overlaid on it, is the tendency of the organism to develop asymmetrically. In humans we see this tendency in "handedness": Virtually everyone has a preferred side, usually the right. We write with the hand on the preferred side, throw a ball with that hand, kick with the foot

terconnectedness by eating more later. But malnourishment after about age 2 does seem reversible if you catch it soon enough. The child can regain the lost height, muscle tissue, and so on after a period of good nourishment.

Illness also has an impact on the child's growth rate. During periods of serious illness, the child's rate of growth slows markedly. The longer the child is ill, the more she will fall behind the level of growth that she would have achieved under healthy circumstances. But in most cases once the period of illness is past, the child catches up by growing more rapidly than before the illness, until the original pattern of growth has been reestablished, after which the rate slows down again. If the illness is prolonged or occurs very early, the child may not catch up completely, so that her eventual size will be smaller than it would have been without the illness.

SOME CORRELATES OF GROWTH PATTERNS

Throughout this chapter I have emphasized that although the sequence of physical development is essentially the same for all children, the rate at which they go through that sequence is not, either because of hereditary differences or because of environmental differences such as diet. What are the implications of those differences in development rate for the child?

Physical Growth and Mental Development

There is a large body of evidence showing that children who are more rapid in physical growth are also slightly advanced in mental growth. They score somewhat higher on standard IQ tests and do somewhat better in school than do their more slowly developing peers. For exon that side, and so on. Accompanying such motor asymmetry is an equivalent neural asymmetry: If you are right-handed, you are "left-brained," and if you are left-handed, you are "right-brained." One-half of the brain is dominant over the other half.

The Principle of Self-Regulating Fluctuation. Development, according to Gesell, does not proceed at the same even pace along all fronts simultaneously. Although one system is developing vigorously another may be dormant, and later the two may reverse activity levels. A good example of this, which will be discussed later, is in the relationship between motor development and language development. Usually the child doesn't begin talking extensively until after she has learned to walk; the two skills are rarely developed together. Later, after the language system is more firmly established, there are more advances in motor skills.

Gesell may have used somewhat old-fashioned language, but these are still valid descriptions of much of prenatal development and of many aspects of motor development as well.

ample, in one study conducted in London (and described by Tanner), 10-year-old girls who were in the top 25 percent in height for their age had IQ scores that were, on the average, 9 points higher than those for 10-year-old girls in the bottom 15 percent of the height distribution. Among older girls those who have begun menstruating have slightly higher IQs than do those girls of the same age who have not yet begun to menstruate. (Bear in mind that these are *average* differences; not all shorter people have lower IQs!)

Many of you, I'm sure, will have already thought that diet explains part of this difference: Shorter children are often, though by no means always, children whose diet is less good. We have other evidence that malnutrition has an adverse effect on the child's ability to learn, either directly through early interference with brain development or indirectly through effects on her levels of energy and motivation. But diet won't explain all the relationship between height and IQ score. We know, for example, that there is no eventual difference in height between boys who are early maturers at puberty and those who are late maturers, yet the earlier maturers continue to have a slight IQ advantage. It is by no means clear why this should be true, but it is an intriguing fact. One possibility is that children who are taller and faster developers during their early years and adolescence acquire a kind of confidence about themselves and all their abilities that carries over into adulthood. Alternatively, children who have been fast developers throughout their lives may have been treated differently by adults and peers during their childhood and adolescence, and the impact of that difference in attitudes or behavior by others may still be felt in adulthood.

125   Physical Growth and Development

BOX 8
Body Build and Personality

In the main part of this chapter I have pointed out that there is some relationship between height or rapidity of physical maturation and personality. There appears also to be some connection—at least in men and boys, on whom the research has been done—between the type of body build and some kinds of personality characteristics. One of the original exponents of this view was W. H. Sheldon, who identified three components of human body types: the endomorphic, the mesomorphic, and the ectomorphic. Each man's physical build, according to Sheldon, can be described in terms of its degree of endomorphy, mesomorphy, and ectomorphy.

Very generally, endomorphy is the amount of fat, mesomorphy the amount of muscles, and ectomorphy the length of bone. An endomorphic man is generally soft and round. A mesomorphic man is close to the classic "all-American boy" image: well muscled, thick-chested, broad-shouldered, squarely built. The ectomorphic man is tall, thin, and somewhat stoop-shouldered. Most men, of course, have elements of all three, but in many cases it is possible to identify a dominant theme.

Sheldon was not satisfied, however, merely to classify the types of build. He also believed that there are personality traits to go with the various kinds of build. In children there is some slight evidence that he is correct.

Endomorphic preschool boys in one study (Walker, 1962) were rated by their teachers as aggressive and assertive; the ectomorphs were thoughtful and considerate but lacked energy and assertiveness. The mesomorphs were leaders in play and had lots of self-confidence, but they were also difficult to handle because they were quarrelsome. Other research (for example, Cortes & Gatti, 1965) suggests that these patterns continue through adolescence and perhaps into adulthood. Among adolescents the ectomorphic types (the tall, skinny boys) are not dominant in their peer groups; they are more likely to go along with the gang than to try to

Either of these alternatives receives some support from the fact that among boys, at least, the largest are most likely the leaders, and that is particularly true of the solidly built, well-muscled boy.

Body Build, Rate of Maturing, Self-Image, and Personality

As you can see from the discussion in Box 8, the particular body build a child or adult has is related in some ways to personality characteristics. The *rate* of physical development, independent of body type, is also a factor in a child's self-image and personality.

In our society physical appearance seems to be particularly important in adolescence, no doubt partly because the changes in the body that occur at puberty are signs of maturity, of reaching adult status. At this stage girls worry about whether or not their breasts are going to develop. When they do, the girls worry about whether they will be too small or too big or the wrong shape. They also worry about their height, and so on. Boys worry about such outward signs of puberty as height, whether or not they need to shave, whether or not they have developed hair on their chest and in the pubic area, whether or not their penis and testes have developed fully, and so on. These changes are exciting and important events in teenagers' lives, as the 12-year-old son of one of my friends demonstrated. He rushed up to his mother in

push their own interests. The mesomorphic types are more likely to be the leaders, to make the decisions, and to give orders to the group. Notice that it isn't tallness per se that is associated with leadership. Rather, it seems to be body type.

Where do these kinds of differences come from? One possibility is that, for some reason, in our society we have fairly clear expectations about people with different sorts of body build. Muscular boys are viewed as athletes and we expect them to be "stars" in their group. The thin, ascetic-looking child we may think of as a future professor, and we may encourage him to read. Perhaps we force children into personality molds, to some extent, because of their body build.

An alternative possibility is that body build is itself the result of particular patterns of hormones in the child's bloodstream and that the hormones also have an effect on personality. The data on this question are not at all good, but what evidence we have is at least consistent with the notion that hormonal differences among men and boys or women and girls may well influence both physique and personality. What we do know is that hormones affect personality (in both monkeys and men, there is some indication that those with the highest concentrations of male hormones in the blood are the most dominant and aggressive) and that they affect growth patterns. The ectomorphic types—the tall, lean men—are likely, for example, to have begun puberty rather late and to have continued growing over a longer period of time rather than in a single spurt, which suggests the presence of somewhat less massive doses of male hormones at the beginning of the pubertal period. What we don't know is whether or not both the personality characteristics and the differences in physique come from the same kinds of hormone differences.

great excitement, crying, "Mom, I've got three pubic hairs!" It's a period in life when one is extraordinarily conscious of one's body and whether or not that body measures up to the standards of physical maturity held by our society.

Given that kind of preoccupation with the body, it's not surprising that there are major psychological effects on those teenagers who arrive at puberty later than usual. At age 13 or 14 some boys and girls are smaller than their classmates or have not yet developed any of the secondary sex characteristics. They often see their own bodies as inadequate, particularly in comparison to those of their more rapidly developing friends. Parents and other adults treat them as being younger than children who have matured earlier and who look more like adults.

Among boys the early maturers are more likely to be class leaders, are looked up to by other teenagers, and appear to develop generally a positive image of themselves. As adults they are likely to be more sociable and less neurotic. Later maturers, on the other hand, are often more anxious about their bodies, their slow development, and their acceptance by the group. They may find it difficult to get attention because of their physical prowess, so they try to attract attention in other ways, for example by talkativeness, bossiness, or physical restlessness. But all these methods of attracting attention and approval apparently don't work terribly well, for late-maturing boys are frequently not popular, and as adults they have greater difficulty in social relations. So the anxiety and feelings of inadequacy that accompany very slow physical growth carry over into adulthood in a man's image of himself; he still thinks of himself as inadequate and unlikeable even after he has changed and grown physically. (See papers by Jones and her associates listed in the References.)

Among girls very early puberty is not highly valued. Girls who begin menstruating in the sixth grade, for example, are not objects of admiration, because social status in the sixth grade is still determined by other factors. Beginning in the seventh grade, however, girls who have begun to menstruate are accorded higher status. In junior high school and high school the more fully developed girls do have higher status and are more likely to be leaders among the girls (see, for example, the 1960 study by Faust). Longitudinal research at the University of California (see Jones & Mussen, 1958) suggests that in the long run the early-maturing girl is slightly more self-confident and more relaxed in personal relationships, although the differences are by no means as great as among boys.

Before you come to the conclusion that early and more rapid maturation is always a good thing, remember that some costs are involved. The child who matures exceptionally early may appear much older and may be expected to have the emotional and mental maturity to go with her physical maturity. Such expectations can create considerable strain, both for the child and for the adults around her. Then, too, there are some negative physical aspects of puberty, such as acne, that plague the early-maturing child as much as the late maturer.

SEX DIFFERENCES IN PHYSICAL GROWTH

From birth through the period of growth, boys and girls differ in important ways in the amount and pattern of physical growth. The facts, as we know them, are as follows.

1. As I pointed out earlier, girls are more advanced—as much as four weeks—at birth in the development of bone ossification and muscle development, and they remain advanced in these dimensions throughout the early years. This difference is often referred to as a "faster maturational timetable" for girls.

2. Girls begin their adolescent growth spurt sooner and stop sooner, which may be yet another example of the faster maturational process in girls.

3. Girls' physical growth is steadier and more predictable than that of boys. You can get a better estimate of final height from looking at the height of a young girl than you can for a boy.

4. Girls and boys do not differ markedly in physical strength or endurance until adolescence; after about ages 12 to 14, boys experience

a sharp increase in strength as a result of major changes in musculature, whereas a girl's physical strength remains about the same. Put another way, a 10-year-old girl has nearly as much strength as an adult woman, whereas a 10-year-old boy has only about half as much strength as an adult man.

5. At about the same time as boys are developing extra muscle tissue during adolescence, they are also developing a larger heart and lungs relative to their size and a greater capacity for carrying oxygen in the blood (they develop a greater density of red blood cells, in which oxygen is carried). None of these events occurs in the growth of girls. What all these changes mean is that the male, after adolescence, is better adapted for physical activities requiring strength and speed, like running, fighting, carrying heavy objects, and so forth.

6. Girls from birth onward have a thicker layer of fat directly below the skin than do boys. It gives girls their "softer" appearance; the bones don't show through as much. It also gives girls and women greater tolerance for extremes in temperature. Women can withstand extreme cold, for example, much longer than can men because of this extra layer of insulation.

SOCIAL CLASS DIFFERENCES IN PHYSICAL GROWTH

Aside from the ethnic differences in early motor development that I discussed in Box 6, there are no clear and consistent social class differences in rate of physical growth. Most "infant IQ tests," which are made up primarily of motor and perceptual items, reveal no social class differences in early years of life. Motor and other physical development seem to be heavily dependent on maturation and on opportunity for minimal practice. Virtually all environments appear to provide this minimal practice, so there are few consistent differences among social class groups in physical development.

CONCLUSIONS

I hope that at least I have persuaded you that physical growth and development can't be ignored when we think about the child's overall development. I've tried to show that motor skills depend on muscle growth, brain growth, and bone growth, and that the child's unique rate of growth and body build may have profound influences on her self-image and self-confidence. I think you will see in the chapters on cognitive development that physical growth—particularly of the nervous system—sets limits there too. It is certainly not accidental that the child begins to talk at about the same time that cortical growth approaches completion.

As you read all the later chapters, you should keep in mind the general outline of these facts about physical growth, for the child's body always sets limits. A child cannot do what her body is not yet developed to do, and we are foolish to expect her to. Physical readiness does not, of course, guarantee that she will learn. In most cases it is a necessary but not sufficient condition. But it is necessary, and that fact should not be forgotten.

SUMMARY

1. It is important to know something about physical growth and development because the child's level of physical development sets limits on the kinds of interaction she may have with the environment and because her feelings about her own body may also affect her very broadly.
2. Changes in height are very rapid during the first year and level off to a steady rate of increase until adolescence, when there is a sharp increase in rate.
3. Muscles and bones develop in a similar pattern, with an increase in muscle density and in length of fibers, particularly during adolescence. During the early years, the bones harden in sequence, first in the hands and arms, then in the feet and legs.
4. The nervous system develops substantially during the first year or two of life, with myelinization of the nerves and an increase in both the number and density of brain cells being the important developments.
5. The brain develops in a particular sequence, with perceptual areas first, followed by motor areas involved in the hands, arms, and trunk before development of nerves to the legs.
6. Maturation is the most important process underlying all physical growth and development, although some practice is needed just to maintain the organism. Children with severely restricted opportunities for movement and other practice may be substantially retarded in motor development, for example.
7. During adolescence, in particular, the influence of hormones is of special importance. Increases in excretion of hormones from the pituitary gland at the very beginning of adolescence in turn trigger increases in the hormone output of various other glands, including the sex glands.
8. There are great differences in rate of maturation among children. These are particularly noticeable during adolescence, when some children may go through puberty four or five years sooner than their late-developing peers. Such individual differences, however, are *not* related to the social class of the child's family.
9. Early or late, rapid or slow development has an impact on the child's relationships with her peers. In general, larger, faster-developing children are more likely to be leaders in their groups.
10. There are some consistent differences between males and females in both rate and pattern of physical growth. Girls are accelerated in physical growth in some respects from infancy onward and go through puberty sooner. In adolescence boys show more growth of heart and circulatory system, lungs, and muscle tissue.

REFERENCES

Suggested Additional Readings

Dennis, W. Causes of retardation among institutional children: Iran. *Journal of Genetic Psychology,* 1969, *96,* 47–59.
An oft-quoted study, partly because the method is unusually good for a study of institutionalized children; the results are of great interest, and the paper is not difficult to read.
Garn, S. M. Body size and its implications. In L. W. Hoffman & M. L. Hoffman (Eds.), *Review of child development research* (Vol. 2). New York: Russell Sage, 1966.

A good, only moderately technical review of the literature on prediction of body size, effects of diet on body size and rate of growth, and related subjects.

Jones, M. C. The later careers of boys who were early or late maturing. *Child Development,* 1957, *28,* 113–128.
The classic study of early- and later-maturing boys and of the psychological impact of variations in rate of maturing.

Tanner, J. M. Physical growth. In P. H. Mussen (Ed.), *Carmichaels' manual of child psychology* (Vol. 1). New York: Wiley, 1970.
A very detailed, very technical, but excellent presentation from which much of this chapter is derived; the most complete and up-to-date presentation of the material that I know.

Other Sources Cited

Ainsworth, M. D. S. *Infancy in Uganda: Infant care and the growth of love.* Baltimore: Johns Hopkins Press, 1967.

Bayley, N. Comparisons of mental and motor test scores for ages 1–15 months by sex, birth order, race, geographical location, and education of parents. *Child Development,* 1965, *36,* 379–412.

Brazelton, T. B., Robey, J. S., & Collier, G. A. Infant development in the Zinacanteco indians of southern Mexico. *Pediatrics,* 1969, *44,* 274–293.

Cortes, J. B., & Gatti, F. M. Physique and self-description of temperament. *Journal of Consulting Psychology,* 1965, *20,* 432–439.

Faust, J. S. Developmental maturity as a determinant in prestige of adolescent girls. *Child Development,* 1960, *31,* 173–181.

Gesell, A. The ontogenesis of infant behavior. In L. Carmichael (Ed.), *Manual of child psychology* (2nd ed.). New York: Wiley, 1954.

Gesell, A., & Thompson, H. Learning and growth in identical twins: An experimental study by the method of co-twin control. *Genetic Psychology Monographs,* 1929, *6,* 1–123.

Jones, J. C., & Mussen, P. H. Self-conceptions, motivations and interpersonal attitudes of early and late maturing girls. *Child Development,* 1958, *29,* 491–501.

McGraw, M. C. *Growth: A study of Johnny and Jimmy.* New York: Appleton, 1935.

Mussen, P. H., & Jones, M. C. Self conceptions, motivations, and interpersonal attitudes of late and early maturing boys. *Child Development,* 1957, *28,* 243–256.

Sheldon, W. H. *The varieties of human physique.* New York: Harper & Row, 1940.

Walker, R. N. Body build and behavior in young children: I. Body and nursery school teachers' ratings. *Monograph of the Society for Research in Child Development,* 1962, *27* (Whole No. 84).

Washburn, W. C. The effects of physique and intrafamily tension on self-concept in adolescent males. *Journal of Consulting Psychology,* 1962, *26,* 460–466.

Williams, J. R., & Scott, R. B. Growth and development of Negro infants: IV. Motor development and its relationship to child rearing practices in two groups of Negro infants. *Child Development,* 1953, *24,* 103–121.

6

Perceptual
Development

For the infant perceptual skills are of foremost importance. She cannot yet walk or even crawl. She cannot grasp things with her hands or fingers, nor has she developed the mental capacity that will enable her to think about things that aren't there. All she really can do in the beginning is perceive. For the first two years or so the child's major mode of interaction with the environment is through her eyes, ears, nose, tongue, and fingers. Of course, in some sense your major interactions with the environment are perceptual as well, but you have a great many other abilities not shared by the young child. You can imagine, you can compare events to those that have happened before, you can overcome perception with thought ("That can't be true. My eyes are deceiving me"). And, of course, you also have the motor skills that make it possible to go out to experience more than the baby can. It is important for us to know something about the perceptual skills of the infant and young child because those skills are so crucial for the child; we need to know what the child can and does experience.

The study of perception in infants and young children has also been of considerable interest because it touches on one of the most fundamental issues in psychology, the "nativism-empiricism" issue. The essence of this issue is whether we as humans are born with already-developed systems for dealing with experience (the nativist position) or whether our methods of analysis and our skills are developed as a result of experience (the empiricist position). If a child were raised in a black box without any perceptual experience, but were fed and cared for, would the child develop normal perceptual skills? Or is experience necessary for the child to develop the repertoire of perceptual skills that you see in the normal 6-year-old or the normal adult? This question is, of course, really a restatement of the question that I've been asking all along about every aspect of behavior: How much is determined internally and how much by external events and experience?

In order to answer both the factual and the theoretical questions, let me as usual begin with the descriptive material. Just what can the infant do, and how do her skills change over time? Then we can take a look at what we know—and don't know—about the role of experience in all those changes.

Over the first few months of life the child's visual acuity—her ability to distinguish one shape or pattern from another at various distances—improves greatly. Total adult-like acuity isn't reached until about age 10, but the 4-month-old infant has vision that is perfectly adequate for any normal needs.[1]

There is evidence that some other changes with age go in the opposite

[1] Incidentally, beginning in middle age nearly all of us become more farsighted; that is we become better able to see things far away and less able to see things close up. Someone who starts out nearsighted may actually have better far vision in the middle years and later, but someone who starts out farsighted may become more so and may require bifocals eventually in order to focus on close objects.

direction, with young children being more acute than older children. For example, some research suggests that babies and young children are more sensitive to contrasts and contours than are older children— perhaps because contrasts and contours are more important features of the visual world of the infant. Later, possibly, the child focuses more on the objects and their uses and meaning, and less on the contours.

Auditory acuity appears to improve steadily until adolescence; older children are able to hear and discriminate more high and low tones, very loud and soft sounds, and all sound levels not well discriminated by the young baby. As I pointed out in Chapter 4, newborn babies are already highly sensitive to touch. But an infant is not as able to discriminate the location of touch as is an older child or an adult. One of the standard ways to measure the individual's touch discrimination is to touch her in two places at once. In young children often the child doesn't report feeling both, or if she feels both, she'll mistake the location of one of the touches. By about adolescence both these kinds of errors are rare. In addition there cannot be equal sensitivity all over the body in the infant and toddler as there will be later, for full cortical development isn't completed until about age 4.

PERCEPTUAL CONSTANCIES

A more interesting set of findings is related to a collection of skills called *constancies.* When you see someone walking away from you, the image of the person on your retina actually becomes smaller. But you don't see the person as smaller. You see him as the same size but moving farther away. When you do this, you are demonstrating size constancy; you are able to see the size as constant, even though the retinal image has become smaller or larger. One of the skills required for size constancy is depth perception. Unless you can estimate the distance of an object, you can't make any guesses about how big it is and can't maintain size constancy. Next time you're in an airplane, just before landing or just after takeoff, when you can still see the cars and people on the ground, take a good look out the window. The usual experience is that the cars look like toys and the people like midgets. Because you have no way of estimating the distance, you can't maintain your size constancy either. You know they are real people and cars, but they look smaller to you.

Other constancies include shape constancy (the ability to recognize that shapes are the same even though you are looking at them from different angles) and color constancy (the ability to recognize constant colors, even though the amount of light or shadow on them may change). Taken together, the several specific constancies add up to the larger concept of object constancy, which is the recognition that objects remain the same, even when they appear to change. Although some rudimentary forms of these several constancies are present at birth or in the early months of life, most have a developmental course that continues through the first several years.

Depth Perception

There is quite a lot of disagreement among researchers and theorists about whether infants have any kind of depth perception at birth or whether they develop this skill later, after some interactions with the environment, or with further neurological growth. Let me approach this problem by working backwards in time.

Gibson and Walk's work with 6-month-old infants on the visual cliff apparatus, which is described in detail in Box 9, shows that 6-month-old infants respond to cues of depth. But what about younger infants? Using a quite different research strategy, T. G. R. Bower has shown depth perception and size constancy in 2 to 3 month old infants. Bower first trained each infant to turn her head toward the side of an infant seat each time she saw a 12-inch cube in front of her eyes. When this response was clearly established, Bower then presented the infant with a series of alternative cubes, some bigger, some the same size but farther away, and some bigger and farther away. What Bower was doing, in this instance, was seeing how the original response *generalized*. What sorts of cubes would the child respond to *as if they were the same* as the original cube? Would the infant continue to turn her head when she saw the original cube, no matter how far away from her it was? Or would she turn her head when she saw a larger cube at a greater distance? The large-cube-farther-away creates the same *retinal image* as did the original cube the baby had been trained to respond to. So, if the infant is *not* responding to depth, she should treat this cube as "the same" as the original one. In fact, the infants in this study responded in a way that showed they were paying attention to the

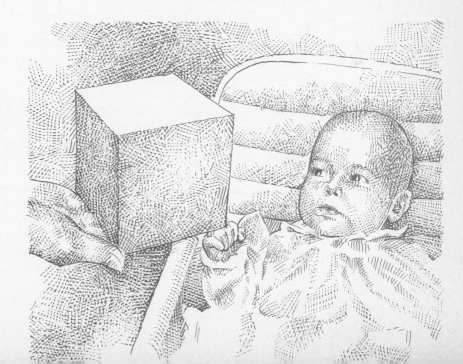

BOX 9
Experiments with the Visual Cliff

A fascinating series of experiments for exploring the development of depth perception has been done by E. J. Gibson and R. D. Walk, and involves an apparatus they call the "visual cliff." The apparatus includes a large table with a barrier around the outside edges. In the center is a slightly raised runway, and on either side are slightly lower sheets of glass. On one side, immediately under the glass, is a checkerboard pattern. On the other side, as you can see in the photograph, the checkerboard pattern is considerably below the glass. The glass is kept very clean, and since the lighting is arranged so that the glass doesn't reflect light, presumably the baby doesn't see the glass. Under these circumstances will the baby go out on the "cliff side," the side with the deep checkerboard? If she has no depth perception, there should be no difference in her willingness to crawl out on either side of the table. But if she has some depth per-

ception, some ability to use the depth cues contained in the checkerboards, then she should be unwilling to go "over the cliff."

The procedure has been used with babies as young as about 6 months but no younger, for a child has to be able to crawl in order to participate. The baby is placed on the raised center runway, and her mother goes around the table, first to one side and then to the other, trying to coax the baby to crawl toward her. The results indicate that virtually all babies of this age will refuse to crawl out on the cliff side, even when coaxed by their mothers, thus indicating that they have noticed the difference and have drawn the conclusion that the cliff side is dangerous.

This series of studies, which was among the first undertaken on depth perception in the very young infant, shows that by 6 months the baby has clear discrimination of some of the needed cues for depth.

depth cues. But even this fairly clear finding is open to some question. Let me give you some sense of the kind of complexity that can creep into issues of this kind. When flat pictures of cubes rather than the cubes themselves are used, 2- and 3-month old infants do *not* show response to depth cues. What this probably means is that at this very early age one of the critical cues for depth for the infant is what is called *motion parallax*. When you look at a three-dimensional object, the view of it changes when you move your head or look at it from a different position. The nearer the object is to you, the more different the views will be as you move your head or body to different viewing positions. These cues are missing, however, when you are looking at flat pictures (two-dimensional objects) at varying distances. Since the 2-month-old infant shows depth perception when responding to three-dimensional objects, but not when responding to two-dimensional objects, it suggests that the infant is using motion parallax as a major cue for depth.

With still younger infants the question of the presence of depth perception skills is even more complicated. I don't want to load you down with unnecessary research detail, but I think it important for you to get some feeling for the difficulties involved in answering an apparently simple question. Let me sample the literature briefly: Fantz observed that infants a few days old would look at a sphere rather than a disc.

An infant on the "visual cliff" apparatus. (Source: Gibson, E. J., & Walk,
R. D. The "visual cliff." *Scientific American*, April 1960, p. 65. Photo courtesy
William Vandivert.)

The existence of this preference suggests that they could respond in
some way to the difference. But the sphere may have had sharper looking edges than did the disc, and we know from other research that a
newborn's attention is "caught" by sharp contours. White observed
that infants would blink their eyes when a disc was looming closer to
them, but the eye-blink response was not clearly seen in infants
younger than 5 months, which suggests either that infants younger
than 5 months do not have depth perception, or that they do not show
their perceptual skill by blinking. Finally, Bower, Broughton and
Moore showed that infants a few days old would put their hands in
front of their faces as a looming disc approached, which *may* indicate
some depth perception.

Let me sum up all this complexity. Six-month-old infants clearly
have depth perception, and it is present in at least some form in 2- to
3-month-old infants as well. Whether depth perception is present in
the newborn is still an open question.

**Shape
Constancy**

Bower has studied shape constancy using an operant conditioning procedure similar to the one he used to study depth perception. He found
that 2-month-old babies responded to *actual* shape. If they have been
trained to turn their head when they see a rectangle, they will continue
to turn their head when they see the same rectangle turned slightly,

even though the retinal image under those conditions becomes a trapezoid. So babies do have some shape constancy.

Research by Gollin and others, however, suggests that experience with specific shapes is necessary for more nearly complete shape constancy. If you show children pictures of objects that have been partly erased, for example, they have more difficulty than do adults in figuring out what the pictures are. So recognition of shapes based on incomplete information is not very good among young children but improves with age.

OBJECT CONCEPT

The infant has to learn at least three different things about objects. She has to learn that objects remain the same even when they appear to be different. It is this set of skills I have just been discussing and have called *object constancy*. But she also has to develop an *object concept*, which has two facets. The infant must learn that objects continue to exist even when she can't see or feel them any longer—that when her mother goes out of sight through a doorway, the mother continues to exist, or that when a toy disappears beneath the sofa it still exists. This understanding is usually called *object permanence*. Finally, the infant has to learn that individual objects retain their unique identity from one encounter to another. When the mother goes away and then comes back again, it is the same mother both times; the crib is the same object each time she is placed in it, and so on. This understanding is usually called *object identity*.

These understandings about objects and people may seem so basic that you may not be able to imagine the child's not having them. But she does not, at least not at first. And the three aspects develop at different speeds. Object constancies such as size constancy, brightness and color constancy, although probably present in some rudimentary forms in the very young infant, may not be completely developed until the child is 2 or 3 years old. Object identity by contrast seems *not* to be present at birth. It apparently develops first at about 5 months of age. For example, Bower has studied infants' reactions to an artificial situation in which the infant, seated in an infant seat, looks at her mother through a window. The mother's image is then artificially multiplied, so that the infant sees three mothers. Young infants show no signs of surprise at this multiple image. If anything, they seem to be more delighted with three mothers than with one. But at about 22 to 24 weeks of age, infants begin to be extremely upset at this multiple image, which suggests that they have in some sense understood that there should be only one, and the multiple image violates this expectation.

Object permanence also develops over the first year or two of life, apparently through a series of moderately distinct stages. Through the first month of life, there is little evidence that infants respond to anything that is not immediately present and visible or touchable. By about 2 months of age there are some signs that the infant is developing a rudimentary notion of object permanence. If you have an infant this age look at a toy, then put a screen between the child and the toy, remove the toy and then remove the screen, the 2-month-old infant will show some surprise, which suggests that she has some expectation that the toy will continue to be there. But infants of this age will not try to search for the missing toy if you leave the screen there or if you cover a toy with a cloth.

By about 6 months the infant is showing still more signs of object permanence. For example, if she drops a toy over the edge of her crib, she will look over the edge to see the toy. Occasionally she will also look to see if she can find something that someone else dropped, although this is slower to develop (which may suggest that things the infant has handled herself are in some sense more "real" to her than those other people have handled). At this same age an infant will search for an object that has been *partially* hidden. If you put a favorite toy under a cloth but leave part of it sticking out, the infant will reach for the toy, which suggests that in some sense the infant "recognizes" that the whole object is there, even though she can see only part of it. But if you cover the toy completely with the cloth, the infant will stop looking at it and will not reach for it, even if she has seen you put the cloth over it.

This changes somewhere between 8 and 12 months; infants this age will reach or search for a toy that has been covered completely by a cloth or hidden by a screen. There are further refinements of object permanence, which develop during the second year of life, but by 12 months most infants appear to grasp the fact that objects continue to exist even when they are no longer visible.

What I have just given you is the "standard version" of the development of object permanence. There is quite a lot of research and observation that supports this description, and the sequence is quite widely accepted as valid. But once again I want to alert you to the fact that the process is probably more complex than the standard version would suggest. T. G. R. Bower, in a recent paper (1975), has raised some intriguing questions about the process of development of the object concept. Let me touch on some of his arguments, not because I particularly want you to become expert on the subject of object concept development, but because I want you to have some feeling for the intricacy of the developmental process and of the theories we will need to develop to account for that process.

Bower points to a series of incongruities. First, there is an earlier study by Mundy-Castle and Anglin, which showed that a 16-week-old infant will follow visually the *presumed* path of a moving object. The experimental situation is illustrated in Figure 20. The infant can see the object through the two portholes. The object moves from the bottom to the top of the left porthole, and from top to bottom in the right porthole, with a pause between the two appearances. What the 16-week-old infant does, in this situation, is to move her eyes in an oval pattern, following the presumed path of the object behind the screen. The child *anticipates* the reappearance of the object in the next porthole. This is a sophisticated response and seems to show that the infant of this age *does* grasp the fact that the object continues to exist

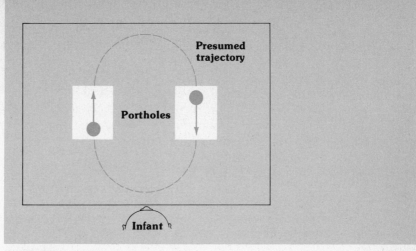

FIGURE 20

Schematic drawings of the apparatus used in the Mundy-Castle and Anglin experiment. (Source: Mundy-Castle, A. C., & Anglin, J. The development of looking in infancy. Paper read at the meetings of the Society for Research in Child Development, Santa Monica, Calif., April 1969.)

while out of sight. A second incongruity is found in the fact that while 5-month-olds will not reach for an object that has just been covered in their sight, the same infants *will* continue to reach for an object if you turn out the lights. Finally, a third puzzle is that 5-month-old infants will stop reaching for an object if it is placed on *top* of another object, even if it is still in plain sight.

These puzzling findings do not fit nicely into the developmental sequence I sketched earlier; very young infants may have far more grasp of object permanence than we have given them credit for. In fact, the concept of object permanence probably is not a unitary concept at all, and the infant may develop different aspects of it at different rates. Bower suggests, for example, that for the infant an "object" may be something that is set apart from other things. When you cover the child's toy with a cloth, the child may consider that cloth and toy have somehow unified and are now a single object. This is consistent with Bower's observation that the child will stop reaching if you put one toy on top of another one; the infant may somehow consider this a *new* object and not simply a new placement of the original toy.

What does seem clear is that the infant does not come into the world equipped with a full scale concept of object permanence. This concept develops gradually over the first year or so of life, but the precise order and stages through which that development occurs is still under study.

I do not want to leave you with the impression that all infants go through this process at exactly the same speed. They do not, and the differences in rate of development of object permanence may be related to the particular environment the child encounters. Research by Sylvia Bell suggests that infants may develop the concept of "person permanence" before they develop "object permanence." That is, the infant may grasp the fact that the mother continues to exist before she grasps the fact that her toy continues to exist. Bell found that approximately 70 percent of the babies in her study acquired person permanence before object permanence; the remaining 30 percent either had acquired object permanence first or had learned both at about the same rate. Bell thought that the warmth and adequacy of the child's relationship with her mother might have something to do with difference among babies in the pattern of developing the concept of permanence. She argued that for a baby with a good, warm, responsive relationship with her mother, people would be the most salient objects in the environment; hence, permanence would develop first in connection with people. Babies with less adequate relationships with the people in their environment might focus more on interactions with objects and hence might develop permanence in connection with objects earliest. Bell's findings provide strong support for this possibility. All the babies in her study who were ahead in person permanence were strongly and positively attached to their mothers, whereas the majority of the babies who were ahead in object permanence had ambivalent or negative relationships with their mothers. Furthermore, Bell found that the babies who were ahead in person permanence were also faster in overall mental development.

Bell's research is important for several reasons. First, her findings underline the important point that in the young child there is no automatic generalization of a principle from one area to another. In fact, we cannot even say during the early months that the child is operating with a "principle" at all. The baby's early expectations about the permanence or uniqueness of objects, for example, are highly specific. She learns about individual people, individual toys, and objects in her world. Only gradually does she develop rules, which we may think of as generalized expectations, to cover new experiences, new objects, and new people. These more general expectations, or more general object concepts, are still developing well into the second year of life.

Second, Bell's study illustrates again the intricate interconnections between the development of perception or cognition and the development of interpersonal relationships. A positive and responsive relationship between the child and the mother can have a pervasive effect on all the child's interactions with the world.

ATTENTION AND EXPLORATION In Infants

A great deal of research attention has been devoted to the pattern of an infant's attention. What sorts of things will an infant choose to look at? What does she look at first? What sort of preferences does she have? These questions are interesting in themselves, I think, but much of the

142

research on these issues has been motivated by broader concerns. Since the young infant cannot talk and has such a limited range of responses by which she can "tell us" what is happening internally, psychologists have searched for techniques that may reveal something about the infant's earliest development. Looking at the child's patterns of attention is one way of approaching such questions. Perhaps by observing what the infant looks at, we can draw some tentative inferences about what she "likes" to look at, and from there we may begin to develop better understandings of the earliest stages of cognitive development.

There is quite a lot of evidence that there are substantial changes at about 2 months of age in infants' responses to objects and pictures. During the first few months of life the infant's attention is "captured" by corners and edges of figures. Kessen and Salapatek, whose work I have described in some detail in Box 5 (page 87), have noted that newborn infants spend the most time visually exploring the parts of a figure that have the sharpest contrast. Newborn infants also respond to movement and will look longer at pictures with large figures than at pictures with lots of smaller figures. They seem to look mostly at the outer edges of figures, *not* at the centers.

By about 2 months some of these patterns have changed. In Kessen and Salapatek's studies, 8-week-old infants showed scanning of the *whole* figure, with more eye movement back and forth across the figure. Two-month-old infants also shift to a preference for figures with many small pictures (See Box 10 for a discussion of research on preferences). So, by 2 months of age the child's attention has become, in some sense, less fixed. Piaget, too, was struck by the very great fixity of the young infant's early attention to objects. He called this behavior *centration*. Decentration—the ability to decenter—he thought came only slowly through a process of cognitive as well as perceptual development. The "decentration" process does seem to begin, though, during the earliest months of life, since 2-month-old infants are already showing less concentrated focus on single objects or spots on a picture or an object.

By 2 or 3 months of age an additional salient feature of a stimulus appears to be its degree of novelty or complexity. But it is not the *most* novel objects or pictures that the infant is likely to prefer to look at. Rather, the preferred objects are those that are *moderately* novel. Jerome Kagan calls this preference the *discrepancy principle*. A baby will look at, listen to, or touch things that are moderately different (moderately discrepant from) things she has already experienced.

Piaget, too, emphasizes the importance, from the very earliest months, of a moderate level of novelty. The child's interactions with the world, according to Piaget, always include a process of assimilating the new to the old, of responding to new objects and events, and relating these new things to earlier experiences. If she is confronted with something completely novel, she has nothing to connect it to, nothing

BOX 10
Perceptual Preferences

The research technique most often used by investigators exploring the development of attention in infants is a preference technique developed by Fantz. If an infant is shown two pictures simultaneously, or several pictures in series, the experimenter can measure the amount of time the infant spends looking at each picture and the number of shifts back and forth from one to another. If there are differences in the amount of time the infant gazes at each picture, this can be taken as evidence that the infant can discriminate between the two pictures. So the preference technique can be used to study early visual discriminations. But it also may tell us something about the sort of visual features the child "chooses" to focus on.

Since Fantz first began using the preference technique in the late fifties, a large number of researchers have used this strategy to explore a whole series of perceptual dimensions with infants. Infants have been shown checkerboards with varying number of squares, bull's-eyes versus striped patterns, patterning with varying numbers of corners, pictures of faces with pieces of the face left out or rearranged, and nearly endless other combinations. Let me select just one example from this array to give you some feeling for the research and for the results that emerge from research of this sort.

Fantz, Fagan, and Miranda (1975) have done a series of experiments exploring infants' preferences for curved versus straight contours. Some

to "assimilate" it to, so she will examine and explore it less than something that she can hook up in some way to an earlier experience.

Recent research on visual preferences in young infants provides some (but not universal) support for the discrepancy principle. The discrepancy principle seems to hold for changes in an existing figure, such as changing color or moving the figure 90 degrees. Infants of 2 months prefer medium-sized changes of this sort to larger or very small changes. But for completely new pictures or objects, the discrepancy principle may not hold. Infants seem to look longest at pictures or objects that are most novel. So once again we may discover that the processes involved are more complex than we had supposed.

In Older Children

Although there is some agreement among researchers and theorists about the factors that influence attention and exploration in the very young infant, that agreement decreases as the child's age increases. Kagan has suggested that an additional point of change in the "rules" that govern the child's attention occurs at about 1 year of age, when something he called a *hypothesis* enters the picture. The younger baby can, in some sense, recognize that a picture is different from what she has experienced before, but according to Kagan, only the older child has some ability to interpret that difference; such interpretation is in the form of a hypothesis. It is as if the child generates ideas about why and how a thing is different. Kagan suggests that objects, pictures, and events that provoke many hypotheses should attract the greatest amount of the child's attention.

of the pairs of stimuli used are a bull's-eye versus a series of straight lines or arcs versus straight lines or circles versus rectangles.

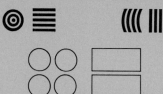

On all three of these pattern pairs there was little clear preference among newborn infants, but there was a clear preference for the curved figures by 8 to 10 weeks, sometimes sooner. This preference for curved lines is most marked at about 12 weeks, after which it declines. By 4 months the preference for curved lines is still detectable, but smaller.

All of this research is focused primarily on "what" questions. Just what do infants look at, what will they look at when given a choice, and how may we characterize those choices? The more interesting question is why. Why are there preferences at all? Most researchers in this area assume that these preferences are, in some way, built into the organism. The child comes equipped with scanning strategies and neurological systems that lead to the behavioral preferences we observe. But just what sort of neurological patterning is involved is still being debated.

Underlying both Kagan's concepts (the discrepancy principle and the development of hypotheses) is the assumption that the very young infant develops expectations (which Kagan calls *schemas*), which, if violated, provoke attention. Eleanor Gibson, one of the major theorists in the area of perceptual development, takes issue with the notion of schema or expectation. She suggests instead that the schema is a sort of end result, a final concept that follows all the attention and exploration, rather than guides it.

Gibson proposes, as an alternative view of the development of attention, that the process of "optimization of attention" has four dimensions.

1. From Capture to Activity. Young infants, as already mentioned, have their attention "captured" by things; gradually attention becomes more voluntary, although Gibson acknowledges that we have as yet little understanding of how voluntary control is achieved.

2. From Unsystematic to Systematic Search. From the earliest hours of life there is some system to the child's visual searching (see Kessen), but the very young infant and even the child of 2 or 3 does not examine an entire figure systematically, but rather tends to get stuck on a particular part. Because of inefficient exploration strategies, the young child is also less good at picking out the same thing later on.

3. From Broad to Selective Pickup of Information. With increasing age children become better and better able to focus on a single aspect of a complex situation. For example, in one series of experiments Eleanor Maccoby and her colleagues had children listen through earphones (or on loudspeakers) to a man's voice and a woman's voice speaking words at the same time. The child was asked to report what either the man or the woman had been saying. Six-year-olds can perform this task, but they have a great deal more difficulty and make more errors than do older children.

4. Ignoring Irrelevant Information. Focusing attention on one source of information is not the same thing as shutting out everything else. It is possible both to focus attention and to pick up a lot of additional information as well. But in complex situations the ability to shut out completely the unwanted information may become important, and this ability develops gradually with age. The 12-year-old is better at it than is the 5-year-old, and the very young child has little ability to ignore what is irrelevant.

Obviously, in suggesting these four main dimensions of perceptual development, Gibson is attempting to describe processes that cover a much longer age span than is Kagan, and the two theories need not be mutually exclusive. Gibson does describe the development of strategies of search and exploration, which may be not unlike the hypotheses defined by Kagan. The increasingly voluntary nature of the child's exploration and attention is also consistent with the interpretive quality of hypotheses.

Before we leave the very complex and controversial area of attention development, one final word is necessary. As I am sure you have already gathered, it is extremely difficult to draw a line between perception and cognition. Object constancy, for example, is not just a perceptual achievement; it is a mental achievement as well. It is a question not just of noticing similarities but also of coordinating information over time and space. And the whole trend in the development of attention appears to be toward more voluntary control of attention. The year-old or older child prefers to pay attention to certain objects; she chooses to examine or explore in a particular way. Such preferences, choices, and strategies are presumably governed by cognitive accomplishments as much as by increased perceptual acuity. Because of the intimate relationship between the two processes, many of the same issues will come up again in Chapter 9, when cognitive development is discussed more thoroughly.

INDIVIDUAL DIFFERENCES IN PERCEPTUAL DEVELOPMENT

There is some individual variation in the rate at which perceptual skills are acquired, but on the whole the child's chronological age is the best predictor of her perceptual abilities. Retarded children, for example, have about the same amount of depth perception as do children of the same age with normal intelligence.

But there are some interesting individual differences in style and preference. Kagan, for example, has suggested that children differ—from birth perhaps—in something that he calls *conceptual tempo.*

Some children, when confronted with something moderately new, pause, examine it carefully, and look at it quietly. They appear to be calm and slow in responding. The child with a faster tempo becomes excited, may move around physically, and doesn't examine the new thing for as long. This same contrast can be observed in babies; the baby with the slower tempo will remain still and look at something new with fixed concentration, whereas the baby with the faster tempo will thrash around, become excited, gurgle, and look away after only a short period of examination. We see the same difference in older children. If you give children from 4 to 8 years of age a picture of a chair and then ask them to pick out a picture just like it from a collection on another page (see Figure 21), some will look at all the alternatives very carefully, comparing each one to the original chair picture, before selecting one as the same. They are slow to respond and are likely to give the correct answer on the first try. Children with the faster tempo (who are often called *impulsive*) look quickly over the alternatives and simply choose one. They make their choices sooner, but they're more likely to choose incorrectly.

In older children this tempo dimension is fairly stable. That is, an impulsive child at age 4 is likely to be a perceptually impulsive child at age 5. It is less clear whether or not there is consistency from infancy on. We just don't know whether the quiet, contemplative 3-month-old

FIGURE 21

Sample item from Kagan's test of "reflection-impulsivity." The child must try to select the picture that exactly matches the figure at the top. (Source: Kagan, J., Rosman, B. O., Day, D., Albert J., & Phillips, W. Information processing in the child: Significance of analytic and reflective styles. *Psychological Monographs*, 1964, 78(1, Whole No. 478). Copyright © 1964 by the American Psychological Association. Reprinted by permission.)

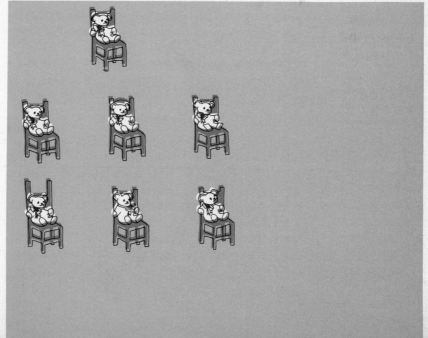

BOX 11
Field Independence and Field Dependence

Another conceptualization of individual differences in perceptual cognitive style has been proposed by H. A. Witkin and his associates. Their primary task is called the *rod-and-frame test*. The subject is seated and looks at an empty picture frame in the center of which a rod is mounted. The frame and the rod can be moved independently. In the test the room is darkened, but the rod and frame can be seen, for they are painted with luminous paint. The frame is tilted off center and the rod is tilted in the opposite direction. The subject is to adjust the position of the rod until she thinks it is directly upright. Because the lights are off and the subject doesn't know that the frame has been tilted off center, she could use the frame as a guide to tell her where upright is. But the information from the frame is at variance with the information from her own body, which also tells her where upright is. Some people in this situation are more tuned to the cues from the frame, whereas others are more tuned to the cues from their bodies. Those who pay more attention to the frame—and who thus adjust the rod to position off the upright—are called *field dependent* because they are influenced more by the context of the stimuli; those who use their own body cues and ignore the context or field are called *field independent*.

Witkin and his group have devised many

turns out to be the reflective 4-year-old, although it's an interesting hypothesis and one that has received some exploration (see Kagan, 1971). We do know that the children who have slower tempos at age 4, whom Kagan calls *reflective*, have a somewhat easier time learning to read than do the impulsive children, perhaps because they examine the letters more carefully before deciding what a word is (see Kagan, 1965).

Several other groups of researchers have attempted to identify stable individual differences in perceptual or conceptual style (see Box 11 for a second theoretical perspective). In each case the assumption is that people differ systematically in the ways in which they pay attention and the things that they pay attention to. Among older children and adults there is some support for this notion, but we simply don't know how early such differences in style start, whether or not they are present at birth, whether or not they are learned through interaction with parents or others, and whether or not they are related to some aspect of physical development.

EXPLANATIONS   As I emphasized at the beginning of this chapter, one of the issues that has run through all the research on perceptual development, particularly in infancy, is the old question of internal versus external causes. In this case the issue is stated in terms of nativism versus empiricism. Does the baby have to learn what to pay attention to, how to see depth, and so on, or are these skills present at birth? Even if skills are present at birth, does practice matter? Does it matter what kind of learning experiences the child has?

As with most psychological issues originally stated in black-and-other tests for measuring this dimension of individual difference, including one called the *embedded figures test*, in which the subject must find a simple figure that has been embedded in the midst of a more complex drawing. Again, the question is whether or not the subject can ignore the context and focus on the shape of the simple figure.

Using any of these tests, Witkin finds that older children and adults are more field independent than are younger children but that at all ages there are some consistent individual differences. That is, some adults and some children tend to be consistently more field dependent, others consistently more field independent.

Witkin has gone further and suggested that there are personality correlates, that people who are field dependent are also more dependent in other ways too. The evidence for this assertion, however, is not very strong nor do we know much about where the individual differences Witkin talks about may come from or what their implications may be for other aspects of perception or cognition.

Still, the possibility that there may be systematic differences in style of perceptual exploration may have great relevance for teachers, because children with different styles may require very different kinds of teaching or different materials.

white-terms, we rapidly discover that the answer is a sort of gray. Neither the extreme nativist position nor the extreme empiricist position is entirely correct. As usual, experience and initial abilities are involved, yet both are affected by the continuing maturation of the body. Let me review some of the findings.

First, we know that at birth the baby has considerable perceptual acuity, probably some depth perception and perhaps some rudimentary constancies. More important, Kessen and Salapatek's work shows very clearly that babies do not have to be taught what to look at.

Kagan puts this point very nicely: "Nature has apparently equipped the newborn with an initial bias in the processing of experience. He does not, as the nineteenth century empiricists believed, have to learn what he should examine." (Kagan, 1971, p. 60) The initial biases include the tendency to look at movement and contour. These basic tendencies change during the early months of life. In particular, there seems to be a shift of some kind at about 2 months of age, as well as gradual changes over the early months and years.

Some of these changes seem quite obviously to be maturationally based. Quite a number of researchers, noting the collection of changes in visual attention patterns at about 2 months, have suggested that there may be important neurological changes taking place at about that time that permit the child to shift from a set of primitive, reflex-like, looking patterns to more advanced patterns of behavior, which seem to be governed more by cortical action. (See, for example, the discussion of this by Salapatek, 1975.)

Other changes in the child's perceptual skills are equally obviously affected by the child's specific experience. First of all, we know from research with cats and monkeys (such as the work of Hubel and Wiesel) that a basic minimum of visual stimulation is needed in order for any perceptual development to occur. For example, animals deprived of all light during the early months of life experience deterioration or nondevelopment of portions of the eye. Dennis' study of orphanage babies in Iran (described earlier) suggests that such research with animals may be generalizable to human subjects as well. Infants required at least minimum opportunity to practice, or both perceptual and motor skills were retarded. On the other end of the scale extra enrichment may help to speed up the process, as in the orphanage babies studied by Burton White (described in Chapter 4, page 97). The babies with extra visual and tactile stimulation were more rapid in their development of good eye-hand coordination than were the less stimulated babies. But more than merely the amount of physical stimulation may be involved. Bell's study points to the importance of the quality of the child's relationship with her mother, and research by Leon Yarrow and others suggests that the complexity and variety of stimulation, as well as the sheer quantity, affect the child's perceptual and motor development.

The important dimensions of the necessary stimulation are only imperfectly understood at this point. In fact, I think it is fair to say that exploration of the environmental variations involved in early development (perceptual, motor, cognitive, and interpersonal) is one of the major research tasks of the 1980s.

Can there be overstimulation? If so, of what might it consist? Does it matter if the stimulation is contingent on what the child does, rather than being merely there? Some work by Yarrow, Lewis, and others suggests the importance of contingent stimulation, but further work is needed.

How large a role does the child's emotional and interpersonal development play in the acquisition of perceptual and cognitive skills? There are many such questions, all of them now being vigorously addressed by researchers.

It is important, however, in the midst of all the unanswered questions, to keep in mind that the research of the 1960s has taken us a long way already. For so many decades—even centuries—psychologists, parents, and educators had thought of babies as formless creatures, certainly without much in the way of perceptual skills or learning abilities. What recent research has shown us is that the newborn baby has complex abilities and that she comes into the world already programmed to search and examine in certain ways. This is important new knowledge to be built on by still further research.

SEX DIFFERENCES

There is relatively little information about possible sex differences in perceptual skills or preferences. What information is available points to two fairly consistent sex differences and a host of areas in which there are no differences at all.

The two apparently consistent differences are in sensitivity to pain and in responsiveness to taste. Girls appear to have lower tolerance for pain and to be more responsive to taste differences than are boys.

A number of researchers have also suggested lately that beginning in infancy girls are more responsive to or prefer auditory stimuli, while boys are more responsive to or prefer visual stimuli. Garai and Scheinfeld, for example, in their 1968 review of sex differences, say, "One might postulate a 'visual stimulus hunger' of the boys and an 'auditory stimulus hunger' of the girls. From the foregoing studies we may conclude that boys tend to be showing an inherently greater interest in objects and visual patterns, while girls are congenitally more interested in people and facial features." (Garai & Scheinfeld, 1968, p. 193) This hypothesis was seized upon as fact by many researchers and theorists. It seemed to explain the apparently faster rate of early language development in girls and possibly the advanced spatial skills in boys (both of which I will discuss at greater length in Chapter 9). But the more recent data on infant attentional preferences or discriminations simply do not support Garai and Scheinfeld's suggestion. There are *no* consistent sex differences in response to sounds or pictures, either in infancy or later childhood, and there is no indication that girls are more interested in such "social" stimuli as faces or voices.

SOCIAL CLASS DIFFERENCES

As I have already pointed out in the discussion of social class differences in physical development (Chapter 5, page 129) there is little evidence for *any* kind of social class differences in the rate of development of early perceptual and motor skills. Among school-age children there is *some* indication that children from poverty backgrounds are more likely to be "impulsive" on Kagan's test of reflection-impulsivity, so the perceptual and cognitive style of approaching tasks may differ. But there is no evidence that I know of showing that such style differences are preceded by any systematic differences in scanning strategies or preference patterns during infancy.

SUMMARY

1. The study of perceptual development is important because of the great role that perception plays in the early life of the child and because of the important theoretical issues involved.
2. Perceptual acuity in infants is not perfect at birth; it improves over the first four years or longer.
3. The development of perceptual constancies also begins early, with some research showing babies as young as 4 to 6 weeks of age having some form of size constancy and depth perception, as well as some shape constancy.
4. Object permanence and object identity are slower to develop; the child probably does not have complete object permanence until age 2 or older. Rudimentary forms of object

permanence—recognition that the object continues to exist even when you can't see it—are present in infants as young as 3 or 4 months, but take some years to become general.

5. Findings from one recent study by Bell suggest that development of the concept of permanence is somewhat more rapid for most infants in relation to people than in relation to objects, perhaps because of the great importance of people in the infant's early life.

6. In the development of attention the newborn's apparently innate preferences for edges, contours, and movement give way to other strategies, including a frequent tendency to prefer to look at and explore objects and pictures of moderate novelty.

7. Overall, the development of attention may be guided by four major principles, suggested by Gibson: a shift from the tendency to be "captured" by stimuli to more voluntary exploration, a shift from unsystematic to systematic search, a shift from broad to more selective pickup of information, and a shift from inability to ignore irrelevant information to the ability to do so.

8. Several authors, among them Kagan and Witkin, have suggested the possibility of pervasive individual differences in style of perceptual exploration. There is some evidence for such stable differences among children and adults.

9. Although more of the child's perceptual skills are present at birth than had previously been thought, the important role of learning and experience cannot be underestimated. So both the nativists and the empiricists are correct to some extent.

10. There are few consistent sex differences in perception; girls are less tolerant of pain and somewhat more sensitive to tastes. No social class differences in early perceptual development have been found. Older poverty level children may be somewhat more likely to be "impulsive" in visual scanning.

REFERENCES

Suggested Additional Readings

Bower, T. G. R. The visual world of infants. *Scientific American*, 1966, *215* (6), 80–92.
A report of the research on depth perception and shape constancy discussed in this chapter, written in language that should be fairly understandable. The pictures and figures are excellent.

Cohen, L. B., & Salapatek, P. (Ed.). *Infant perception: From sensation to cognition* (Vols. 1 and 2). New York: Academic Press, 1975.
The first of these volumes focuses on visual perception, the second on perception of space, speech, and sound. Many of the individual papers are very technical and difficult, but there are some good overviews of recent work, including one by Fantz and one by Salapatek.

Gibson, E. J. *Principles of perceptual learning and development*. New York: Appleton, 1969.
An encyclopedic presentation of all of the literature on perceptual development up to that time, along with Gibson's own theoretical interpretations; not recommended in its entirety, but individual chapters may be helpful, particularly Chapters 16 and 17, which cover some of the material I have discussed rather briefly.

Kagan, J. *Change and continuity in infancy*. New York: Wiley, 1971.
A long report of a single longitudinal study; fairly technical, but includes discussions of the discrepancy principle, hypotheses, and schemas.

Maccoby, E. E., & Jacklin, C. N. *The psychology of sex differences*. Stanford, Calif.: Stanford University Press, 1974.
The best single source of current information on sex difference. The relevant section on differences in perception is pp. 17–40.

Pick, H. L., Jr., & Pick, A. D. Sensory and perceptual development. In P. H. Mussen (Ed.), *Carmichael's manual of child psychology* (Vol. 1, 3rd ed.). New York: Wiley, 1970.

Another detailed discussion of perceptual development, which may be a helpful source of specific references. The level is technical and fairly difficult.

Other Sources Cited

Bell, S. M. The development of the concept of object as related to infant-mother attachment. *Child Development*, 1970, *41*, 291–311.

Bower, T. G. R. Infant perception of the third dimension and object concept development. In L. B. Cohen & P. Salapatek (Eds.), *Infant perception: From sensation to cognition* (Vol. 2). New York: Academic Press, 1975.

Bower, T. G. R., Broughton, J. M., & Moore, M. K. Infant responses to approaching objects. *Perception and Psychophysics*, 1970, *9*, 193–196.

Fantz, R. L., Fagan, J. F., III, & Miranda, S. B. Early visual selectivity. In L. B. Cohen & P. Salapatek (Eds.), *Infant perception: From sensation to cognition* (Vol. 1). New York: Academic Press, 1975.

Garai, J. E., & Scheinfeld, A. Sex differences in mental and behavioral traits. *Genetic Psychology Monographs*, 1968, *77*, 169–299.

Gibson, E. J., & Walk, R. D. The "visual cliff." *Scientific American*, 1960, *202* (4), 80–92.

Gollin, E. S. A developmental approach to learning and cognition. In L. P. Lipsitt & C. C. Spiker (Eds.), *Advances in child development and behavior* (Vol. 2). New York: Academic Press, 1965.

Hubel, D. H., & Wiesel, T. N. Reception fields of cells in striate cortex of very young, visually inexperienced kittens. *Journal of Neurophysiology*, 1963, *26*, 996–1022.

Kagan, J. Reflection-impulsivity and reading ability in primary grade children. *Child Development*, 1965, *36*, 609–628.

Kagan, J., Rosman, B. L., Day, D., Albert, J., & Phillips, W. Information processing in the child: Significance of analytic and reflective attitudes. *Psychological Monographs*, 1964, *78* (1, Whole No. 578).

Salapatek, P. Pattern perception in early infancy. In L. B. Cohen & P. Salapatek (Eds.), *Infant perception: From sensation to cognition* (Vol. 2). New York: Academic Press, 1975.

Walk, R. D. The development of depth perception in animals and human infants. In H. W. Stevenson (Ed.), Concept of development. *Monograph of the Society of Research in Child Development*, 1966, *35* (5, Whole No. 107), 82–108.

White, B. L. *Human infants: Experience and psychological development*. Englewood Cliffs, N.J.: Prentice-Hall, Inc., 1971.

Witkin, H. A., Dyk, R. B., Faterson, H. F., Goodenough, D. R. & Karp, S. A. *Psychological differentiation*. New York: Wiley, 1962.

7

Language
Development

As you've probably gathered from my constant use of examples from language development, I think that a child's learning of language is one of the most fascinating processes of all time. Among other things language is one of the characteristics that separates man from other animals. Chimpanzees and other primates (as well as some other mammals such as dolphins and whales) apparently have vocabularies of individual sounds to be used in particular situations. But human language is more than that. To be sure, we do have a vocabulary of sounds, each of which has a particular meaning, but what makes human language so extraordinary is that these sounds can be put into all sorts of different orders (sentences) and new meanings can thus be created. You and I can say more than just "Help!" or "Danger!" We can say "Please help me," "I have time to help you now," "I thought there was danger here, but there isn't," and so on. There is an infinite number of possible sentences with an infinite number of possible meanings, yet somehow nearly every human child learns to use language in this way.

At 8 months a child makes babbling sounds like "kikiki," "dadada-dadada," and "diddlediddlediddle." Only a few months later you hear the first words. Vocabulary explodes, and by 18 months or 2 years the child is beginning to put words together into the first two-word sentences. Of course, many of the "sentences" that the 2-year-old constructs are not what you and I would consider to be very good grammar. The child says, "Daddy show" or "A celery" or "That Adam," or (from an older child) "Why it can't turn off?" or one of my favorite child sentences—"Cowboy did fighting me."

How on earth does all this change take place? Why does a child stop babbling at all? Is it because her needs are better met if she talks? Probably not. The first word of one child I know was the sound k, which meant "Spook"—the name of the family cat. I doubt that the child's needs were better met in any way by being able to say "k" for "Spook," though she crawled eagerly around the floor after the cat calling "k!" "k!" So why should words develop? Is the child taught to use words by parents who reinforce the child's near-words? Does the child learn words by imitating adults' language? If so, why doesn't it begin earlier? Why don't words appear right away? What about the first combination of words into a sentence? Although many of the early two-word sentences seem nonsense to us, they have marked regularity and predictability. What kind of regularity? Where does it come from?

There are many questions. Language in a child is one of those things that seems simple and obvious at first; the longer you think about it, however, and the more you learn, the less simple and obvious it becomes. In the past fifteen years there has been an enormous burst of interest in and research on children's language, so that we now know a good deal more than we used to about how it sounds, and the phases the child goes through. But the more we learn, the more complex the process seems; we are still a long way from a good explanation.

To summarize all this information, let me go back as usual to the level of description. Just what is the sequence of events in a child's language? What does it sound like? The task of explanation I will leave to Chapter 8.

BEFORE THE FIRST WORD

The sounds a child makes before age 10 months or 1 year, when she speaks her first words, are really not language at all. Usually linguists call this period the *prelinguistic* phase. Within the prelinguistic phase there is once again evidence that development occurs in rough stages. Although children differ quite widely in the ages at which they pass from one stage to another, and in the abruptness or gradualness of the shift, the stages do appear to occur in the same order for most or all children.

Stage 1: Crying. From birth to about 1 month of age, very nearly the only sound an infant makes is a cry. Infants may have several cries with somewhat different sound patterns, but those different sounds do not seem to be related to different kinds of discomforts or problems. Parents often feel that they can distinguish between a "hungry cry" and a "wet diaper cry," but when children's cries are recorded and played back to parents, the parents are unable to tell the cause of the cry.

Stage 2: Cooing. Starting at about 1 month (although, as I pointed out, the age varies quite a bit), the baby begins to make some noncrying sounds, of which a kind of "cooing" sound is the most common—the vowel sound *uuuuuuuuuu* is heard sometimes for quite protracted periods. The sound *seems* to be associated with more pleasurable times for the child, but that is an inference drawn by the observers.

Stage 3: Babbling. By about 6 months the infant begins to use a quite wide range of sounds, including a lot of what we would call *consonants*, such as *k* and *g*. Frequently, the baby combines a consonant sound with a vowel sound and produces a kind of syllable, such as *ba* and *ga*. Toward the end of the babbling period, the baby frequently repeats such syllables over and over, so that you may hear "dadadadadadada," or "gigigigigigi," or more complex combinations. This apparently endlessly repetitive game is called *echolalia:* the child echoes herself.

Several features distinguish the babbling period from what has gone before. First, the child simply spends more time making noises. Often she will "talk to herself" when alone in her crib just after waking up or for a short time before going to sleep. Second, the sounds the infant makes begin to have *intonational* patterns that are something like speech. The baby may use rising inflections or use the rhythm of speech, even though she is still babbling apparently "meaningless" sounds.

Stage 4: Patterned speech. Sometime around 1 year of age (give or take a few months), the infant begins to use sounds consistently to refer to objects, people, or events—her first words. But she doesn't suddenly stop making nonword sounds at the same time. The toddler continues to make a variety of other sounds, often called *jargon*, for another 6 months or so. The jargon sounds are less echoic, more variable, and seem to have stress and intonation patterns like that of the adult speech the child is hearing. If you hear a 12- or 14-month-old child vocalizing in her crib, but are too far away to hear the actual sounds, the babbling or "jargoning" may sound like sentences or conversation, since the sounds rise and fall and have question-mark types of intonation.

Some of the arguments about the significance of babbling and other early sounds, and the relationship between the early sounds and later development, are discussed in Box 12.

THE FIRST WORDS

The first word is an event that parents wait for eagerly, and often they imagine consistency when it isn't there. Equally often, parents miss the very earliest words because they are frequently sounds that are not at all like the words in the language the child hears. A baby does not one day say "dog" in a loud, clear voice. Even "dada" is often unrecognizable, or it may not mean "Daddy" at all. To give you some idea of the sort of words a child may "invent," take a look at Table 4. This is a partial list of words produced by young Hildegard Leopold during her first year. Hildegard's father, Werner Leopold, is a linguist, and he kept a running account of her language development.

TABLE 4
Hildegard Leopold's First Words

Sound	Child's age	Apparent meaning of the sound
dididi	9 months	If she said it loudly, meant disapproval; if she said it softly, used to comfort herself
mama	10 months	Refers to food; also means tastes good, and hungry
nenene	10 months	Scolding
tt!	10 months	Used to call squirrels

Source: McNeill, D. The development of language. In P. H. Mussen (Ed.), *Carmichael's manual of child psychology* (Vol. 1, 3rd ed.). New York: Wiley, 1970, p. 1075, after Leopold, 1949.

BOX 12
Babbling and Later Development

Many linguists have concluded that the child's early sounds, such as babbling, have little or nothing to do with the later development of words and sentences. We know, for example, that deaf children babble, although they do not spontaneously form words or sentences, which suggests that babbling may be a quite independent phenomenon. Perhaps the child is merely exercising her vocal cords or "playing" with her sounds. In addition, analysis of the actual sounds children use in babbling and in the early words shows that while babbling may involve quite a wide range of sounds, the early words use only a few sounds. So there is a sharp *reduction* in the infant's sound repertoire (at least those she uses) between the babbling and the word stages. The sound repertoire heard in babbling is very similar among infants exposed to different languages, but the sounds the child uses in forming her first words tend to be those used in the actual language she is hearing.

Erik Lenneberg and others have suggested that the shift from stage 3 to stage 4—from babbling to words—occurs as a result of fundamental changes in the child's neurological development. She can't learn to create words and sentences until a certain amount of brain growth has taken place, and that necessary growth has not occurred until about the end of the first year. Before this development the baby's babbling and other sounds may be more in the nature of play, as wiggling her fingers is a kind of play. With the beginning of real language—words and sentences—her activity seems to be more purposive, more guided by the intent to communicate.

But there are *some* connections between the early babbling and later language and between the early babbling and other types of development. It looks as if the *rate* of progress through the several phases of prelinguistic development may be predictive of the child's overall sensorimotor development. For example, Roe has recently found that male infants who babbled a lot

For a sound or a collection of sounds to be considered a word it doesn't have to be the same as any word spoken by adults. The crucial factor is that the child must use the sound or sounds consistently in some situation, or to refer to a particular person or thing or to a collection of persons or things. Obviously, Hildegard used some sounds to refer to whole situations. She used "Mama" for food, hunger, and good tastes. But she didn't say "Mama" in other situations, so the sound was restricted in its usage.

The first words are also often described as *holophrases.* They are whole phrases in that they appear to contain a whole sentence in a single word. When we use a word like "milk," we mean a white liquid that comes from a cow and is drunk by most children and by many adults. We don't ordinarily use the word by itself. Rather, we use it in any one of an infinite number of possible sentences: "Pass me the milk" "We're out of milk," "The milk tastes sour," and so on. But the year-old child doesn't yet create sentences in this way. What she does instead, or so it seems, is to use a single word to convey a whole sentence. If the baby slams her cup down on the highchair and says "Milk!" a whole message is involved: "Bring me my milk right now!" or some such. If the baby sees the milk bottle being brought out of the

at early ages (3 to 5 months) had higher scores on "infant IQ tests" at 9 months than did infants whose babbling peaked later, at 7 months. Other investigators, such as Kagan, Moore, and Bayley, have found that infant girls who vocalize a lot during testing situations have higher IQ scores at ages 2 and 3 than do those infants who vocalize less. Such findings are generally consistent with Lenneberg's position, since children who babble early may be on a somewhat faster maturational timetable.

Evidence that *would* be inconsistent with Lenneberg's maturational position would be any that indicated that the sequence of prelinguistic development could be speeded up by extra stimulation during infancy. Do infants who are talked to a great deal arrive at stage 4 sooner than infants who are stimulated less? This seems like a fairly straightforward question, but there are not a lot of good data. Two types of information are available. First, the frequency of vocalization in young infants can be increased by direct reinforcement, such as smiling at the baby when she makes sounds or rubbing her tummy (Haugen and McIntire). Second, infants who are talked to a great deal are likely to score somewhat higher in later years on IQ tests or on measures of later language ability. But neither of these pieces of information tells us that extra verbal stimulation, or direct reinforcement of vocalizing, has any effect on the rate with which a child passes into the "first word" stage of language development. Once words occur, talking to the child does seem to help to increase the vocabulary at a faster rate, but it is not clear that lots of early vocal stimulation speeds up the first word. This is not to say that talking to an infant has no effect. It seems to have positive effects on the child's overall cognitive development. But there is no good evidence that early linguistic stimulation speeds up *language* during the first year of life.

refrigerator and says "Milk" in a quieter tone, something like "There's my milk" is conveyed. To be able to understand this earliest language it's necessary not only to hear what the child says but to see what she is doing or what situation she is in.

Ordinarily, the first ten words or so are slow to develop. Nelson found that for the 18 children she studied, most had a ten-word vocabulary at 15 or 16 months of age, so it had taken most of these children three or four months to get this far. But past this point, words are added quite rapidly. In Nelson's study the average age at which the children had 50-word vocabularies was about 19 to 20 months. Children differed in the age at which they began the vocabulary growth process, but nearly all of the children in this study showed the pattern of slow initial growth followed by a kind of spurt after about the first ten words.

But what *kind* of words does the child use in the early months of this stage? The old-style attempts to study this problem involved analyses of the child's speech into the same parts-of-speech categories as those used by adults. The numbers of nouns, adverbs, adjectives, and verbs in the early vocabulary were totaled. But such a procedure artificially applies an adult category system to the child's language. A better

strategy is to group the words into categories that appear to represent different functions in the child's speech. Nelson did this in her recent study and arrived at six categories: (1) specific nominals—words the child uses to name unique objects, such as people and animals; (2) general nominals—words the child uses for classes of objects, animals, and people, such as ball, car, milk, doggie, girl, he, that; (3) action words—the child uses these to describe or accompany actions or to express or demand attention: go, bye-bye, up, look, hi; (4) modifiers—words that refer to properties or qualities of things: big, red, pretty, hot, all gone, there, or mine; (5) personal-social words—these say something about the child's feelings or social relationships: ouch, please, no, yes, or want; and (6) function words—words that have only a grammatical function, such as what, where, is, to, or for.

Among the first 50 words used by each of the 18 children whom Nelson studied, these six categories were represented as follows:

Specific nominals	14 percent
General nominals	51 percent
Action words	13 percent
Modifiers	9 percent
Personal-social words	8 percent
Function words	4 percent

Clearly, the vast majority of the child's earliest words are used to name or refer to classes of objects.

When Nelson looked at the specific words learned by these children, she found still further clarification. Most of the earliest words, even those that named objects or people, had something to do with action, with things that the child could do. It was fairly common for a young child to have the word *shoe* or *sock* in her vocabulary, but much less likely for her to know *pants* or *diaper* (perhaps because the child can do something with shoes and socks herself). Names of the child's toys are quite common (ball), as are names of foods (milk, cookie). The interesting point is that it appears to be not only the amount of exposure to the object or word that determines whether or not the child will learn the word at this early stage. Each child's selection of words is different, but each seems to contain a great many labels for things the child can play with or manipulate, that make interesting noises, or that move in interesting ways. Perhaps, like that of the very young infant, the toddler's attention is still captured to some extent by things that move. But she also learns early the words for things she can act on herself in various ways.

Nelson also found some indication that there are two different types of early vocabulary. Some children, whom Nelson calls *referential*, have vocabularies heavily weighted with nominals but with very few personal-social words, fewer action words, and fewer still specific names for people and things. The other group she calls *expressive*, for their vocabularies seem to consist more of words that relate to interactions with people, naming people, or expressing feelings. Her group of 18 children was about equally divided between these two types of early vocabularies. It is to be hoped that further research will tell us whether or not these earliest styles of language development persist and whether or not they represent pervasive styles of interaction with the environment.

| Later Vocabulary Growth | Past the first 50 words, vocabulary growth continues at a rapid pace. Figure 22 shows some old data on vocabulary growth, showing the rapid addition of words from about 18 months onward, with particularly large spurts from 18 to 24 months and from 30 to 36 months. |

| THE FIRST SENTENCES | Much more interesting than the mere addition of words to the child's vocabulary is her growing ability to string those words into sentences. The first two-word sentences usually appear at about 18 months. For some months after this, the child continues to use single words as well as two-word sentences. Eventually, the one-word utterances drop out almost completely, and the child begins to use three- and four-word sentences and to create more complex combination of words. |

Again, there seems to be order in the process of the development of grammatical skill (or *syntactic* skill, to use the more technical term). Linguists now commonly divide the process into two stages.

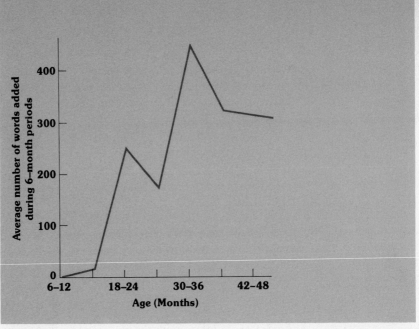

FIGURE 22
The number of vocabulary words *added* during each six-month period for the first four years. Note the very large spurt in vocabulary between 18 and 24 months, and between 30 and 36 months. (Source: Adapted from Smith, M. E. An investigation of the development of the sentence and the extent of vocabulary in young children. *University of Iowa Studies in Child Welfare*, 1926, 3,(5).)

Stage 1 Grammar

There are several distinguishing features of the earliest sentences. First, they are shorter—usually two or three words. Second, the first two- and three-word sentences are *simpler*. Nouns, verbs, and adjectives are usually included, but virtually all the other grammatical markers (which linguists call *inflections*) are absent, including the *s* for plurals, the *ed* for verb endings, the possessive markers, and auxiliary verbs. Because only the really critical words are present, the sentences of the very young child are sometimes referred to as *telegraphic speech.* The child's language is rather like what we use when we send a telegram. We keep in all the essential words—usually nouns, verbs, and modifiers—and leave out all the prepositions, auxiliary verbs, and so on.

Roger Brown makes this point about the early telegraph speech very nicely.

Words in a telegram cost money, and so that is a reason to be brief, to say nothing not essential. If the full message were: 'My car has broken down and I have lost my wallet; send money to me at the American Express in Paris' the telegram would be: 'Car broken down; wallet lost; send money American Express Paris.' The telegram omits 10 words: *my, has, and, I, have, my, to, me, at, the, in.* These words are pronouns, prepositions, articles, conjunctions, and auxiliary verbs. The words retained are nouns and verbs. The adult user of English when he writes a telegram operates under a constraint on length and the child when he first begins to make sentences also operates under some kind of constraint that limits length. The curious fact is that the sentences the child makes are like adult telegrams in that they are largely made up of nouns and verbs (with a few adjectives and adverbs) and that they generally do not use prepositions, conjunctions, articles, or auxiliary verbs. (Brown, 1973, pp. 74–75)

Not only is the child's spontaneous speech simpler in this way, but her imitations are as well. If you ask a child of 20 to 24 months to say *"I am playing with the dogs,"* the child is like to say *"Play dog"* or *"I play dog"*—thus omitting the auxiliary verb (*am*), the verb ending (*ing*), the preposition (*with*), the article (*the*), and the plural ending (*s*).

The other feature of this earliest sentence construction that I want to underline is that from the beginning the child's sentences are *creative*. Just as you and I can create totally new sentences following the rules of our grammar, so the very young child seems to construct totally new sentences as well. Children make sentences they could not have heard, as for example, "A more water," "Out a car" (both of which were recorded by a student of mine listening to a 2-year-old boy), or "Allgone sticky." Older children construct more complex, but still novel, utterances, such as the example I gave earlier: "Cowboy did fighting me." What all of this sounds like is that the child has a grammar of her own, and that she is constructing sentences that conform to that grammar, to those rules, just as you or I would following our rules.

Following this logic, linguists have attempted to study the child's earliest sentences as if they were a foreign language, and to write a grammar for it. What kind of rules does the child seem to be following? Do all children use the same kind of rules? And how do the rules change?

Martin Braine was one of the first to attempt to write a kind of grammar for the sentences of young children. He listened to three children—Gregory, Andrew, and Steven—all of whom were in the beginning stages of concocting two-word sentences. He began by simply collecting as many different sentences as he could from each child and then tried to see if there was regularity or rules built in. You can see his preliminary analysis of Gregory's first sentences in Table 5. You can see that he has a small collection of words that he uses in many different combinations: *see, pretty, my, it, nightnight, byebye, hi, big, more,* and *allgone*. Each is a kind of catchword; the child uses most of the other words he knows with it. And each of this small collection of important words always appears in the same place in the child's "sentences"; *see* always comes at the beginning, whereas *it* always comes at the end. Braine called this small list of especially important words

TABLE 5
Gregory's First Sentences

14 combinations	pretty boat	nightnight office	allgone shoe
with *see*	pretty fan	nightnight boat	allgone vitamins
see boy			allgone egg
see hot	my mommy	hi plane	allgone lettuce
see sock, etc.	my daddy	hi mommy	allgone watch
	my milk		
31 combinations		big boss	Plus 20
with *byebye*	do it	big boat	unclassified
byebye plane	push it	big bus	mommy sleep
byebye man	close it		milk cup
byebye hot, etc.	buzz it	more taxi	ohmy see, etc.
	move it	more melon	

Source: Braine, M. D. S. The ontogeny of English phrase structure: The first phase. *Language*, 1963, *39*, 5.

pivot words; the bigger group of words, which the child combines with the pivot words, he called *X words.*

After studying Gregory's sentences, as well as those of Steven and Anthony (which are very similar to Gregory's), Braine came to the conclusion that there is great regularity in the child's sentence construction and that we can write a sort of grammar to describe what the child is doing. At the simplest possible level the child seems to use a rule something like this: Pick a pivot word, and then combine any X word with it. If this description of what the child is doing is valid, then you or I should be able to follow that rule and "speak childese" as well as the child does.

One of the most intriguing aspects of this approach to the study of child language, to me at least, is that it begins to make sense out of the really peculiar combinations that a child comes up with. Look again at Gregory's sentences. "Byebye hot" is a combination that you and I would never make, as are "Allgone shoe" and "Allgone vitamins." But those sentences make perfectly good sense, given the child's grammar.

While a pivot grammar (as Braine's description came to be called) seemed to be a good first approximation of what young children were doing, it became clear rather quickly that the early sentences were more complex than this. While most of the children studied by linguists and psychologists did seem to have some words that were used more frequently, not all children regularly used these pivot words in the same places in sentences. A child may say both "Byebye cat" and "Daddy byebye" at different times. While *byebye* seems clearly to be a pivot word for this child, it sometimes occurs at the beginning and sometimes at the end. So Braine's idea that pivot words had fixed positions seems not be correct.

164

More importantly, the pivot grammar concept seems to gloss over some interesting *semantic* distinctions that occur in the child's first sentences. For example, young children frequently use a sentence made up of two nouns, such as "Mommy sock" or "Sweater chair" (to use some examples from Bloom's analysis). In a simple pivot grammar the word *Mommy* would probably be considered a pivot word. But such a classification misses what the child was saying in some instances. The child in Bloom's study who said "Mommy sock" said it on two different occasions during a day. The first time was when she picked up her mother's sock, and the second was when her mother put the child's sock on her foot. In the first case mommy sock seems to mean mommy's sock—a possessive relationship. But in the second instance, the child seems to convey mommy putting on my sock, which is an *agent* (mommy)-*object* (sock) relationship.

So, hidden within the apparent simplicity of the pivot grammar are important complexities. The child appears to be able, from the very earliest two-word sentences, to express a series of different relationships. She can express location, as in "Sweater chair"; possessive, as in "Mommy coat"; recurrence, as in "More milk"; relationship between agent and action, as in "Sarah read"; or between object and action, as in "See sock"; and so on. In adult language each of these different relationships is expressed with different grammatical forms. Since the young child often uses the same kinds of word combinations to express these different relationships, it is easy to miss this complexity. But if you listen to the child's language in *context*, you can see that the child is indeed expressing a rich array of relationships from the very earliest sentences.

Stage 1 continues for perhaps a year. During this time the child's sentences get longer; she uses fewer single-word utterances and more

MOMMY
SOCK

3- and 4-word sentences. But the distinguishing feature of this stage is the *absence* of the plurals, past tenses, prepositions, and other "inflections."

Stage 2 Grammar

The beginning of stage 2 is defined by the first use of any of the grammatical markers and continues for several years. Children do not go swiftly from simple two-word sentences to completely "correct," adultlike sentences. The process takes years and is not fully complete at school age. (In fact, I might even argue that it is not fully complete among adults, since most of us make grammatical errors quite regularly!)

Roger Brown, who has been a major figure in the study of early language development, has found that among English-speaking children there is a very distinct regularity in the order with which they add the grammatical complexities to their language. Prepositions are added very early, as are plurals. Irregular verb endings come fairly early (as in *went* or *saw*), with the possessive and auxiliary verbs (*am*, *do*, etc.) developing later.

One of the intriguing things that often happens in the development of these complexities is a phenomena called *overregularization*. Take the development of the past tense as an example. It happens that in English most of the most frequently used verbs have irregular past tenses (*go/went; see/saw; am/was; come/came; do/did*, etc.), while most of the less common verbs have regular past tenses, adding *ed* (e.g., *play/played*). Many young children learn a small number of the irregular past tenses and use them correctly for a short time. But then, rather suddenly, the child "discovers" the rule of adding *ed* and overgeneralizes this rule to all verbs. It is precisely this process that I illustrated on the first page of this book, when my 4-year-old daughter said *beated* instead of *beat*. She was making the English language more regular than it really is. The period of overregularization may last for several years; only slowly does the child learn the exceptions to the rule. Dale says the following about this particular overgeneralization:

The crucial point here is that the irregular verbs, even though they are the most frequent verbs in English, do not follow a pattern; we can only conclude that the child is fundamentally a pattern learner. Once a pattern is acquired, it will be applied as broadly as possible, even if this results in the production of words the child has never heard. (Dale, 1976, pp. 34–35)

During the long stretch of stage 2 grammatical development, the child not only needs to learn how to use the several grammatical markers, she also needs to learn how to form different types of sentences, such as questions and negatives. The development of questions has been quite widely studied, and it provides a delightful illustration of the sequence of changes that occurs. Let me focus on only one type of question, those questions that begin with a *wh* word—*who, what, when, where, why*. Take the sentence

The liberated woman is wearing blue jeans.

How do we turn that into a question with a *wh* word at the beginning? There are three necessary changes:

1. We must add a *wh* word.

The liberated woman is wearing what?

2. We must move the *wh* word to the beginning of the sentence.

What the liberated woman is wearing?

3. We must move the auxiliary verb (in this case *is*) to a position just after the *wh* word.

What is the liberated woman wearing?

Obviously, when we create questions of this kind, we are totally unaware of having gone through those three processes. We simply transform the statement into a question in one step in our head. But the child doesn't go from statements to questions in one fell swoop. In fact, she goes through the three steps I've outlined separately.

In the very earliest stage of questions the child doesn't add the *wh* word at all. She simply speaks ordinary two- or three-word sentences and raises her voice at the end, such as:

See hole?

Adults do this all the time too. It's perfectly legal in adult English to imply a question with the tone of voice, as in "You're coming?" rather than "Are you coming?" But all the child's early questions take this form.

Somewhat later—the timing varies enormously from one child to another—the earliest *wh* questions emerge, but what the child apparently does is to stick the *wh* word onto the beginning of one of her ordinary sentences without changing the sentence around at all.

Where my mitten?[1]
What me think?

A child at the same age says things like "Me think" or "My mitten" as separate sentences, so all she's done is to add the *wh* word for a question. Still later the child begins to cope with the auxiliary verbs, *is, do, are,* and so on. These words show up in the child's questions but not in the right place.

What my trailer he should pull?
Why it's resting now?

Finally, as a last stage, the child manages to turn the verbs around the right way and produces *wh* questions that sound more or less like those of an adult.

[1] The examples of sentences in this section are all taken from McNeill, D. *The development of language.* In P. H. Mussen (Ed.), *Carmichael's manual of child psychology* (Vol. 1, 3rd ed.). New York: Wiley, 1970, pp. 1111–1112.

The development of questions is more complex than I've presented it because all sorts of other developments are occurring at the same time, and they confuse the problem of questions somewhat. For example, the child is learning about negatives at about the same time and may try to create a negative *wh* question, coming up with such tongue twisters as

Why not me can't dance?
Why not me break that one?

Still later the child learns the rules for transforming a simple sentence into both a negative and a question.

Cross-cultural Similarities in Language Development

Obviously, all the examples I have given of early language development have come from studies of children hearing and learning English. Do the same kind of regularities occur among children learning other languages? Although the amount of research on early language acquisition in children speaking languages other than English is not vast, it does look as if most of the same kinds of regularities occur cross-linguistically. Children learning Russian and Finnish have a stage 1 grammar, which seems to be virtually identical to what has been observed in English-speaking children, as you can see in Table 6. Children in other language communities show overregularizations too. The order of development during stage 2 may be somewhat different in different languages, since different languages vary in the difficulty or complexity of their rules for forming plurals, past tenses, or possessives. But there do seem to be two broad phases, and children do seem to show rule-governed behavior in their language learning in all cultures studied.

Overview of Grammatical Development

Several points deserve emphasis:

1. From the very earliest point in the child's sentence construction, there are clear regularities. The child constructs sentences by some kind of rule system, however simple.
2. The rule system is not the same as that for adult English (or adult Urdu, Greek, or any other language) but is unique to children.
3. As far as is known now, the same kinds of rules, in roughly the same order, are used by children learning all sorts of different languages. We find something like a stage 1 grammar in children learning Russian, French, or whatever.
4. The child's grammar changes gradually in a sequence that seems the same for all the children who have been studied. There are vast differences among children in the rate of language development, but the sequence seems to stay about the same.
5. Children's language is creative from the very beginning. The child is not just copying sentences that she has heard; she is creating new ones, according to the rules of her own grammar.

TABLE 6
Comparison of Stage 1 Grammar in Children Learning English, Russian, and Finnish

Type of sentence: Relationship expressed	Sentences heard from children speaking:		
	English	Russian	Finnish
Recurrence	more milk	yesche moloka (more milk)	lissa kakkua (more cake)
Attribution	big boat	papa bol-shoy (papa big)	rikki auto (broken car)
Possession	mama dress	mami chashka (mama's cup)	tati auto (aunt car)
Agent-Action	Bambi go	mamo prua (mama walk)	Seppo putoo (Seppo fall)
Action-Object	hit ball	nasbla yaechko (found egg)	ajaa bmbm (drives car)
Question	where ball	gdu papa (where papa)	missa pallo (where ball)

Source: Adapted from Dale, 1976, p. 40, who in turn adapted it from D. I. Slobin, Universals of grammatical development in children. In G. B. Flores d'Arcais & W. J. M. Levelt (Eds.), *Advances in psycholinguistics.* Amsterdam: North-Holland Publishing Company, 1970, pp. 178–179.

SEMANTIC DEVELOPMENT: WORD MEANINGS

Thus far I have been talking primarily about the development of *grammar* (syntax), the way in which words are put into different orders to create sentences. But an equally important issue, which has only lately drawn the attention of psychologists and linguists interested in language development, is the problem of semantics, of word meaning. How does the child come to understand the meanings of words? What kinds of words does she use in the early months and years?

There have been various attempts to describe the quality of a child's early words. Some psychologists have suggested that the child begins by referring to very specific things and only gradually comes to use words for more general categories of objects. Others have suggested exactly the opposite—that children begin with global, diffuse word usage and only gradually make these global categories more specific and particular.

The fundamental difficulty in studying the question, and perhaps the basis for disagreement and misunderstanding, is that we cannot tell what concepts the child may have simply by knowing what words she uses. Because a child uses a particular word in roughly the correct situation (the adult situation) does not mean that she has attached the same concept to the word that an adult does. To assume that she does ensures some communication difficulties with the child. My daughter at age 4 would come to me and ask when "Sesame Street" was going to be on. "In a little while," I would say. Thirty seconds later she would be back asking again. She used the word little and the phrase *little while* herself, but she did not attach the same meanings to them that I did. Partly, the problem is that she did not yet comprehend time in an adult way, but also it is simply that we defined our terms differently. Fifteen minutes is a little while to me, but it was a long time to her.

The whole issue of word meaning for children is an enormously complex one, with competing (and incomplete) theories. But let me touch on several aspects of the question briefly to give you some feeling for the issues being raised.

The fundamental task for the researcher is to discover how the *child* uses a particular word. What meaning does it have for her? The largest amount of research has been focused on two types of words—the earliest nouns and opposites.

In the case of the earliest nouns the issue has been whether the child attaches too specific meanings, or too general meanings. Does the child, for example, use the word *dog* to refer only to the family collie (which would be a too-specific usage), or does she use the word to refer to all four-legged creatures, including cats, cows, horses, and others (which would be a too-general usage)? The answer seems to be that most children do some of both. Many children do apply the word *dog* to all four-legged creatures, but this is not universal. Most children have some words they use in very limited ways. Bloom, for example, observed that one of her daughter's earliest words, the word *car*, was used only to refer to cars moving in the street; she did not use the word when she was riding in a car or for cars that were standing still.

Nelson's study of the first words of children also provides some information about the generality or specificity of children's earliest words. She found that all of the children in her study had at least some words among their first 50 that were *general* terms, covering general (usually overgeneralized) categories. At the same time all the children Nelson studied had at least some parts of their vocabularies that were highly specific, highly differentiated. Paul, at 18 months, included the words *bear, duck, frog, bird,* and *fish* among his 30-word vocabulary, whereas Jane, at age 15 months, had seven words for different kinds of food in her 50-word vocabulary: *cracker, cookie, cake, water, noodles, turkey,* and *pea.*

What these several bits of information tell us is that the earliest vocabularies of children are neither entirely general nor entirely specific, neither entirely diffuse nor entirely particular.

One apparently valid conclusion is that among these early words there are no superordinate words, that is, words for all the separate items in a single category. Paul has no word for *animals* as a class, nor does Jane have the word *food* or any equivalent in her vocabulary. So,

170

although the very young child's vocabulary does contain words that refer to many separate individual things, the concepts behind them are not yet organized hierarchically. To be sure, there have been comparatively few good studies of this aspect of early language development, and my conclusion can only be tentative. But the lack of superordinates, the absence of a hierarchical organization of concepts, would fit very well with what else we know about the child's cognitive development at this same age. As you will see in Chapter 8 hierarchical classification does not appear to develop until the child is perhaps 5 or 6 years old.

Another area of semantic development in which there has been considerable interest has been the development of words for opposites, such as *more* and *less*, or *big* versus *little*, *long* versus *short*, *wide* verus *narrow*. Palermo found that in the case of *more* and *less*, the word *more* was learned first; nearly all the 3- and 4-year-olds he studied could correctly pick *more water*, or *more weight*; but only half could pick *less*. Most of the children who made "errors" on the word *less* used it as a synonym for *more*. So whichever word you used, these children picked on the basis of *more*.

Clark has developed a theory that predicts just this sort of confusion in children's word meanings. She suggests that words like *more* and *less*, or *high* and *low*, have a great deal of common meaning. For example, both *more* and *less* refer to amount. If the child learns the concept for amount first, then there may be a period when *more* and *less* are used interchangeably. Later, the child discovers the dimension on which the two terms differ and begins to use them correctly. This theory has some appeal, but there are a number of research findings that do not conform to expectations from Clark's theory.

Other researchers have found that general terms such as *big* and *little*, which can subsume many other dimensional terms (such as *short*, *tall*, *wide*, and *narrow*) are learned earliest, with the more specific descriptive terms learned later. But even this generalization needs some qualification, since Maratsos found that the word *big* was used more correctly by 3-year-olds than by four- or five-year-olds. The younger children seemed to use the word *big* to refer to global size, but the older children confused the words *big* and *long*, and frequently picked the *longer* item, even if it was not the largest in overall size. So as the child's concepts and word usage become more complex, there may actually be a kind of regression or deterioration in performance.

The process of semantic development seems to be a gradual process in which the child slowly comes to match her meanings to those of the adults around her. At the same time she learns the rules for combining meanings into sentences. She learns for example that adjectives go with nouns, and that some adjective-noun pairs are more common and more acceptable. *The red hat* is "legal," but *the red donkey* is an unlikely combination. There are similar semantic restrictions on other kinds of word combinations in sentences, and children seem to learn these restrictions gradually. By age 9 or 10 most children have quite detailed semantic information, although naturally it is limited to the range of the child's vocabulary.

In sum, the process of semantic development seems to be less regular and more individual than that of syntactic development. Whether this is because we have not yet devised the techniques that will reveal the underlying orderliness or whether there really *is* less systematic order is just not clear at the moment. What we do know is that meanings children attach to their early words are different from the meanings used by adults, and that the development of full adultlike semantic understanding is a long and apparently gradual process.

INDIVIDUAL DIFFERENCES IN LANGUAGE DEVELOPMENT

I have emphasized throughout this chapter that the *rate* of development differs considerably from one child to the next. The range of "normality" is quite large. The first word usually is heard when the child is somewhere around 1 year old. Yet it's not at all uncommon for a child to delay the first words until she is 14 or 16 months, and a few children don't speak a single word until they are 18 months old. These children are normal, not retarded or brain damaged. On the other side there are a very few children who begin saying words as early as 7 or 8 months. The range of normality, then, is almost a full year, from 8 to about 18 months.

The spread is even wider in the construction of early sentences. The earliest two-word sentences recorded for any child studied thus far were uttered at about 10 months. The average age is about 18 months, but again it is quite normal for the first sentences to be delayed until perhaps 24 months, or even 26 or 28 months.

Sex Differences

One of the standard psychological generalizations over the decades from the 1940s to the 1960s was that girls were "more verbal." There were fragments of early data that suggested that girls talked sooner, had larger vocabularies, and were generally more skilled at all linguistic tasks. Recent reexaminations of the evidence, however, suggest that although there may be some advantage for girls in the early years of life, the advantage is small and disappears by about age 3 when boys have generally caught up (although in adolescence girls again show superiority to boys on a variety of verbal tasks). Among very young children girls may be slightly ahead in vocabulary development. Katherine Nelson, for example, found in her recent study that the girls in her sample were about four months ahead of the boys in developing a vocabulary of 50 words. Studies of grammatical development, however, have not ordinarily shown sex differences in complexity of sentences or the rate at which the child adds various new fea-

172

tures to her grammar. However, all the
young children have involved very sma
class children, so we must be cautious
ings too broadly.

Among older children girls are ahe
more boys wind up in elementary so
faulty pronunciation (such as saying "
girls ordinarily pronounce clearly fror
3 onward there appears to be no over:
tence length, complexity, and vocab

There are similar findings about the effects of
ferences as the social class of the child's family. It has long bee
serted that children from middle-class homes are more skilled verbally
in every respect than are children from working-class or poverty
homes. Whether or not you find support for that assertion depends very
heavily on the measures of language development that you use. Measures of vocabulary size do show differences. Children from
working-class or poverty families have smaller vocabularies than do
children from middle-class families (see, for example, Stodolsky &
Lesser). But it is much less clear that there are differences in the grammatical complexity of sentences spoken by the children.

The most recent and linguistically sophisticated studies of grammatical complexity comparing social classes have compared black
ghetto children and white middle-class children (see Dale for a review
of this material). We know that many children from minority groups
who are growing up in poverty homes have difficulty in school, and
many social scientists have concluded that the difficulty arises from a
broad deficit in language ability, including inability either to understand or to construct complex sentences. However, as several linguists
have pointed out, earlier studies of language complexity in black children all involved applying the rules of "standard English" to the language spoken by black children. In fact, a distinctly different dialect is
spoken by many ghetto black children. They are learning a language
with different grammatical rules. Some of the contrasting sentence
structures are shown in Table 7.

It may appear from the sentence contrasts in Table 7 that Black
English (BE) is simply less complex than Standard English. But Dale
and other linguists caution against that simpleminded analysis. The
use of *come* as the past tense, in the sentence "She come home", does
not mean that there *is* no past tense in Black English; rather it merely
means that both the present and past tense are formed with come.
Although Black English sometimes forms sentences with fewer grammatical markers (as in "He going home" versus the "He is going
home" in Standard English), there are times when Black English uses

TABLE 7
Comparison of Standard English and Black English Sentence Structures

Standard English version	Black English version
He is going home	He going home
I have lived here	I have live here
	or
	I lived here
This is John's mother	This is John mother
Didn't anybody see it?	Didn't nobody see it?
She has a bike	She have a bike
She came home	She come home

Source: Based on examples in Dale, 1976, p. 274.

more markers, as in the double negative sentence, "Didn't nobody see it?"

When comparisons of the language of children exposed to Black English and those exposed to Standard English are made, the usual finding is that the two groups use language of about equal grammatical complexity.

However, most of the studies comparing grammatical complexity between black and white, or between poor and middle class, have been done with children aged 5 or older; we still lack good evidence about the very earliest stages of grammatical development. There is also a need for more research on the early grammatical skills of poor *white* children who are primarily exposed to Standard English.

Overall, however, the several lines of research suggest that vocabulary size is probably more influenced by family situation than is grammatical development. Middle-class children are talked to more from the earliest weeks of life, which appears to make a difference in their rate of vocabulary growth. But the development of sentences and the stage-by-stage changes in the construction rules for sentences appear, at this point, to be much less influenced by environmental variations.

To get ahead of myself a little and to talk about explanations, it's worth asking why vocabulary might be influenced by environment when grammar is not. I can think of two kinds of explanations. One suggestion is that grammar development is tied to a maturational process; the development of grammar is limited by the development of certain neurological structures. We do know that children seem to develop grammar in the same order, apparently regardless of what they're listening to, and such consistency among children always makes a maturational explanation seem very sensible. But maybe it's just that to learn a grammar you don't have to be listening to a very rich or varied language. New words can't be learned unless you hear them, but even the simplest language contains most of the various forms of grammatical rules that the child will have to learn.

I can't select at this point between these two explanations. They are probably both correct to some extent.

SUMMARY

1. The earliest sounds that a child makes are probably not a part of language development proper; they appear instead to be mere exercise of her vocal cords.
2. During this early period the most interesting development is the process called babbling, in which the baby repeats "syllables" over and over and rehearses other sounds.
3. At about 1 year of age, on the average, the earliest words begin to appear. A word is defined as any sound or combination of sounds that the child uses consistently with a clear referent.
4. Vocabulary grows rapidly during the second year, particularly during the second half of the year. By age 2 most children have a vocabulary of about 50 words, and many children have much larger vocabularies at that age.
5. The first two-word sentence is usually heard when the child is between 18 months and 2 years of age. These early sentences appear to have a grammar of their own, with perhaps two "parts of speech"—the pivot words and the X words.
6. From the time of these earliest sentences, the child's language is creative. She constructs new sentences that she has never heard.
7. Subsequent development of grammar involves sequential addition of crucial parts of sentences such as prepositions, plurals, past tenses, questions, and negatives.
8. There are marked individual differences in the rate at which children develop language, with some indication that girls develop slightly more rapidly in the early years.
9. The development of word meanings (semantic development) seems to follow a less predictable course. Most children use both overgeneralized and undergeneralized words in their early vocabularies. Later understanding of words such as *big, little, narrow,* and *wide* seems to run primarily from the general to the specific, although even this generalization may be open to some question.
10. Social class (and racial) differences in language development seem to be largely confined to vocabulary growth, which is faster in middle-class children than in the poor. Grammatical development occurs at a similar rate across social class and racial lines.

REFERENCES

Suggested Additional Readings

Braine, M. D. S. The ontogeny of English phrase structure: The first phase. *Language,* 1963, *39,* 1–13.
Although Braine's analysis is now somewhat out of date, I think you would find this paper interesting and very easy to read. It has been reprinted in a number of places and should not be difficult to obtain.
Brown, R. *A first language: The early stages.* Cambridge, Mass.: Harvard University Press, 1973.
The material in this book is moderately technical, but Brown's writing style is easy and informal; this would be an excellent second source if you are interested in this area.
Dale, P. S. *Language development: Structure and function* (2nd ed.). New York: Holt, Rinehart and Winston, 1976.

This brand new edition of Dale's excellent overview of language development is the very best single source I know. The first edition is also excellent, but the 1976 edition is more up to date, particularly in the area of semantic development.

Lenneberg, E. H. *Biological foundations of language.* New York: Wiley, 1967.

I hesitate to recommend this since it is *extremely* difficult reading. But it is a good source if you are interested in the possible maturational underpinnings of language.

Nelson, K. Structure and strategy in learning to talk. *Monographs of the Society for Research in Child Development,* 1973, *38* (1–2, Whole No. 149).

The level of presentation in this monograph is fairly complex and detailed, but I think this is a good example of first rate research in a difficult area.

Other Sources Cited

Bloom, L. *Language development: Form and function in emerging grammars.* Cambridge, Mass.: M. I. T. Press, 1970.

Bloom, L. *One word at a time.* The Hague: Mouton, 1973.

Cameron, J., Livson, N., & Bayley, N. Infant vocalizations and their relationship to mature intelligence. *Science,* 1967, *157,* 331–333.

Clark, E. V. What's in a word? On the child's acquisition of semantics in his first language. In T. E. Moore (Ed.), *Cognitive development and the acquisition of language.* New York: Academic Press, 1973.

Haugen, G. M., & McIntire, R. W. Comparisons of vocal imitation, tactile stimulation, and food as reinforcers for infant vocalizations. *Developmental Psychology,* 1972, *6,* 201–209.

Kagan, J. *Change and continuity in infancy.* New York: Wiley, 1971.

Maratsos, M. P. Decrease in the understanding of the word "big" in preschool children. *Child Development,* 1973, *44,* 747–752.

McNeill, D. The development of language. In P. H. Mussen (Ed.), *Carmichael's manuel of child psychology* (Vol. 1, 3rd ed.). New York: Wiley, 1970.

Moore, T. Language and intelligence: A longitudinal study of the first eight years. *Human Development,* 1967, *10,* 88–106.

Palermo, D. S. Still more about the comprehension of "less." *Developmental Psychology,* 1974, *10,* 827–829.

Roe, K. V. Amount of infant vocalization as a function of age: Some cognitive implications. *Child Development,* 1975, *46,* 936–941.

Smith, M. E. An investigation of the development of the sentence and the extent of vocabulary in young children. *University of Iowa Studies in Child Welfare,* 1926, *3* (5).

Stodolsky, E., & Lesser, G. Learning patterns in the disadvantaged. *Harvard Educational Review,* 1967, *37,* 546–593.

PROJECT 2
BEGINNING TWO-WORD SENTENCES

Find a child as close to age 20 to 24 months as you can. He or she should be speaking at least some two-word sentences. Arrange to spend enough time with the child so that you can collect a list of 50 different sentences, each at least two words long. If the child uses longer sentences, fine. What you need are 50 sentences. Write them down in the order that they occur and stop when you have 50. It may take several sessions with the child before you get this many, and you may find that it would be helpful to have the child's mother, some other adult, or an older child play with the subject while you just listen and write things down.

When you have your list of 50 sentences, go back and look again at the groupings of Gregory's early speech given in Table 5 in this chapter. See if you can come up with a similar grouping for your child's sentences.

1. Are there pivot words? Which words are they?
2. What are the X words in your child's grammar?
3. Is your child at stage 1 or stage 2? What evidence is there of either?

Supplementary reading for the project:

Braine, M. The ontogeny of English phrase structure: The first phase. *Language*, 1963, *39*, 1–13.
Brown, R., & Bellugi, U. Three processes in the child's acquisition of syntax. *Harvard Educational Review*, 1964, *34*, 133–151.

8

Theories of Language
Development

In Chapter 7 I have given quite a detailed description of the development of language during the early years; the remaining task is to explain it. Why does the child's language develop in the way that it does? How does she learn language at all?

In devoting a separate chapter to theories of language development I do not mean to suggest that theory in this area is particularly well developed. But the theoretical alternatives for explaining language development are at least unusually clear-cut, which affords a good opportunity to compare a number of different views of development.

IMITATION

As I suggested on the very first page of this book, the common-sense answer to the problem of language development is that the child learns by imitating. Obviously, this has to be true to some extent. A child growing up in a family speaking English learns English, not Chinese or Greek. And there are some other kinds of direct imitation. When a child asks, "What's that?" and you say "Light" (or whatever), she may say the word after you. This type of imitation may well be involved in vocabulary growth.

A form of imitation is also illustrated in the following exchange I had with my daughter (then about age 3½) while we were watching a golf match on television:

Child: Who winned putting the ball in the hole?
Me: Who *won* what?
Child: Who winned putting the ball in the hole?
Me: Nobody *won* yet.
Child: Did he won it?

You can tell that I was vigorously trying to emphasize the word *won*, rather than winned, in the hope that I could get some corrective imitation. She imitated, all right, but the wrong thing! She put the word won into a sentence requiring win. You can't win them all!

Clearly, children do imitate some of what they hear. Accents are obviously learned through imitation, for example, and some kinds of grammar may be learned through imitation. But imitation cannot possibly account for all language development. Let me list some of the reasons why not.

1. From the very beginning children create sentences that are quite unlike any that an adult would construct and use forms of grammar that cannot be imitations because no adult uses them. The *ed* endings (*wented, goed, beated*) are good examples, as are sentences like "Byebye hot" or "Allgone vitamins." It's virtually impossible to construct a reasonable adult sentence with the words in this order, although we can come up with such unlikely sentences, such as "Say byebye to the hot burner" and "They are all gone, your vitamins." The child's language is creative from the beginning, and she creates sentences using her own rules, not those of adults.

2. When children do imitate sentences spoken by adults, they reduce or convert the sentence to conform to their own then-current grammar. I have already made this point in talking about the "telegraphic" quality of children's language; their imitations are as telegraphic as their spontaneous speech. This is illustrated nicely in the following exchange quoted by Dan Slobin:

Mother: It fits in the puzzle someplace.
Adam: Puzzle? Puzzle someplace?
Mother: Turn it around.
Adam: Turn around?
Mother: No, the other way.
Adam: Other way?
Mother: I guess you have to turn it around.
Adam: Guess turn it round. Turn round. (D. I. Slobin. Imitation and grammatical development in children. In N. S. Endler, L. R. Boulter & H. O. Osser (Eds.), *Contemporary Issues in Developmental Psychology.* New York: Holt, Rinehart & Winston, 1968, p. 441.)

3. If a child learned language entirely through imitation, no one would ever learn to speak "correct" English (or French, German, or whatever one is listening to). Much of the language that adults speak to one another and much of what we say to children is highly ungrammatical. We start sentences one way and end them another, we forget halfway through whether the subject is plural or singular and wind up with verbs that don't agree, and so forth. I'd always thought of myself as very articulate and clear and was sure that I always spoke in complete grammatical sentences until I read the transcript of a public lecture I had given. I only hope it "listened" better than it read, since most of the sentences were incomplete or ungrammatical. If that is a sample of what the child hears around her all the time—and I can only presume that it is—how could she ever come up with reasonable grammatical sentences by imitation? Even though I do not always speak grammatically, I know what a grammatical sentence is and can (usually) write grammatically. How could I do so if I had acquired all my language through imitation?

4. As a final blow to imitation as an explanation, there is at least one documented case of a child who was totally unable to speak but could hear and was quite normal mentally. This boy was obviously unable to imitate anything that was said to him, but he nonetheless learned language. That is, he was able to understand what was spoken to him and could follow complex directions given to him. So imitation can't be required for the child's comprehension of language, and it's probably not required for the child's expression of language either.

REINFORCEMENT

A second, apparently reasonably, common-sense answer to the question of how children learn language is that they are somehow directly trained to do so through reinforcement from parents or others. Skinner made an early attempt to specify a reinforcement theory of language acquisition, emphasizing that the child is shaped into forming more and more grammatically correct sentences through systematic changes in the rewards given by parents.

For this theory to be valid at least two things have to be true. First, we must observe that parents do *in fact* show systematic shaping of the child's language. Do parents pay more attention to a child when she speaks in grammatically correct sentences? Do they correct the grammar directly? Do they withhold treats like cookies until the child says, "I want a cookie" instead of just "Want cookie?" The presumed sequence is illustrated (somewhat facetiously, I confess) in Figure 23.

Second, assuming that parents *do* use some kind of system of reinforcement to shape language, do such patterns of reinforcement have any noticeable effect on the child's grammar?

The available evidence suggests that neither of these things is true. Brown, Cazden, and Bellugi examined the recorded exchanges between mothers and children from several of their studies to see if the mother's responses to the child depended on the grammar of the child's

"Cookie"

"Want cookie"   "Say it better"   "I want cookie"

FIGURE 23
A reinforcement view of language learning: The child is shaped into better and better sentences.

language or on the presumed *meaning*. They found that in nearly all cases, the mothers seemed to be responding to the "truth value" of what the child said, and not at all to the grammatical complexity of the child's sentence. Mothers appear to be willing to interpret and extract meaning from rather incomplete and primitive sentences. They provide little observable pressure on the child to improve the quality of her sentences.

Brown and Hanlon, in a later study, tried to discover whether mothers were more likely to respond to a child in some relevant way (by answering a question, giving the child what she wanted, or simply by carrying on the conversation) if the child's sentence was grammatically correct rather than not. They found that mothers responded in this relevant way about half the time whether the child's sentence was grammatically correct or not. These findings certainly do not provide any support for the notion that parents are consistently reinforcing better and better grammar.

But assuming that one *did* attempt to shape the child's language, would it lead to improvement? Braine provides a lovely anecdote about an attempt of this kind of his own:

I have occasionally made an extensive effort to change the syntax of my two children through correction. One case was the use by my two-and-a-half-year-old daughter of *other one* as a noun modifier . . . I repeatedly but fruitlessly tried to persuade her to substitute *other* + N for *other one* + N . . . the interchange went somewhat as follows: "Want other one spoon, Daddy"—"You mean, you want THE OTHER SPOON"—"Yes, I want other one spoon, please, Daddy"—"Can you say 'the other spoon'?"—"other . . . one . . . spoon"—"Say . . .

182

other"—"Other"—"Spoon"—"Spoon"—"Other . . . spoon"—"Other spoon. Now give me other one spoon." Further tuition is ruled out by her protest, vigorously supported by my wife. (M. D. S. Braine. On two types of models of the internalization of grammars. In D. I. Slobin (Ed.), *The ontogenesis of grammar*. New York: Academic Press, 1971, pp. 160–161.)

Nelson looked at this type of parental behavior fairly systematically in her study of early vocabulary growth (described in some detail in Chapter 7) and observed that those mothers who engaged in systematic correction of poor pronunciations of words and provided reward for good pronunciations had children who developed vocabulary *more slowly* than did children whose parents were more accepting of the child's pronunciation.

Another version of the reinforcement theory places emphasis on the fact that the child may learn to talk because it ensures that her needs will be met better. This argument crops up particularly in the common observation that the youngest children in large families talk somewhat later. You will hear it said that in such a family the littlest child doesn't have to talk; everyone leaps to take care of her every need without her having to say a word. Yet such children do learn to talk and without enormous delay.

This general hypothesis is *not* supported by the findings from the Brown and Hanlon study I just described. They did not find that mothers were any more likely to respond relevantly or contigently to the child's requests if they were framed in good as opposed to poor sentences. If a child is just as likely to get a cookie saying "Want cookie" than saying "I want a cookie," why does her language ever become more complex? If a reinforcement theory were correct, it shouldn't. But it does.

As a final argument against reinforcement theories of language acquisition, let me call your attention once again to the genuinely *creative* aspect of the child's language. She puts together things she hasn't heard before, just as you and I constantly create sentences that we have never heard. Furthermore, remember that the child's early language, like yours and mine, is apparently governed by rules—it is nonrandom. How could a child whose language learning has been entirely governed by the parents' reinforcements be creative and nonrandom? How can we account for the fact that the child continues to produce sentences in the "wrong order" or to use the "wrong grammar"? And how can we explain the fact that all children apparently go through very similar stages in their sentences?

Reinforcement probably does make a difference in some areas, such as pronunciation of individual words. My daughter said "Lebis" instead of "Levis." I could probably have trained her to say "Levi" by withholding the Levis each time until she said it correctly, although there was little point in my bothering, however, since she learned to pronounce the word correctly without my intervention.

Overall then, neither imitation nor reinforcement theories are adequate to account for what actually happens between parents and children, and neither accounts well for the child's own liguistic achievements.

THE ROLE OF PARENTS

Even if imitation and reinforcement, taken alone, are insufficient to account for language acquisition, it is still quite possible that parents (and other adults) *facilitate* language development in various ways—by using simpler language with the child, by emphasizing or calling attention to important grammatical features in their own speech, and by simply talking to the child regularly.

At the most basic level it is clearly critical that the parents (and other adults and siblings) *talk* to the child. In general it seems to be the case that children who are talked to a lot have somewhat more rapid language development than do children who are talked to less. So the quantity may make some difference.

But are there some kinds of "talking to" that are more useful to the child, that are more likely to foster rapid grammatical development? Here the answer is fuzzier. We do know from several recent studies that adults talk in simpler language to young children, and that their speech gets gradually more complex as the child gets older. For example, Phillips found that when speaking to either 8- or 18-month old children, mothers used shorter sentences, fewer different verb forms, fewer modifiers, and fewer of such "inflections" as conjugations and prepositions than was true when these same women spoke to adults. The sentences used with young children were strikingly shorter. Mothers used sentences that averaged about three to four words in length with the young children, while their sentences to adults averaged about eight to nine words. Phillips also found that mothers of somewhat older children (28 months) had moved up a notch in complexity; the sentences were slightly longer, and there were more verbs and modifiers used. Moerk and others have also found that mothers gradually increase the length and complexity of their language with the child to match the increasing complexity of the child's grammar.

Other researchers have tried to discover if a child, given a choice, will prefer to listen to such simplified language as opposed to normal adult speech. The limited evidence suggests that she will, but it is not clear from this whether it is the shorter, less complex quality of the speech-to-child that is preferred or the greater tonal variation that adults use with children. Imagine youself reading a story to a child and then to an adult, and you may be able to get some feeling for the difference in emphasis and pitch you would use in the two situations. Perhaps it is the greater tonal variety the child prefers to listen to; if complex adult sentences were spoken with the same tonal richness, children might be as happy listening to them.

184

My point is that while it *is* true that parents use simpler speech with their children than they do with each other, we don't know if this simpler speech is in any way *necessary* or *helpful* to the child. There is some indication that children will choose to listen to language that is somewhat more complex than their own grammar, but again we don't know whether a child who heard *only* the most complex adult speech would develop language at the same rate, or faster, or slower.

Another thing that parents do with their children, which *may* have some impact on early language development, is to *expand* on the child's sentences. If the child says "John shoe," the mother might say "This is John's shoe" if the child's meaning seemed to be possessive. What the mother does in this expansion of the child's sentence is to add the inflections, the grammatical elements that make a complete adult sentence. Perhaps this kind of activity on the part of parents aids the child by demonstrating the relationship between the child's more primitive forms and the "correct" adult forms.

There have been several attempts to check on the importance of expansions experimentally by exposing some children to a concentrated dose of expansions every day and comparing them to children who had had an equivalent amount of conversation without expansions. Of the three studies to date on this question, two found that expansions had no clearly positive effect on the rate of language development. In a third study the children who had had "recast sentences" (as these authors called it) showed significantly faster development of grammatical complexities than did those children who simply had had conversation with the experimenter. There is no way at the moment to add up these discrepant findings to some meaningful conclusion about expansions. We know that parents do expand children's sentences (although only in a small fraction of their sentences), and it looks as if this activity *may* be helpful to children, but the case is simply not proven.

THE CHILD'S CONTRIBUTION

All of the theories and hypotheses about the child's language development I have discussed thus far focus primarily on what the environment does *to* the child. What is left out of this equation is what the child is doing with the linguistic information she is getting. Since "external" theories seem to be largely inadequate, we must turn to theories that focus on the inner workings of the child.

Rehearsal

One of the things that many children do is a kind of systematic practice or rehearsal of their language by trying out new combinations and new kinds of grammatical order. One linguist, Ruth Weir, made a recording of her son Anthony practicing in this fashion by putting a tape recorder, set to turn on automatically when he started to talk to himself, in his room. Anthony did a lot of talking before his nap, at night, and just after waking up. Some of the sequences of his soliloquies appear to be rehearsals of various grammatical patterns in which he seems to be trying out different words in a single place in the phrase:

What color
What color blanket
What color mop
What color glass

or the following, in which he seems to be rehearsing negatives:

Not the yellow blanket
The white
It's not black
It's yellow
Not yellow

These and other examples from Weir's observations suggest that Anthony enjoyed playing with the sounds of the language. But they also seem to show that Anthony had noticed particular features of grammar or word relationships, and he was trying out the alternatives.

The Child's Linguistic Hypotheses

One preliminary proposal is that the child develops her grammar by means of noticing regularities in the speech she hears and then applying those regularities to her own speech. In the early stages she may notice only a few significant features, so her own language has only a few important variations. Gradually, she notices the more subtle aspects of adults' language, and her own language begins to mirror them.

There are several serious drawbacks to such a proposal. First, remember that much of what the child hears consists of incomplete and badly constructed sentences. Second, recall the discussion of the development of questions forms from Chapter 7. In passing through the several stages from no questions to a complete form of *wh* questions, the child passes through stages not represented in any adult language she is hearing. If she is proceeding by some sort of analysis of adult speech, why would these intermediate stages be so unlike adults' speech? Finally, consider what an incredible mental feat we are so casually attributing to the child. The process would be not unlike that of breaking a code. The child is given a variety of examples of the code and is somehow supposed to make sense of it. To assume that the 1½-year-old child can accomplish such an analysis is to assume abilities that are not seen in children until much later.

The Innateness Hypothesis

The "solution" to these difficulties to which most linguists now subscribe is some variation of an "innateness hypothesis." The child is thought to come into the world already programmed, in some ways, to learn language. Built in may be a kind of "language acquisition device," which contains some of the basic elements or structures of language. To explain this concept more fully, I need to take a short side trip into the topic of *transformational grammar.*

Nearly two decades ago Noam Chomsky first suggested that the type of grammar we ordinarily write for adult language, which is usually called *phrase sturcture grammar,* was for various reasons an insufficient account of how we as adults go about forming correct sentences. Many of you (at least those of you who are of my generation or older) are familiar with the process of "parsing," or analyzing sentences, which was often taught in high school English classes. Words were classed into "parts of speech," and phrases within sentences were analyzed. Chomsky argued that this analysis of the *surface structure* of a language simply misses a lot of what is going on. The more important relationships in a sentence, he thought, were the basic ones, such as those between subject and object, subject and predicate.

As an alternative view Chomsky proposed that sentences may be thought to have both a surface structure and a *deep structure.* That is, sentences have some basic, essential meaning (the deep structure), and that basic meaning is *transformed* into an acceptable adult sentence by means of certain rules. Let me see if I can make this somewhat clearer with an example, taken from Dale's discussion of transformational grammar.

Suppose that the deep structure—the basic meaning—is

John prefers steak

This deep structure may be turned into any one of several surface structures by applying certain *transformational rules.* For example, I can turn it into a question,

Does John prefer steak?

or into a passive sentence;

Steak is preferred by John.

or into a passive question;

Is steak preferred by John?

If we also assume that in the deep structure there is a restriction attached to the verb *prefer,* so that the verb can only take *animate* subjects, then this additional restriction forbids some other transformations, such as

John is preferred by steak.
Steak prefers John.
Is John preferred by steak?

and so forth.

The theory of transformational grammar is enormously complex and obviously I have only scratched the surface. But this brief view

BOX 13
Spontaneous Language in the Deaf

Further evidence that some kind of "language program" exists comes from an intriguing study by Goldin-Meadow and Feldman. They have studied a group of four congenitally deaf children, each raised by parents who do not know or use sign language. None of these children had enough residual hearing to be able to hear spoken language, and none was exposed to any deaf adults using sign language. Goldin-Meadow and Feldman observed these children in their homes over a period of months, beginning when the children were about 1½ year old. Each child was videotaped once each six weeks in a play session with the parents and with the experimenters.

The videotapes show clearly that these children *created* sign language. Each of the four children invented signs, first for individual objects and actions (similar to the one word, or holophrase stage, in a hearing child), and then later combined the signs into what appeared to be two-word sentences. The characteristics of this second stage in signing made it look very similar to the stage 1 grammar described in the last chapter. The oldest of the four children, by the end of the observations, appeared to have gone on to still more complex sentences.

Of course, these findings do not tell us that such deaf children would construct a complete language without any input at all. It is extremely

may give you some feeling for the sort of "language acquisition device" with which linguists now think children may come equipped. Perhaps children have some kind of built-in system of analysis of language, which focuses attention on the *transformations* that occur.

We know that all languages are transformational in nature. That is, they all have specific rules for forming negatives or questions out of basic meaning or deep structure. So it seems possible that the child has some built-in tendency to "scan" for transformational rules, just as the newborn infant seems to have a built-in tendency to "scan" edges and contours.

I realize that the suggestion made by Chomasky, Lenneberg, and others that there may be some built-in programming for language seems a bit farfetched. Most of us are accustomed to thinking of language as something learned after birth, so it is hard to imagine that any part of it may be built in to the child. But there are several lines of evidence that make some "innate transformational system" look very plausible.

First, there is good evidence that there is a maturational underpinning to language development. It is not until the later part of the first year, when cortical development is greatly advanced, that language begins to be noticeable. So *something* may have to develop in the neurological system before language is possible.

Second, the fact that children learning to speak diverse languages go through enormously similar early grammatical stages points to some important common ground. All children thus far studied have gone through a stage 1 grammar, and all the stage 1 grammars seem to share important features. Linguists have also found that adult languages

unlikely that they would. All the signs and sentences these children devised referred to objects and events that were immediately present. There was no evidence of signs to refer to events that were distant from the child in time or space, and it is doubtful whether such language would develop without some kind of input—signs or otherwise—from those around the child. But these findings *do* suggest that the child will begin the language process on her own with essentially no encouragement from parents or other adults. These data and findings from studies of deaf children whose parents use sign language with them (such as Schlesinger and Meadow) also point to the fact that "language" need not be oral language. Children learning sign language appear to go through the same stages in their language development as do children learning the usual oral language. So the "language learning system" appears to be a very powerful one and a very central process.

have important features in common. Every known language has some kind of division between nouns and verbs, some way of expressing the negative, and so on. This universality of language features suggests that language has some common root. Perhaps languages are alike in some ways because all humans are built in certain ways.

It might help, at this point, to think of the analogy of a computer. Not all computers are alike. Each is built in a particular way to be able to perform particular kinds of operations. Simple desk computers can add, subtract, multiply, divide, and perform other simple operations; more elaborate computers can perform these and many more complex operations. The computer is programmed to handle incoming information in a particular way. Because of the way it is constructed, it starts by sorting, or adding numbers or ideas in a specific fashion. Perhaps in a similar way the human child's brain is already programmed to handle incoming sounds in particular ways as well, just as the newborn baby is apparently programmed to respond to visual scenes in particular ways. The child's brain, after it has developed sufficiently (at about age 1), may be programmed to sort incoming vocal sounds into words, questions, negatives, action words, labels, and so on. In order for this language program to be activated, the child has to hear some language (as a desk computer, for example, has to be given numbers to add or subtract before it does any calculating), but once she starts listening to a language she may atuomatically analyze in certain ways. The child's early grammar may thus be the product of her first analysis of the language she's hearing. As she hears more and more, her analysis and subsequently her grammar become more and more complex.

What many linguists are now suggesting is that the inborn "program" focuses the child's attention on *transformations*. (Indeed some linguists have suggested that the inborn programming may generate language even if the child doesn't hear it, as you can see in Box 13.) All of what I reported to you about the development of *wh* questions, and indeed all the rule-governed aspects of children's early language, are consistent with this general notion. The child appears to go through a series of steps, with each stop involving the application of a particular rule. Gradually the child's rules become more sophisticated and more closely parallel to the adult's rules, and gradually the child comes to be able to apply those transformational rules two or three at a time, as in generating passive or negative questions.

Clearly, all of this is not yet a full theory of language development. Even the existence of an innate "language acquisition device" is still purely hypothetical. But the general notion that the child has inborn "language scanning strategies," and that what she learns over time is a series of transformational rules, seems to be consistent with what we observe in children's actual language development.

SUMMARY

1. Theories of language development are of interest because some of the central issues in the several major developmental theories can be highlighted by examining theories of language.

2. The first and most obvious theory is that language results from the child's imitation of adults. This theory is weak for a number of reasons, among them the fact that the child's language is creative from the beginning, that children do not imitate sentences wholly but "reduce" them, and that much of what the child hears is imperfect language.

3. A second alternative is that the child is shaped into language by some reinforcement pattern. Although reinforcement principles undoubtedly apply to some aspects of language—such as perhaps pronunciation—there is no good evidence that reinforcement is systematically applied to the child's grammar or that the child could learn grammar that way even if it were. Reinforcement theories also tend to ignore the rule-governed aspects of the child's early language.

4. A third alternative places emphasis on the child's ability to analyze adult speech and to extract rules from it. These rules are then believed to be copied in simplified form. No doubt some such copying takes place, but the complexity of such an analysis seems well beyond the abilities of the 1½-year-old child.

5. A fourth alternative, proposed recently by several psychologists and linguists, is that the child is born into the world already programmed to react to and analyze language input in particular ways. In particular, the child may have an inborn tendency to sort into and to learn rules for *transformations*.

6. No one of these alternatives is yet a full theory of language development; none accounts for all of what is observed, and none deals extensively with the development of word meaning. There is some agreement, however, that some kind of biological underpinning is involved in language learning.

REFERENCES

Suggested Additional Readings

Dale, P. S. *Language development: Structure and function* (2nd ed.). New York: Holt, Rinehart and Winston, 1976.
 By far the best single source for a more detailed exploration of the issues raised in this chapter. Particularly if you find the concepts of transformational grammar difficult, there is no better next source than Dale.

Lenneberg, E. H. *Biological foundations of language.* New York: Wiley, 1967.
 I hesitate to recommend this because it is so *very* difficult; but there are good discussions of the maturational timetables underlying language development.

Schlesinger, H. S., & Meadow, K. P. *Sound and sign.* Berkeley: University of California Press, 1972.
 If you are interested in language in the deaf and in the development of deaf children generally, there is no better first source than this book.

Slobin, D. I. Imitation and grammatical development in children. In N. S. Endler, L. R. Boulter, & H. Osser (Eds.), *Contemporary issues in developmental psychology.* New York: Holt, Rinehart and Winston, 1968.
 A fairly easy discussion of the role of imitation in early language development.

Other Sources Cited

Braine, M. D. S. On two types of models of the internalization of grammars. In D. I. Slobin (Ed.), *The ontogenesis of grammar.* New York: Academic Press, 1971.

Brown, R., Cazden, C., & Bellugi, U. The child's grammar from I to III. In J. P. Hill (Ed.), *Minnesota symposium on child psychology* (Vol. 2). Minneapolis: University of Minnesota Press, 1969.

Brown, R., & Hanlon, C. Derivational complexity and order of acquisition. In J. R. Hayes (Ed.), *Cognition and the development of language.* New York: Wiley, 1970.

Chomsky, N. *Syntactic structures.* The Hague: Mouton, 1957.

Chomsky, N. *Aspects of the theory of syntax.* Cambridge, Mass.: M.I.T. Press, 1965.

Goldin-Meadow, S., & Feldman, H. *The creation of a communication system: A study of deaf children of hearing parents.* Paper presented to the Society for Research in Child Development, Denver, April 1975.

Moerk, E. L. Verbal interactions between children and their mothers during the preschool years. *Developmental Psychology,* 1975, *11,* 788–794.

Nelson, K. Structure and strategy in learning to talk. *Monographs of the Society for Research in Child Development,* 1973, *38* (1–2, Whole No. 149).

Phillips, J. R. Syntax and vocabulary of mothers' speech to young children: Age and sex comparisons. *Child Development,* 1973, *44,* 182–185.

Skinner, B. F. *Verbal behavior.* New York: Appleton-Century-Crofts, 1957.

PROJECT 3
CONVERSATION BETWEEN MOTHER AND CHILD

Find a child between $2\frac{1}{2}$ and $3\frac{1}{2}$ and arrange to spend time with the child while the mother is around. If you are working in a nursery-school or day-care setting or have access to such a setting, it is all right to study a child and the teacher, but you'll have to get the teacher alone with the single child for a period of time.

Record the conversation between mother (or teacher) and child, making sure that you have the sentences of the two people in the right order. Continue to record the conversation until you have at least 25 sentences from each.

When you have collected the sentences, reread the sections on imitation and on the parents' role in the child's language development. See if you can detect any of the following patterns in your adult-child conversation:

1. **Expansions:** instances in which the adult repeats what the child has just said, expanding it into a complete adult grammatical sentence.
2. **Child's Imitations:** instances in which the child imitates what the adult has just said either exactly or with some kind of simplification so that her sentence is less complex than the adult's sentence.
3. **Reinforcement from the Adult:** responses by the adult to the *form* of the child's sentence.

Turn in your record of the conversation, along with a page or two of analysis and comment, focusing on the questions above. Supplementary reading for the project (if needed):

Slobin, D. I. Imitation and grammatical development in children. In N. S. Endler, L. R. Boulter & H. Osser (Eds.), *Contemporary issues in developmental psychology.* New York: Holt, Rinehart and Winston, 1968.

9

Cognitive Development I:
Development of Thinking

Daddy, please cut down this pine tree—it makes the wind. After you cut it
  down the weather will be nice and mother will let me go for a walk.
Mother, who was born first, you or I?
Mommy, the nettle bites me?
Well, in a way . . .
Then why doesn't it bark too?

These conversations with children are taken from Kornei Chukovsky's book *From Two to Five*. Chukovsky (a poet and not a psychologist at all) was struck by the delightful logic typical of a child from 2 to 5. Psychologists as well as poets have found the child's thinking delightful and fascinating—and puzzling. How does thinking arise in the very young baby? Where does the kind of logic that prompted the first quotation above come from and how does it change?

When we begin to look at the development of children's thinking, we have to examine three quite separate bodies of research and theoretical tradition, which do not mix very comfortably together. First, there is the whole testing movement. During the past 70 years extensive efforts have been made to devise and perfect measures of individual differences in intellectual skill. This particular aspect of the problem is important enough to have a separate chapter (see Chapter 10).

A second thread in the study of children's thinking is the literature on learning in children. The learning theorists, their students, and followers who have worked with children have emphasized that the processes of learning are the same, regardless of the age of the child or the particular task to be learned. Child psychologists who have been trained in this tradition have studied the whole gamut of developmental problems (personality, socialization, language, perception, and so on), in each case trying to demonstrate that a fundamental set of laws of learning could account for the child's acquisition of skills and traits in all areas of development. The heaviest emphasis in learning research, however, has been on a set of problems that would ordinarily be considered part of the problem of the development of thinking. There are extensive studies, for example, of the child's developing ability to make discriminations among objects that vary in color, shape, size, or whatever. Such research touches on perceptual development but also on conceptual development, for discrimination may be based on concepts, as well as on purely physical differences among objects. Still closer to the problem of thinking are studies of concept acquisition, of the learning of oddity problems, of the learning of the concept of intermediate size, and so on. In much of this learning research there has been no attempt to compare the performance of children of different ages, for it has been presumed that the same rules, or laws, apply to learning at any age. But increasingly this body of research has been cast in a developmental framework, and experimenters have begun to include children of several ages in the same study. And, increasingly, differences both in performance and apparently in strategy of learning have been found among age groups. It begins to seem inescapable that the same set of "laws of learning" cannot encompass the manner of learning of children of all ages. The way a 3-year-old tackles certain kinds of problems is different from the way a 7-year-old or a 12-year-old goes at it.

A third tradition, and the one that I will emphasize most heavily in this chapter, is that of Jean Piaget. His work has focused precisely on the question of the child's changing strategies and logic.

In order to explain just what it is that Piaget has contributed to the study of the development of cognition, let me go back to some of his own history. Although he was trained as a biologist, in his student days Piaget worked briefly on the development of some of the first mental tests. His job was to give a whole series of children the same test and to determine whether or not each child had given the "correct" answer on each item. But he soon discovered that it was not the correct answers but the wrong ones that were interesting. He noticed that children of the same age often gave the same wrong answers and that children of different ages gave different kinds of wrong answers. Piaget drew a number of important conclusions from these early observations:

We should be interested not in the quantity of what a child knows or in how many problems she can solve but in the quality of her thinking: her manner of solving problems, the kind of logic that she brings to bear, the way that she uses information, and so on. These qualities of thinking may be better revealed by the child's mistakes than by her correct answers.
Children of different ages may have different qualities of thinking; that is, they may have uniquely different ways of going about solving problems.

This apparently simple set of assumptions, with which most developmental psychologists would now agree, was fundamentally different from those that governed American child psychology during the 1930s, 1940s, and 1950s. Learning theorists assumed that the same rules, the same qualities, applied to all people, no matter what their ages. Classical conditioning was believed to operate in the same way for an infant or for an adult; the rules didn't change just because age changed. The testing movement, too, was based fundamentally on a measure of quantitative rather than qualitative difference. So Piaget's basic theoretical assumptions did not fit into our thinking until we had gone through the process of extensive experimentation with children of various ages and had begun to discover for ourselves that there are some differences in the way children of different ages approach the same problems.

Since approximately 1960 Piaget's ideas have exerted a major theoretical influence on developmental psychology in the United States. His views have been blended with other theories and extended, elaborated, and modified by other theorists. What has evolved is a series of basic theoretical understandings about the development of thinking in the child with which most (though not all) current theorists would agree.

THE BASIC
ASSUMPTIONS Let me try to extract those current basic assumptions in a simplified form.

1. Every child is born with certain strategies for interacting with the environment. We know that the normal newborn can see and hear. She can also touch, suck, lick, and grasp objects. I have already described some of Kessen's work on visual-scanning procedures in newborn infants, so you know that babies are apparently programmed at birth to explore sights in particular ways, and it's reasonable to assume that their exploration through touch and other senses may be subject to similar programming from the beginning.

2. These primitive strategies are really the beginning points for the development of thinking. The child interacts with the environment through the basic strategies, and the strategies change as a result of those encounters. A child grasps a square block and makes certain adjustments of her hand to the shape of the block. When the child is given a ball to grasp, the hand has to make a different adjustment. Slowly, the child's repertoire of coping skills improves, as, of course, does her body control.

3. Over a period of months and years the basic strategies become less and less automatic or reflexive and more and more subject to the child's voluntary control. The child explores things on purpose and experiments with new ways of exploring and manipulating. In this way each child, in some sense, rediscovers the wheel. Each child rediscovers that objects are constant, that they can be grouped and classified, that things can be added to and subtracted from, and so on.

4. These rediscoveries appear to occur in sequence. For example, a child can't discover the principles of adding and subtracting until she has figured out that objects are constant. Progress through this sequence of discoveries occurs slowly. At any one age the child has a particular view of the world, a particular logic for exploring and manipulating it. This basic logic changes as she encounters objects or events that don't fit into her system, but the change is slow and gradual.

5. The environment that the child grows up in does affect the rate with which she goes through the sequence. If she shifts from one set of strategies to another only when confronted with things that don't fit, then she will develop more slowly in an environment that doesn't encourage or require many accommodations. A child needs "food for thought," and some environmental diets are richer than others, just as are some food diets. Piaget calls the examination of environmental effects on the rate of development the "American question" and has himself been little interested in it. Yet it is an important question, particularly in any society in which there is inequality of opportunity. We need to know whether or not some features of the environment are particularly important for the child's cognitive progress. The data on this question are not extensive, but I'll report to you what we do know later in the chapter.

PIAGET'S TERMINOLOGY AND CONCEPTS

Before going on to describe the sequence of development Piaget proposes in some detail, I need to pause briefly to give you some exposure to the specific language and theoretical concepts Piaget uses. You will encounter these terms and concepts in other reading and need to have some familiarity with them.

Piaget calls his theory a theory of *genetic epistomology*. That is, he is concerned about the development of knowledge within the individual over her lifetime. How does the child come to "know" the world? How do ideas and concepts develop? In order to understand the sort of theory Piaget has suggested to explain the development of knowledge, you should understand that since he was trained as a biologist, he uses a kind of biological analogue for much of what he has to say about the development of thinking in man. Specifically, he suggests that in the functioning of man's intellect, as in biology, there are two invariant processes: *adaptation* and *organization*. It is the nature of human beings, Piaget says, to organize their experience and to adapt themselves to what they have experienced. Organization of experience includes integrating experiences from several senses, as when the baby combines looking and grasping or looking and sucking, and it includes the tendency to classify, to group into sets of systems, which we see in the older child. Adaptation, at its most basic level, is simply the process of adjusting to the environment. The chameleon adapts by changing color so that its body matches the environment it is in. When you eat breakfast, your body adapts to the food you have taken in by digesting it, by adding fat tissue, utilizing the vitamins and minerals, and so on.

The process of adaptation, however, is broken down in Piaget's theory into two further important aspects of functioning, which Piaget calls *assimilation* and *accommodation*. Assimilation is the process of taking in, of incorporating happenings and experiences into your existing strategies and systems. When you eat something the food is changed by your body into a form that it can manage: The stomach acid breaks it down so that it can pass into the body tissues in a usable form. The food has thus been assimilated. It has been taken in and changed to fit the existing capacities and structures of the body. Accommodation is the twin process, that of adapting the body (or the concept or idea) to conform to what has been taken in.

When a baby sees a block and reaches to grasp it, she is assimilating. She is taking in the experience and fitting it into a category or strategy she already has, in this case grasping and reaching. When she changes the way she holds her hand so that she can grasp a particular block, she is showing accommodation. When you read this page, you are assimilating the words to your already existing ideas. You are taking in the words, and you are categorizing them and relating them to ideas, concepts, and terms that you have already encountered. Your understanding of the words on the page depends on what you have already understood. If you have nothing to which to relate the words—no available concept or idea to which they can be connected—you can't assimilate them at all. They will "go over your head," to use the common phrase. But you do some accommodating, too, when you read these words. Your already existing ideas and concepts are changed because of what you have read, just as your body changes because of what you eat.

The essence of Piaget's ideas is that it is the nature of human functioning to organize and adapt, whether physically or mentally, biologically or intellectually.

There is one final concept with which you should have some familiarity, the concept of the *scheme* or *schema* (Piaget has used both spellings at different times). It was difficult to describe the baby assimilating the block without saying what she was assimilating it to. When you eat your body structures do the assimilating. A schema is the intellectual analogue of a bodily structure. The infant begins with a set of reflexive schemas such as sucking, looking, and hearing. Experiences are assimilated to those schemas, and the schemas change (accommodate) as a result of the experiences. In the infant, because there is no internal representation, all the schemas are actions: grasping, pulling, sucking, looking, crawling, and so on. They change, they become integrated, they become classified—but they are still actions. Later, when some kind of internal representation begins, the child's schemas may be representations of actions or concepts, but new experiences are assimilated to them, too, and they accommodate as a result of the experiences. In the child of about 7 a whole series of more complex schemas, which Piaget calls *operations*, are developed. These are complex mental actions, like adding, subtracting, classifying, ordering, and so forth. New experiences are assimilated to these more complex methods of analysis, and the child's methods of analysis in turn become more and more refined (accommodated) because of the encounters with new experiences.

THE SEQUENCE OF DEVELOPMENT

The emphasis in Piaget's theory and in most other theories of cognitive development (see, for example, the theories proposed by Bruner, Vygotsky, Kagan, Werner, and others) is on a gradual progression through a fixed sequence of skills and discoveries. The sequence, presented largely as Piaget sees it, is as follows.

198

From Birth to Age 2

Piaget calls the first two years the *sensorimotor stage*; Bruner calls it the *enactive stage*. Vygotsky, an important Russian psychologist, saw this period as the *prelanguage period*. There are different labels and descriptions, but nearly everyone agrees that this very early period is one during which the child's interactions with the environment are governed by overt actions, either sensory actions like seeing and hearing or physical actions like grasping, touching, reaching, sucking, and so on. At the beginning the baby does not "think" in the sense of planning or intending; rather, her explorations are governed by reflexes and by chance—someone puts a mobile over the crib and the baby swats at it.

In the thinking of an adult objects and events are mentally represented in some way. You have a word for an object and a mental picture of the object, and you can use that word and image in various ways. You can remember the object, compare it mentally with some other object, or figure out how to fix it—all in your head. During the sensorimotor period the baby can only begin to do these things in very primitive ways. Over the first 18 months of life, she gradually acquires some rudimentary internal representations, as demonstrated, for example, by her developing concept of object permanence, which I described in Chapter 6. But until about 18 months she does not have the ability to manipulate these images or representations in her head, to move them around in her mind, as it were, and examine them in new combinations. During the first 18 months her primary means of representing objects is not through internal images but through the actions she can perform on them. A ball is the feeling of grasping, the feeling of the texture of the ball on the tongue, the color seen by the eyes. Gradually, during the sensorimotor period internal images of objects develop as well. When language begins to be available words can be used as labels for objects, which provides a rich new form of representation for the child.

Through the period from birth to 2 years the child does progress slowly in various ways. Her earliest strategies change and become more intentional. Piaget suggests six substages, which are worth sketching briefly.

STAGE 1: BIRTH TO 1 MONTH

During the first month the baby is mostly restricted to the practice and perfection of the reflexes that she has at birth. According to Piaget, the child of any age does what she can do; she practices and exercises whatever kinds of interactions are possible to her. In the newborn the reflexes of sucking, looking, and so on are all that are available, so the baby practices and exercises them. But, of course, the baby does learn. For example, she learns how to search for the nipple—where to look for it, how to turn her head in order to get it into her mouth, and so on. She has adapted (or "accommodated," to use Piaget's term) her basic reflex to the demands of the situation in which she finds herself. And such first simple adaptations are the beginning of cognitive growth.

Suppose that by accident the baby makes something interesting or
pleasurable happen; for example, she accidentally gets her thumb in
her mouth. If you take her thumb out she may make attempts to put it
back in. This behavior is not a reflex. The baby does have sucking and
rooting reflexes that will cause her to turn her head toward a touch on
the cheek. But bringing her hand up to her mouth to put the thumb in
is not a reflex. So the baby, by about 1 month, is showing something
new. She is apparently trying to repeat an act that produced an interesting or pleasurable result, and she improves her technique as she goes
along.

It is also during this second substage that the baby's visual exploration begins to be more selective and more systematic (see Chapter 6).
She looks more at things that are moderately novel or discrepant, and
she scans entire objects, and not just their contours.

It is during the third stage that we see the beginning of what we might
call intention; the baby seems to set out to do things on purpose. As in
the second stage, though, the baby's actions may be initially prompted
by something accidental. If her thrashing arm happens to hit the mobile and the mobile moves, that's accidental. But what happens next is
apparently not. The baby of 4 months or so will now try to repeat the
event and will slowly learn how to control her arm movements enough
to make the mobile move on purpose. Notice that she has to have understood, at some level, that there was a connection between her
movement and the result—between her hand and the movement of the
mobile. That recognition is apparently not present in a younger baby,
but we do begin to see it in very rudimentary form at about 4 months.

Other important related discoveries occur during this same period.

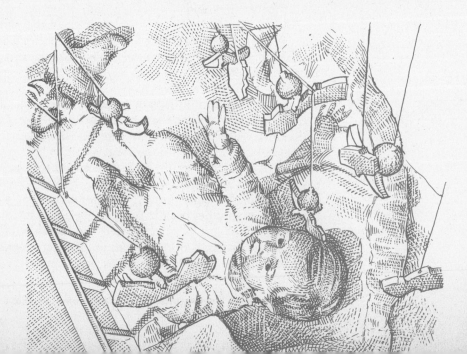

You know already that the development of the concept of permanent objects begins during these months. The baby will search for a missing object, for example, and she will anticipate the positions of objects to some degree. If I move a ball behind a screen on the left side of the child's vision, she will move her head or eyes to look for the ball's reappearance on the right side. She apparently recognizes both that the ball still exists behind the screen and that its movement will continue, which is quite an accomplishment.

STAGE 4: 10 TO 12 MONTHS

Something new and important happens at about 10 months. The baby figures out how to use old and familiar strategies in a new situation. According to Piaget, there is a clear intention on the baby's part to solve some kind of problem, and she invents, as it were, a strategy that will work. She no longer just responds to something that happened accidentally at first. Rather, the baby makes it happen. If you show her a familiar toy like a ball, she may reach for it. So far, she is just practicing an already learned skill. But now put your hand or a pillow in front of the ball. What happens? The baby may try to push the hand or the pillow aside in order to get to the ball. This event may seem simple, but it reflects an enormously significant advance: The baby is using one behavior in the service of another. Hitting the pillow aside is not the goal; getting the ball is. Hitting occurs only in order to reach the ball.

STAGE 5: 12 TO 18 MONTHS

Keep in mind that a baby in stage 5 is walking and exploring the world in a much more active manner and with a vastly greater range of possible experiences. What Piaget has observed during this period is the beginning of what may reasonably be called experimentation. The child seems to explore an object in a new way, experimenting, for example, with new ways of holding it or dropping it. A younger baby may have found pleasure in picking up and dropping the soap in her bath and may have become skilled at doing it. Now she may try to drop the soap from different heights, slide it along the edge of the tub, or other modifications. This experimentation opens up all sorts of new skills and strategies for her. The object concept is also fully developed during this period. If you show the baby an object, make it disappear, show it again in a new place, and so on, she will search for it where she saw it last, not where she had found it last.

STAGE 6: 18 MONTHS TO 2 YEARS

Finally, we come to the beginning of what we normally call thought, the beginning of the child's ability to manipulate her primitive representations in new ways. Piaget has made one wonderful observation of his own daughter, which suggests what may happen in the very beginning of this stage. At the time of this observation Piaget was playing with Lucienne and had hidden his watch chain inside an empty box. He describes what happened then.

BOX 14
Language and Thought

One of the classic, and as yet unresolved, arguments among theorists of cognitive development is about the role that language plays in the development of thought. We can't help but note that a major change in the child's thinking takes place at about the time that language is really taking hold. Are these two events related? If so, how? Is the child able to represent things internally because she has language? It seems a reasonable supposition. Adults use words as a major vehicle in their own internal representation, so it's sensible to extrapolate to the child and to assume that it is the advent of language that makes internal representation possible. But perhaps the reverse is true, that only with the development of the ability to represent things internally does language really make sense to the child. Another alternative is that the two have little or no relation to one another, that neither causes the other, but that both develop separately, at least in the early years.

Piaget has taken the general position that language is merely another reflection of thought, that the language the child uses can be only as abstract as her thinking is. Piaget points out, for example, that in a conservation experiment the child who is not yet able to conserve may say something like "This ball is wide; this ball is thin." The child who is able to conserve may

say, "This ball is wider but thinner." Both children know the words wide and thin, but they are using them differently in sentences. In the case of the conserving child they are used as comparatives.

It is also clear from the research on verbal mediation, which I will discuss later in this chapter, that the mere presence of particular words in the child's vocabulary does not mean that they will be used in complex learning or memory tasks. So at least language does not seem to be leading cognition by the hand, and cognitive advances do not have to be heralded by new advances in language.

An alternative position, propounded by Jerome Bruner and others, is that language and thought are essentially separate until about age 6 or 7, at which time they come together; the child then is able to use language as an aid in memory, problem solving, and analysis. Bruner argues that language acquires complexity at a very early age. The child of 3 or 4 is able to put together sentences with clauses and subordinate relationships long before she is even able to form consistent classes in a classification task. The child's language, almost from the beginning, operates with complex classification, but her thinking apparently does not. Bruner is so impressed with this disparity between the two do-

I put the chain back into the box and reduce the opening to 3 mm. It is understood that Lucienne is not aware of the functioning of the opening and closing of the match box and has not seen me prepare the experiment. She only possesses two preceding schemas (strategies): turning the box over in order to empty it of its contents, and sliding her fingers into the slit to make the chain come out. It is of course this last procedure that she tries first: she puts her finger inside and gropes to reach the chain, but fails completely. A pause follows during which Lucienne manifests a very curious reaction. . . .

She looks at the slit with great attention; then, several times in succession, she opens and shuts her mouth, at first slightly, then wider and wider! (Then) . . . Lucienne unhesitatingly puts her finger in the slit, and instead of trying as before to reach the chain, she pulls so as to enlarge the opening. She succeeds and grasps the chain. (Reprinted from *The Intelligence of Children*, pp. 337–338 by J. Piaget. By permission of International Universities Press, Inc. Copyright 1959.)

mains that he concludes that they must have quite separate roots, language having a primarily biological root and thinking a primarily experiential root. It is only at about age 6 or 7, when the child's thinking has, in some sense, caught up to her language, that she is able to use language effectively. The findings from verbal mediation research are consistent with Bruner's position as well. There is an age below which the child does not use language spontaneously in her problem solving, followed by an age in which she can be induced to do so but does not do so spontaneously, followed by an age at which language is used spontaneously in problem solving of various kinds.

Still others, like Vygotsky, have emphasized the important role that language may play in the development of internal representation at about age 2. Vygotsky sees the discovery that each thing has a name as a crucial instant in the child's developing intellect. And, of course, the child of this age does seem to use verbal labels to represent objects. The issue is whether the existence of language is necessary for the development of internal representation or whether the discovery that things have names comes because the child has already reached a level of internal representation.

A series of studies by Hans Furth and his associates on the development of thinking in the deaf, who have no oral language during the crucial period, seems to show very clearly that the child can and does develop internal representation without the aid of spoken language. Deaf children go on to develop classification skills and many operations as well, although they appear to lag somewhat behind their hearing peers. Whether or not deaf children have developed some system of abstract symbols other than spoken language we don't know, but they certainly can and do develop complex logical operations without language as we normally understand it.

Thus language, for the normal-hearing child, is an extremely useful tool, which may simplify many complex mental operations, but it appears not to be absolutely essential. And even in children who develop language naturally the existence of language does not lead automatically to the use of language in thinking. As Philip Dale puts it in his book on language, "Mastering the linguistic system is not the same thing as putting it to work. Language is not used for many functions—memory, classification, inner speech—until a point in development considerably later than the essential mastery of structure." (Dale, 1972, p. 235)

Try to see the really enormous discovery this child has made. Faced with a new situation, instead of going immediately to experimentation, to trial and error, she paused and appears to have discovered the solution through some kind of analysis. To be sure, she used her mouth to represent the box—she didn't do all the analysis inside her head—but this behavior is nevertheless the very beginning of the child's ability to manipulate and combine, to experiment and explore with images instead of real objects.

Some of you may be thinking that this transition to internal representation occurs at about this time because the child begins to develop language then. It may be that way, but then again it may not. Some of the arguments and positions on the relationship between language and thought are presented in Box 14.

I want to emphasize that the transitions from one stage to another during infancy are gradual. The baby doesn't suddenly wake up at age 1

month with a whole new set of skills. But, although the change is gradual, major new accomplishments are apparently acquired in sequence and at a fairly standard rate. This continuous progress is broken down into stages because they are helpful for description and because the child who is in the middle of one of the stages really is functioning qualitatively differently from a child in the middle of another stage.

From Age 2 to Age 6

Piaget calls this period the *preoperational stage;* Bruner calls it the *ikonic stage,* highlighting the importance of images (ikons) in the child's representation at this age. They agree, as do other theorists, that the really important feature of this period is the child's achievement of a rudimentary ability to represent objects and events to herself, but that such internal representation is still tied to specific events and not yet organized into complex systems. This period is, in many ways, a time of transition. The child has made it over the first enormous hurdle—she is able to represent things to herself—but there is a very long way yet to go.

It is perhaps easiest to describe the child's growth during the period from 2 to 6 years by dealing separately with a series of topics and describing the changes in each domain, rather than being entirely chronological.

THE DEVELOPMENT OF SYMBOLS

As I have emphasized, starting at about age 2 the child discovers the possibility of representing an action or object by some kind of internal symbol. At first, according to Piaget, these internal symbols may be a kind of abbreviated form of the action itself, like Lucienne's opening and closing of her mouth to represent opening and closing the box. Some visual imagery may also be involved, as Bruner has emphasized. The young child probably uses a mental picture of an object to represent it, rather than some more abstract kind of representation like a word or sentence. Words, too, may be used as symbols at this stage, however.

THE DEVELOPMENT OF REASONING

The child's reasoning, particularly during the early part of this stage, from about 2 to age 4, is heavily influenced by her own wants and desires. It's as if she sees the world through her own wishes and tries to reason her way around the obstacles. Piaget gives an example from the behavior of his daughter Jacqueline. Jacqueline, at age 2 years 10 months, wanted an orange. Piaget explained that the oranges were still green. A little later Jacqueline was drinking orange-colored camomile tea. She said: "Camomile isn't green, it's yellow already. . . . Give me some oranges." There is *some* logic here: She understands that the oranges need to be yellow to be ripe. But she has gone from the yellow of the tea to the expectation that therefore the oranges must be yellow also.

A related type of reasoning that occurs during this period is what Piaget calls *transductive reasoning.* The child reasons from the specific to the specific: Two things that happen together are taken to have some causal relationship. Piaget gives an example. Lucienne announced one afternoon when she had not taken her nap, "I haven't had my nap so it isn't afternoon." Afternoon and nap do usually go together, but she had the relationship between them wrong. The child Chukovsky observed (see the quote at the very beginning of this chapter) who thought that the wind would go away if you chopped down the tree was showing a kind of transductive logic. It is a kind of correlational logic, not altogether unlike what an adult does when concluding that because there is a correlation between two things, there must be a causal relationship. There is a correlation between smoking and prematurity; what most people do is to leap to the conclusion that smoking causes prematurity, just as the child concluded that the tree causes the wind. The difference, among others, is that although the adult may be in some sense caught by the apparent importance of the correlational relationship, she or he is capable of understanding other possible logical relationships, whereas the child of age 4 or 5 is not.

EGOCENTRISM

Piaget has suggested that one of the overriding characteristics of the child's thought during the preoperational period is a quality he calls *egocentrism.* He does *not* mean egotistical in the sense in which we usually use that word. The child is not preoccupied with herself, but rather she is *self-centered* in a very literal way. She is centered in herself and experiences everything in terms of herself.

In one of Piaget's early studies of egocentrism he showed children three toy mountains, three-dimensional, and of a size to fit on a table. The child could explore the mountains, look at them, and walk around them. Then with the child standing and looking at the mountains from a single perspective, Piaget placed a doll in different places around the mountains and asked the child to select a picture that would show how the mountains looked to the doll. That is, he asked the child to try to put herself in the place of the doll—to step out of her own perspective. Piaget and Inhelder's research on this, reported in their 1958 book on *The Child's Conception of Space,* showed that 4-year-olds were totally unaware that the doll would see the mountain differently than they did; 6-year-olds had some awareness that the doll saw it differently, but were unable to pick out the correct picture. Only at age 9 was there apparently a complete ability to take the doll's perspective.

Recent American research, however, seems to show that 3- to 5-year-old children are less egocentric than Piaget thought. It turns out that the task Piaget and Inhelder used was unusually difficult; if the task is made easier, the younger children show some ability to take another person's perspective. If the child is allowed to show her understanding by moving another three-dimensional scene on a turntable, rather than selecting a two-dimensional picture as Piaget has his subjects do, then 3- and 4-year-old children *can* select the perspective seen by another. (See, for example, the study by Borke in the References.) There is also some evidence that children in the preoperational period can identify other people's emotions from facial cues or from knowing the situation they are in. So a 4-year-old will say that another child is "happy" if she sees a picture of that child smiling or at a birthday party.

Once again, then, we find that we may have underestimated the child's cognitive abilities. At the same time we must be careful not to overgeneralize these early abilities. The preoperational child may be less egocentric than Piaget believed, but she is still quite a lot more egocentric than she will be later. So it is still true that one of the major threads running through cognitive development is a progressive *decentering,* a progressive ability to step farther and farther from one's own perspective or experiences. The decentering process continues throughout the lifespan. Adolescents still show some types of egocentrism, as do adults under some circumstances. But the overall movement is toward more and more decentering.

REVERSIBILITY   Another feature of thought in the preoperational child is the absence of the quality that Piaget calls *reversibility.* In your own thinking you are able to go both backward and forward. You can go back to the beginning of a chain of reasoning and go through it again to see where you went wrong; you can visualize undoing an action and can imagine what it would be like to be back at the beginning. But a young child apparently cannot do these things. Her reasoning moves forward only;

there is no reverse. If I pour water from a short, squat glass into a tall, thin glass, the 4-year-old sees that the level of the water is higher and is caught by that; she thinks that now there is more water. If the child could visualize or imagine the reversal of the process—the pouring of the water back into the short glass—she might be able to see that the amount of water hadn't changed.

The beginnings of reversibility are seen at about age 5 or 6, and the development of this ability is an important landmark in the child's development of reasoning.

CLASSIFICATION   Another reasoning skill present in only rudimentary form in the young preoperational child is the ability to classify—to put objects, events, or whatever into groups and to use those groups consistently. Most studies of children 2 to 5 years old show that 2-year-olds do little classifying (although see Box 15 for some counter evidence), but that classification skills develop rapidly and sequentially during the preoperational period.

The usual way of exploring the child's classification abilities is to give her a batch of blocks or paper cutouts of various sizes, shapes, and colors, and ask her to "put the things together that go together." This procedure is nicely illustrated in a recent study by Denney. She studied 2-, 3- and 4-year-old children, asking each to group a set of 32 cardboard figures, which included four different shapes, two different sizes and four different colors. The different sorts of groupings the children used are shown in Figure 24. You can see that some children merely make

BOX 15
Classification in Very Young Babies

Whether or not the child younger than age 2 has any kind of classification skills is still being debated. Piaget suggests that during the first year the child has something analogous to classification in the sense that she appears to respond to objects on the basis of what actions she can perform on them or with them, but he does not say that classification of the objects by function is in any way conscious at this age. The baby is not saying to herself, "Ah yes, there is something I can pull on." But, if the baby is shown something that can be pulled on, she may make small, pulling motions, as if she "recognizes" that the object is pullable.

Some recent research by Katherine Nelson, however, suggests that classification of some sort may begin very early. She found that children from 12 to 24 months of age did create groups of objects out of a total set, and that the function of the objects—what could be done

designs out of the material, while others group the cutouts in various ways. In order to analyze the responses of the children Denney divided the children's groupings into three types: (1) groupings that did not seem to be based on similarity at all, such as the designs, (2) groupings based on some kind of similarity, but in which only part of the objects were grouped, which she calls "incomplete similarity," and (3) groupings based on similarity in which *all* of the objects were grouped into one cluster or another, either along one dimension or two. Denney calls this latter category "complete similarity." Table 8 shows the percentage of children of each age who made one or another of these types of groupings. You can see the shift with age very clearly in these data. The 2-year-olds create far fewer groupings in which all the cutouts were organized along some dimension, and half of the 2-year-olds form no grouping based on similarity at all. But you should notice here that half of the 2-year-olds *do* form some kind of grouping, so there is at least rudimentary classification skill present as early as age 2 and quite well-developed classification skills among most children by age 4.

But even by age 4 or 5, the child's understanding of classification is not complete. The 5-year-old still has not developed what Piaget calls the concept of *class inclusion*.

Suppose the child puts all things with sharp corners together and then makes subgroups of triangles and squares. That sounds very advanced, and, of course, it is an enormous advance over the kind of classification the child showed only two or three years earlier. But Piaget has shown that the 5- or 6-year-old doesn't yet completely understand the relationships among the squares, triangles, and the larger class of "things with sharp corners." At that age she does not yet see that the two groups of squares and triangles are included in the larger class of things with sharp corners.

Piaget's classic example was an experiment in which children were

with them—was the most salient feature in classification. The children had an easier time, for example, grouping objects that differed in function (for example, four animals and four eating utensils) than grouping toys that differed only in size, color, or shape.

The fact that classifications before age 2 are apparently based on function is certainly consistent with Piaget's description of the sensorimotor period and with his insistence that objects during this period are defined by what can be done with them. But the fact that the child as young as 12 months is forming classes, or at least groups of some kind, is highly suggestive. It appears that the child forms these rudimentary classes before she has the word or label to attach to the group, and that the whole process of classification begins much earlier than we had supposed.

given a set of wooden beads, most of which were brown but a few of which were white. The children of ages 5 to 6 could apparently understand that all the beads were wooden and that some were white and some brown. But when asked, "Are there more brown beads or more wooden beads?" the 5-year-old child would say that there were more brown beads. The child hadn't really understood yet that the class of brown beads is included in the class of wooden beads and thus has to have fewer in it. Only at about age 7 or so does this important concept appear in the child's reasoning.

LEARNING TASKS FROM AGE 2 TO AGE 6

So far I have talked about the child's thinking during the preoperational period as Piaget has seen it, using his terminology and his illustrations. The description of this period would not be complete, however, without some exploration of the view of this same period to be found in the learning literature. As I have already pointed out, a whole series of tasks that touch on processes of reasoning and conceptualization has been extensively studied by researchers interested in children's learning. For most of these tasks developmental differences have been found: Younger children do not always respond to the tasks in the same way as do older children. Let me give some illustrations.

In an *oddity* learning problem the subject's task is to learn always to respond to the one of three stimuli that is different from the other two. Adults can learn this response easily, but young children have more difficulty. On complex problems only about 20 percent of 4-year-olds can learn to choose the odd one, about 50 percent of 6-year-olds can learn the concept, and virtually all 12-year-olds can learn it.

In a *reversal-nonreversal* learning task the subject is given two problems in sequence. In the classic sequence, originally adapted for research with children by Tracy and Howard Kendler (1962), the child

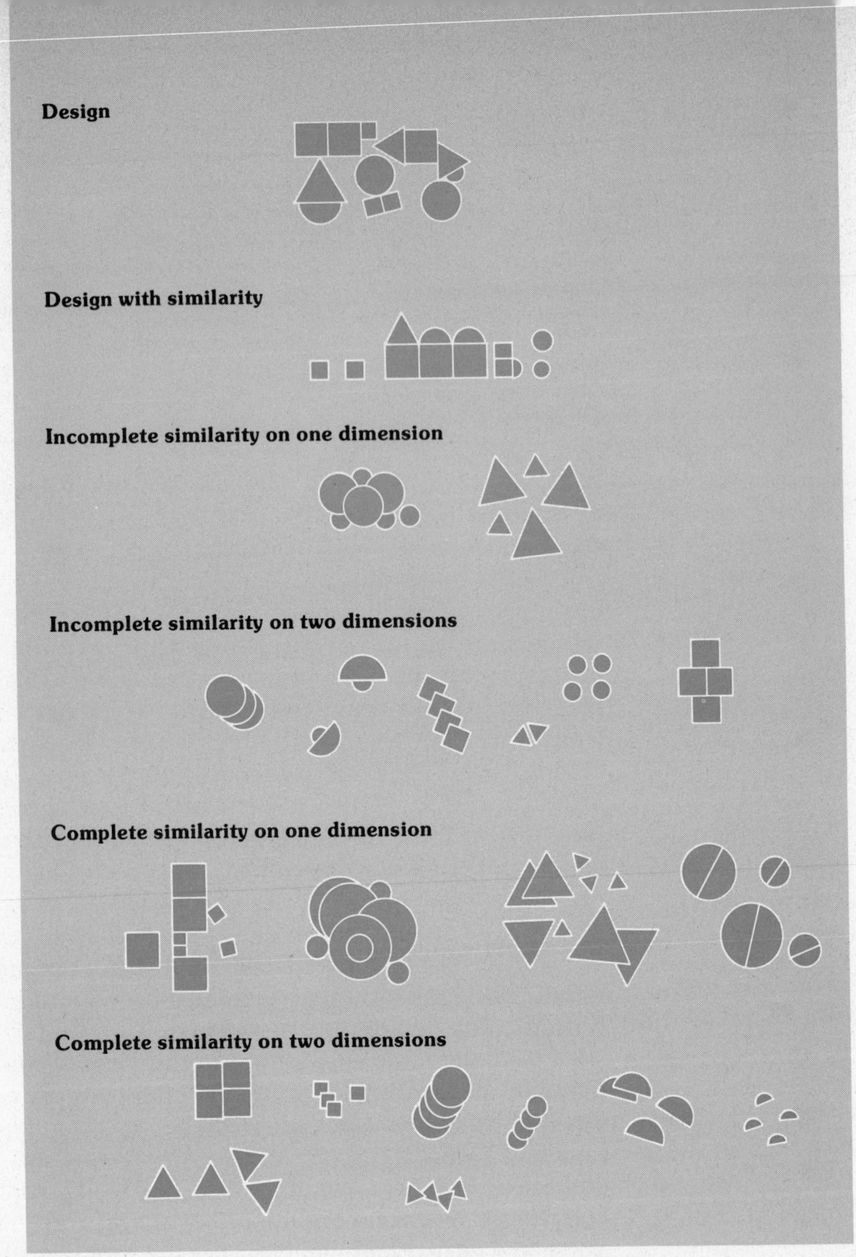

Design

Design with similarity

Incomplete similarity on one dimension

Incomplete similarity on two dimensions

Complete similarity on one dimension

Complete similarity on two dimensions

FIGURE 24
Schematic drawing of the different types of classification of geometric figures created by children 2 to 4 years old. (Source: Denney, N. W. Free classification in preschool children. *Child Development,* **1972,** *43,* **1161–1170.)**

TABLE 8
Percentage of Groupings of the No Similarity, Incomplete Similarity, and Complete Similarity Types on a Classification Task Among 2-, 3-, and 4-year-old Children

Category	Age of child		
	2	3	4
No similarity	50.0%	11.1%	11.1%
Incomplete similarity	44.5%	52.8%	25.0%
Complete similarity	5.5%	36.1%	63.9%

Source: Based on data in Denney, N. W. Free classification in preschool children. *Child Development* 1972, *43*, 1161–1170.

is shown a pair of pictures on each trial. For example, she might be shown the following pairs of pictures:

Pair 1   Pair 2

That is, on each trial, the child sees one of these two pairs and is told she should choose one picture. If she selects the right one she gets a reward, such as a marble. How is the child to go about this task? There are at least two strategies. First, she could simply learn which specific picture in each pair will pay off with a reward. Suppose, for example, that she is rewarded for the small black picture in pair one and for the large black picture in pair two. She might learn each of these separately, by trial and error. Alternatively, she may try to determine if there is some common feature to the correct choices. Perhaps the size of the picture is what she should pay attention to, or the color. In this instance color is correct, so the child could learn that black is always right, regardless of the size of the picture. Either of these procedures will lead to consistently correct choices on this part of the problem.

In order to find out which strategy the child has used, a second part is added to the procedure. In this part the same pairs are used, but now the payoffs are changed. Some children now get rewarded if they choose the *white* pictures instead of the black, while other children now get rewarded if they choose the *large* pictures. The switch to rewarding white pictures is called a *reversal shift*, since the same *dimension* (color) is still the right one to pay attention to, but the payoff has been reversed. The switch to rewarding large pictures is called a *nonreversal shift*, since the dimension has been changed. The child experiencing this shift has to change from paying attention to color to paying attention to size.

The Kendlers, and others who have used tasks similar to this one, have argued that the amount of trouble a child will have with the second half of this task will depend on which strategy she used on the first part. Suppose the child approached the task by learning each "correct" choice by rote. She learns to choose the small black picture in pair one and the large black picture in pair 2. When you now *reverse* these, so that white is now the correct dimension, both of the responses the child has learned are now wrong. But if you now present a nonreversal shift, only *one* of the original choices is now wrong. That is, in the nonreversal shift, the large white one is now correct in pair 1, but the large black one is still correct in pair two. So the rote-learning child only has to "unlearn" one of her original choices in the nonreversal shift. If all of this logic is correct then we might conclude that a child who has more difficulty with a reversal shift than with a nonreversal shift learned the original problem by learning the correct choice in each pair separately.

The task for the child who had learned originally by paying attention to the *dimensions* is somewhat different. If this child learned that color was the relevant dimension the first time, then when the correct choice is reversed so that white pictures are now correct, color is still the relevant dimension. With the nonreversal shift, however, this child must learn to ignore color and begin to pay attention to size. So we might expect that a child who has more difficulty with a nonreversal shift than with a reversal shift was paying attention to the dimensions, and not just to the specific stimuli.

When children of different ages are given problems of this kind, the usual finding is that 3- to 5-year-old children find the nonreversal problem easier than the reversal problem, which suggests that they were approaching the task by attending to the specific pictures in each pair. Older children ordinarily find the reversal problem easier, which suggests that they are approaching the task by paying attention to the dimensions. Although not every study shows precisely the same age effects, the overall results point to the possibility that there is a difference between the way the preoperational-aged child (2 to 6) and the older child approach learning tasks of this kind.

One of the suggestions made to explain the apparent change in performance from the 2- to 4-year-old to the 4- to 7-year-old is that the older child is somehow using language as a reminder or guide to her learning behavior, that language mediates the behavior of the older child. The Kendlers and others have suggested that the older child is able to perform the reversal shift more easily because she has put a label on the dimension—she thinks of it in terms of the verbal label of size, shape, or color. The younger child may not be able to use words in this way. John Flavell and others have suggested instead that whereas the young child knows words like *big* and *small* and can use them as mediators, she simply does not produce these words in learning situations in which they might be helpful to her. If you provide the 5-year-old child with the mediation words, she is able to use them.

At the moment the findings of the several research studies directly addressed to the question of changes in the role of verbal mediation with age suggest that there may be several stages. In the first stage, perhaps at about age 3, the child knows the words (*big, small, red, green,* and the like) but does not produce them in learning situations or on memory problems when they might be helpful as labels or memory aids. And if the words are suggested, the very young child does not or cannot use them as mediators. Somewhat later, perhaps at around age 5, although she still doesn't produce the mediating words spontaneously, she can and does use them when they are provided and when she is reminded that the words might be helpful. So, if you suggest to a 5-year-old that she might find it helpful in remembering a set of pictures if she named the pictures and then said the names over to herself while she was trying to remember them, her ability to remember the pictures will improve. But if you stop reminding her to name and to rehearse, she will stop doing so, and her memory for the pictures will decline. At about age 6 or 7 the third stage begins: The child spontaneously produces and uses words in memory or learning tasks.

If this description turns out to be valid, it may give us some clues to the changing relationships between language and thought (see Box 14), as well as underlining the important fact that while children of different ages may all be able to *solve* the same learning problems, they may go about it in quite different ways.

From Age 6 to Age 12

Virtually all theorists and researchers agree that there is a major change in the child's thinking and way of learning somewhere between ages 5 and 7. For Piaget this change marks the beginning of the period of *concrete operations;* Bruner calls the new period the *symbolic stage.* Both agree that the child is moving away from the specific to the more general. In addition, the child is able to go beyond mere internal representations and can begin to manipulate those representations in various ways.

Piaget calls the set of skills that the child begins to show at about age 6 concrete operations—mental actions of complex sorts, like addition, subtraction, classification, putting things in serial order, relating one thing to another, and so forth. All these operations are reversible. The child can not only add; she can also subtract and understands that subtracting is the reverse of adding. But at this age the operations are still concrete, still tied to particular experiences. She cannot yet think about thinking or imagine things she has not experienced.

Neither Piaget nor other theorists have broken down this period into substages. Piaget assumes that the child gradually acquires a whole range of new and complex skills over the five or six years of the concrete operations stage. The focus of interest in this particular period of time has been on a set of tasks that the 6- or 8-year-old can perform and that the younger child cannot. Let me touch on a few of these tasks.

CONSERVATION By far the most famous of Piaget's tasks is the problem of conservation. The classic experimental situation begins with two equal balls of clay. I ask the child to hold them and to feel them in any way that she wishes and ask her whether or not there is the "same amount" of clay in each. When she agrees that they are the same, we go on. As a next step, I change the shape of one ball into a pancake or a sausage shape. I again ask the child, pointing to each of the two shapes in turn, "Is there the same amount here as here or is there more here, or more here?" A child in the preoperational period will tell you that the amount of clay has changed. Usually she will say that the pancake has more because "It's bigger." The child in the concrete operational stage will say that they are still the same and may give any one of several reasons: "If you put it back into the ball, it would be the same" or "It's bigger around, but it's thinner, so it's the same" or "You haven't added any or taken any away, so it must be the same."

The fundamental principle is that certain properties of objects—their quantity, number, weight, and so on—stay the same, even when the shape or spatial arrangement is changed. The number of pennies in a row is not increased by spreading them out, the amount of water doesn't change when it is poured into a glass that's shaped differently, and so forth. But the preoperational child has not yet grasped this principle. Her attention is too much focused on one thing at a time. In the first part of the experiment she sees that the two balls of clay are the same, but she can't keep that fact in mind during the second part. She gets caught by the compelling sight of two differently shaped objects. It is only when she is able to step back from the immediate moment and take into consideration what has already happened and what can happen in the future that she begins to be able to conserve.

There has been a vast amount of research on conservation, not only to determine the age at which children typically acquire conservation, but also to discover just what kinds of experiences lead the child from nonconservation to conservation. The findings, in general, show that conservation of quantity and conservation of number are acquired first at about age 5 or 6. Conservation of weight comes later, at about age 8, and conservation of volume (the amount of space that each of the two balls of clay takes up is the same, regardless of shape) comes last, at about age 11 or 12, or later.

The extensive research on conservation has also underlined the fact that to teach a nonconserving child to conserve is not a straightforward

matter. One group of training studies has emphasized that what the child needs to do is learn to ignore the compelling but irrelevant cues in the situation, such as the shape of the ball or the shape of the glass into which water is poured. For example, Bruner and his associates used the sequence of presentations of a conservation problem shown in Figure 25. In this study, without the screening, none of the 4-year-olds showed conservation, but with the screening about half of them did.

FIGURE 25

Schematic drawing of the procedure used by Bruner in his study of the effects of screening on children's ability to conserve quantity. (Source: Adapted from Bruner, J. On the conservation of liquids. In J. S. Bruner, R. R. Olver, & P. M. Greenfield (Eds.). *Studies in cognitive growth.* **New York: Wiley, 1966.)**

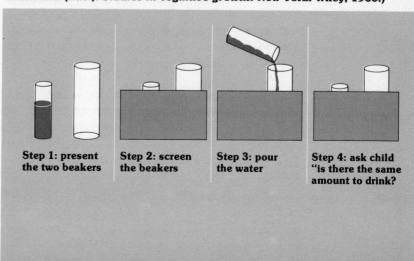

Step 1: present the two beakers

Step 2: screen the beakers

Step 3: pour the water

Step 4: ask child "is there the same amount to drink?

But when the screen was again removed and the child checked for conservation again, the 4-year-olds reverted back to nonconservation. The visual presence of the level of water in the beakers dominated. Five-year-olds in this same study, however, showed some improvement in conservation as a result of the screening. After the screening experience some of the children who had not conserved initially were able to maintain their conservation even with the beakers fully in sight.

Other researchers have also found that training the child to ignore irrelevant dimensions may help the child to acquire conservation. Piaget would agree that developing the ability to go beyond compelling perceptual cues is part of the important transition from preoperational to concrete operational thinking, but he also emphasizes that conservation is something "discovered" by the child as a unifying principle that brings sense to a whole series of experiences and that discovery of conservation is made possible in turn by the child's "discovery" of reversibility and similar principles. So Piaget would emphasize that acquiring conservation is more than just ignoring perceptual cues; it also requires some basic reorganization of the child's thinking. Some researchers have devised training procedures that confront the child with dilemmas that may trigger the discovery of some basic principles; this sort of training may also bring about a shift from nonconservation in some children.

The aim of most training studies is to discover what sorts of experiences are needed for the child to progress from one step in cognitive development to the next. The research has provided some suggestive answers. But one fundamental difficulty is that often the researchers do not have a very good assessment of where each child is at the start of the experiment. An experience that brings about conservation for a child who is just on the verge of acquiring it naturally may have no effect on the child who is further away from discovering the concept to begin with. We may find, then, that there is no single experience or kind of experience that is both necessary and sufficient for all children to achieve conservation (or any similar concept). The helpful experiences may vary from child to child. If so, the research problem is infinitely more difficult, for it requires a very fine-grained analysis of the child's status before the experiment begins, as well as ingenuity in devising experiences that can trigger the appropriate mental adaptation by the child.

SERIAL ORDERING AND TRANSITIVITY

Another task that the concrete operational child can perform that the child in the preoperational stage cannot is arranging objects in a serial order: a set of blocks by height, by shades of blue from pale to dark, by size, and so on. The younger child may be able to arrange three things in a serial order, but five or seven or eight things cannot be arranged in serial order until about age 6. Since numbers represent a serial order, it's clear that until the child understands about serial systems she won't understand or be able to use numbers either.

A related concept, which the child usually grasps during this same period, is the concept of transitivity. If Jane is taller than Sarah and Sarah is taller than Ann, then Jane is taller than Ann. Or, more generally, if X is greater than Y and Y is greater than Z, then X is greater than Z. Transitivity thus describes one of the relationships that exist within a serial order. Most children discover this property some time around age 7.

CLASS INCLUSION

I have already mentioned this concept in discussing classification in the preoperational child. The development of the notion of class inclusion in many ways marks the beginning of the concrete operational period. The child has begun to understand the relationships among classes of things, that some classes can be included in others, that a dog is both a dog and an animal, and that there are more animals than dogs. She has reached an important level of abstraction, which makes possible new kinds of reasoning.

MEMORY

A shift in the way the child approaches a memory task also occurs between the preoperational and concrete operational stages. I have already touched on this transition in discussing verbal mediation earlier in this chapter, but the transition deserves further emphasis.

Flavell and his several associates, and Hagen and his colleagues, have both focused a great deal of research attention on the development of memory strategies in children. How do children remember things? How do they recall lists, or what to get at the store, or where they last saw their favorite toy? Flavell has most often approached this task by giving children a set of pictures to remember in a particular order. There is usually then a period of delay, during which the child has to remember what she saw, and then the child has to reproduce the set of pictures in the right order. The experimenter observes and listens to see if there are any signs of the child's mnemonic strategies. Does the child rehearse the order of pictures out loud? Does she mutter them to herself? Flavell's research shows that in children below age 6, there appears to be a *production deficiency*. That is, the child does not spontaneously use rehearsal or other mnenomic procedures. But 4 to 5-year-olds will use rehearsal if you suggest this strategy to them. So they have the *ability* to rehearse, but they do not do so spontaneously. Six- to 7-year-olds often show spontaneous rehearsal, although they are not terribly efficient at it, and by 9 or 10, most children use rehearsal efficiently and more silently. Among adults the rehearsal is usually entirely silent, entirely "in the head."

But the ability to use mnemonic devices such as rehearsal is not all there is to the shifts in memory ability. As the task gets more complex, simple rehearsal may not be enough to help you remember something.

BOX 16
Bruner and Kenney's Experiment

An experiment by Jerome Bruner and Helen Kenney offers a particularly good illustration of some of the changes that take place around age 6 or 7 in both memory and general conceptual level. The materials for their experiment consisted of a set of nine beakers, which varied in width and height, as you can see in the figure.

Children aged 3, 4, 5, 6, and 7 were asked to do three different things with the set of beakers. First, a child was asked to replace individual beakers that had been removed. As the child watched, the experimenter would take one beaker away and then ask her to put it back where it had been. The replacement task was then made harder by removal of two beakers and finally by removal of the three beakers on one of the diagonals. Note that this task can be performed without attention to both height and width; the child can replace any single beaker, any pair of beakers, or the beakers on the diagonal by using either the height or the width, but she needn't look at both.

Next, the child was asked to reproduce the whole array. The whole set of beakers was scrambled, and she was asked to "make something like what was there before." This task is obviously much more difficult, for the child has to pay attention to both height and width to do it. Of course, this task can be accomplished successfully if the child has a good mental image of the set of beakers. Then she needn't have figured out that the beakers vary in height and width; she can follow a picture in her mind and reproduce it in that way.

Finally, the child was asked to transpose the matrix of beakers. The beakers were again scrambled, but this time the shortest, thinnest one was placed on the other side of the front row, and the child was asked to make something like what was there before, leaving the one beaker where it had just been put. In order to do this the child had to have understood and remembered the basic principle that underlay the matrix, namely, that it was arranged systematically by height and width. If the child understands this principle, then she can begin with the short, thin one in any corner and can reproduce a matrix that has the same basic features as the original: the glasses becoming wider in one direction and taller in the other.

We would expect that the youngest children should be able to do the replacement task. The 4- and 5-year-olds ought to be able to reproduce the array, for their skills at visual imagery are up

If you have a list of 30 things to get at the store, you will need to organize the list into some kind of system or create categories that will help you recall. The sort of conceptual scheme the child can come up with is going to be heavily dependent on the child's general level of cognitive accomplishment. This interaction between the conceptual level and memory is illustrated very nicely, I think, by the experiment by Bruner and Kenney described in Box 16.

Flavell has also explored the development of something he calls *metamemory* (see the paper by Kreutzer, Leonard, & Flavell in the References). Metamemory refers to the child's *awareness* of her own memory processes. A child may be able to remember a list of pictures or words fairly well, but not be able to tell you how she went about it. To find out if there was any kind of age change in the child's awareness of her memory strategies, Kreutzer and her colleagues asked kindergarten, first-, third- and fifth-grade children a series of questions about how they would remember various things. For example, the experimenters showed the child a row of 20 pictures and said,

to that kind of task. But the preoperational child should not be able to do the transposition task, for it requires a level of abstraction not yet available to her. To do the transpositional task, the child must be able to step beyond the specific array that she sees and to grasp the abstract properties of the array.

The results of the experiment confirm this prediction. The 3- and 4-year-old had trouble with all the tasks, although a few could do the replacement task. The 5-year-olds could do the replacement task, and many could do the reproduction task, but none could do the transposition. Among 6-year-olds about 25 percent could do the transposition task, and among 7-year-olds about 80 percent were able to do it. Bruner and Kenney summarize these findings as follows:

Younger children tend to be strongly guided by the perceptual nature of the tasks, and by only a single perceptual feature at a time. As they grow older, they seem no less perceptual in their approach to our tasks, but they are now able to deal with several features of a task at once. But while (at age six, for example) they can reproduce complex perceptual displays, they are poorly equipped to do tasks that require a translation of a perceptual array into a verbal formulation of a more general type. (Bruner & Kenney, 1966, p. 163)

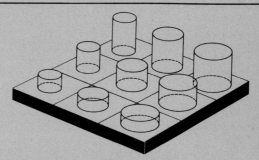

The array of nine beakers used in the Bruner and Kenney experiment. Source: Adapted from Bruner, J. S., & Kenney, J. J. On multiple ordering. In J. S. Bruner, R. R. Olver, & P. M. Greenfield (Eds.), *Studies in cognitive growth*. New York: Wiley, 1966.)

The other day I asked two children to look at and learn some pictures because I wanted to see how well they could remember. I asked them how much time they would like to learn the pictures before I would take them away and ask them how many they could remember. One child said 1 minute. The other child said a longer time, 5 minutes. (1) Why do you think he wanted as long as 5 minutes? (2) Which child remembered the most, the one who studied 1 minute, or the one who studied 5 minutes? (3) Why? (4) And what would you do, study 5 minutes or 1 minute? (5) Why? (Kreutzer, Leonard & Flavell, 1975, p. 18. © Society for Research in Child Development.)

Virtually all of the children in first grade or older said that more could be remembered with five minutes, and most of these children explained this by referring to the very large number of pictures to be remembered. They indicated that it would take a certain amount of time to recall each picture, and that one minute was not enough. Among the kindergartners three-quarters correctly said that five minutes study would produce better performance, but they did not do very well at explaining why. Still, the kindergartners in this study did display quite considerable awareness of the sorts of things that would be hard to remember, and they had some strategies for trying to recall things. But most often, these youngest children would resort to *external* aides in recall—writing a phone number down, or asking their mother to remind them of something. Older children, when asked how they would go about remembering, more often describe *internal* strategies, such as rehearsal. The older children were also more planful in their approach to the hypothetical memory problems.

From Age 12 On

Piaget has emphasized that the level of concrete operations is not the end of development. He suggests another major shift at about age 11 or 12, approximately at the beginning of puberty. Piaget calls this new period *formal operations,* to distinguish it from that of concrete operations. The concrete operational child can perform complex mental operations, but only with experiences or objects she has had or seen. She is not yet able to go beyond the observable or the observed, beyond the actual to the possible. The difference is nicely illustrated in a task devised by Mosher and Hornsby, which involves the game of Twenty Questions. In their first task they used a set of 42 pictures of animals, people, toys, machines, and so forth. Each child was told that the experimenter was thinking of one of the pictures and that she was to figure out which one by asking questions that could be answered "Yes" or "No." Many of you have played this kind of game before and already know that there are several ways to go about it. One way, especially with a set of pictures, is simply to start at one end of a row and ask, "Is it this one?" about each in turn until you hit the right one. Another way is first to classify the pictures into groups, hopefully hierarchically. You notice that there are red and blue toys. You can start by asking, "Is it a toy?" If the answer is "Yes," then you might ask whether or not it is a red toy and so on. If the answer is, "No, it's not a toy," then you go on and ask about other kinds of categories.

Six-year-olds, who ordinarily do not yet have the ability to classify hierarchically, do not ask questions like, "Is it a toy?" They use almost entirely the first kind of strategy, going from one picture to another, often in an apparently random order, hoping to guess the right one. Eight-year-olds, on the other hand, do fairly well at narrowing down the possibilities through a series of more general questions, as do 11-year-olds.

To make the problem more difficult, in a second task, instead of using pictures, Mosher and Hornsby used a story. The child was told, "A man is driving down the road in his car, the car goes off the road and hits a tree. Find out what happened." To approach this task systematically, the child has to be able to imagine all the possible reasons for such an accident, and then to organize those possibilities into categories, such as weather, illness, or auto breakdowns. It is precisely this ability to imagine and organize unseen or unexperienced possibilities that the concrete child does not yet have, so she reverts to guessing, such as, "Was the man stung on the eye by a bee?" On the other hand, the 11-year-olds, who are just beginning formal operations, can begin to think up all the possibilities and organize them into some kind of system. They ask whether the accident had anything to do with the weather, a malfunction of the car, or the man himself.

The 8-year-old thus has the ability to classify, and to classify fairly complex things—but only if the things have been experienced. The 11- or 12-year-old can imagine and then organize the possibilities.

Another feature of the child in the formal operations period is the ability to search systematically for an answer to a problem. The 8- or 9-year-old may cast about rather haphazardly, whereas the older child thinks through the possibilities and tries them out in an order that will be helpful.

Piaget and Inhelder explored this type of systematic search with a task that has since been used by quite a number of researchers—the pendulum problem. The child is given a long-ish string and a series of weights, or objects or varying weights, that can be attached to the string. She is shown how to hold the string at various distances from the weight, how to swing the object on the end of the string starting from various heights, and how to push the object with differing strengths at the beginning of the swing. The child's task is to discover which of these four factors—the length of the string, the weight of the object on the string, the height from which the swing starts, and the amount of push—singly or together affect the rate at which the pendulum swings. (Those of you who have forgotten your physics might try this experiment yourself!) Piaget, as usual, was far less interested in whether the child arrived at the correct answer than in how the child went about trying to solve the problem.

Concrete operational children, when presented with this task, design very inefficient experiments. For example, they may try a heavy object on a short string and then a light object on a long string. They have thus confounded two of the dimensions and cannot possibly draw accurate conclusions. Children of this age *do* sometimes come to the correct solution, but only after fairly random or unsystematic attacks on the problem.

But adolescents approach the problem differently. They apparently recognize that the only way to solve the problem is to vary only one of the factors at a time. So a 12- to 15-year-old may try a heavy object with a short string, with a medium string, and with a long string, and then a light object with the same three string lengths. Of course, not all adolescents (and not all adults) approach this task in a perfectly organized and systematic way, but there is a very sharp difference in the overall strategy between the formal operations and concrete operational child.

Another facet of the change from concrete to formal operations is the shift from *inductive* to *deductive* logic. The concrete operational child can go from the particular to the general—she can eventually arrive at general principles, based on a lot of individual experiences. But only at formal operations is the child able to go from the general to the particular. The 11- or 12-year-old can understand *if-then* relationships: "If all men are equal, then you and I must be equal." Much of scientific logic is deductive. We begin with a theory and propose, "If this theory is correct, then I should observe such and such." In doing this we are going well beyond our observations. We are conceiving things that we have never seen but that *ought* to be true or observable. Clearly this is a next step in the decentering process Piaget talks about. Now the child can be largely free not only of her own narrow perspective, but of her reliance on specific experience as well. Now she can imagine things never seen and draw inferences from general principles.

One of the particularly interesting things about the formal operations stage is that not everyone reaches it at all. Unlike the preceeding stages, which seem to occur widely in many cultures, formal operations is achieved by only about half or two-thirds of the people in our culture, and by far fewer in less complex cultures. I think that most researchers and theorists agree that there *is* a stage after concrete operations, and that formal operations as Piaget has described it is at least an approximate description of that stage, but it is not clear why everyone does not master this final stage. The most likely explanation is that formal operations, like all the earlier stages, is only achieved when the child is somehow "forced" to accommodate earlier, less complex, logical systems. And if the child exists in an environment in which concrete operations are sufficient, then there is no need for more advanced logical forms.

Cross-Cultural Studies of Piaget's Stages

If the specific environment affects the accomplishment of formal operations, then perhaps major environmental variations would affect the rate or even the sequence of development of the earlier stages. Put another way, how universal are the basic stages of cognitive development as Piaget has described them? How much do major cultural variations affect the developmental pattern?

Questions of this sort have led a number of investigators to study cognitive development among children being reared in widely different cultural environments. As you might imagine, the technical problems involved in such research are immense. How do you translate Piagetian tasks into native languages? How do you make the instructions understandable to the child? Do you modify and use only materials familiar to the child in her own culture? If you make changes of this sort, how do you then compare the results across cultures? In view of these difficulties it is hard to be very confident about conclusions, but a few general findings seem to stand up.

First, the general order of the stages seems to be roughly as Piaget described it. The concrete operations skills do develop later than the preoperational skills, and formal operational abilities—if they develop at all—come later than concrete operations. There are some indications of reversals of order *within* a given stage; in some cultures, for example, children seem to learn conservation of weight before conservation of mass. But the overall order seems to be about right.

Second, the rate at which the child progresses and the final stage achieved is affected by cultural variables, including schooling. In cultures in which children do not attend any kind of school, some of the more complex cognitive skills are far less likely to develop. Cole and his associates, for example, conclude that schooling is critical in "learning to learn."

In school the child is most often talking about things that are not present, about *classes* of things rather than particular objects. So schooling forces the child to deal at a higher level of abstraction. The child learns to generalize from one problem to another that is like it. Without schooling, this level of abstraction, of generalization from one problem to the next, is less likely to develop. In Piaget's terms what this means is that the development of some aspects of concrete operations, and most of formal operations, is probably dependent to some extent on the kinds of experiences children have in school.

Overview of the Stages

Think back to where all this development started—with the newborn baby who has a repertoire of reflexes and some basic perceptual skills. In only about 11 years the child has reached the point of being able to perform complex logical operations, to think about thinking, to imagine things that she has never seen. That's a long way in a comparatively short time. The progress seems to be steady, but there are some major accomplishments along the way that mark off convenient stages. The development of internal representation is one of the milestones; the development of the concepts of classification and reversibility are others, as is the freeing of oneself from the confines of concrete experience.

The general outlines of this series of changes are not much disputed. The reasons for development in this pattern are still argued rather heatedly. Does the child progress in this way, as Piaget has suggested, because of her explorations and manipulations of the environment, which prompt new discoveries, new understandings? Or is the child taught these concepts in some way? Is there a change in the child's thinking at ages 5 to 7 because that's when she goes to school and encounters all sorts of new ideas and new teachings? Or have we arranged things so that she begins school at ages 5 to 7 because we recognize that children's thinking changes markedly at those ages and that only then are they ready for school? It's a difficult set of questions, one that theorists and researchers will be a long time in answering.

SOME PROBLEMS WITH PIAGET'S THEORY

I have used Piaget's theory and his description of the progress of cognitive development as the basis for most of the discussion in this chapter partly because his theory is by *far* the most influential one in this area, and partly because so much of what Piaget has said has been validated by others' research. But I don't want to leave you with the impression that there are no difficulties with or challenges to Piaget's view of the world. As you might imagine, there are extensive (and sometimes abstruse) theoretical arguments about some of Piaget's basic premises, as well as about his description of specific sequences. There is certainly no room to go into most of the arguments here, but I do want to point at least briefly to a few puzzles and difficulties.

1. Not all children develop at the same rate. In fact, of course, there is nothing in Piaget's theory that says they must, only that the *sequence* should be the same. But Piaget has had little to say about the possible reasons for differences in rates of development. For American researchers this is often the critical question, so there has been some dissatisfaction with Piaget's theory because it offers us so little in this

area. (I'll be discussing some of the American research on this question in the next section.)

2.   Children don't seem to be at a given "stage" on every task or in every situation. Piaget's theory seems to suggest that a child should be at least somewhat consistent in her approach to different tasks or problems at a given age. If the child's approach to a problem arises from her overall level of logical development, then the 7-year-old should go at a whole series of problems or tasks in the same general way, demonstrating the same level of logic in each. There has been relatively little research exploring the generality of strategy at a given age, but what little there is does *not* seem to point to very much consistency in the child's approach to sets of apparently similar problems. For example, Uzgeris explored this set of issues in a group of infants and found that each individual sequence, such as the development of the object concept, occurred in pretty much the order Piaget had described. But an individual child's achievement of this sequence was *not* very strongly related to other contemporaneous sequences (such as the sequences for the development of means-ends understandings). So it doesn't look like a child is consistently "at a stage" in all respects. Others have found similar lack of generality among older children (see Achenbach & Weisz, 1975). What Uzgiris has suggested is that there may be stretches of time in which the child is achieving new understandings in each of a series of areas or tasks, but that there are then periods of consolidation, when many of the threads are brought together and coordinated into a more unified, new, logical system. This appears to occur at the *end* of each of Piaget's major stages. So at the end of the perceptual motor period, there is fairly good generality from task to task. But then in the early years of the preoperational period, the child is again functioning at quite different levels on different tasks. Quite obviously we need to know a great deal more about the *overall* functioning of children at different points in development if we are to be able to refine Piaget's theory properly.

3.   Some of the ages Piaget proposes seem to be wrong. You should keep clearly in mind that Piaget has *always* defined the several stages with broad age ranges. He has never suggested that everyone reaches these stages at the same time. But there is quite a lot of recent research suggesting that even Piaget may have underestimated children, and that many of the ages he suggests are too old. As research techniques have been refined, researchers have found younger and younger children showing evidences of more complex cognitive accomplishments. The research on egocentrism in preoperational children, which I discussed earlier in this chapter, is a good example of this. Oddly enough, Piaget may have been wrong in the other direction in the case of formal operations. Here it looks as if his suggested ages are too young. Most American researchers have *not* found 11- to 12-year-old children showing much sign of formal operations.

These brief looks at some of the problems should alert you to the fact that Piaget's theory should not be viewed as immutable. It is in a state of constant revision, by both Piaget and other theorists. But the general outline of his view has been widely accepted.

THE EFFECTS OF ENVIRONMENT ON THE DEVELOPMENT OF THINKING

I have already pointed out that schooling seems to make some difference in the cognitive level a child eventually achieves. But among children going to school, there are quite wide variations in the rate of progress through the stages Piaget describes. What might account for these differences in rate? Obviously there may be genetic differences, but setting this possibility aside for the moment, what kind of environmental variations might make a difference? This question has been approached in at least two ways. A number of researchers have compared children from different social class groups on standard Piagetian tasks. Other researchers have focused more on the specific quality or quantity of interaction between the child and the parents as a source of variation in the child's rate of development. Let me explore each of these.

Social Class Differences in Performance on Piagetian Tasks

The rate of development during the sensorimotor period does *not* appear to differ among poor versus middle-class children. This should not be surprising in view of everything I have already pointed out about the lack of social class differences in either motor or perceptual development. Wachs, Uzgiris and Hunt, as well as Golden and Birns, have found essentially no differences among children as a function of social class level up to about the beginning of the preoperational period. There *is* some indication that infants from poverty level families are more difficult to test; it is harder to get them to display their best performance. But when the experimenter is persistent, he or she can elicit good performance from the subjects, regardless of family background.

The picture is different among older children. The consistent finding among older subjects is that children from poor families perform at a developmentally lower level than do children from middle-class families. For example, Gaudia found that poor children were slower in developing concepts of conservation; other researchers (including Wei, Lavatelli, & Jones) have found poor children to be slower in the development of classification skills as well. These lower performances could be the result of the poor child's greater discomfort in the testing situation (a possibility I will be discussing more fully in the next chapter) or of other conditions of testing, or they could reflect a genuinely slower rate of cognitive growth.

Family Variables Affecting Children's Performance

Much more interesting are those few studies in which the researcher has tried to examine the specific kinds of experiences available to the child and the effect they might have on the child's cognitive progress.

One of the best studies of this type has been carried out by Leon Yarrow and his colleagues. They made lengthy observations of

226

mother-child interactions in the home and then tested the child on a Piaget-based test. The home observations were first made when the children were 6 months old; additional observations and testing were done when the children were 18 months old.

At 6 months Yarrow found that both the amount of social stimulation the baby experienced (being talked to, picked up, cuddled, moved around, carried, and the like) and the amount of inanimate stimulation provided (number and variety of toys and other objects) made a difference, but in somewhat different ways. Six-month-old babies whose mothers talked to them a lot and gave them lots of physical stimulation, holding, and cuddling showed faster development in several areas. Their language was somewhat more advanced, and they showed more goal directedness and more object permanence than did babies who experienced less social contact. Babies who received lots of inanimate stimulation (lots of varied and complex toys) were somewhat faster in motor development, explored more (looking at and manipulating new things), were more goal-directed, and exhibited more reaching and grasping and more "trying to make good things happen again," which Piaget describes as an important part of stage 2 in infant development.

At 18 months, when the mothers and children were again observed, Yarrow found that what the mother had been doing with the child at 6 months was still predictive of the child's behavior at 18 months. Mothers who had used a lot of social stimulation, and whose behavior toward the infant had been highly contingent on what the infant did, had 18-month-old children who explored their environment more extensively and vigorously.

Several other investigators (including Clarke-Stewart and Burton White) have approached this problem by identifying children who seem overall to have high levels of *competence*. Competence is conceived of as including not only the kinds of cognitive skills Piaget discusses, but also language ability and skills in relating to adults and peers. Differences in competence among children emerge quite clearly during the second year of life and become more pronounced thereafter. Compared to mothers of less competent children, mothers of competent children seem to do several things: provide richer language stimulation, provide more *contingent* stimulation—that is, they gear their behavior toward the child's requests, needs, or behavior—encourage and provide opportunity for exploration, and provide affection and warmth to their children.

These several findings suggest a number of conclusions. First, we must stop thinking very grossly about stimulating or unstimulating environments. At the very least we have to think about environments that are socially stimulating and those that provide a lot of object stimulation, for the results seem to be somewhat different. Second, these findings do point to the possibility that very specific aspects of the child's early experiences may either help or hinder her development —a finding that is at least consistent with what Piaget has said. But let me caution you about going too far with information of this kind. All of these studies are entirely correlational. (Recall all my earlier cautions about correlational research.) They point to a set of relationships between the baby's degree of development and the baby's environment. But we can't conclude that the environment caused the baby's development. It could be that more rapidly developing babies call forth more responses from their parents, so that they talk to the babies more, provide more toys, and so on. More likely there is an interaction between what the baby and the parent bring to the relationship. Still, research like Yarrow's, White's, or Clarke-Stewart's seems to me to be an enormous advance over mere comparisons of groups of poor and middle-class children. We are beginning to get some sense of the sort of early experiences that may stimulate or retard intellectual growth.

SEX DIFFERENCES IN COGNITIVE DEVELOPMENT

Most of the research on sex differences in cognition has been based on measurements on standardized IQ or achievement texts, and I will deal with that sort of evidence in Chapter 10. Comparisons of males and females on tests or tasks based on Piagetian theory are scarcer, but the findings are quite easy to report. There is essentially *no* evidence showing that either sex is consistently faster in development of preoperational, concrete operational, or formal operational skills.

SUMMARY

1. Three groups of researchers and theorists have been concerned with the development of thinking: those devising intelligence tests, those interested in children's learning, and the cognitive-developmental theorists, who have focused on systematic and sequential changes in the child's logic in the course of development.
2. Most current researchers working in the area of cognitive development would agree on a set of basic assumptions that emphasize the child's active role in development and the sequential changes in her strategies for interacting with her environment.
3. The sequence of development, which appears in general outline to be the same for all children, can be broken down into four periods.
   a. From birth to 2 years, the "sensorimotor period" in Piaget's terminology, is marked by gradual movement from reflexive to intentional behavior and from absence of internal representation to the beginnings of such representation.
   b. From age 2 to age 5 or 6, the period that Piaget calls preoperational, is a period of transition in which the child's thinking gradually becomes less egocentric, reasoning is less tied to specific experience, and ability to classify concepts and objects gradually becomes more complete.
   c. From ages 5 to 6 to age 11, the period that Piaget calls concrete operations, the child becomes able to make complex classifications and to perform various operations like addition, subtraction, and seriation on sets of objects or experiences. In this period she is still tied to actual experiences or objects, however, and is not yet able to perform operations on possibilities or potentials.

d. From age 11 or 12 onward, the period that Piaget calls formal operations, is the time when the child becomes capable of deductive as well as inductive logic and becomes more systematic in her exploration and search. She is able to think about thinking.

4. Over the same period there are changes in the child's observed approach to classical learning problems of various kinds, including reversal-learning problems, oddity problems, and other tasks apparently requiring verbal mediation.

5. Some recent research has focused on the effects of environmental variation on the rate with which the child progresses through the sequence. In children over 3 years of age there is evidence that middle-class children are a year or two more advanced than are children from poverty environments, although similar differences among infants have not been consistently found.

6. More detailed analyses of mother-infant interactions suggest that some very specific aspects of early stimulation, such as the variety and complexity of toys and the amount that the child is talked to or stimulated, may hasten or retard the child's rate of early mental development.

7. No sex differences in rate of progress through these stages have been consistently found.

REFERENCES

Suggested Additional Readings

Bruner, J. S., Olver, R. R., & Greenfield, P. M. (Eds.). *Studies in cognitive growth.* New York: Wiley, 1966.
A fascinating book, although very tough going in some parts; in the first two chapters Bruner presents his own theory of cognitive development; the remainder of the book includes descriptions of individual studies on aspects of the theory, including some especially interesting cross-cultural studies.

Chukovsky, K. *From two to five.* Berkeley: University of California Press, 1963.
An absolutely delightful book, by a Russian poet, about children's language and thinking. Chukovsky has captured much of what is fascinating, whimsical, and special about both language and thought during the early years in a nontechnical and enjoyable book for anyone.

Dale, P. S. *Language development: Structure and function.* Hinsdale, Ill.: The Dryden Press, 1972.
There is a first-rate discussion of the problem of language and thought in Chapter 8.

Ginsburg, H., & Opper, S. *Piaget's theory of intellectual development.* Englewood Cliffs, N.J.: Prentice-Hall, 1969.
In my opinion the best overview of Piaget's theory available in English; difficult but not impossible reading for those of you who are especially interested in Piaget's theory.

Maccoby, E. E., & Jacklin, C. N. *The psychology of sex differences.* Stanford, California: Stanford University Press, 1974.
A first-rate book, which I have suggested to you in earlier chapters. The material particularly relevant here is on pages 105–110.

Neimark, E. D. Intellectual development during adolescence. In F. D. Horowitz (Ed.), *Review of child development research* (Vol. 4). Chicago: University of Chicago Press, 1975.
If you are interested in formal operational development, this is the very best current review.

Piaget, J. Development and learning. In R. Ripple & V. Rockcastle (Eds.), *Piaget rediscovered.* Ithaca, N.Y.: Cornell University Press, 1964, pp. 7–19. Reprinted in C. S. Lavatelli & F. Stendler (Eds.), *Readings in child behavior and development* (3rd ed.). New York: Harcourt Brace Javanovich, 1972.
I find this relatively brief paper to be one of the clearest, most "chatty" of Piaget's writings. It presumes that you know something about his terminology, but it is the only

place I know in which Piaget has discussed the roles of experience and maturation in cognitive development.

Piaget, J., & Inhelder, B. *The psychology of the child.* New York: Basic Books, 1969.
This book is usually considered to be the most concise and easiest of the several summaries of his theory that Piaget has written. I still find it difficult, but it *is* easier than his other writings. I recommend, though, that you try the Ginsburg and Opper book first.

Schantz, C. U. The development of social cognition. In E. M. Hetherington (Ed.), *Review of child development research* (Vol. 5). Chicago: University of Chicago Press, 1975.
Contains an excellent review of research on egocentrism.

Stevenson, H. W. *Children's learning.* New York: Appleton, 1972.
By far the most up-to-date and comprehensive discussion of learning in children and developmental changes in the pattern of that learning, written for a professional or advanced audience but not very difficult; an excellent source of further references on the subject.

Vygotsky, L. S. *Thought and language.* New York: Wiley, 1962.
The major book by a famous Russian developmental psychologist, actually written in the later 1930s just before Vygotsky died; delightful and easy to read. Vygotsky was a major influence on Bruner's thinking and influenced many others as well.

Werner, H. *Comparative psychology of mental development* (Rev. ed.). Chicago: Follett, 1948.
The major work of another great theoretical figure in developmental psychology, one overshadowed by Piaget, whose theories resemble Werner's in many respects although Piaget has much more detailed descriptions of the child's mental development; very difficult.

Other Sources Cited

Achenbach, T. M., & Weisz, J. R. A longitudinal study of developmental synchrony between conceptual identity, seriation, and transitivity of color, number, and length. *Child Development*, 1975, *46*, 840–848.

Borke, H. Piaget's mountains revisited: changes in the egocentric landscape. *Developmental Psychology*, 1975, *11*, 240–243.

Bruner, J. S. On the conservation of liquids. In J. S. Bruner, R. R. Olver, & P. M. Greenfield (Eds.), *Studies in cognitive growth.* New York: Wiley, 1966.

Bruner, J. S., & Kenney, H. J. On multiple ordering. In J. S. Bruner, R. R. Olver, & P. M. Greenfield (Eds.), *Studies in cognitive growth.* New York: Wiley, 1966.

Clarke-Stewart, K. A. Interactions between mothers and their young children: Characteristics and consequences. *Monographs of the Society for Research in Child Development*, 1973, *38* (Whole No. 153).

Cole, M., & Schribner, S. *Culture and thought: A psychological introduction.* New York: Wiley, 1974.

Denney, N. W. Free classification in preschool children. *Child Development*, 1972, *43*, 1161–1170.

Flavell, J. H. Developmental studies of mediated memory. In H. W. Reese & L. P. Lipsitt (Eds.), *Advances in child development and behavior* (Vol. 5). New York: Academic Press, 1970.

Furth, H. G. *Thinking without language.* New York: Free Press, 1966.

Gaudia, G. Race, social class, and age of achievement of conservation of Piaget's tasks. *Developmental Psychology*, 1972, *6*, 158–167.

Golden, M., & Birns, B. Social class and cognitive development in infancy. *Merrill-Palmer Quarterly*, 1968, *14*, 139–149.

Golden, M., Birns, B., Bridger, W., & Moss, A. Social-class differentiation in cognitive development among black preschool children. *Child Development*, 1971, *42*, 37–45.

Kendler, H. H., & Kendler, T. S. Vertical and horizontal processes in problem solving. *Psychological Review*, 1962, *69*, 1–16.

Kendler, T. S. Development of mediating responses in children. *Monographs of the*

Society for Research in Child Development, 1963, *28* (Whole No. 86), 33–48.

Kreutzer, M. A., Leonard, C., Sr., & Flavell, J. H. An interview study of children's knowledge about memory. *Monographs of the Society for Research in Child Development,* 1975, *40* (Whole No. 159).

Mosher, F. A., & Hornsby, J. R. On asking questions. In J. S. Bruner, R. R. Olver, & P. M. Greenfield (Eds.). *Studies in cognitive growth.* New York: Wiley, 1966.

Nelson, K. Some evidence for the cognitive primacy of categorization and its functional basis. *Merrill-Palmer Quarterly,* 1973, *19,* 21–40.

Uzgiris, I. C. Patterns of cognitive development in infancy. *Merrill-Palmer Quarterly,* 1973, *19,* 181–204.

Wachs, T. D., Uzgiris, I., & Hunt, J. McV. Cognitive development in infants of different age levels and from different environmental backgrounds: An explanatory investigation.

Merrill-Palmer Quarterly, 1971, *17,* 283–318.

Wei, T. T., Lavatelli, C. B., & Jones, R. S. Piaget's concept of classification: A comparative study of socially disadvantaged and middle-class young children. *Child Development,* 1971, *52,* 919–928.

White, B. L. Critical influences in the origins of competence. *Merrill-Palmer Quarterly,* 1975, *21,* 243–266.

Yarrow, L. J., Klein, R. P., Lomonaco, S., & Morgan, G. A. Cognitive and motivational development in early childhood. In B. Z. Friedlander, G. M. Steritt, & G. Kirk (Eds.), *The exceptional infant: Assessment and intervention* (Vol. 3). New York: Bruner/Mazel, 1974.

Yarrow, L. J., Rubenstein, J. L., Pedersen, F. A., & Jankowski, J. J. Dimensions of early stimulation and their differential effects on infant development. *Merrill-Palmer Quarterly,* 1972, *18,* 205–218.

THE GAME OF TWENTY QUESTIONS

**General
Instructions**

The first step is to locate a child between the ages of 5 and 10. Tell the parents that you want to play some simple games with the child as part of a school project, reassuring them that you are not "testing" the child. Obtain their permission, describing the games and tasks if you are asked to do so.

Arrange a time to be alone with the child if at all possible. Having the mother or siblings there can be extremely distracting, both for the child and for you.

Come prepared with all the equipment you will need. Tell the child that you have some games you would like to play. Play with the child for a while to establish some kind of rapport before you begin your own experimenting. At the appropriate moment, introduce your "game."

The Task

I am thinking of something in this room, and your job is to figure out what I am thinking of. To do this, you can ask any question at all that I can answer by saying Yes or No, but I can't give you any other answer but "Yes" or "No." You can ask as many questions as you need to, but try to find out in as few questions as you can.

Choose the door to the room as the answer to your first game. (If there is more than one door, select one particular door as correct; if there is no door, use a particular window.) If the child asks questions that cannot be answered Yes or No, remind her (or him) that you can't answer that kind of question, and restate the kind of questions that can be asked. Allow the child as many questions as needed (more than 20 if necessary). Write down each question verbatim. When the child has reached the correct answer, praise her and then say,

Let's try another one. I'll try to make it harder this time. I'm thinking of something in the room again. Remember, you ask me questions that I can answer Yes or No. You can ask as many questions as you need, but try to find out in as few questions as possible.

Use your pencil or pen as the correct answer this time. After the child has solved the problem, praise her. If the child has not been successful, find something to praise ("You asked some good questions, but it's a really hard problem, isn't it?"). When you are satisfied that the child's motivation is still reasonably high, continue:

Now we're going to play another question-asking game. In this game I will tell you something that happened, and your job will be to find out how it happened by asking me questions I can answer Yes or No. Here's what happened: A man is driving down the road in his car, the car goes off the road, and hits a tree. You have to find out how it happened by the way I answer questions you ask me about it. But I can only answer Yes or No. The object of the game is to find out the answer in as few questions as possible. Remember, here's what happened: A man is driving down the road in his car, the car goes off the road, and hits a tree. Find out what happened.

If the child asks questions that cannot be answered Yes or No, remind her that you cannot answer that kind of question and that you can answer only Yes or No. If the child can't figure out the answer, urge her to try until you are persuaded that you are creating frustration, at which point you should quit, with lots of positive statements.

The answer to the problem is that it had been raining, the car skidded on a curve, went off the road, and hit the tree.

Scoring

Score each question asked by the child on each of the three problems as belonging to one of two categories.

1. Hypothesis. A hypothesis is essentially a guess that applies to only one alternative. A Yes answer to a hypothesis solves the problem, whereas with a No answer all that has been accomplished is to eliminate one possibility. In the first two problems a hypothesis would be any question that applied to only one alternative, only one object in the room:

Is it your hair?
Is it the picture?

In the third problem a hypothesis would be any question that covers only one alternative:

Did the man get stung in the eye by a bee?
Did he have a heart attack?
Was there a big snow bank in the middle of the road that the car ran into and then skidded?

2. Constraint. A constraint question covers at least two possibilities, often many more. A Yes answer to a constraint question must be followed up. ("Is it a toy?" "Yes." "Is it the truck?" "Yes.") A No answer to a constraint question allows the questioner to eliminate a whole class of possibilities. On the first two problems, any of the following would be constraints:

Is it in that half of the room?
Is it something big?
Is it a toy?
Is it something red? (Assuming there is more than one red thing in the room.)

For the third problem any of the following (or equivalent) would be constraints:

Was there something wrong with the car?
Was the weather bad?
Did something happen to the man?

For your own analysis or for an assignment to be turned in to a course instructor, you should examine at least the following aspects:

1. How many questions did the child ask for each problem?
2. On each problem how many were hypotheses and how many constraints?
3. Did the child do better (ask more constraint questions) on the concrete problem than on the abstract (story) problem? Or was the performance the same on both?
4. Is the child's overall performance on this task generally consistent with the findings from Mosher and Hornsby's study? Does your subject behave in a way that would be expected on the basis of her age? If not, what explanation can you offer?
5. What were the conditions of the testing? Did you feel the subject was comfortable and motivated? Have you learned anything about the way one might go about doing research of this kind with children? Are there any special conditions that you might like to impose on any testing circumstances? If so, what and why?

PROJECT 5
CONSERVATION OF NUMBER, MASS, AND WEIGHT

General Instructions

For this project you will again need a child between 5 and 10 years of age, as well as the following materials: two balls of clay, Play-doh or plasticine, and a bag of M & Ms or a set of identical buttons.

As indicated in the text the concept of conservation involves the understanding that some features of objects remain invariant, despite changes in other features. The weight of an object remains the same, regardless of how its shape is changed, and the number of objects in a row remains the same, regardless of how widely spaced the objects are. In this project you'll be testing your subject for three kinds of conservation: number, mass, and weight. Typically, number and mass conservation occur at about age 5 or 6, and conservation of weight occurs later, at about age 8 or 9. If your subject is between 5 and 8, you may find that he or she can manage the first two conservations but not the last.

The Task

Begin with the two balls of clay. Handle each of them yourself, and then hand them to the child, asking, "Is there the same amount of clay in each of these balls? Are they the same?"

If the child agrees that they are, proceed. If not, say to the child, "Make them the same." The child may just want to squash them a little or she may actually shift some clay from one ball to the other. That's quite all right. When she's done, ask her again, "Is there the same amount of clay in each of these balls? Are they the same?"

Once she has agreed that they are the same, proceed with the actual test. Say to the child, "Now I'm going to squish this one into a pancake" (and proceed to do that).

Then place the two objects—the ball of clay and the pancake—in front of the child, asking, "Is there the same amount of clay in this one (pointing to the pancake) as in this one (pointing to the ball), or is there more here (pointing to the pancake), or is there more here (pointing to the ball)?"

Record the child's answer, and then ask her for an explanation. "Why is there more here?" or "Why are they the same?" (depending on the answer).

Record the child's answer.

After this procedure, mold the pancake back into a ball and set the two balls of clay aside for the moment. Bring out your M & Ms or buttons and place them between yourself and the child, spaced equally in two rows of five, as follows:

X X X X X

X X X X X

Ask the child, "Are there the same number of buttons (candies) in this row as in this row (pointing), or are there more here (pointing to the child's row) or more here (pointing to your own row)?"

Record the child's answer.

Now spread the objects in your row (the row on your side) so that your row is now noticeably longer than the child's row but still contains the same number of objects:

X X X X X

X   X   X   X   X

Ask the same question again. "Are there the same number of buttons (candies) in this row as in this row or are there more here, or more here?"

Record the child's answer and ask, "Why are they the same?" or "Why are there more here?"

Now spread out the child's row and add two objects to each row, so that your row and the child's row are again exactly matched, with seven items equally spaced in each. Ask the same question. Record the child's answer.

Now move the objects in your row closer together, so that the child's row is longer. Ask the same questions and record the child's answers.

Remove the buttons and bring the balls of clay out again, saying, "We're going to play with the clay again." Again, show the two balls to the child, asking, "Do these two balls weigh the same? Do they have the same amount of weight?"

If the child agrees, proceed. If she does not, say, "Make them the same," and give her the balls to manipulate, proceeding as in the first part of this project. After she's through again ask her if they weigh the same, and do not proceed until she agrees.

Once she has agreed that they are the same, say, "Now I'm going to make this one into a hot dog" and roll out one of the balls into a hot-dog shape. When you have completed the transformation, put the two pieces of clay in front of the child and ask, "Does this one (pointing to the hot dog) weigh the same as this one (the ball), or does this one weigh more or does this one weigh more?"

Record the child's answer and probe for a reason, asking, "Why do they weigh the same?" or "Why does this one weigh more?"

At the end of this trial, the test is complete. You should thank the child and offer to give her the clay and candies or buttons.

Scoring

Record verbatim the child's own words in answer to each question on the score sheet, and for each of the crucial questions indicate whether the child conserved or not. A conservation response requires both that the child say that the objects (or rows) remain equal and that she give a good reason for thinking so. For example,

You haven't added any or taken any away.
One's longer, but it is still the same.
If I made it back into a ball it would be the same.

236

You may find it useful in sorting out the child's responses to use a score sheet similar to the one that follows.

SAMPLE SCORE SHEET FOR PROJECT 5

Experimenter_____

Subject_____

Age of subject_____

Sex of subject_____

		Conserved	Did not conserve
Conservation of Mass	Test question answer_____ _____ _____	_____	_____
Conservation of Number	**1.** Initial equality with 5 objects_____ _____ _____		
	2. First transformation—your row longer _____ _____	_____	_____
	3. Second equality stage, with seven objects per row_____	_____	_____
	4. Second transformation—child's row longer_____ _____	_____	_____
Conservation of Weight	Test question answer_____ _____ _____	_____	_____

Analysis

As in the Twenty Questions project, you should think about a series of questions. For example,

1. Did the child show conservation on any of the tasks?
2. If so, on which tasks? Is the pattern of correct conservation responses consistent with the age of the child and with the usual age of acquisition of the various conservatons?
3. If the data are not consistent with what I have reported to you or what you have read elsewhere, how can you explain the discrepancy?
4. What, if anything, have you learned about procedures that would be useful in designing and carrying out an experiment of this kind?

10

Cognitive Development II:
Measurement of Intelligence

When Piaget uses the word *intelligence* he is talking about a quality. The child at a given age has a particular *kind* of intelligence, a kind of thinking, a kind of logic. The quality of logic changes as a result of the child's interaction with the environment, and it is with the sequence and process of that change that Piaget and his followers are concerned. Most of the research on cognitive development now being done in the United States embodies a similar emphasis.

But there is a much older tradition in American research, focusing on the problem of individual differences, including individual differences in thinking and their origins. Such a concern with individual differences leads to a different sort of question. Instead of asking, as Piaget does, how thinking changes over time, we ask how children of the same age differ in their thinking skills and how we can measure such differences. Given that some children are quicker, more knowledgeable, or better able to learn new things, how did those differences come about? The important point for now is that the word *intelligence*, as it is commonly used in discussing tests of individual differences, does *not* mean the same thing as it does when Piaget uses it. When the word *intelligence* refers to the score on a standard test of intelligence, it means not a *kind* of thinking but a relative *amount* of thinking skill. The constructors of intelligence tests recognized that children change in the number of things that they know, but they did not ordinarily assume that the manner of thinking changes. So the concept of intelligence that lies behind the development of the intelligence test is vastly different from the concept of intelligence that Piaget has advanced. They both have value, but you should be careful not to confuse them.

Because the concept of intelligence as exemplified in an intelligence test has been so pervasive in American psychology and education and because there is continuing controversy about it, it seems worthwhile to devote an entire chapter to it. It is important for each of you, particularly as prospective teachers or parents, to have a very good understanding of what an intelligence test is, what it is not, what influences it, and what kinds of biases are built into it.

SOME HISTORY

Two Frenchmen, Binet and Simon, published the first of what we ordinarily call intelligence tests in 1905, although there had been some earlier attempts to develop a global test of intellectual functioning. There was general agreement at the time that people do differ in some overall quality of brightness or ability; what was needed, it was thought, was a test that could measure such differences reliably. Binet was asked by the French government to devise such a test for the express purpose of identifying retarded children. From the beginning, as is still true today, the fundamental purpose of the tests was to predict school success.

The earliest tests consisted simply of a set of problems arranged approximately in order of difficulty. But the very first revision of the test in 1908 altered this format to the one that is now most common: a set of problems for each of a series of ages. There is a set of problems for the 4-year-old, a set for the 5-year-old, and so forth. In the usual procedure the child is given the tests for the year below her own chronological age, then given all the tests for her actual age, and on up as far as she can go. The purpose of this procedure is to discover what her mental age is. If she can do the problems normally solved by the typical 6-year-old but not the problems for the 7-year-olds, she has a mental age of 6. The IQ score is basically a comparison of the child's actual age (chronological age) with her mental age. The child who is able to do problems normally solved only by children older than herself is above average in IQ, whereas the child who is unable to solve problems suitable to her own age is below average in IQ. The actual formula is

$$\frac{\text{Mental age}}{\text{Chronological age}} \times 100 = \text{IQ}$$

Suppose, for example, that a child whose chronological age is 5 can solve all the problems for 5-year-olds and all the problems for 6-year-olds but nothing above that level. She thus has a mental age of 6 and a chronological age of 5, which gives an IQ of 120:

$$\frac{6}{5} \times 100 = 120$$

A child of 6 who has a mental age of 4 would have an IQ of 67, and so forth.

The items for each age level have been selected carefully to represent the average ability of children of that age, so that the average child will be able to solve problems at her own age level but not those above. The average child thus has a mental age the same as her chronological age and an IQ of 100. The average IQ is 100 for children of any age. There's nothing magical about the figure 100 as an average; it is a convention only.

The selection of tasks or items to be included on the tests has been heavily influenced by Binet and Simon's thinking. They believed that intelligence is basically judgment:

It seems to us that in the intelligence there is a fundamental faculty. . . . This faculty is judgement, otherwise called good sense, practical sense, initiative, the faculty of adapting oneself of circumstances. To judge well, to comprehend well, to reason well, these are the essential activities of the intelligence. (Binet & Simon, 1916, p. 24. © The Williams & Wilkins Co., Baltimore.)

The tests that they devised, based on this conception of intelligence, were heavily loaded with tests of comprehension, reasoning, words, definitions, and so forth.

The Binet-Simon test was soon brought to the United States, trans-

240

lated, and revised by several researchers. The best-known revision is the Stanford-Binet, done primarily by Terman and his associates at Stanford University.

Because the Binet tests and their offspring in the United States relied heavily on verbal skills, there was some movement among those interested in intelligence testing to devise tests that might tap the same fundamental abilities without relying on verbal ability. So-called "performance" tests were included in Wechsler's test batteries, the best known of which is the Wechsler Intelligence Scales for Children, or WISC. Wechsler's tests, in fact, are half performance and half verbal tasks. The child's performance on the two halves of the test can be evaluated separately, so that it can be seen if the child is doing much better or less well on one kind of item or the other.

Other performance tests were designed to be "culture free" or "culture fair." It was argued by some that any verbal test is inherently unfair to children from cultural backgrounds different from those of the children for whom the test had originally been standardized. The hope was that it would be possible to discover some kind of nonverbal test that would be equally fair to all children, no matter what their cultural backgrounds. Of these tests, the most famous is F. Goodenough's Draw-a-Person test (see Figure 26), which simply requires the child to draw a picture of a man or a woman. The child's drawing is evaluated in terms of the normal amount of detail and elaboration found in the

FIGURE 26

Examples of children's drawings from the Goodenough Draw-a-Person test. (Source: From *Measurement of Intelligence by Drawings* by Florence L. Goodenough, copyright 1926 by Harcourt Brace Jovanovich, Inc.; renewed 1954 by Florence L. Goodenough. Reproduced by permission of the publishers.)

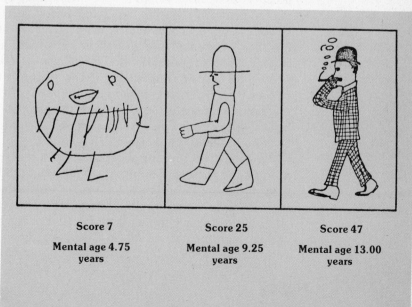

Score 7

Mental age 4.75 years

Score 25

Mental age 9.25 years

Score 47

Mental age 13.00 years

drawings of children of that age. Since all children have observed people, it is assumed that they all have had the basic experience necessary to perform this test. There are other such culture-fair tests, although none is very widely used today for the simple reason that they have proven to be less predictive of various other kinds of performance than have the more standard IQ tests.

SOME ASSUMPTIONS

Binet himself did not assume that intelligence, as measured by the tests, is a fixed thing. He argued that a child's intelligence is a product of experience and could be modified. All he was trying to do was to assess it at a given time. But in the United States those who devised and revised intelligence tests by and large did assume that intelligence is fixed. A child was presumed to inherit some amount of ability from her parents, and that ability was thought to be only slightly affected by the subsequent environment (see J. McV. Hunt's excellent discussion of this problem). There is nothing in the concept of intelligence as measured by the standard tests that requires us to believe in fixed, predetermined intelligence. It's perfectly possible to hold, as did Binet, that the tests measure merely the child's (or adult's) current status, not her status forever. But you should realize that most test developers and theorists in this country did believe in fixed intelligence and that their belief has somehow become attached to the tests themselves. Consequently, when a parent is told that her child has been tested and has, say, an IQ of 85, she is likely to be very distressed. The parent thinks that her child is somehow permanently stupid. Whether or not that is in fact the case—whether IQ is fixed or not—is something I will deal with at much greater length later in this chapter.

Another assumption underlying most tests, in some form or another, is that the development of intelligence is more a quantitative than a qualitative process. Binet and Simon, as well as other test constructors, did recognize that there are changes in the manner of thinking that lies behind the growth of knowledge and information, but their interest was primarily in the *rate* at which the child accumulates knowledge and information, not in the processes by which she accomplishes that. Such an emphasis on differences in rate of development inevitably places great emphasis on the quantitative aspects of intellectual growth: How many things does the child know in comparison to other children of her age?

Again, there is nothing about the assessment of intelligence that requires us to place this emphasis on the amount of knowledge or information instead of on the processes by which knowledge is achieved. We can devise tests of relative functioning based on Piaget's theory, and such tests have in fact been developed. As on standard tests, the child's performance on these Piagetian tests is compared to the "normal" or "expectable" performance for a child of her age, but the test results are not intended to label a child smart, retarded, or average. Rather, the Piaget-based tests are designed to allow us to diagnose the child's level of thinking, to say something about where she is in the sequence of development.

An additional difference between tests based on Piaget's theory and the standard intelligence tests is the kind of items that are selected for the tests. On standard IQ tests there is an effort to include items that tap the general realms of reasoning and judgment. But individual items are chosen because they have a particular property: Half of the children of a given age can pass them, most younger children cannot, and most older children can. Figure 27 illustrates this pattern of scores for an imaginary IQ test item. In this case the item would be a "6-year-old item," since about half of the 6-year-olds passed it, while only a small percentage of the younger children did.

Among items that meet this general criteria, the Stanford-Binet includes vocabulary items, questions that measure the child's reasoning, her classification (such as, "How are an apple and an orange alike?"), and memory. These items may touch on aspects of the sequence of cognitive development that Piaget has outlined, but they are chosen not *because* they relate to important developmental sequences but because they have the property of being passed by only about half the children at any given age. Tests based on Piaget's theory, on the other hand, involve items chosen specifically because they reflect the se-

FIGURE 27

The prefered "shape" of test results for a good IQ test item. The line shows the percentage of children passing the item at the several adjacent ages.

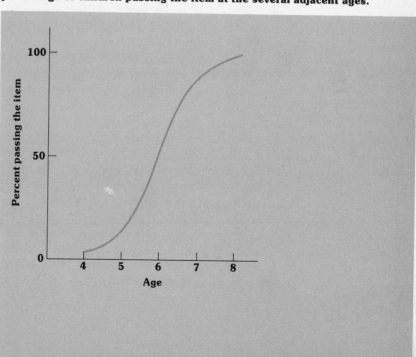

quence of cognitive development. For example, Uzgiris and Hunt have devised a set of scales that measure an infant's progress through the several stages of the sensorimotor period. The end result of the Uzgiris and Hunt test is not a single IQ score, but a statement of the step in the sequence of development achieved by the child. The contrast between these two approaches is nicely drawn by Uzgiris and Hunt. In this quotation they refer to their own test as an *ordinal scale.*

The traditional tests rest on an assumption of incremental progress, without much consideration of the interrelationships between achievements at one level and those at the next. In contrast, ordinal scales imply a hierarchical relationship between achievements at different levels, so that in principle the achievements of the higher level do not incidentally follow, but are intrinsically derived from those at the preceeding level and encompass them within the higher level. (I. C. Uzgiris & J. McV. Hunt. *Assessment in Infancy,* p. 11. Urbana: University of Illinois Press. © 1975 by the Board of Trustees of the University of Illinois.)

Thus Piagetian (and similar) tests are based on a theory of development, whereas most standard IQ tests are not. Piagetian tests emphasize the child's placement in a hierarchical sequence of development, whereas the standard tests emphasize differences among children at a particular age.

PERFORMANCE VERSUS COMPETENCE

If you believe in fixed intelligence—some kind of ability that is determined at birth—then what you aim for is a test that will somehow tap that fundamental inherited capacity. Even if you believe that the tests measure only the child's current ability, you still hope for a test that gets at the child's underlying skills—what she can do under the best of circumstances. But inevitably any test can measure only performance. We can see only what the child does when we ask her a question or give her a problem to solve. We can't see inside to determine how well she could do under ideal circumstances.

It's important to keep in mind at all times that all tests are measures of performance and that the child's performance will be affected by a whole host of factors beside her underlying competence. The child may not care about you or your test. Or she may be enormously anxious to please, and her anxiety may interfere with her ability to do well. So the child's motivation, whatever it is, is going to make a difference. There is also the possibility of various kinds of bias entering. If you, as the examiner, have to make a judgment about the correctness of a child's answer, then your feelings about the child may sway you. Unless you are careful, irritation with a particular child or spontaneous liking for another child may affect the way you score the test or the amount of time that you give the child to come up with the answer. The tests are supposedly standardized to avoid such bias, but undoubtedly some does creep in.

244

Another kind of bias can be built into the test itself. If, in seeking some understanding of the child's language competence, we use a vocabulary test originally developed for middle-class children, we may receive an altogether false idea of the vocabulary size of ghetto children. The ghetto child may know just as many words, but not the words on that particular test. There have been enormous arguments in the literature on exactly this basis about the fairness to poor children of most standard tests. It's argued that the poor child, even if she is motivated in the testing situation and even if her fundamental competence is as high, is inevitably going to look bad on middle-class tests.

Some of these biases and motivational problems have been studied directly, so we have some idea how big the effects of such variables may be. But even when every effort is made to equalize motivation and to remove biases whenever possible, we are still only measuring performance. When we eliminate some of the motivational and biasing factors, we may bring performance and competence closer together, but performance is all we can actually see and assess.

WHAT THE TESTS PREDICT

For many psychologists the really crucial question about any test is, What does it predict? A test that is beautifully based on theory, with clearly defined subject matter, but that does not predict anything is of little use. I could probably measure the length of your little finger with great precision and reliability. But what good is the information? The same is true of an IQ test; unless a given test score is related somehow to other behavior of the child, it has limited interest.

IQ tests, on the whole, have been excellent predictors of school success. The correlation between IQ tests and children's performance in school is about 0.60. What that means is that although some children with high scores on the IQ tests may do poorly and some with low scores may do well, on the whole the children who have the top scores will also be among the higher achievers in school and those who score low will be among the low achievers.

There are several aspects of this relationship that must be understood. First, by saying that there is a correlation of 0.60 between IQ scores and school performance, I am not saying that IQ causes or makes possible school performance. All we know is that the two things tend to vary together. Second, in traditional schools IQ is related to achievement and grades, but we don't know whether or not there would be a similar correlation between IQ and performance in a "free" school or in one of a more unconventional makeup. I suspect, however, that there would be at least a modest correlation, for any kind of school demands some kinds of cognitive skills, just as the IQ test does. Overall, the IQ test seems to measure something that is necessary but not sufficient for school performance.

IQ scores have been useful predictors of factors other than school performance. Performance in any competitive situation requiring reasoning and comprehension is likely to be predicted, in some measure, by IQ scores. Success in various kinds of jobs, for example, may be partly predicted by IQ. But again, the IQ test seems to measure only one of many factors that is needed for achievement in school or in a job.

Overall, I think it is fair to say that IQ tests are measuring something of interest, but I am not suggesting that they are measuring all that we might be interested in about cognitive development or about the child's motivation to achieve, her anxiety, or any other factor that may affect learning and achievement. But the fact that an IQ test doesn't measure everything important doesn't mean that we should cast it out. At the very least the score is a useful indicator of a child's current intellectual performance in comparison to the performance of her peers.

FACTORS INFLUENCING IQ TEST SCORES
Genetic Influences

Genetic influences on intelligence are an enormously complex and controversial issue, as you are no doubt aware. The question comes down to something like this: How much of the variation in IQ score from one person to another is due to different inheritances and how much to different environments? Put this way, the basic issue is obviously one that I've raised repeatedly: Is the source of the behavior we see largely internal, largely external, or some combination of the two?

Answers to the question about the genetic influence in IQ scores are based on a series of facts:

1. Identical twins reared together have IQ scores that correlate very highly with one another.
2. Identical twins are much more like each other in IQ than are fraternal twins, even when we include only fraternal twins of the same sex.
3. When identical twins are reared apart from each other from an early age they still have remarkably similar IQ scores, though not as similar as if they had been reared together. There is, however, some suggestion that pairs of identical twins who have been raised in widely differing families have scores that are more different from one another than is the case for twins raised in families of similar income and education.
4. If a child born to a relatively uneducated or poverty level mother is adopted by a better educated, middle-class family, the child's IQ is likely to be considerably higher than the IQ of her natural mother or father. At the same time the IQ of an adopted child can be *predicted* somewhat better by knowing the IQ of the child's real mother than by knowing that of the adopting mother. That is, among a group of women who have given their babies up for adoption, the mothers with higher IQs are likely to have chil-

dren with higher IQs, regardless of the kind of family in which the child is brought up. But *all* the adopted children are likely to have higher IQs than their mothers.

Clearly, both the environment in which the child is raised and the specific genetic inheritance affect the test score, although the relative contribution of the two and their interaction is still hotly debated. (See the Scarr-Salapatek paper for one presentation of the issues.) Estimates of the proportion of test score variation that may be attributed to genetic differences vary from about 80 percent (which Jensen and many others have suggested) to a lower estimate of perhaps 50 percent. But no one has suggested that there is no genetic influence at all.[1]

But just what is it that we inherit? Obviously, we don't inherit a score. We must inherit instead some kinds of capacities, capabilities, speed of reflexes, speed of habituation, or whatever, and these inherited skills in turn affect the rate at which we learn things, our ability to reason quickly and correctly, our ability to notice discrepancies, and so on. We have much to learn before we can be more precise about the genetic influence on intelligence as measured by our tests. What we can say with some assurance now is that there is such an influence.

But even if the influence of heredity is strong, there is a great deal of room for environmental effect. The child is presumably born with potentials determined or limited by genetic factors. How those potentials are realized or if they are realized at all is a function of the environment.

Environmental Influences
SOCIAL CLASS DIFFERENCES

By far the most consistent finding in studies of IQ is that children from poor or working-class families have lower average IQs than do children from middle-class families. The difference is on the order of 10 to 20 points.

These differences are *not* found in studies of infants, as you could have gathered from the discussions of social class differences in earlier chapters. The rate of a child's sensorimotor development seems to be largely unrelated to the education or income of the family. But by age 3 consistent differences are found between children from poor and those from more affluent families. A short-term longitudinal study by Golden and Birns provides the best evidence for this transition. They studied a group of black children from poor, working-class and middle-class families beginning when the children were a year old, and

---

[1] Since I wrote this paragraph, I have come across a fascinating, excellently argued, book by Leon Kamin, who *does* argue that there may be *no* genetic component at all in measured IQ. After detailed reanalysis of all the early studies on twin similarities and adopted children, he concludes that the case for a genetic factor is just not proven, and that at least some of the early studies are highly suspect methodologically. Kamin has not entirely persuaded me that there is no genetic component, but it does begin to look as if an estimate of 50 percent is way too high, and that a "heritability" of 80 percent is completely undefensible. Those of you who are interested in this issue will find Kamin's book fascinating.

tested them at regular intervals. No differences on any measures of infant development were found until the children were 3. But at age 3 the children from the middle-class group had an average IQ of 112, while the children from the poorest families (all on welfare) had an average IQ of 94.

The disparity between social class groups, which Golden and Birns found at age 3, persists thereafter and occurs for a wide variety of tasks, including tasks based on Piagetian theory (as I pointed out in Chapter 9). So there may be something about the overall environment of the middle class, compared to the overall environment of the poor, that leads to consistent differences in performance. Whether or not the difference in performance reflects a difference in competence is hotly argued. Some have suggested that the major difference is really not in competence but in motivation (see, for example, Ginsburg). The child from poverty circumstances doesn't come into a testing situation with the same desire to achieve—to do the best she can—as is typical of the middle-class child. Others have pointed out that even when great pains are taken to try to equalize the motivational differences, differences in performance are still found (see the paper by Lesser, Fifer, & Clark). Precisely the same arguments are offered to deal with observed racial differences in measured IQ as well, as you can see in some detail in Box 17.

Obviously the existence of social class differences in measured IQ and in school performance (since the two usually go hand in hand) has major policy implications. Whether or not you believe that there are "real" differences in intellectual competence between the poor and the middle class is going to have a major impact on the kind of educational system you advocate. But I do not think that answers to the questions involved are going to emerge from further comparisons of poor and middle-class children on tests. What we need to know more about are the *specific environmental conditions* that promote maximum intellectual growth. What are the specific qualities of families from which brighter children emerge? What particular things can we detect about environments that foster or impede general cognitive progress? There are at least two ways to go about answering such questions. First, we might look in some detail at families interacting with their children and try to ferret out those dimensions of interaction or environment that are correlated with high test scores. Second, we can design intervention programs of various types: We can take children out of poverty level families for parts of the day and give them different experiences to see what effect that has. Let me explore each of these.

SPECIFIC FAMILY
CHARACTERISTICS
I have already discussed some of the evidence on family characteristics and cognitive development in Chapter 9. The results of studies by Yarrow, White and others pointed to the importance of contingent social stimulation and of involvement of the mother with the infant in

promoting the child's cognitive development. Studies focused more specifically on prediction of IQ scores point to similar kinds of family variables.

Some of the most interesting recent research has been done by Caldwell and her colleagues (Bradley & Caldwell and Elardo, Bradley & Caldwell). They studied a group of 77 infants, both black and white and both poor and middle class, from 6 months to 3 years of age. At regular intervals the children were tested, first with a standard "infant intelligence test" and later with the Stanford-Binet. At the same time the environment provided for the child was assessed using an instrument developed by Caldwell, called the Inventory of Home Stimulation. An observer/interviewer visits the home, talks with the parent (or other caregiver) about various things, and observes the kind of materials available to the child. The observer also notes the kind of interactions the caregiver has with the child and whether or not a whole series of things are present or absent in the home.

For example, there is a set of items on the inventory that relates to the "provision of appropriate play material." The observer notes some of the following. Does the child have some muscle activity toys or equipment? Does she have a push or pull toy? Does the mother provide toys or interesting activities for the child during the interview? Does the mother provide learning equipment appropriate to the child's age? Other sets of items describe the emotional and verbal responsivity of the mother to the child, her avoidance of restriction and punishment, her organization of the physical and temporal environment, her involvement with the child, and the opportunities she provides for variety in daily stimulation.

When the ratings of the child's home environment are compared with the child's tested IQ, some extremely interesting results emerge. First, the kind of home stimulation the parents provide to the 6-month-old infant does not tell us very much about the child's rate of development during those early months. Families do differ in the amount of stimulation they provide, but those differences are not matched by the differences in children's early progress. But the early home stimulation differences *do* predict the child's IQ at age 3. Parents who provided appropriate play materials and had a well-organized physical and temporal environment for their 6-month-old infant had children who at age 3 had higher IQs. Home stimulation at 1 and 2 years also predicted the later IQ, and these correlations are quite large. The strongest predictors over the full three-year period seem to be the provision of appropriate play materials and the mother's involvement with the child. Regardless of the race or social class level of the family, families that provided play materials geared to their child's needs and level of development and who spent time with the child and encouraged her development, had children with higher IQs at age 3.

These same dimensions of family stimulation emerge from studies

BOX 17
Racial Differences in IQ

I have mentioned in the main part of the text that there are consistent differences in IQ scores between children raised in middle-class families and those raised in poor families. The average difference from the highest social class group to the lowest is about 20 IQ points. There is also a consistent difference between blacks and whites on standard IQ tests. White children, on the average, score about 15 points higher than blacks. Obviously, this difference has aroused enormous controversy, and rightly so, for the way you explain or interpret such a fact will have a major influence on social attitudes and policy. To clarify the situation, if I can, let me first give you the set of facts as we now know them and then describe some of the alternative explanations that have been offered.

FACTS

1. The average IQ difference between blacks and whites is found in numerous studies, those conducted in the North as well as in the South.
2. The difference is not found among infants, however, at least on any test now available. There are essentially no differences among racial and social class groups during infancy, except that black children exhibit somewhat faster motor development than do white children. The difference between blacks and whites on IQ tests is first seen when the children are between 2 and 4.
3. Within both the black and white groups there are social class differences: Middle-class blacks, on the average, achieve higher scores than do poor blacks, just as among whites.
4. School performance is about equally well predicted by the IQ scores in each group: Black children who have high IQ scores are more likely to do well in school than are black children with low scores, again just as among whites.

EXPLANATIONS

1. The most controversial explanation of these findings is that there is a genetic difference between the two racial groups. The genes that tend to produce high IQ scores are said to be more common in the white community. We do know, as I have discussed elsewhere in the chapter, that there is an important genetic contribution to the measured IQ score. On that fact some people have based the assumption that because heredity is an important determinant of measured IQ, differences between blacks and whites in measured IQ must be due to heredity. It sounds somewhat logical on the face of it, but it is not. It is entirely possible that individual IQ scores may be heavily influenced by heredity and that group differences may be entirely or largely the results of environmental differences. Let me give you an example that may make this point clearer. Suppose that you go to a very poor village in Mexico (or any other underdeveloped country) and study the relationship between parents' and children's height. You will find, to no one's surprise, that height is highly heritable: Genetic factors account for 80 or 90 percent of the variations among the heights of people in the village. Tall parents have taller children than short parents. Now go to Mexico City and do the same thing. Again, you will find a strong genetic effect. But now measure the average height of the children in the village and of the children in the city. You will find that the village children are, on the average, quite a lot shorter than the children in the city, and this difference between the average heights of the two groups we know to be mostly a function of diet. The people in the village are not as well nourished so they do not grow as tall as the people in the city. So we have a situation in which there is a major genetic effect on height within each group but a group difference that is entirely or largely a result of an environmental variable. The same may well be true of

the difference between blacks and whites in IQ scores. Within each group there is still an important genetic influence, but the difference between groups may be entirely the result of environmental differences.

2. Test bias has also been suggested as an explanation of the observed difference. The argument is that the tests were originally devised for middle-class whites and have never been standardized for the poor or for blacks. Then, too, as the tests tend to be heavily verbal and as many black children do not speak "standard English," the children may look bad on the test when in fact their competence is equal. This explanation is probably true to some extent. Some of the difference is probably due to some kind of test bias, in the sense that many standard IQ tests are not designed to assess children from different cultural backgrounds. (The tests are still adequate predictors of school performance, however, for most schools aren't equipped to handle children from different cultural backgrounds either.) But in my opinion test bias can't explain all the differences for the following reasons. First, every test that I know of, no matter how "culture fair," shows both social class and racial differences. Second, contrary to the usual expectation, it is not necessarily the case that the largest differences are obtained on verbal tests. In some studies there are smaller differences on verbal tests than on performance tests.

I am not trying to suggest that there is no bias. Rather, I want to emphasize that even when heroic efforts are made to overcome such bias, a difference is still found. In the best-known such study, by Gerald Lesser and his co-workers, the children were tested by adults of their same race and cultural background. The tests were rewritten to include only words equally available to both groups, the testing was done in many sessions, with lots of time for each child to get to know her examiner, and so on. Under these testing conditions—the very best and fairest that could be devised—there

were very large social class differences as well as differences among ethnic groups.

3. What we are left with is the very general notion that the environments of the two groups—blacks and whites—must differ in some ways that have important influences on test scores. Diet may well be one such environmental influence. The evidence on malnutrition points to the importance of nutrition for proper physical development, which may in turn affect the child's cognitive functioning, either directly by affecting the growth of the brain or indirectly by influencing alertness and motivation. Whether or not blacks, on the whole, have less nutritious diets than whites, I don't know. Of course, there are proportionately many more poor among the black population in this country, and we know tht the poor tend to have inadequate diets. We need more research on the question.

Alternatively, there may be aspects of the physical or interpersonal environment that are different in important ways. The typical statement is that the early environment of the black child is "impoverished," although precisely what impoverishment means in this context is not at all obvious. It is clear that the black child is likely to experience a different family structure (more often lacking a male figure), is more likely to be poor, and is likely to experience more prejudice and rejection from others, which may lead to a very different kind of self-image. There may also be different teaching and interaction styles in black families, and different values may be assigned to learning and education, although the evidence here is not as clear.

Overall, although we cannot on logical grounds reject the possibility of a genetic difference, it seems to me that there is ample reason to suppose that the difference is largely, if not entirely, the result of environmental differences. However, we are a long way from being able to describe environmental effects with any precision.

of a similar sort by other researchers. Tulkin and Covitz, for example, found that the number of play materials provided to children at 10 months was related to the children's intellectual test scores at age 6. Hanson, in an elaborate analysis of a longitudinal study of the relationship between parental behavior and children's IQ, finds that the parents' involvement with the child, their emphasis on school achievement, and their encouragement of the child's verbal expression are all quite strongly correlated with the child's IQ scores from age 3 through age 10.

Each of these groups of researchers has approached the task of assessing the environment in a different way, so adding up the results is complex. But there do seem to be some very consistent threads running through all the findings. Children who show the most rapid cognitive progress or highest IQ seem to be those whose parents do several things:

1. They provide *appropriate* play materials for the child. It is not the sheer quantity of play materials that is significant; rather, it is the appropriateness of the play materials for the child's age and developmental level that seems to be critical. Yarrow's research, which I discussed in Chapter 9, (page 227) also points to the importance of variety and complexity in the toys and materials provided for the child.

2. They are *involved* with their child. They spend time with the child, encourage the child's play and problem solving, talk with

the child frequently, and respond to the child's questions, actions, or activities.

3. They *expect* their child to do well and to develop rapidly. They emphasize and press for school achievement.

These patterns of parental behavior seem to begin when the child is still in infancy, but the full impact of these parental behaviors on the child's IQ is not felt till age 3 or older.

Another way to look at the impact of environment on the child's IQ is to look at the family interactions of children whose IQs have increased or decreased substantially. One such study is described in some detail in Box 18. Other research, including some by Caldwell and her colleagues, points to a similar set of conclusions. Children whose IQs increase during childhood are likely to be those whose parents push for achievement and are involved with their children.

SCHOOLING AND SPECIAL INTERVENTIONS

Is a child's IQ score affected by schooling or by other sorts of group experience or even institutional care? The whole Head Start program is based on the assumption that cognitive progress can be speeded up or augmented by special school experiences before regular school. Other special interventions have been designed to supplement the early experiences of children thought to be "at risk" for poor academic performance (usually children from poverty environments). What effect do these major environmental variations have on the child's IQ?

At the very least we know that the change in IQ can be quite dramatic if a child is shifted from a severely impoverished environment to one that is richer. Harold Skeels has provided some of the most fascinating data.

During the 1930s Skeels had been serving as staff psychologist for several orphanages and for schools for the retarded in Iowa. The orphanage children were nearly all illegitimate and had been placed in the institutions because adoptive placements had been impossible or because there was some concern—on the basis of infant testing—that they were retarded in development. The institutions were overcrowded and provided very little in the way of personal attention or intellectual stimulation. The eventual study was suggested by a chance occurrence. Two little girls, both about 1½ years old at the beginning of Skeel's observation, had been moved from an orphanage to a home for retarded children, as they were both functioning at about a 6-month-old level and seemed clearly "retarded." By chance they were placed in a ward of older retarded girls. The infants were the only babies in the ward and great attention and stimulation were lavished on them. Several months later when Skeels visited the institution for the retarded, he was startled to see two normal-looking little girls. When retested, they scored at about the normal level for their age and continued to seem normal for the next two years. Eventually they were

BOX 18
IQ Changes During Childhood

I have already mentioned that there is comparatively little consistency in test performance between infant tests and later IQ tests. It has been thought, however, that past age 4 or 5, there was quite considerable stability in test scores. For example, the correlation between IQ at age 6 and at age 10 is about 0.75 (see Honzik, MacFarlane, & Allen), which suggests a marked degree of consistency over time.

Recently, however, an intriguing analysis by McCall, Appelbaum, and Hogarty of the test scores from the Fels longitudinal study suggests that hidden in the apparent consistency over time are both patterns of change in test scores and some interesting developmental patterns.

McCall and his associates looked at the test scores of all the children who had been tested at regular intervals from age 2½ to age 17. When they examined the pattern of test scores for these subjects, they found that the majority showed shifts of 20 to 30 points over the age span studied, and that nearly 15 percent of the children showed shifts of more than 40 points. Furthermore, the shifts followed distinct patterns. Some children showed fairly steady declines in IQ scores with age, some showed sharp increases during the preschool and early school years and then declined somewhat after age 10, and others' scores remained fairly steady throughout the period. You can see these patterns in the figure.

Two additional findings make the results of this analysis particularly interesting. First, the investigators found reliably different patterns of parent behavior in families that had children whose IQs increased compared to families in which the children showed some sort of IQ decline. The children whose IQs had increased had parents who were both moderately strict and who pushed their children to develop rapidly and to succeed. The children whose IQs had decreased tended to come from families that placed little stress on the importance of children's development and that were either very severe or very mild in their punishment of their children. These findings are consistent with other evidence suggesting that family emphasis on achievement is associated with higher test scores.

Second, McCall and his associates found two

sent back to the orphanage and were then adopted. This chance event suggested the possibility that something similar might be done intentionally with other children from the orphanage, and Skeels was able to persuade administrators and state officials that something so radical should be tried. As a result 13 children from the orphanage—all with IQs between 35 and 89—were transferred to the institution for the retarded when they were about 1½ years old. All the children were considered unsuitable for adoption because of obvious mental retardation and probably would have been transferred eventually to the home for the retarded anyway. Skeels merely had them transferred early and placed in wards with older children. At the same time he followed an approximately comparable group of children who remained in the orphanage. Two years after the transfer the children who had been placed in the home for the retarded (the experimental group) had shown an average increase of about 28 points in IQ, but the group that had remained in the orphanages (the control group) had shown an average decline of about 26 IQ points. As before, because the children in the experimental group had shown such marked improvement, most (11 of

inflection points in the patterns of test scores for all their groups. Children's test performances tended to change at about age 6 and again at about age 10. There are obviously several possible interpretations of such findings, but it is at least interesting that these inflection points are similar to the points Piaget has stressed as important transitions in the child's cognitive development.

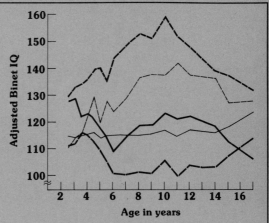

Mean IQ test scores over time for five groups of children with different patterns of IQ change. Note that there is a tendency for the test scores to change at age 6 and again at about age 10. (Source: McCall, R. B., Appelbaum, M. I., & Hogarty, P. S. Developmental changes in mental performance. *Monographs of the Society for Research in Child Development*, 1973, *38*, (3, Whole No. 150).)

the 13) were placed for adoption. Skeels didn't stop there, however. Twenty years later he managed to find all the subjects to see what the long-term effects of his "experiment" had been.

He found that all 13 of the people who had been in the experimental group were self-supporting; none was in an institution. Of the control group four were still in institutions of some kind, and one had died in an institution for retarded adolescents. The experimental group, on the average, had completed high school (one had completed college), whereas the subjects in the control group, on the average, had completed less than three years of school. The subjects in the experimental group had thus become educated, self-supporting adults. Subjects in the control group were still a drain on society in one way or another; when employed, they were usually employed in unskilled jobs, and in most cases barely eked out a living.

There are several morals to be drawn from this study. First, it is *very* difficult to make any kind of accurate prediction about eventual IQ test scores based on the child's rate of development in infancy. Infancy test scores do *not* correlate highly with later IQ scores. Second, the environment in which the child is raised clearly matters a great deal. This does not mean that all children who are subnormal in functioning could be normal if raised in "optimum" environments. There are some children whose potential is low, no matter what the environment. But most children will achieve higher levels of cognitive development if raised in more stimulating environments.

An ongoing study by Heber and his associates at the University of Wisconsin provides additional fuel for this same point. They have designed what amounts to a total intervention for a group of 20 children born to poverty level, low IQ mothers. All the mothers had measured IQs below 75, all lived in a slum area, and all were black. A second, matched group of 20 mothers served as the control group.

Beginning when they were 3 months old the infants were cared for during the day by Heber and his group. Each infant had a single caregiver (usually a black paraprofessional) who was completely responsible for the infant's care and stimulation. When the infants were about a year old, they began to spend more time in groups, although there was still one caregiver for every two children. The ratio was gradually increased and the groups of children became larger, until by preschool age the children were in a school-like setting. The intervention itself focused on perceptual-motor, cognitive, linguistic, and social-emotional development. Beginning at age 2 there was also instruction in prereading and reading, mathematics, and problem solving.

Obviously the purpose of the program was to show that a group of children otherwise highly likely to have low IQs and serious problems could achieve normal or above-normal cognitive development with special stimulation. The infants in both the experimental and control groups were tested regularly with standard IQ tests. The results can be seen in Figure 28. All the children started out with fairly high scores at 1 year of age. This is not particularly surprising in view of all the things we know about the lack of social class differences in infancy. But after age 1 the experimental and control groups begin to diverge quite sharply, with the control group showing a fairly steady decline in measured IQ and the experimental group a slow but fairly steady increase. By age 5½ the children in the experimental group had an average IQ of about 120, while the control group was at about 95. At this point the two distributions do not overlap at all; that is, the lowest-scoring child in the experimental group has a higher score than the highest-scoring child in the control group. Similar differences were found on measures of language development.

The number of children involved in this study is small, but the results are a bit startling. Certainly these findings point to a very large potential impact of rearing conditions on the child's cognitive development. Heber's results do not tell us what specific kinds of experience are critical, since they did *everything* they thought would make any

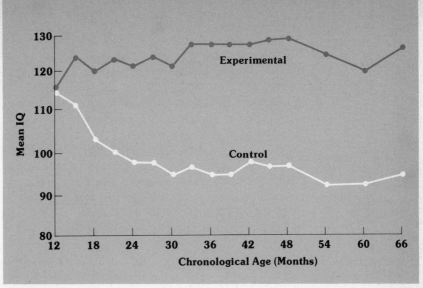

FIGURE 28

Results from Heber's intervention program, showing the IQ test scores for the experimental and control children over a five-year period. (Source: Heber, R., Garber, H., Harrington, S., Hoffman, C. & Falender, C. *Rehabilitation of families at risk for mental retardation.* Unpublished progress report, Research and Training Center, University of Wisconsin, Madison, Wisc., December, 1972, p. 49a.)

difference. But everything obviously can make a very large difference. It will be extremely interesting to see what happens to the 20 children in Heber's study as they reach school.

Shorter-term, less massive schooling interventions, such as those typically found in Head Start programs, have had much smaller effects, and the effects rarely last very long. Children in most Head Start programs show an initial increase of about 10 to 15 points in IQ, but this drops gradually later so that by the end of the second grade or so there are no measurable residual effects of the Head Start experience.

A few of the more intensive experimental programs for 3 to 4-year-old children—such as Gray and Klaus's program in Tennessee, or Weikart's program in Ypsilanti, Michigan—have found that children with Head Start-like experiences are still somewhat better in school performance in second or third grade, but the lasting effects are small.

What these studies seem to be telling us is that massive interventions begun in infancy can have a major impact, while smaller-scale interventions begun later have only a small effect. A great many people have gone on to argue that we must begin in infancy if we are going to help those children who are likely to have school difficulties without intervention. But I want to caution you about this conclusion. Heber's study does *not* tell us whether the intervention had to begin at age 3 months to have the effects it did. It is possible that the same intervention begun at age 2 or some other age could have had equally long-term effects. Phyllis Levenstein, for example, has devised a program of home training of poor mothers, which she begins ordinarily when the child is 2. Mothers and children are visited once a week or so by a "toy demonstrator" who brings specially selected toys designed to foster verbal interaction between mother and child. Children who have been involved in this program from ages 2 to 4 show *persisting,* and quite substantial, gains in IQ and in school performance. So in this case a later intervention was quite potent. Clearly, there are still a great many unanswered questions about both the specific sorts of schooling or other intervention that makes the biggest difference and the proper or most effective timing of such schooling or intervention.

THE TESTING SITUATION

In addition to all the general environmental influences, the manner in which the IQ test is given may also have an impact. There are two kinds of related findings.

First, the nature of the child's relationship with the tester can make a marked difference, particularly for a young child. If the examiner is known to the child, better still if she is someone with whom the child has a warm relationship, the child does better on the test than when she is tested by someone unknown. The difference may be as much as 10 or 15 points (see, for example, Sacks).

Second, the way the test itself is given makes an equivalent difference. For example, when you give the Stanford-Binet test in the standard fashion, you begin with questions and problems that are typically passed by a child a year younger than the child you are testing. If your subject can handle these problems, you increase the age level of the problems, continuing until the child fails all the tasks or questions for a given age level. One consequence of this procedure is that the child has most success at the beginning. As you proceed failure becomes more and more common until toward the end she is unable to do any of the problems. An alternative procedure is to mix the easy and the hard items so that each time the child fails a task or problem, you give her an easy one to be sure that she has some feelings of success throughout the test. You can also provide a little encouragement (or a lot) and give the child a little time (or a lot) to come up with the answer. When you combine all the most encouraging things—lots of praise, lots of time, and successes mixed with failures—the child typically achieves a higher score, as much as 10 or 15 points higher in many cases (see Zigler & Butterfield).

Both these findings suggest further caution in interpreting the results of testing on a single day. Unless you know a good deal about the child's feelings and health and about the quality of the testing, it will be difficult to interpret results. Is the test score representative of the best performance that she can give under optimal conditions, or is it a kind of lower limit to her performance under discouraging, or even standard, conditions? The fact that the child's score varies from one testing situation to another because of her own feelings and the quality of the testing itself does not mean that test scores, overall, are not good predictors. An individual score may still be (in fact probably is) predictive of the child's performance in other situations. But you may be able to make a better prediction if you know something about the conditions of the test and the child's feelings.

Characteristics of Children with High Versus Low Scores

Are there any ways in which high-scoring children are systematically different from low-scoring children? We know that the two groups are likely to differ in social class, but are they different in style, in behavior, and personality? The amount of research on these questions is not vast, but there are a few conclusions that seem reasonable. First, children who are *highly* active—who move a great deal or fidget—are likely to score somewhat *lower* on standard IQ tests than do children with more moderate rates of movement. It is possible that the hyperactive child has suffered some kind of very minimal brain damage, and that both the high activity level and the lower IQ score are the result of the dysfunctioning of the brain. Halverson and Waldrop have recently found, for example, that among a group of school-age children, those who are the most physically active are also likely to have more "minor physical anomalies," which *may* point to some kind of irregularity in development prenatally. It is also possible, of course, that the highly active child simply spends less time in focused attention on those kinds of tasks that relate to cognitive development.

Second, higher IQ children seem to be those who from an early age get more intensely involved in intellectual tasks and get pleasure out of exploration and experimentation. Birns and Golden, for example, found that children who scored highest on an IQ test at age 3 were those who had been rated as having the greatest pleasure from and persistence at cognitive tasks at age 2.

Third, there is evidence from several studies that children who *increase* in IQ over childhood are more emotionally independent from parents and more competitive and aggressive with peers than are children who show decreases in IQ. Let me emphasize, as usual, that these are all *correlational* results. We do not know what casual links there are, if any, between the child's temperament or personality and her measured IQ. But it is at least reasonable to hypothesize that the child who approaches tasks with vigor and interest is likely to have different kinds of, and perhaps more informative, encounters with the world than is a more passive, less exploring child.

Finally, healthy children score higher than unhealthy children, and this is true for short-term ill health as well as long-term physical disability. I've already discussed malnutrition at great length in Chapter 3, so I needn't belabor that point again here, except to point out that the child's nutrition will affect her performance on an IQ test. But we also have evidence that on a given day a child who has a cold or is run down for some reason will not score as highly on an IQ test as she will on another day when she feels better (see, for example, the work of Honzink, McFarlane, & Allen).

FIGURE 29
The relationship between birth order and IQ. The chart shows the IQ test scores of children from families of varying sizes. Each line represents of family of a particular size, while each dot represents the mean IQ for the first, second, third or nth child in a family of that size. The data come from a study of over 400,000 Dutch males. (Source: R. B. Zajonc. Dumber by the dozen. *Psychology Today*, January 1975, *8*, 37–43. Copyright © 1974 Ziff-Davis Publishing Company. Reprinted by permission of *Psychology Today* magazine.)

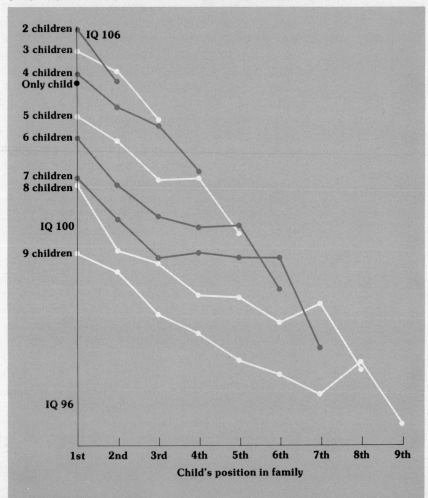

There is a *lot* of evidence showing that the IQs of children are related to their position in a family. Firstborn children have the highest average IQs, and the mean IQ declines steadily as you go down the family. Secondborn children have lower average scores than do firstborns, thirdborns have lower scores than secondborns, and so forth. Some sample results are given in Figure 29. How can such a finding be explained?

One possibility is that a mother's general health declines with repeated pregnancies, so that the prenatal environment of each succeeding child is less good. There is some support for this hypothesis in the fact that the second child in two very closely spaced pregnancies has somewhat more difficulty on IQ tests than does the second child from two wider spaced pregnancies. The "tired mother" hypothesis may also make some sense in the case of *very* large families. But it is difficult to see how physical fatigue or depletion could account for average differences in two-and three-child families in which the children are reasonably well spaced.

A second hypothesis, recently advanced by Robert Zajonc, is that the child's intellectual development is influenced by the particular combination of adults and children around her during her early years. Zajonc suggests that we might think in terms of the average developmental level of the people the infant contacts. The lower the average developmental level in the family, the slower the child's cognitive development will be. The firstborn child in a family encounters a very high average developmental level, since only the parents are involved. But the second child has the parents plus the older sibling. Suppose, for example, that an infant has a 3-year-old sibling. She has interactions both with the parents, who are at their full intellectual development, and with her preoperational sibling. The average developmental level is thus probably about concrete operations (to use Piaget's terminology). With each succeeding child the average drops, and so does the IQ of the child.

Zajonc's hypothesis makes a certain amount of intuitive sense, since we know that second-, third-, or later-born children do spend more time with other children than is the case with firstborns. And if we follow Zajonc's suggestion further, we would expect that a child born after a large gap in the family should do *better* intellectually, since the older siblings are now quite a lot older and can provide higher levels of intellectual stimulation. In fact such later-born children have higher IQs on the average than we would expect from their family position.

Still, I am not at all sure I am ready to buy Zajonc's rather simplified conception of the influence of the environment; I don't think that the effects of the environment are additive in the way he suggests. But most researchers who have looked at environmental effects on IQ have ignored the potential impact of older siblings, and Zajonc has quite rightly pointed us in a new direction.

On measures of overall IQ there are *no* consistent sex differences at any age. But when the IQ score is broken down into several components, some patterns of sex differences emerge.

Beginning at about adolescence boys are better on the average at tasks requiring spatial visualization, and often (but not always) better at mathematical reasoning problems. Girls are somewhat better on many tests of verbal skills, including measures of verbal reasoning, both in infancy and early childhood, and again at adolescence and among adults. Girls also get better grades in school.

Except for the difference in spatial ability, the sex differences in intellectual abilities are far smaller than the sex-role stereotypes would suggest. Girls and women are as good or better than are men and boys at most kinds of reasoning tasks, the exception being reasoning tasks involving mathematics. And men are not a whole lot less verbal than are women. Most of these differences emerge clearly only at adolescence. The differences at that age do not appear to be only the result of different school experiences—with boys taking more math and science courses. Rather, it seems likely that differences in spatial ability may underlie the observed differences in math skill, since many math problems require some kind of spatial visualization.

The sex difference in spatial ability *may* have genetic roots, and the genes involved may be located on the X chromosome and may be recessive. For a girl to inherit "high spatial ability," since she has two X chromosomes, she would have to receive the recessive "good space" gene from both mother and father; since a boy has only one X chromosome, which he receives from his mother, he need only inherit the recessive gene from her to have high spatial ability. The results from several studies of parent-child similarity in spatial skills make this look like a very likely hypothesis. Still, there are many girls who have high spatial ability and many boys who do not, so despite the *average* difference, the distributions overlap considerably.

OVERVIEW

It is important to remember than an IQ test is inevitably a measure of the child's performance. It is *not* a measure of capacity or competence. What it tells us is how well the child is doing at the moment of the test and under the circumstances of the test. Since children do not change all that much from day to day, the test score is also likely to predict how well she will perform in a similar situation, such as school. But it does *not* tell us much about how well that child can do two years from now or how well she would have done had she been raised in a different environment.

SUMMARY

1. Standard IQ tests do not measure all the aspects of the child's cognitive development that might interest us. They don't as a rule tell us where the child is in some sequence of logical development, as would a test based on Piaget's theory. But they do tell us something about the child's performance relative to that of her peers, and they do predict such nontest performance as school success with some reliability.

2. Test scores are influenced by the child's heredity, although we do not yet know precisely what inherited factors affect her performance. There is some agreement, however, that between 50 and 80 percent of the differences in IQ scores among individuals are attributable to differences in their genetic makeup.

3. The environment plays a major role. It may be helpful to think that while the child inherits a range of potential abilities, where she will actually function within that range depends on the kind of environment she grows up in. Some environments can encourage maximum growth, others may inhibit it, and still others may fall between. Children who test higher on standard tests more often come from middle-class families.

4. Regardless of the social class of the family, those parents who provide appropriate play materials, are involved with their child, and expect success tend to have children with higher scores.

5. Major environmental interventions, such as all-day enriched day care from infancy, can have a substantial positive effect on test scores; smaller amounts or shorter duration enrichments have smaller, or shorter-term, effects on test scores.

6. Children with high scores are likely to be those who are more intensely involved and interested in exploration and experimentation, and may be more independent and assertive. They are more likely to be first- or earlyborn children in a family.

7. No sex differences are found in total IQ scores, although males are somewhat higher in spatial ability and mathematical reasoning, and females are higher in some verbal abilities, including verbal reasoning.

8. The test score achieved by a particular child on a particular day will be influenced by the child's health and by the conditions of testing.

REFERENCES

Suggested Additional Readings

Ginsburg, H. *The myth of the deprived child.* Englewood Cliffs, N.J.: Prentice-Hall, 1972. A beautifully written, elegantly argued attempt to demonstrate that there is no fundamental difference in competence among children from different social classes; an argument against IQ tests as currently standardized and in favor of a more Piagetian approach.

Hunt, J. McV. *Intelligence and experience.* New York: Ronald Press, 1961. This book was a landmark, representing the turning point in our thinking about intelligence, from the view that IQ is largely fixed to the view that intelligence is malleable and heavily influenced by experience; reflects the theoretical influence of Piaget and includes an excellent discussion of the history of intelligence testing and the origins of the notion of fixed intelligence.

Kamin, L. J. *The science and politics of I.Q. Potomac, Maryland; Lawrence Erlbaum Associates, 1974.* An absolutely fascinating analysis of the data on inheritance of intelligence from a strongly environmentalistic point of view. There is some technical statistical language, but generally it is easy and engrossing reading. This book has very nearly made me change my mind about the inherited portion of intelligence.

Lewis, M. (Ed.). *Origins of intelligence: Infancy and early childhood.* New York: Plenum Press, 1976.

A very recent collection of papers on intelligence in infancy, including several discussions of "infant intelligence tests." A good first place for references and for recent thinking on intelligence and its measurement.

Maccoby, E. E., & Jacklin, C. N. *The psychology of sex differences.* Stanford, Calif.: Stanford University Press, 1974.

Once again, I refer you to this already classic work for more detailed information on sex differences, in this instance sex differences in intellectual functioning. See particularly Chapter 3.

Other Sources Cited

Binet, A., & Simon, T. *The development of intelligence in children.* Baltimore: Williams & Wilkins, 1916.

Birns, B., & Golden, M. Prediction of intellectual performance at 3 years from infant tests and personality measures. *Merrill-Palmer Quarterly,* 1972, *18,* 54–58.

Bradley, R. H., & Caldwell, B. M. Early home environment and changes in mental test performance in children from 6 to 36 months. *Developmental Psychology,* 1976, *12,* 93–97.

Elardo, R., Bradley, R., & Caldwell, B. M. The relation of infants' home environments to mental test performance from six to thirty-six months: A longitudinal analysis. *Child Development,* 1975, *46,* 71–76.

Golden, M., Birns, B., Bridger, W., & Moss, A. Social class differentiation in cognitive development among black preschool children. *Child Development,* 1971, *52,* 37–46.

Gray, S. W., & Klaus, R. A. The early training project: A seventh-year report. *Child Development,* 1970, *41,* 909–924.

Halverson, C. F., Jr., & Waldrop, M. F. Relations between preschool activity and aspects of intellectual and social behavior at age $7\frac{1}{2}$. *Developmental Psychology,* 1976, *12,* 107–112.

Hanson, R. A. Consistency and stability of home environmental measures related to IQ. *Child Development,* 1976, *46,* 470–480.

Heber, R., Garber, H., Harrington, S., & Hoffman, C. *Rehabilitation of families at risk for mental retardation.* Unpublished progress report, Research and Training Center, University of Wisconsin, Madison, Wisc., December 1972.

Honzik, H. P., MacFarlane, J. W., & Allen, L. The stability of mental test performance between two and eighteen years. *Journal of Experimental Education,* 1948, *17,* 309–324.

Jensen, A. R. How much can we boost IQ and scholastic achievement? *Harvard Educational Review,* 1969, *39,* 1–123.

Lesser, G. S., Fifer, G., & Clark, D. H. Mental abilities of children from different social class and cultural groups. *Monographs of the Society for Research in Child Development,* 1965, 30(4, Whole No. 102).

Levenstein, P. Cognitive growth in preschoolers through verbal interaction with mothers. *American Journal of Orthopsychiatry,* 1970, *40,* 426–432.

Madden, J., Levenstein, P., & Levenstein, S. Longitudinal IQ outcomes of the mother-child home program. *Child Development,* 1976, *47,* 1015–1025.

McCall, R. B., Appelbaum, M. I., & Hogarty, P. S. Developmental changes in mental performance. *Monographs of the Society for Research in Child Development,* 1973, 38(3, Whole No. 150).

Sacks, E. Intelligence scores as a function of experimentally established social relationships between child and examiner. *Journal of Abnormal and Social Psychology,* 1952, *46,* 354–358.

Scarr-Salapatek, S., & Weinberg, R. A. *IQ test performance of black children adopted by white families.* Paper presented at the biennial meeting of the Society for Research in Child Development, Denver, 1975.

Skeels, H. M. Adult status of children with contrasting early life experiences: A follow-up study. *Monographs of the Society for Research in Child Development,* 1966, 31(3, Whole No. 105).

Tulkin, S. R., & Covitz, F. E. *Mother-infant in-*

teraction and intellectual functioning at age six. Paper presented at the biennial meeting of the Society for Research in Child Development, Denver, 1975.

Uzgiris, I. C., & Hunt, J. McV. *Assessment in infancy. Ordinal scales of psychological development.* Chicago: University of Illinois Press, 1975.

Weikart, D. P. Relationship of curriculum, teaching and learning in preschool education. In J. C. Stanley (Ed.), *Preschool programs for the disadvantaged.* Baltimore: Johns Hopkins University Press, 1972.

Zajonc, R. B. Birth order and intelligence: Dumber by the dozen. *Psychology Today,* 1975, 8(8), 37–43.

Zigler, E., Abelson, W. D., & Seitz, V. Motivational factors in the performance of economically disadvantaged children on the Peabody Picture Vocabulary Test. *Child Development,* 1973, 43, 294–303.

Zigler, E., & Butterfield, E. C. Motivational aspects of changes in IQ test performance of culturally deprived nursery school children. *Child Development,* 1968, 39, 1–14.

11

The Development
of Interpersonal Relationships

Mommy, I *need* you.

You're a big dummy, Mommy. I hate you!

Don't you hit your sister.

You don't need me to help you; you can do it yourself.

Teacher, teacher, look what I drawed!

I don't want to play with *them*. They're *boys*.

If you are going to talk back to me like that, you can go to your room!

Most of you, I'm sure, have heard adults and children say such things to each other; I've even said some of them myself! All reflect aspects of the child's developing relationships with the people around her—her attachments to her mother and to others, her aggression or nonaggression toward others, and her relationships with her peers. Interactions with adults and other children are important for the growth of the child's intellectual skills and language, as I have emphasized in earlier chapters, but they are important in themselves as well. The child needs more than mind and tongue to survive. She also needs effective and satisfying relationships with the other people around her, and she must develop styles of interacting that will produce those satisfactions.

The development of the child's interpersonal behavior is also of critical importance to her parents. In many ways the child's aggression and dependency are among the most visible of her behaviors, the ones that parents feel most compelled to control. A child's cognitive accomplishments can be noticed, enjoyed, and gloated over, but they are not likely to compel action in the way that an excessively clinging child may. Most parents consider their major business as parents to train their children to fit into the prevailing society in some ways, to shape them so that their behavior with others falls within some kind of acceptable range. Of course, parents differ enormously in their views on what is acceptable behavior, but for all parents the problem of socializing the child is ever present.

In exploring this important area, we ask at least three kinds of "what" questions:

1. Do children change systematically with age in the ways they relate to others? Are there observable developmental progressions, as in cognitive development?
2. How much do children differ from one another in interpersonal behavior? Are some more aggressive or more clinging than others?
3. How do the experiences of highly aggressive or dependent children differ from those of their less aggressive or dependent peers?

The fourth question, the "why" question, I will take up in Chapter 12.

Because theory and research on the development of interpersonal relationships are not focused on broad changes with age, an overall sequential discussion is less relevant here than in the case of cognitive development. Instead, I will look at each of three areas separately: the development of attachment and dependency, of aggression, and of peer relationships.

ATTACHMENT
AND
DEPENDENCY
Developmental
Trends
THE EARLIEST
INTERACTIONS

In the past five or ten years there has been a rather astonishing outpouring of interest in and research effort on the earliest relationship of infant and caregiver. Many of the patterns of later interaction between parent and child seem to be set in the earliest days and weeks, when the infant and the mother (or father) develop important, reciprocal patterns.

Until quite recently most psychologists had thought of the early interactions in terms of the *infant's* attachment to the mother; there is now quite a lot of good research on this process—which I will be describing shortly. But in the earliest weeks and months an equally critical process seems to be the *mother's* attachment to the child. I have come to think of these earliest interactions as a kind of dance. The infant has certain signals—she cries, she smiles, she looks alert, she cuddles her body into the mother's when she is picked up, she looks the mother in the eye—and the mother has certain responses to those signals. The mother goes to the child, picks her up, jiggles or jounces her, holds her to the shoulder, feeds her, changes her diaper, looks her in the eye, and so forth.

The mother initiates interactions with the child as well, by talking to the baby, picking her up, smiling at her or looking her in the eye. And the child responds to these signals in characteristic ways. What results, even between a mother and a newborn infant, is a chain of signal and response between the two. Kenneth Kaye points out that one of the critical elements in this early pattern of interaction is the turn-taking that is built into it. The mother and the infant, in some sense, take turns, just as adults do in conversation. First I say something, then you say something, then it's my turn. Since the infant can't talk, the turn-taking occurs with actions. Kaye sees this sort of turn-taking in the earliest feedings of the child. The baby sucks for a while, then stops; the mother jiggles the baby a bit, presumably hoping to get the baby started sucking again. The mother stops jiggling, and then the baby starts sucking again. So they have taken turns: Suck-pause-jiggle-pause, suck-pause-jiggle-pause.

This early reciprocity of relationship seems to be critical in the mother developing a sense of being attached to her own infant. Infants who do *not* signal in these ways, who do not respond or smile or cuddle, are *far* harder to relate to. Selma Fraiberg has done a series of observations of mother-infant attachment in blind infants, described in Box 19, which illustrates the kind of difficulties that can occur when the child does not provide clear signals to the mother.

One of the more important signals, from the point of view of the mother, seems to be *mutual gaze*—an encounter in which mother and infant look at one another's eyes for some period of time. This seems to occur first some time around 1 to 2 months of age in the infant, or more fleetingly in younger infants. Many mothers report that the moment when their child first "looked at them" was the moment they felt the baby was really *their* baby. By 3 to 4 months of age mutual gaze seems to be quite firmly estblished, but research by Stern shows that it is the *infant,* and not the mother, who is primarily in control of the mutuality. In the "play" interactions that Stern observed the mother looked at the child most of the time and talked to her as well. It is the infant who makes and then breaks off eye contact. A good deal of the mother's behavior in these sessions seems to be designed to entice the child into looking at her. The best combination of behaviors on the mother's part is talking to the infant while looking at her; this is most likely to elicit mutual gaze in the child.

There is no reason to believe that at this early age the infant looks at the mother because she is attached to her. But the infant's looking has an effect on the *mother's* attachment to the child. If the child is unable to manage or maintain mutual gaze—as in the case of the blind infants Fraiberg studied—or is unable to enter into the "dance" of interaction in the early months, then the mother is likely to feel estranged from the child. Such feelings of estrangement on the part of the mother may have powerful effects on the long-term quality of the relationship between mother and child.

BOX 19
Blind Infants and Their Mothers

The importance of the child's signals, particularly her eyes and her facial expressions, in "hooking" the parent into interaction and into attachment to the child is underlined by a series of fascinating studies by Fraiberg of blind infants. Blind infants do not smile as early as do normal infants, and they do not smile in response to a smile the way sighted infants do. Even in older blind infants, who do show some kind of "social smile," the smile is somehow less intense. Blind infants also do not engage in mutual gaze and have a much smaller repertoire of facial expressions.

Fraiberg has studied ten blind infants in interaction with their mothers, and has found that the mothers nearly always interpret the child's less expressive face as a sign of depression, de-tachment, or even rejection. The blind baby does not turn her head when you come into the room; instead, she may *stop* playing. What she is obviously doing is listening to the sounds of your entering. But parents don't automatically figure that out. Instead, they are likely to react to the absence of any kind of greeting by feeling rejected or they consider the child unresponsive. Fraiberg's observation was that eight of the ten mothers she studied had to be helped to "read" the child's other signs, since the visual signals were all missing. Without help, these mothers felt less attached and less close to their infant. Two of the mothers managed to learn on their own to interpret the child's body movements and other signs, but these were both mothers with extensive experience with infants.

THE INFANT'S ATTACHMENT TO THE CAREGIVER

The other half of the process is the child's development of specific and exclusive attachment to the mother or other caregiver. Studies by Ainsworth and by Schaffer and Emerson point to a clear sequence in the development of such early attachments. Schaffer and Emerson identified three basic phases.

Indiscriminate Attachment. This begins quite early. The baby may protest at being put down or separated, but it doesn't seem to matter who holds her or puts her down. She protests as much over being put down by a stranger as by her mother. In Schaffer and Emerson's study this period lasted until about 7 months of age (although there were differences among babies on this point). Other researchers have suggested that perhaps this period ends sooner, at about 5 months of age.

Specific Attachment. This begins at about 7 months of age or earlier and becomes quite intense for three or four months or more. The baby is usually attached to just one person, most commonly her mother, and shows distress when her mother leaves or puts her down. Fear of strangers—shown by such behaviors as crying at the approach of a stranger—usually appears about a month after the child begins to show this specific attachment. There seems to be a wide range of individual differences in the age at which this stage begins. The youngest child in Schaffer and Emerson's study showed a strong specific attachment at about age 22 weeks, but several babies did not show any such attachment until about 1 year old.

Multiple Attachments. Several months after the beginning of specific attachments, the child begins to show a broadening of attach-

Fraiberg and her staff found that they, too, responded differently to a blind infant, despite their great awareness of and sensitivity to other signals. Fraiberg describes one experience in which a sighted child had come to the laboratory for a visit:

When a sighted child comes to visit, there is spontaneous rapport and we trot out our repertoire of antics with babies. We are back in the tribal system where the baby plays his social game and we play ours. If one has worked very largely with blind babies for many years, as we have, the encounter with a sighted baby is absurdly like the experience of meeting a compatriot abroad after a long stay in a country where the language and customs are alien. The compatriot, who can be a perfect stranger asking for directions, is greeted like a friend, his regional accent and idiom are endearing, and with nothing more in common than a continent two strangers can embark upon a social exchange in which nearly all the tribal signs are understood and correctly interpreted.

What we miss in the blind baby, apart from the eyes that do not see, is the vocabulary of signs and signals that provides the most elementary and vital sense of discourse long before words have meaning (Fraiberg, 1974, p. 271).

It is precisely this sense of "discourse" that seems to form the earliest basis for attachment of the parent to the infant. In any infant—blind, deaf, cerebral palsied, or otherwise impaired—for whom this discourse is altered, there is likely to be an alteration in the pattern of early mother-infant attachment as well.

ments, first perhaps to one other person, then to several other people. By 18 months most babies have some attachment to several people (the mother, father, brothers and sisters, grandparents, the usual babysitter, and so on). In the Schaffer and Emerson study only 13 percent of the babies were still attached exclusively to a single figure at 18 months of age.

It is worth emphasizing that the ages Schaffer and Emerson have suggested as division points between stages are only approximate. Babies differ markedly in the ages at which they move from one stage to another. Furthermore, the age at which a child is said to have developed a specific attachment may depend partly on how the attachment is measured. Schaffer and Emerson used the child's protest at separation from her mother and her reaction to the strange experimenter as measures of the child's attachment to her mother. Mary Ainsworth, who has done extensive and fascinating work in this area, used the child's smiling and vocalization to others as additional measures, and she suggests that exclusive protests over the departure of the mother (or other major caregiver) often comes fairly late, after the child has already shown signs of specific attachment by smiling and vocalizing more for her mother than for others. But regardless of the arguments over the precise chronological age of the beginning of specific attachment, there does seem to be general agreement that there are three phases, and that most children pass through them in the order described by Schaffer and Emerson.

There is far less information on the developmental patterns of attachment or dependency after early infancy. There is a distinct discontinuity in the research in this area between those studying attachment in infants and those interested in dependency in older children. It is not at *all* clear what the relationship between the two behaviors may be. In preschoolers dependency is defined in terms of clinging, being near, and seeking attention or approval. There is quite an extensive literature on such dependency behaviors among preschool children, but nearly all of the studies have been done in nursery schools or similar settings, and there is little information about the continuing changes in the child's attachment to or relationship with the mother or major caregiver. So we have two rather unconnected sets of research, one on early attachment, and one on dependency in preschool-age and older children.

One study that bridges this gap somewhat is an analysis of attachment behaviors in 2- to 3-year-old children by Maccoby and Feldman. They studied children in a laboratory procedure that has come to be called the "strange situation," which was first devised by Ainsworth. The procedure consists of a series of episodes, all occurring in a playroom stocked with a wide variety of toys. In different episodes, the child is alone in the room with the mother. A stranger enters, the mother leaves the child with the stranger and then returns, and then leaves the child totally alone. Finally, the mother again returns. From observing children in this setting we may get some sense of the way in which they react to strangers, the way they handle the stress of being alone with a stranger or being totally alone, and the kind of attachment or dependency behaviors (being near, clinging, asking for attention or approval) they show toward the mother or the stranger. (An example of a child's reaction to a stressful situation is shown in Figure 30.)

Maccoby and Feldman used this procedure in a short-term longitudinal study beginning with an observation when the children were 2, and then reobserving the children at $2\frac{1}{2}$ and 3 years. Later, they were also able to observe some of these same children in a nursery school setting with teachers and other adults.

Over the period from age 2 to age 3 the children were better and better able to cope with the mother's departure. The older children cried less when the mother left and were friendlier to the stranger when alone with her. Older children handled being left entirely alone differently as well, crying and calling for the mother less. But at all ages, when the stranger first came into the room, the children drew closer to the mother. These findings suggest that there may well be further "stages" or "phases" in the *de*tachment process past the point of multiple attachments that Schaffer and Emerson describe. Three-year-olds still use the mother as a "safe base" when they are under stress, but it takes more stress to produce this and they are able to handle the presence of the stranger more quickly.

272

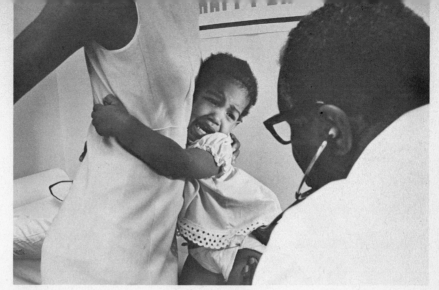

FIGURE 30
A young child showing a clinging attachment in the face of stress.

What can we conclude from all of this? First, children appear to become progressively more *de*tached from the mother over the period up to age 3. They spend less time being near or clinging and more time in independent play. Periodically, their play is punctuated by bids for attention or approval, such as "Mommy, look at my picture," or by merely showing something constructed, or by talking to the mother about something else. Second, children continue to show attachment to the mother through this period and continue to use her as a safe base from which to explore new or strange things.

These findings are consistent with what has been observed about developmental shifts in dependency behavior among nursery school children. In nursery schools or comparable settings 2- to 3-year-olds show more clinging to the teacher and more "proximity seeking" than do the 3- to 4-year-olds, while the older children show more attention seeking, both from teachers and from peers. So there seems to be good agreement that there is not only a *spread* of attachment—from mother to several other adults and from adults to peers—but also there is a shift in the way in which attachment, or dependency, is displayed—from clinging and being near to approval and attention seeking.

Past age 4 or 5 the information on developmental trends in attachment or dependency dries up almost completely. What little we know about this comes from studies of changes in peer relationships, which I will touch on later in this chapter.

Individual Differences

Within the limits of the developmental trends just described, there are enormous differences among children, both in the timing of their shifts

from one stage to another and in the strength and "feeling tone" of their attachments. Ainsworth has distinguished three groups of infants in her studies of early attachment: the securely attached, the insecurely attached, and the unattached. The securely attached baby shows all the positive signs of attachment to the mother. She smiles when she sees her, holds out her arms to be picked up, vocalizes more to her mother, looks at her mother when she's in the room, and so on. At the same time she is able to leave her mother for brief periods to explore the environment, returning occasionally for reassurance, and she does not always protest when her mother leaves her alone for a period of time. The securely attached baby cries less overall and seems generally content. Insecurely attached babies, as Ainsworth describes them, cry a great deal, even when held by the mother. They demand the mother's attention, cling to her, and show considerable distress when she leaves. Finally, Ainsworth suggests that some children never develop attachments to their mother or other individual adult figures at all. All of Schaffer and Emerson's subjects showed some single attachments, although apparently the strength and duration of such attachments varied considerably. It seems reasonable to conclude that children differ in both the strength and the quality of this primary attachment as well as in the speed at which they show spread of attachment to others.

Additional evidence of individual differences can be found in work with nursery school-age children. There appear to be at least two independent clusters of behavior. First is the clinging, being near, touching-and-holding pattern. Some children show their attachment to and dependency on the nursery school teacher (and probably on the mother as well) by sitting near her, by wanting to climb on her lap, by hanging on to her, clinging to her, and so forth. Other children seek the teacher's attention and approval for their activities but don't seem to want or need to be near her or to have physical contact with her. Within each of these clusters of behavior children seem to be fairly consistent over at least short periods of time. That is, a 2-year-old who seeks a lot of approval from the teacher is likely to show the same behavior at 4, and a 2-year-old who clings and holds a lot is likely to show a lot of such behavior later, too.

There is also some evidence that the child who seeks approval and attention from the teacher is likely to seek both from other children as well, whereas the clinging child is not. The clinging child is in some sense showing a less mature form of dependency; she has not yet shifted her major attachments to include her peers. Also, the child who seeks attention from peers is likely to give attention and help to them as well, whereas the clinging child is not. So the attention-seeking child is developing reciprocal relationships with her peers from the age of 2 or 3, while the child who is still strongly (and perhaps insecurely?) attached to adults is delayed in developing peer relationships.

But what about the stability of attachment or dependency over time? There are two related questions. First, what kind of individual consistency is there between the early infant attachments and the nursery school-age dependency behaviors? And second, what kind of longer term, life-time consistency is there in dependency-type behaviors?

The Maccoby and Feldman study gives us the best information on the first question. Over the one-year period in which they observed the children in the "strange situation" there were individual consistencies. The children who cried a great deal at age 2 when the mother left also cried a great deal at age 3 when she left. These same children were also more likely to show a lot of "being near" toward the teacher in the nursery school. So there is *some* indication that a more tearful, and *perhaps* less mature or less secure, attachment to the mother is followed by less mature forms of dependency in the school setting. But these relationships are still highly tentative. We really do not know whether the "insecurely attached" infant goes on to become a more clingy, less independent preschooler.

The best life-span study of consistency in dependency is one done at the Fels Research Institute by Kagan and Moss. They reviewed the available information on a group of children who had been subjects in a longitudinal study from birth through adulthood and found that over periods as long as six to eight years there was considerable consistency in many aspects of dependency. For example, children who were high in what Kagan and Moss called "affectional dependency" (seeking acceptance, approval, and affection from adults) at preschool age were likely still to be somewhat higher in this behavior at age 8 and at age 12. In childhood (up to age 14) there was about equal consistency for boys and for girls. But consistency from childhood to adulthood was much more marked for females than for males. That is, if you want to predict an adult's level of dependency and to base this prediction on what kind of child she or he was, you will have more success predicting for a girl than for a boy. Boys show some consistency within childhood but not from childhood to adulthood, with the exception that the passive male infant is likely to be a passive male adult. Among girls, adolescents who were passive and dependent on adults and lacking in independence, as adults themselves were dependent on their parents, withdrew from stress situations, chose secure jobs, and avoided risks in the choice of their vocations.

There is a very sticky methodological difficulty in any research on "consistency of personality," which I should remind you of before you come to the conclusion that consistency is a rare phenomenon. Suppose you observe an infant showing all the signs of an "insecure attachment" (to use Ainsworth's phrase). You assume that behind the crying, clinging behavior is both an important attachment to the mother and also a feeling, perhaps, of fear that this relationship will somehow be lost. Now how would you expect that child to behave at age 2, at age 8, or as an adult? If the fear of loss of relationship stays the same, how will that fear show itself? Is there any reason to suppose that the child will continue to cling? Isn't it just as likely that the child will learn other ways to maintain relationships that are more effective? If so, then there would be a change in the external, observable behavior, while the underlying (inferred) quality remained the same. The problem with trying to study consistency over time is to decide how to measure the same "quality" in children of different ages. When, in a given piece of research such as Kagan and Moss's study, we note that there is only small consistency among men in dependency and passivity, we cannot conclude that there is no unifying thread running through the individual man's behavior from infancy to adulthood. All we know is that our measures have not picked up such a thread. Nonetheless, it is useful to know something about the consistency of behavior and to know that in this area there is more behavioral consistency for women than for men.

Factors Influencing Attachment and Dependency

Where do individual differences in attachment and dependency come from? Are children born with different propensities for attachment? Do the differences in strength of attachment arise out of the baby's early interactions with her mother?

276

Individual differences in babies at birth probably do contribute in important ways to the development of attachments. In Chapter 4 I described a study by Chess and Thomas of temperamental differences among babies. You may recall that they identified three patterns, which they call the "easy" baby, the "difficult" baby, and the "slow-to-warm-up" baby. These three types of infant sound very much like Ainsworth's "securely attached," "insecurely attached," and "unat-tached" babies—which suggests at least the possibility that the child's basic temperamental qualities and the mother's responses to those qualities may provide an important basis for early attachments. That is, secure attachments may not come about just because the mother has been confident, affectionate, and attentive. All those factors may matter, but it may be much simpler to develop a secure attachment with a temperamentally "easy" baby than with a temperamentally "difficult" one. (This is another very good example of the importance of interaction effects in development.)

But the mother's treatment of the child and the timing of her treatment matter as well. Ainsworth has begun to look at this aspect of the development of attachment and has come to some interesting conclusions. She found that mothers who held their babies less frequently (other than for feeding, diapering, or during other routine care) but who held them tenderly and for longer during each holding episode and who responded contingently and consistently to the baby were likely to have babies who appeared "securely attached." The babies in these dyads take the initiative in making contact by cooing, smiling, or holding out their arms. They show pleasure when held and not much distress when put down again.

On the other hand, mothers who have more frequent (but briefer) episodes of holding tend to have babies who do not respond positively when in contact, and yet who protest after they have been put down—an obviously ambivalent kind of behavior. Mothers who are abrupt and interfering in their pick ups tend to have babies who respond negatively to contact and who squirm to get down. (Ainsworth, Bell, & Stayton, 1972, p. 140)

Ainsworth and her colleagues have also found that a mother's response to the infant's crying during the earliest months of life may set a pattern that affects not only the child's frequency or duration of crying, but also the apparent security of her attachment to the mother. These findings are given in some detail in Box 20.

Schaffer and Emerson found that the sheer amount of time the mother was with the infant did not seem to be related to the strength of the infant's attachment, but the amount of time the mother actually spent stimulating or interacting with the infant did. Mothers who were more attentive and responsive to their infants had infants who appeared more strongly attached. They also observed that infants who had several caregivers (e.g., a regular baby sitter, a grandparent, an older

BOX 20
Mothers' Responses to Crying in Babies

One comment that you will often hear from mothers (or fathers) is that you shouldn't pick up a baby immediately when she starts to cry. If you do, they say, you'll spoil her. She'll just get used to the idea that all she has to do is cry and you'll come and pick her up, so she'll cry more and use her crying as a kind of manipulative device.

Mary Ainsworth's research, which I have discussed at some length in the main part of the text, provides us with one of the first empirical tests of these expectations. In her most recent study she observed 26 mother-infant pairs, all from middle-class American families. The homes were visited every three weeks from the time the babies were 3 weeks old until they were 54 weeks old, each visit lasting about four hours. Among the many variables observed were the babies' crying and the speed and style of the mother's response to it. The finding is unusually clear: Mothers who waited to respond to crying had babies who cried more often than did mothers who picked the babies up right away.

Even more interesting, there is some evidence that the direction of cause can be identified. When Ainsworth observed the mother's responsiveness to the baby's crying during one three-month period and related it to the baby's actual crying during the following three-month period, she found a consistent relationship. That is, a baby of, say, 7 months of age who cried often was likely to have a mother who had been unresponsive to her crying when she was 4 and 5 months old. The implication is that a mother can change her style and speed of responding to her baby's crying and that the child's behavior will then change; but it takes a while for the baby's pattern to alter in response to the mother's change in pattern. Ainsworth and her colleagues draw the following conclusion:

These findings are, of course, inconsistent with the views of those who assume that to respond to crying is to reinforce it, so that mothers who respond promptly are likely to have "spoiled" babies who cry more, whereas mothers who refuse to reward this changeworthy behavior by responding to it should

sibling, or a father) showed an earlier and more rapid shift from the single-attachment to the multiple-attachment stage.

It seems clear from these two studies that there is some connection between the mother's behavior and the quality or strength of the baby's attachment to her. But note that the findings in both cases are largely correlational in nature. What we know is that mothers who give lots of attention have more attached babies, but we don't know which way the relationship runs. Is the baby more attached because her mother pays more attention to her, or does the mother pay more attention to the baby because she is more attached (or "easier" in temperament)? In this case, though, we are somewhat better off than usual, for both studies followed mothers and babies over a period of time, and in both cases mothers who paid a lot of attention to their very young infants—before specific attachments had occurred—had babies who were later more securely attached, which makes it seem as if the mother's style of behavior may be influential in this situation.

ATTACHMENT AND DAY CARE   Another line of evidence on the factors that may affect early attachments of the infant are the studies of children in day care. These children are separated from the mother for long periods each day. What ef-

themselves be rewarded by having babies who cry little. According to our data, the reverse is true. (Ainsworth, Bell, & Stayton, 1972, p. 131)

This result can be understood in at least two ways. First, we can refer to all the work on schedules of reinforcement and their effects (see Box 2) and conclude that the mother who responds slowly to her child's cries is establishing a schedule of partial reinforcement. We know that such a schedule is likely to produce vigorous behavior, highly resistant to extinction. Alternatively, perhaps the Ainsworth finding can be understood in terms of the child's developing sense of "trust," to use Erik Erikson's word. Erikson emphasizes that the child's first cognitive-emotional task is to establish a sense of basic trust. If there is no opportunity to do so then a basic feeling of mistrust may develop instead. When the mother responds promptly to her child's cries, she may be reassuring the child that the world (her mother and all the rest) can be trusted to help when help is needed, and she may build the child's confidence and trust in her own ability to control what happens to her. The mother who does not respond promptly may make it more difficult for the child to develop feelings of trust and self-confidence; therefore, the child may be more anxious and more insecure about the world, and she may cry more.

No doubt neither of these two explanations is entirely correct, for, as always, other complex relationships are involved. For example, the mother who responds promptly to her child's crying responds just as promptly to her cooing or smiling and other positive social cries, so she reinforces those behaviors, too, and may help the infant to develop modes of communication that are good alternatives to crying. The important point of Ainsworth's analysis, however, is that prompt response to crying does not encourage crying, as many parents have thought.

fect might such separation have on the child's attachment? Schaffer and Emerson noted that among the infants they studied, those who were cared for exclusively by their mothers were more strongly attached than were babies cared for by others. A number of legislators and other policy makers, along with some psychologists, have argued against day care for young children on precisely such grounds—that the separation of mother and child which accompanies day care will somehow "weaken" the child's attachment to the mother. In the past several years there has been a batch of good studies of this question, and the preponderance of the evidence seems to be pointing to the conclusion that there is *no* negative effect on the child's attachment to the mother as a result of day-care experience. A number of investigators have used a "strange situation" format, similar to that used by Maccoby and Feldman. The majority of such studies show no important differences between home-reared and day-care children in their response to the stranger or to being separated from the mother. In one of these studies Ragozin also observed children in a day-care center first thing in the morning when they were left by the mother, and again in the afternoon when the mother came to pick up the child. The day-care children showed delight at seeing the mother at the end of the day, so there was evidence that they were still strongly attached to the mother, even though these same children showed attachment to day-care workers as well.

Caldwell and her associates have also explored the question of attachment in day-care children, in this instance using observation and interview of the mother and child at home as the major source of information about the attachment of the child to the mother. They could find *no* indication that the day-care children were more weakly attached to the mothers than were home-reared children. In this study the strength of the child's attachment to the mother seemed to be more a function of the quality of the interaction between the two than of the duration of their time together.

The single study showing any kind of disturbance of attachment in children in group care is a study by Blehar. She observed 2- and 3-year-old children in a strange situation and concluded that the 3-year-old day-care children showed a kind of anxious attachment to the mother, which Blehar believed was a sign of serious disruption of the attachment process. The 2-year-old day-care children in the same study were described by Blehar as showing indifference or detachment from the mother, which again Blehar interpreted as a sign of a restriction of attachment. One major difference between Blehar's study and the other explorations of the effects of day-care centers on attachment is that the day-care centers from which Blehar drew her subjects all had large numbers of children for each adult; the adult child ratios were apparently on the order of $1:7$ or $1:8$. In the other studies the day-care subjects all attended day-care centers with adult/child ratios of about $1:4$ or $1:5$. It is entirely possible that the number of adults available to the child makes a critical difference in the child's sense of security or attachment, both to the adults in the day-care center and to the mother.

Although the collective weight of the evidence seems to be telling us that day care is not detrimental to young children, for both theoretical and policy reasons, we need still more data. We need to know far more about the impact of day care on infants. Most of the studies thus far have involved toddlers; there is far less information about the effect of separation for day care during the first year of life. It is possible that the timing of the separation of mother and child may make a significant difference in the effect on the child. In an earlier study by Schaffer and Callender of children hospitalized for elective surgery during their first year, the effects differed depending on the age of the child. Children younger than about 7 months showed little or no distress accompanying or following the hospitalization, but children 7 months and older showed depression and disturbance of attachment after returning home. Perhaps separation during the peak of single attachment is particularly difficult. If this is the case should parents place children in day care before the peak time or wait until a spread of attachment has occurred? At the moment we don't have good data to answer such practical questions.

LATER DEPENDENCY

Beyond infancy, information about the factors that might produce individual differences in attachment or dependency is more scattered and less consistent. In experimental situations children who have been rewarded for dependency increase in dependent behavior, and those who are punished for it show less dependency—at least in the experimental situation. But translating this fact into a home situation is difficult, for it is rare in the extreme to find parents who are that consistent in their responses to any behavior. Typically, a child experiences rewards for dependent behavior at some times and punishment at others. A mother may be perfectly able to handle a child's desire for cuddling when she is sitting down between jobs and can take time for it. But she may be hugely annoyed if the child comes in to demand attention when she is in the middle of breaking eggs for a souffle. This kind of understandable inconsistency in behavior makes it impossible to find really "pure cases" of reward or punishment for dependency in the home, so it is not surprising that research findings on the relationship between parents' child-rearing practices and children's dependency is somewhat inconsistent as well. In some studies "warm" (affectionate, demonstrative, presumably encouraging of dependency) families have more dependent children, whereas in other studies rejection is associated with high levels of dependency. In perhaps the best-known study of the relationship between child-rearing practices and child behavior (by Sears, Maccoby & Levin) the children most likely to be highly dependent came from families who reported that they both rewarded and punished dependency. (Of course, this result makes sense as an effect of a kind of partial-reinforcement schedule discussed in Box 2, page 18).

There is still less information on the kind of home experiences that may bring about a clinging dependency as opposed to a more "mature" dependency, such as seeking attention or approval. As the home-observation studies of mother-child interactions are extended upward in age, we may begin to be able to tease out some of these relationships.

The ultimate breakdown of the entire attachment/dependency process can be seen in instances of child abuse, when a parent intentionally injures a child. Some of the issues and incidences of abuse are discussed in Box 21.

AGGRESSION Developmental Trends

Little research has been focused on developmental changes in aggressive behavior, and what evidence there is relates to changes in the type of aggressive behavior rather than to changes in the strength or amount of aggression.

281 The Development of Interpersonal Relationships

BOX 21
Child Abuse

The incidence of child abuse in the United States is *extremely* difficult to determine. The vast majority of cases are not reported at all, in part because most cases of abuse are never seen by a physician or other social agency. In the widest national survey, involving all cases reported in the country in 1967 and 1968, nearly half were reported by hospitals, suggesting that only abuse with quite severe consequences is reported. In the 1967–1969 national survey by Gil, the rate of abuse was about 8 cases per 100,000 children in 1967, and about 9 cases per 100,000 in 1968. Probably the incidence is *far* higher than this.

Who are the abused children, and what do we know about parents who abuse? Gil found, in the national survey, that about half of the abused children were under age 6, with about a quarter under age 2. One frequently heard (or read) generalization about abused children is that they are usually infants and perhaps incessantly crying infants. The national survey does not show this, since three-quarters of the abused children were past infancy, and almost half were school age.

Boys are somewhat more likely to be abused than are girls, but this is more true among younger children. In adolescence girls are almost twice as likely to be abused as are boys—and in this survey sexual abuse was not included, so the abuse of teenage girls is physical abuse of other kinds.

Minority group children are about three times as likely to be abused (or at least such cases are three times as likely to be reported). But religious affiliation is not a predictor of abuse: All religious groups are represented among the group of abusers in the national survey.

There is considerable argument among psychologists and physicians about the best way to characterize parents who abuse their children. Some researchers, including Gil, have emphasized the social forces at work. Garbarino, in a recent study based on some of Gil's hypotheses, has shown that the rate of child abuse in counties of New York can be predicted quite well by knowing the number of households headed by women, particularly working women, and the average family income in the county. Counties with high rates of employed women who are heads of households have higher rates

One of the better studies on developmental trends is an old one by Florence Goodenough (published in 1931), based not on observations by the experimenters but on diaries kept by mothers, each of whom recorded every outburst of aggression on the part of her child, its probable cause, and the outcome. The accumulated information from these diaries suggested several changes during the period from age 2 to age 5.

1. Older children experienced aftereffects of their aggression. They sulked or appeared to feel resentful longer than did younger children.
2. Temper tantrums diminished during this period and were quite uncommon after age 4.
3. Older children, especially children older than 3 years of age, were more likely to retaliate against other children or even adults if they felt they had gotten the raw end of a deal, like having a toy taken away. (See Figure 31.)
4. The reasons for aggression appeared to change over this age range.

of abuse. Gil and Garbarino both argue that the cumulative stress of insufficient income—and working and mothering at the same time—greatly increases the likelihood of abuse of the children.

It seems entirely reasonable that some conception of family stress may help to predict child abuse. Families under severe economic or emotional stress who do not have good resources to fall back on are more prone to a number of things, including child abuse. But such sociological or ecological factors are clearly not the only answer. Not all poor working women who are heads of households abuse their children. And many abused children come from middle-class, intact families. So other factors are obviously also at work.

Other researchers, who have focused more closely on the interactions of particular mother-child or father-child pairs, have emphasized that abuse represents a lack of sensitivity to the child's needs or a lack of *empathy*. Abusing parents seem to be more focused on their own needs and are less aware of or are less sensitive to the needs of the child. Many abusers, in fact, seem to be trying to meet their own needs through their children. These parents are emotionally immature and are largely incapable of providing the kind of secure base needed by the child. Instead, they turn to the child for their own security, and when the child (inevitably) lets them down, the child may be abused. Many abusing parents were *themselves* abused as children. In Erikson's terms, they probably had not successfully developed a sense of basic trust and thus have great difficulty establishing such a sense in their own children.

Such psychological conditions, when they accompany the environmental stresses Gil emphasizes (or other family stress), seem to have a high probability of resulting in some form of child abuse.

Younger children (2 to 3 years old) most often were aggressive after conflicts with parents in which the parents had imposed their authority. Older children (ages 4 and 5) were more likely to show aggression after conflicts with brothers, sisters, or other playmates, which again shows the shift in focus from adults to peers that seems to occur at about age 4 or 5.

Observations of nursery school-age children show another change, from physical aggression to verbal aggression. Rather than attack physically, a 4-year-old is more likely to shout something like, "You big dummy!" to a child who knocks over her block tower.

At the same time children are making an important shift in the pattern of their play, which has some impact on the amount of aggression. In the youngest nursery school-age children the most common form of play is parallel play, in which several children play near one another but each on her own project. Older children show more cooperative play, in which two or more children play at the same game or work on

FIGURE 31
Aggression between preschool-age peers; aggression typically increases at this age.

the same project. Conflicts over the game or toys are much more common in cooperative play, and there is more quarreling and other aggression. There is no evidence to suggest that the 4- or 5-year-old has become somehow more aggressive overall, but more aggression may be observed simply because there are more frustrating or conflict-laden situations in her life at this age.

Developmental changes in aggression, if any, after age 5 have been studied rarely, so we have little to go on. What information there is suggests that the total quantity of aggression continues to decrease through adolescence, although there is the possibility that "fantasy" aggression increases. That is, older children may learn to be aggressive by imagining aggressive actions of various kinds rather than by showing their aggression overtly.

Individual Differences

Discussions of individual differences in aggression are nearly always dominated by the single important fact that boys, on almost all measures in almost all studies, are more aggressive than are girls. The difference can be shown at least as early as age 2 or 3 and seems to continue through the entire age span. There is some evidence indicating that girls and women are more anxious about being aggressive than are boys and men, but boys and men are more likely to be openly physical in aggression and use more verbal aggression as well.

But not all boys are equally aggressive, nor are all girls equally unaggressive. There are variations within each sex, and there is some indication that the differences are consistent across time. That is, a boy or girl who does a lot of hitting, kicking, and so on at age 6 is likely to exhibit lots of the same kinds of physical aggression at age 10; and a child who shows a lot of aggression toward her mother (either verbal, as in screaming, "I hate you!" or physical, as in hitting, biting, or kicking) at age 4 or 5 is likely to be still showing a fair amont of aggression toward her as late as age 10. Competitiveness, too, shows some consistency across ages. Competitive 4- and 5-year-olds become competitive 10-year-olds, and among girls competitiveness continues to be highly predictable from early behavior as late as age 14. Beyond adolescence, however, predictions are better for men than for women. In the Fels longitudinal study (the Kagan & Moss study I described earlier) boys who were allowed or encouraged to be aggressive toward their mothers during childhood and adolescence were likely as adults to become angry quickly and to retaliate (by shouting, resistance, or other kinds of verbal aggression) when they felt wronged. But these predictions did not hold for girls. That is, it was not possible to tell from a girl's aggression toward her mother at age 6 or age 12 what kind of or how much aggression she was likely to exhibit as an adult woman.

One point deserves emphasis. Dependency and passivity are more consistent from childhood to adulthood for girls, and aggression is more consistent from childhood to adulthood for boys. So the behavior that is "acceptable" for a given sex is consistent over ages, whereas the stereotypically unacceptable behavior is not. This lack of continuity becomes most marked between adolescence and adulthood, suggesting that the impact of the cultural stereotype of "acceptable" behavior may be felt most strongly in adolescence. A girl who has been fairly aggressive at 6 years of age may still be aggressive at age 10, but she may show a decline in aggression during adolescence and may or may not be aggressive as an adult. Kagan and Moss summarized these findings as follows:

Even the children who were reared by families that did not consciously attempt to mold the child in strict concordance with traditional sex-role standards responded to the pressures of the extra-familial environment. The aggressive girls learned to inhibit direct expression of overt aggression . . . the dependent boys gradually placed inhibition on urges toward dependent overtures to others. (1962, p. 268)

Factors Influencing Aggression

For all children of all ages one of the very common antecedents of an aggressive outburst is some kind of frustration. It was suggested some years ago in a famous book entitled *Frustration and Aggression* (by Dollard et al.) that aggression is always preceded by frustration, and that frustration is always followed by aggression. That extreme position seems clearly not to be valid on several counts. First, children can and do learn other responses to frustration besides aggression (for example, cooperation), and second, factors other than frustration (for example, pain) may lead to aggression. But despite the exceptions it does look as if the human child is born with a fairly strong natural connection between frustration and some kind of aggression.

But what about child rearing? Are there some kinds of training that lead consistently to more or less aggressive children?

In experimental situations children who have been rewarded for aggressive responses show an increase in aggression, including aggression toward other people. If you say "good" each time a child hits an inflated doll on the nose and then put that child in a room with another child and ask them to play particularly aggressive games, the child who has been rewarded for hitting is more likely to hit, bite, kick, pull hair, and scratch her companion than is the child who has not been rewarded (see, for example Walters & Brown, 1963).

There is also good evidence, from experimental situations, at least, that merely watching someone else behave aggressively and being rewarded for it increases the likelihood that the watcher will be aggressive, too. The child will learn new aggressive techniques, too, just from watching someone else use them. This is illustrated in the now-classic photographs from an experiment by Bandura, Ross, and Ross, shown in Figure 32.

In studies of real family situations one consistent finding is that children who are rejected or unwanted are likely to be highly aggres-

FIGURE 32
Children imitating aggressive behaviors observed on film. The top picture in each sequence shows the model performing an unusual aggressive activity; the lower pictures show children who have seen the model on film imitating the novel aggression. (Source: Bandura, A., Ross, D., & Ross, S. A. Imitation of film mediated aggressive models. *Journal of Abnormal and Social Psychology*, 1963, *66*, 8. Copyright © 1963, by the American Psychological Association. Reprinted by permission.)

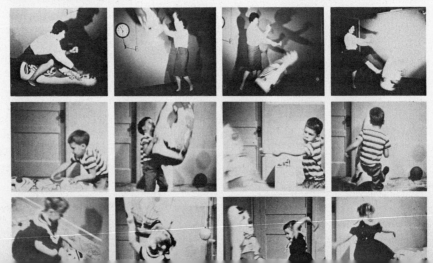

sive. A pattern of rejection by parents combined with large doses of physical punishment is common in the background of delinquent teenagers. The pattern is undoubtedly an interactive one. The child is rejected and frustrated, she strikes out against the parents who retaliate with physical punishment, which in turn provides the child with a model of aggression and brings forth more rejection.

In less rejecting families the most aggressive children appear to come from families who are high in both permissiveness and punishment for aggression (see Sears, Maccoby, & Levin). The sequence apparently runs something like this: The mother (or father) allows the child to beat up her brother or snatch a toy from her little sister, but when the noise level becomes too high or the screams of agony too piercing, she steps in with some fairly severe punishment (spanking, sending the offending child to her room for a protracted period, taking away a cherished privilege, or the like). The parents in such cases may think that they are being consistently severe toward aggression and may be mystified that their children are so aggressive. What they have done, though (in addition to modeling aggression for the child), is to allow aggression some of the time and to punish it at other times. Such a combination may be analogous to the partial reinforcement schedule described in Box 2 (page 18) which we know to be associated with strong and very persistent behavior.

The families with the least aggressive children seem to be those who practice a combination of nonpermissiveness, nonpunishment, and nonrejection. They try to avoid letting potentially explosive situations develop, and they head off quarrels and arguments by separating the children before they begin; but when aggression does occur, they don't punish it severely.

Note that punishment for aggression by itself does not lead to reduction in aggression. Many parents, I suspect, think that spanking a child for hitting her brother is an effective way of handling the situation and that it will make the aggression less likely the next time. But it doesn't work that way. Children who have been consistently punished for aggression may, in fact, be more aggressive than children who have not been punished, either because punishment is a form of frustration that provokes further aggression or because it is itself a form of aggression: The child may think, "When Mommy's mad, she hits me, so when I'm mad, I can hit too."

On the other hand permissiveness toward aggression seems to have a more straightforward relationship to aggressiveness. Children whose parents are permissive toward aggression—who allow it, at least within limits—are likely to be more aggressive than are children whose parents do not permit it. The findings from the Fels longitudinal study are consistent with this conclusion. Mothers who permitted aggression (either physical or verbal) toward themselves by their children had children who were more consistently aggressive throughout middle childhood and into adulthood, whereas those who did not permit it seemed to have children who inhibited aggression in both childhood and adulthood.

TELEVISION AND AGGRESSION

A child's level of aggressiveness is influenced by a number of things other than the parents' reactions to aggressive behavior. One of the major potential influences is television.

Are children more aggressive because of aggression seen on television? This question is of theoretical interest because it relates to the whole issue of observational learning, one of the major concepts in Bandura's theory of learning. But the question is also of considerable social interest as well. There have been innumerable hearings on this subject before Senate committees and other legislative bodies, and substantial amounts of research money have been spent by the government in an effort to answer the question.

Two facts are clear to begin with. First, most children watch a *lot* of television. One recent study indicated that the average preschooler (3- to 5-year-old) watches television for about four hours a day and that the average 9- to 10-year-old watches from four to six hours a day. Of course, not all children spend this much time in front of the TV. In one study of preschoolers the range of hours of watching per week was from 5 to 88 hours. (I find it difficult to imagine any preschooler watching TV for 88 hours a week, but that's what the data show!) And among school-age children and teenagers there are similarly wide variations in the amount of TV watching time. But most children watch at least some TV, and many watch for hours each day.

Second, TV fare *is* violent. In one analysis done for the National Commision on the Causes and Prevention of Violence, violence was define as "the overt expression of force intended to hurt or kill" (Lange, Baker, & Ball, 1969, p. 314). Using this definition the investigators analyzed prime-time and Saturday morning children's programs for violent incidents. They found that about two-thirds of all "comedy programs" included violent incidents as often as four or five times a program. Virtually all the crime and western programs included some violence, averaging 8 or 9 violent episodes in an hour, whereas the children's cartoons averaged about 22 incidents of violence in an hour! Some recent analyses of children's Saturday morning cartoons show that there has been a decline in violence on these programs in recent years (in part in response to parental and legislative pressure) but that the incidence was still at about 17 violent episodes per hour in 1972.

Several points are worth emphasizing about the violence children see. (1) None of the researchers who have counted aggression on television have included verbal aggression; all the violent episodes I have just listed are *physical* aggression. If we were to count verbal aggression as well, the rate of aggression on TV would be many times higher.

(2) The "good guys" are just as likely to be violent as are the "bad guys." (3) Violence on most TV programs is rewarded; people who are violent get what they want. In fact, violence is more often rewarded than are other methods of solving problems. (4) The *consequences* of violence—pain, blood, or other damage—are seldom shown. The networks' own codes forbid the showing of such gore, so the child viewer (and the adult viewer, for that matter) is protected from the painful and negative consequences of the aggression. All that is shown in most instances is the good outcomes of the violence.

What effect, if any, does this barrage of violence have on the child? Is she more likely to be aggressive—for example, to beat up her little brother—because of all this exposure to violence on television? Can she tell the difference between the fantasy of television fare and real-life encounters with others at home, play, and school?

In this case the answers to such questions seem to be becoming clearer, rather than murkier. Let me summarize the findings.

1. A great many laboratory studies have shown that children *do* learn specific aggressive acts from watching someone else perform them, and they will then perform those new aggressive acts in the lab. If they see a model throwing things at another adult dressed as a clown, for example, children will ordinarily imitate this. An extensive series of studies of this kind by Bandura and his associates has shown clearly that *new* aggressive behaviors are learned in this way, and that the effect of seeing a model behave aggressively is to *disinhibit* the child's own aggressive impulses; she will become more aggressive overall after viewing the model.

2. Studies one step closer to "real life" have shown that children who have seen aggressive cartoons or films are more aggressive in free play sessions or in other encounters with peers immediately afterward. This appears particularly true of preschool-age children, who nearly always show heightened levels of aggression after seeing aggressive films or cartoons. Among school-age children and teenagers, who are more able to distinguish the real from the fantasy world of the films, watching aggressive films seems to raise the level of aggression *except* in those circumstances where some situational factors would tend to inhibit the performance of aggression. So if the child is in the presence of an adult she *knows* disapproves of aggression, or if something about the film or the setting arouses her anxiety about aggressiveness, then seeing the film does not have the effect of raising the level of aggression.

3. In general, the effects of viewing aggression are cumulative. The more violent programs the child sees, the higher the level of aggressiveness she shows.

4. There is some indication that the impact of violence on TV is greater for those children whose typical levels of aggression are above average. I am *not* just talking here about children who are already delinquent, or those who are severely aggressive. But those children who are above average in aggression—but still in the "normal" range—appear to be more influenced by the TV aggression they see. This has not been found in all studies; there are several good studies that show the impact of violent TV on children of all aggression levels. So we cannot pass off the effect of TV aggression as something that influences only a highly deviant minority.

5. Stein and Friedrich, in their excellent recent review of this literature, emphasize that except for restricting the number of violent programs a child views, there is relatively little a parent can do to modify the impact of the TV aggression. If the parents consistently follow rearing patterns that discourage aggression, then the impact seems to be somewhat smaller, but still present.

Lest you draw the conclusion that all TV has negative effects, let me emphasize that other kinds of learning can and do occur from television. Children who watch "Mr. Rogers' Neighborhood" regularly, for example, show more sharing, more imaginative play, sometimes more cooperation, and in some studies a *reduction* in aggression. So *all* of what the child (or the adult) watches on television is "educational" in some sense. The issue is what is being taught. Aggression can be (and is being) taught, but so can helpfulness.

PEER RELATIONSHIPS
Developmental Patterns

As I have already pointed out research on dependency and on aggression suggests an important shift in focus away from adults and toward peers as major sources of interaction some time between the ages of 2 and 5.

Very young babies, up to about 6 months of age or so, interact little with one another when they are placed together. Starting at about 6 months, they may explore one another more or less as if they were mutually interesting objects. But between two toddlers placed together you will see various kinds of positive approaches: They may talk, smile, run together, or play with toys separately but companionably. Usually the larger or older of the two children dominates the interaction.

Between ages 2 and 5 there are some major changes. First, the total amount of interaction with peers increases throughout this period. At the same time the kind of interaction changes toward more cooperative play and away from parallel play, and the children begin to show reciprocal relationships through praising each other, sharing toys, giving in when another child asks for (or demands) something, and showing concern over others' cuts and bruises. (See Figure 33 for examples of parallel and cooperative play in children.) All in all, relationships among children begin to take on many of the features that earlier had only been seen in children's relationships with adults, including some apparent attachments formed toward other children. But all is

FIGURE 33
Parallel and cooperative play in preschool children.

not sweetness and light at this age either. I have already emphasized that there is competitiveness and rivalry during this period as well, and these behaviors increase from ages 2 to 5, along with the more positive peer interactions.

There is also a connection between some of the changes that occur during the preschool period and the child's cognitive development. Recall from the discussion of egocentrism that children during this preoperational period find it comparatively difficult to look at the world from someone else's point of view. Altruism and helpfulness toward others require seeing the need for help or assistance, which in turn requires at least a rudimentary ability to step into the other person's shoes. As egocentrism lessens helpfulness should increase, and that is exactly what we see in children's relationships with each other during the period from 2 to 6 years.

By the time they reach school age children have developed fairly clear "in groups," and new children coming into a school or a neighborhood are not welcomed immediately; a new child has to work her way slowly into the group. From this age up to about age 10 the informal gang is the dominant peer experience, and the gangs are almost entirely same-sex groups. At the same time school-age youngsters form individual friendships that may be very strong and lasting.

In adolescence peer groups become still more complex. There seem to be three levels (at least) of relationships. First, there is "the crowd," a largish group of kids who share activities or broad interests or who come from similar kinds of families. The crowd is, in turn, made up of a set of cliques—smaller groups of kids who have strong ties with one another. Finally, within the clique there may be deep personal friendships between pairs of children. At the beginning of adolescence, around ages 11 or 13 or so, cliques are mostly one sex, whereas the crowd includes both boys and girls. Somewhat later, when dating begins to dominate, the cliques shift to include both boys and girls; still later, the cliques may consist of a loose collection of "steady" couples. Through all this development, individual friendships continue, especially among girls, who apparently rely on them for emotional support more than do boys of the same age.

Individual Differences and Influencing Factors

Children differ in their status within a group of peers; some children are markedly more popular than others. Research on popularity and the factors that influence it is largely correlational in nature, and there is the usual problem in interpretation. We know, for example, that friendly children are likely to be more popular, but which way does the causality run? Is the child popular because she is friendly or friendly because she is popular? But keeping in mind this general difficulty, there are several fairly clear findings.

At all ages peer acceptance and popularity seem to be associated with friendliness and outgoingness. Children who are open and positive in their interactions with others are liked by their peers more than children who are not, although a less friendly child won't necessarily be rejected by the group. She just won't be as well accepted or as popular.

At all ages the brighter child is more likely to be popular than is the less-bright child, and this seems to be true within each social class group as well. In the middle-class "crowd" the brighter children are more popular, and the same is true among groups of children from poorer families.

Children who are the last born in their families or who are only children are likely to be more popular, particularly when compared to first-born children, who tend to be more anxious and dependent on others. Children like other kids to be good group members, to go along with the will of the crowd, but they don't apparently like those who are anxiously dependent and anxiously desiring to please, which oldest children are more likely to be.

Physical characteristics also play some role, as I've already pointed out in Chapter 5. At least among boys (on whom most of the research has been done) the bigger and huskier children are likely to be more popular than are the tall, skinny types or the short, fat types. Among girls the most popular are the good-looking (but not *too* good-looking) ones.

Finally, the child's name may take a difference. Several recent studies indicate that children have very clear stereotypes about names. If a child's name is too "oddball," she is likely to have very low status in the group. But at this point we don't know whether the low group status results because the group somehow imposes particular roles on kids with weird names or because parents who choose highly unusual names for their children bring up their children differently, or perhaps both.

What kinds of families do popular children come from? Three factors seem to stand out in the literature: (1) The families discourage aggression and antisocial behavior in their children, (2) they try not to frustrate the children and punish little, and (3) they like their children and tell them so. For a boy to be popular with his peers, a strong father figure, one who is warm and positive toward the son, seems to be particularly important.

This particular combination of child-rearing patterns should help the child to develop positive social behavior and a very positive self-image, and it may be that a positive view of oneself is what makes dominance and popularity possible.

Some Cautions about Studies of Peer Relationships

Two final cautions about the meaning of this information on peer relationships seem necessary. First, virtually all the findings that I have described to you are based on research on children in the United States. Whether or not the same changes in peer relationships occur in other countries with other rearing patterns we don't know. For example, would a child reared in a Russian day-care center from age 6 months through age 6 years have the same kind of peer relationships as does an American child? Do the changes occur in the same order and at about the same rate? If the sequence of changes in the nature of peer relationships, especially during the toddler and preschool ages, is linked to the child's developing cognitive system and to the system of attachments, then the sequence should be the same, regardless of the kind of experience the child has. But among adolescents the age at which same-sex groups give way to heterosexual groups is probably very largely determined by such cultural patterns as whether or not the two sexes attend school together (which they do not in some countries) or whether or not dating is accepted as a teenage activity.

Second, in the vast majority of studies on peer relationships that have been done in this country, only boys have been used as subjects. There is far less information on groups of girls, so we cannot be completely sure that the same generalizations hold for girls as for boys. Until we have more cross-cultural research and more studies of peer relationships among girls we should be cautious about our conclusions.

SEX DIFFERENCES

This is an area in which the sex-role stereotypes are *very* strong. We normally expect males to be more aggressive, competitive, active and independent, while females are expected to be more dependent, nurturant, empathetic, and more oriented toward others in general. But most of these stereotypic expectations are *wrong*. Except for differences in aggression, which I have already mentioned, and which are consistent and fairly large, virtually all of the other "expected" differences are simply not found.

Girls are *not* more dependent, and they are *not* more oriented toward social involvement of one kind or another. In fact, in studies of preschool children, it is the boys who are more "sociable," more oriented toward the activities of peers. Among adults, women more often mention liking others as being a major reason for forming or staying in groups, but it isn't at all clear that this means that women are more sociable or have more friendly interest in others than do men.

Nurturance is also not clearly more common among girls or women. In cross-cultural studies the frequent observation is that girls are more often given the task of caring for younger brothers and sisters, but laboratory studies in this country do not reveal any sex differences in children's tendencies to give help or aid to other children. And there is one very interesting recent study by Parke and O'Leary, which shows that fathers are as nurturant and affectionate toward their newborn infants as are mothers.

Some other nondifferences are that boys are not found to be more motorically active, except during the preschool years when they seem to show more large muscle play. Girls are not found to be more compliant over the whole age span, again except for the preschool age groups, when girls may be readier to comply with requests from mothers or teachers. Girls do not cry more; if anything, preschool-age boys may cry somewhat more than do girls of this age.

Only in aggressiveness and in related characteristics like dominance and competitiveness are there consistent sex differences across ages. Boys are more aggressive, more competitive, and rated higher in dominance across most ages studied.

The most likely explanation of the consistent sex difference in aggression is that there are hormonal or other biological influences at work. Maccoby and Jacklin have summarized this argument concisely:

Let us outline the reasons why biological sex differences appear to be involved in aggression: (1) Males are more aggressive than females in all human societies for which evidence is available. (2) The sex differences are found early in life, at a time when there is no evidence that differential socialization pressures have been brought to bear by adults to "shape" aggression differently in the two sexes. (3) Similar sex differences are found in man and subhuman primates. (4) Aggression is related to levels of sex hormones, and can be changed by experimental administration of these hormones. (Maccoby & Jacklin, 1974, pp. 242–243)

The critical factor here seems to be the level of sex hormones present prenatally. Recall from the discussion in Chapter 3 that for a boy to develop male genitals there has to be an infusion of male hormone at the appropriate point in the prenatal period. Such prenatal hormones appear to affect later behavior as well, particularly aggressive behavior. Female monkeys given male hormones prenatally show increased amounts of aggressiveness and rough-and-tumble play as infants. And among humans, girls who have accidentally received elevated levels of male hormone prenatally also seem to show more "tomboyish" behavior.

I want to emphasize again that despite the average difference in aggressiveness, there is still overlap in the distributions. There are many relatively *un*aggressive boys and many relatively aggressive girls. Whether such differences *within* a sex may be attributed to differences in prenatal hormonal patterning is not known, although research now underway by Maccoby and Jacklin may help to answer some of these questions.

SOCIAL CLASS DIFFERENCES

I know of no evidence showing any systematic differences in attachment, dependency, or aggression as a function of social class. Delinquency is more common among the poor, but it is not at all clear that this means that poor children are, on the whole, more aggressive than are middle-class children.

Social class does seem to have an impact on peer relationships, however. In general, children from poor backgrounds are likely to be less popular in children's groups than are middle-class children, although this finding is confounded in most cases by the fact that academically successful children are likely to be more popular, and lower-class children are less likely to be academically successful. When differences in IQ or grades are controlled there still seems to be some slight effect of the child's social status on group popularity or acceptance, but the effect is not large.

SUMMARY

1. For parents the training of the child's "personality" and patterns of personal relationships are among the main concerns. The child must be "socialized" to fit into her society.
2. Of particular concern to parents are the child's aggression, and attachment or dependency.
3. The earliest patterns of interactions between parent and infant seem to be a kind of "dance" in which the child signals with smiles, cuddles, mutual gaze, and cries, and the parent responds. The parents' attachment to the child may be affected by the ability of the parent-infant pair to achieve a smoothly working communication system.

4. There are clear sequences in the development of attachments, particularly in young infants, who go from diffuse attachment to a single and then multiple attachments. In older children there is a shift away from immature dependent behaviors, such as clinging or touching and holding, toward more mature forms, such as seeking attention and approval.
5. Children differ in the strength and quality of their early attachments and in the speed with which they pass from the less to the more mature forms of dependency. Consistency in dependent behavior throughout the lifetime is, however, more notable in females than in males.
6. Individual differences in early attachments

are partially determined by the mother's child-care practices, although the child's temperament may be influential, too.

7. Among older children the degree of dependency seems to be determined jointly by the amounts of reward and punishment that the parents provide in response to the child's dependency bids.

8. Developmental trends in aggressive behavior are less clear than are those in attachment, but they suggest shifts from physical aggression to verbal aggression in older children.

9. Individual differences among children in aggression are marked; boys show more aggression on the average, particularly more physical aggression, at nearly all ages. Consistency in aggressiveness throughout the lifetime is also more apparent in males than in females.

10. There is good reason to suppose that the baby comes equipped with a link between frustration and aggression, so that aggression is a very common response to frustration in all children. Other responses to frustration, however, can be learned.

11. Some child-rearing practices have been found to be consistently associated with high levels of aggression in children; they include severe rejection, high levels of physical punishment, and a combination of permissiveness and punishment for aggression.

12. Viewing of aggression on television also appears to have the effect of heightening the levels of aggression or violence in the viewer.

13. Peer relationships change in predictable developmental sequences. Very young children have little active involvement with one another. By age 3 or 4 cooperative play begins to replace parallel play, and this shift is accompanied by an increase in empathy and nurturance toward other children—but also by an increase in rivalry and competition.

14. During the elementary school years children band together in clear "in groups," which are nearly always same-sex groups. At adolescence same-sex groups gradually give way to heterosexual groups.

15. Peer acceptance and popularity are associated with friendliness and outgoingness, with brightness, with being born later in a family, and with being large and husky (at least among boys).

16. The only consistently observed sex difference in this domain is in aggressiveness; boys are consistently more aggressive, on the average, than are girls. The most likely explanation of this sex difference is that the level of aggressiveness is partially prepatterned by the amounts of various hormones prenatally.

17. No significant social class differences in dependency or aggression have been found. Poor children may be somewhat less popular in peer groups.

REFERENCES

Suggested Additional Readings

Ainsworth, M. D. S. The development of infant-mother attachment. In B. M. Caldwell & H. N. Ricciuti (Eds.), *Review of child development research* (Vol. 3). Chicago: University of Chicago Press, 1973.
The most comprehensive recent review I know of on the topic of attachment, by one of the major researchers in the field. The level is moderately difficult, but it's a very good first place to look for more detailed information and for references.

Bandura, A., & Walters, R. H. *Social learning and personality development.* New York: Holt, Rinehart and Winston, 1963.
A good source for further theory and information about observational learning, particularly as it influences the development of aggression.

Bee, H. L. *Social issues in developmental psychology* (2nd ed.). New York: Harper & Row, 1977.
If you are interested in the impact of day

care or in the effect of maternal employment on the child, this would be a good source, since I have discussed the evidence in much greater detail. There is also a chapter on sex differences, which is a great deal shorter than the Maccoby and Jacklin volume and might be a good first review.

Feshbach, S. Aggression. In P. H. Mussen (Ed.), *Carmichael's manual of child psychology* (Vol. 2, 3rd ed.). New York: Wiley, 1970.
A full and detailed review of the literature on aggression and its origins in early childhood; assumes a lot of background knowledge but useful to a student particularly interested in the development of aggression.

Hartup, W. W. Peer interaction and social organization. In P. H. Mussen (Ed.), *Carmichael's manual of child psychology* (Vol. 2, 3rd ed.). New York: Wiley, 1970.
A very well-written and thorough examination of the literature on peer interaction, with special emphasis on method; a highly technical paper but worth pursuing if you have a particular interest in this subject.

Lewis, M., & Rosenblum, L. A. (Eds.). *The effect of the infant on its caregiver.* New York: Wiley, 1974.
A marvelous collection of papers describing recent research on very early infant-mother interactions. The papers included vary in technical level, but many should be clear to a beginning student.

Maccoby, E. E., & Feldman, S. S. Mother-attachment and stranger-reactions in the third year of life. *Monographs of the Society for Research in Child Development.* 1972, 37 (1, Whole No. 146).
Most of the monograph concerns a particular study, which I have referred to in the text, but there is also an excellent brief review of the literature on early attachment and an extremely interesting study of attachment in kibbutz-reared children.

Maccoby, E. E., & Jacklin, C. N. *The psychology of sex differences.* Stanford, Calif.: Stanford University Press, 1974.
Once again this is the best source for information on sex differences in personality. See particularly Chapters 5, 6, and 7.

Maccoby, E. E., & Master, J. C. Attachment and dependency. In P. H. Mussen (Ed.), *Carmichael's manual of child psychology* (Vol. 2, 3rd ed.). New York: Wiley, 1970.
Another of the thorough reviews of research and theory contained in the Mussen volumes, to which I have referred you before; assumes considerable theoretical and methodological sophistication and is not to be tackled lightly. I would recommend that you begin with the Ainsworth review listed above and use the Maccoby and Masters review as a second source.

Stein, A. H., & Friedrich, L. K. Impact of television on children and youth. In E. M. Hetherington (Ed.), *Review of child development research* (Vol. 5). Chicago: University of Chicago Press, 1975.
An excellent, comprehensive, and readable current review of all the literature on TV and its effects. The very first place you should go for further data and discussion of social policy issues.

Other Sources Cited

Ainsworth, M. D. S. Patterns of attachment behavior shown by the infant in interaction with his mother. *Merrill-Palmer Quarterly,* 1964, *10,* 51–58.

Ainsworth, M. D. S., Bell, S. M., & Stayton, D. J. Individual differences in the development of some attachment behaviors. *Merrill-Palmer Quarterly,* 1972, *18,* 123–143.

Blehar, M. C. Anxious attachment and defensive reactions associated with day care. *Child Development,* 1974, *45,* 683–692.

Dollard, J., Doob, L. W., Miller, N. E., Mowrer, O. H., & Sears, R. R. *Frustration and aggression.* New Haven: Yale University Press, 1939.

Fraiberg, S. Blind infants and their mothers: An examination of the sign system. In M. Lewis & L. A. Rosenblum (Eds.), *The effect of the infant on its caregiver.* New York: Wiley, 1974.

Garbarino, J. A preliminary study of some ecological correlates of child abuse: The impact of socioeconomic stress on mothers. *Child Development*, 1976, *46*, 178–185.

Gil, D. G. *Violence against children.* Cambridge, Mass.: Harvard University Press, 1970.

Goodenough, F. L. *Anger in young children.* Minneapolis: University of Minnesota Press, 1931.

Kagan, J., & Moss, H. A. *Birth to maturity.* New York: Wiley, 1962.

Kaye, K. *Toward the origin of dialogue.* Paper presented at the Loch Lomond Symposium, University of Strathclyde, September, 1975.

Lange, D. L., Baker, R. K., & Ball, S. J. *Mass media and violence: A report to the National Commission on the Causes and Prevention of Violence* (Vol. 2). Washington, D.C.: Government Printing Office, 1969.

Parke, R., & O'Leary, S. Mother-father-infant interaction in the newborn period: Some findings, some observations, and some unresolved issues. In K. Riegel & J. Meacham (Eds.), *Determinants of behavioral development*, II. New York: Academic Press, 1974.

Ragozin, A. *Attachment in day care children: Field and laboratory findings.* Paper presented at the biennial meetings of the Society for Research in Child Development, Denver, 1975.

Schaffer, H. R., & Callender, W. M. Psychological effects of hospitalization in infancy. *Pediatrics*, 1959, *24*, 528–539.

Schaffer, H. R., & Emerson, P. The development of social attachments in infancy. *Monographs of the Society for Research in Child Development*, 1964, *29* (3, Whole No. 94).

Sears, R. R., Maccoby, E. E., & Levin, H. *Patterns of child rearing.* New York: Harper & Row, 1957.

Stern, D. N. Mother and infant at play: The dyadic interaction involving facial, vocal, and gaze behaviors. In M. Lewis & L. A. Rosenblum (Eds.), *The effect of the infant on its caregiver.* New York: Wiley, 1974.

Walters, R. H., & Brown, M. Studies of reinforcement of aggression. III. Transfer of responses to an interpersonal situation. *Child Development*, 1963, *34*, 563–571.

PROJECT 6
TELEVISION AGGRESSION

Using the definition of violence offered by D. L. Lange and his colleagues, that is, "the overt expression of force intended to hurt or kill," select a minimum of four half-hour television programs normally watched by children and count the number of aggressive or violent episodes in each. Count also episodes of verbal aggression, in which the apparent intent is to hurt the other's feelings, as well as episodes of physical aggression. You may select any four (or more) programs, but I would strongly recommend that you distribute them in the following way:

1. At least one "educational" television program, such as "Sesame Street," "Mr. Rogers," or "The Electric Company."
2. At least one Saturday-morning cartoon. "The Road Runner" is a particularly grisly example, but there are others. If you have time it would be worthwhile to watch a whole Saturday morning of cartoons, so that you can get some feeling for the fare being offered to young children.
3. At least one early-evening adult program that may be watched by young children: a family comedy, a western, a crime film, or one of each.

For each program that you watch record the number of violent episodes, separating the verbal and physical violence in your record.

In thinking or writing about the results of your observations, consider the following questions:

What kind of variation in the number of violent episodes is there among the programs that you watched?

Are some programs more verbally aggressive, some more physically aggressive?

Do the numbers of violent episodes per program correspond to the numbers found by Lange in his 1969 study? (See page 288.)

What about the consequences of aggression in the television films? Are those who act violently rewarded or punished? How often do reward and punishment occur?

In light of the discussion in the chapter, what do you think might be the consequences to a child of viewing the same programs?

PROJECT 7
OBSERVATION OF DEPENDENCY AND AGGRESSION

In Project 1 I suggested that you attempt a particular kind of observation in which you try to record everything a child did over a one-hour period. This time a different kind of observation is in order.

The best setting for this observation would be a nursery school or day-care center, although a school playground will do if necessary. Ideally, you should observe a group of children between the ages of 2 and 5. As usual, obtain permission for the observation from school authorities or their equivalent. Seat yourself at the edge of the play area, so that you will be as unobtrusive as possible.

Select two children to observe. You have two alternatives: Pick either two children of the same sex, one of whom is several years older than the other (perhaps $4\frac{1}{2}$ as opposed to $2\frac{1}{2}$ years old), or two children of different sex who are about the same age. Once you have selected the children, begin your observation, watching first one child for ten minutes, then the other child for ten minutes, and so on for at least one hour. You may find that this observation is tiring and that you want a brief rest between the ten-minute observations. That's quite all right, as long as you end up with at least three chunks of observation time for each child.

For each child count two things:

1. The number of aggressive episodes. Aggression is defined in the same way as for the television assignment in Project 6—the overt expression of force intended to hurt or kill, including verbal aggression as well. Be sure to count verbal and physical aggression separately.
2. The number of dependency bids, which can be of two kinds: (a) clinging to, following, or huddling near another person (usually the teacher) and (b) making bids for approval or attention ("Look at me!"; "Teacher, teacher, come here!").

I do not expect this task to be easy, nor do I expect you to be able to count everything that goes on. But make an attempt.

As you think or write about your experiences, consider the following questions:

Did the two children you observed differ from each other in aggression and dependency? Did those differences follow the lines you would expect based on the information given in this chapter?

What difficulties did you have in doing the observation? Did you have trouble defining the categories of behavior to be counted? Did you have trouble deciding whether or not an act was aggressive? Was it difficult to draw inferences about a child's intent? How would you change the definitions if you were going to do the observation over again?

What factors in the play situation itself might have influenced the child's aggression or dependency?

Would the children you observed be likely to show the same kinds of behavior in other situations?

12

Theories of Personality
and Interpersonal Development

In the area of cognitive development I have discussed really only one theory, Piaget's, since his theory and description are quite widely accepted as the best available. But in the area of the development of personality or interpersonal relationships there are many theories, no one of which has wide acceptance. I want to discuss four such theories in this chapter.

Any theory of the development of interpersonal relationships should account for at least two kinds of things. First, it ought to deal with any developmental progressions that are observed, such as the sequence in the development of early attachments. Second, a theory in this area should account for individual differences in characteristics such as aggression or dependency. Of the four theories I will be discussing, only psychoanalytic theorists—both Freud and Erikson—have dealt with both questions in any detail. Social-learning theorists, on the whole, have been much more concerned with accounting for individual differences than with developmental sequences, while both ethological theorists like Bowlby and cognitive-developmental theorists like Kohlberg have done the reverse.

My hunch is that over the next decade, this is an area in which there will be a good deal of theoretical ferment. There are a number of researchers now trying to marry social-learning views and cognitive-developmental views, and that combination may turn out to be a particularly powerful one in the future. But for now let me look separately at what each of the four current approaches has to offer.

ETHOLOGICAL THEORY

John Bowlby has provided the most complete statement of an ethological theory, although he has discussed only the development of attachment and not other aspects of interpersonal relationships. The ethological approach to the study of dependency and attachment is based very heavily on studies of animals in natural settings. Such studies led to the realization that many behaviors in animals, birds, and fish are instinctive and that even patterns of relationship can be instinctive. Mating rituals in many species, for example, consist of intricate instinctive sequences, each action by one member of the pair triggering off the next action of the other member. Bowlby has suggested that the same kind of mutually instinctive pattern might be involved in the early attachment between human baby and mother. The work of both Mary Ainsworth and H. R. Schaffer is partially based on such an assumption.

The fundamental notion is that the baby comes into the world equipped with a set of signals and responses to others that make up what Bowlby calls "attachment behavior." The baby signals the need for help or contact by crying, fussing, smiling, and so forth and then maintains contact with the caregiver by clinging, holding, or, in the crawling or walking stage, following her mother around. Bowlby

thinks that in early infancy the baby's actions are triggered by various fixed signals like separation or threat. Later, her attachment behaviors become more adaptive, so that she can direct them more precisely toward her mother or other caregiver. As she develops, she comes to use her repertoire of attachment behaviors intentionally.

Bowlby, like Ainsworth, does suggest that whether or not the instinctive pattern is maintained depends on the responses of the people around the baby. It takes two to do this particular waltz, and if no one responds, or if the responses are not properly tied in with the baby's signals, then the instinctive patterning may not persist.

A concrete example may help to make this particular theoretical approach clearer. Let's look at smiling in the infant from this perspective. There is quite a lot of research indicating that for an infant past about the first four weeks of life, the sight of a human face is one of the major "elicitors" of smiling. At this age it doesn't have to be any particular face, just "faceness" will elicit or "release" smiling in the infant. The infant's smile in turn triggers any one of a series of responses on the part of the adult. Usually the adult smiles back, talks to the child, and perhaps most importantly, *maintains contact* with the infant. So the sequence is like this: face appears, infant smiles, face smiles back, talks, infant smiles again, and so on. The infant's smile is the critical element in an apparently "instinctive" interaction sequence. This sequence, in the view of the ethologists, has important survival value for the infant, since the infant's smiling tends to keep the adult nearby and providing care.

The contrast between this "normal" sequence and what happens with the blind infant is striking (recall Box 19, page 270). While blind babies do smile, sometimes to the sound of a familiar voice for example, there is no single behavior on the part of the parent that regularly and reliably elicits a smile from the blind infant the way the human face does with the sighted infant. And imagine what happens when the blind infant does smile: The mother smiles back and talks to the infant, but the infant cannot *see* the mother's smile and is not likely to continue smiling. So the whole sequence, which helps to maintain contact and caregiving for the sighted infant, breaks down with the blind infant.

In ethological terms the smile is both an automatic response (a "fixed action pattern") on the part of the infant and a trigger or releaser for more behavior on the part of the adult. It is possible that there may be similar instinctive origins for some aggressive responses. Aggression may be triggered initially by a particular range of events, including frustration. Such original elicitors may then be modified through experience, just as the particular elements in the ritualized attachment behavior between mother and infant change over time.

There are several attractions to ethological views, particularly the ethological view of early attachment. This kind of approach seems to me to do better than any other at explaining the very earliest communications and mutuality that develop between infant and caregiver. As the child develops physically and cognitively, we would quite naturally expect that the sorts of signals she can give and receive will alter, too. So, built into Bowlby's theory is some ability to handle the developmental changes that may occur in the quality of caregiver-infant relationships.

But there are some drawbacks as well. In the first place the theory is not yet complete, and it offers no very detailed explanation for the shift to multiple attachments during the second year. Why should children show such a shift, especially after developing so effective and complex a dance with the major caregiver? Bowlby suggests, in general, that there continues to be one *central* attachment figure through the first 2 to 3 years of life, and that the number of secondary or subsidiary attachment figures is a function of the number of other adults (or children) with whom the child has regular contact. Descriptively, that seems to be more or less true. Infants do seem to maintain somewhat stronger attachment to the central figure, even when a spread of attachment occurs. But that still does not tell us why the child is now willing to "dance" with others when she was not willing to do so at 6 to 8 months.

A second potential problem with this approach is accounting for variations among children in the strength or security of attachment. Bowlby suggests that there may be some genetic differences in such things as the age at which smiling first occurs. Although Bowlby himself does not emphasize them, surely the temperamental differences I described in Chapter 4 (page 93) will affect the earliest reciprocal relationships. Beyond such built-in differences, however, Bowlby lays individual differences at the door of "environment." He merely points out that institutionally reared children, who are deprived of a single mother-figure and of rich stimulation, often show deviations in attachment behaviors. So, some minimal amount of contact with a single caregiver seems to be critical if the whole intricate mutual pattern is to develop.

Obviously this is not (or not yet) a complete theory. But at the very least, ethological approaches like Bowlby's have focused our attention once again on the patterns of behavior the infant brings with her and on the earliest, often ritualized, interactions of infant and environment.

PSYCHO-ANALYTIC THEORIES
Freud

Sigmund Freud, like the ethologists, emphasized the instinctive basis of behavior. According to Freud the baby comes into the world equipped with several sets of instincts, including one having to do with self-preservation (breathing, hunger, and the like) and one having to do with sexual gratification (the word *sexual* is used very broadly in this context). In several of his later writings Freud also suggested that there may be a kind of aggressive instinct, or "death wish," although this portion of his theory has found the least support among his followers.

Freud saw attachment to others as one manifestation of the child's sexual instincts. The sexual instinct, as a whole, is directed toward various objects in a fixed sequence during the individual's lifetime. At each stage sexual energy (which Freud called *libido*) is invested in a single part of the body, a single *erogenous zone*. I want to emphasize that the psychosexual stages, as Freud saw them, have a distinct maturational basis. The shift from one stage to the next is triggered by changes in sensitivity of different regions of the body. But within each stage the specific experiences a child encounters will affect her resolution of the conflicts that accompany each phase. The five main stages, as Freud outlined them, are very briefly as follows.

THE ORAL STAGE: FROM BIRTH TO 1 YEAR

The baby's first contacts with the world are through her mouth, and she has great sensitivity there. Freud emphasized that the oral region—the mouth, tongue, and lips—becomes the center for pleasure for the baby. Her earliest attachment is to the one who provides pleasure in the mouth, usually her mother. Freud does not assume that the baby has any concept of mother at this very early stage or even that she has recognized that her mother is a separate entity. But there is some primitive attachment to she-who-brings-pleasant-things-to-the-mouth.

THE ANAL STAGE: AGE 1 TO AGE 3

As maturation progresses and the lower trunk becomes more developed and more under voluntary control, the baby becomes more and more sensitive in the anal region and begins to receive pleasure from bowel movements, both in themselves and because they eliminate discomfort. At about the same time that the baby's anal sensitivity increases, her parents begin to place great emphasis on toilet training and to show pleasure when she manages to perform in the right place at the right time. These two forces together help to shift the major center of sexual energy from the oral to the anal erogenous zone.

THE PHALLIC STAGE: AGE 3 TO AGE 5

At about 4 years of age there is another shift, away from the anal region and toward the genital erogenous zone. Again, there is a maturational basis for the shift; only at this point is the genital area fully developed, and only about then does the child begin to receive pleasurable sensations from stimulation of the genital area. It is during this period that children of both sexes quite naturally begin to masturbate.

According to Freud the most important event that occurs during the phallic stage is the so-called *Oedipal conflict*. He described the sequence of events more fully (and more believably!) for boys, so let me trace that pattern for you.

The theory suggests that first the boy somehow becomes "intuitively aware of his mother as a sex object." (Rappoport, 1972, p. 74) Precisely how this occurs is not completely spelled out, but the impor-

tant point is that the boy at about age 4 begins to have a sort of sexual attachment to his mother and to regard his father as a sexual rival. His father sleeps with his mother, holds her and kisses her, and generally has access to her body in a way that the boy does not. The father is also seen by the boy as a powerful and threatening figure who has the ultimate power to castrate. The boy is caught between desire for his mother and anxiety about his father's power. This conflict is resolved, so Freud thought, by the boy's repression of his feelings for his mother and his *identification* with his father. The process of identification is a process of taking in, of "incorporating," all that the father is: his behaviors, mannerisms, ideas, attitudes, and morals. By doing so the boy makes himself so like his father that the father will not aggress against him. The process of identification results in the boy's adoption not only of the appropriate male sex role but also of the father's moral system.

Just how the process occurs in girls is not as clear either in Freud's work or in that of his followers. Supposedly, the girl sees her mother as a rival for her father's sexual attentions, but her fear of her mother is less (perhaps because she assumes that she has already been castrated), and there may be less full identification. For the girl the situation is different in still another way. Her original love attachment is also to her mother; but whereas the boy shifts his attachment (identification) to his father but continues to love his mother, the girl must shift her love to her father while continuing to be attached to her mother. Altogether, the psychoanalytic interpretation of the phallic stage for girls is not terribly satisfactory. The phallic stage is thought to be of great importance for both boys and girls, however, because of the development of identification, a process that Freud believed to be at the heart of the development of morality, of sex roles, and of attachment. The child replaces immature oral attachment to the mother with more mature attachment to the parent of the same sex. For a discussion of what may happen to both boys and girls reared during this, or later periods, *without* a father, see Box 22.

THE LATENCY STAGE: AGE 5 TO AGE 12

Freud thought that after the phallic stage there is a sort of resting period before the next major change in the child's sexual development. The child has presumably arrived at some preliminary resolution of the Oedipal crisis, so that there is a kind of calm after the storm. Then, too, the child starts school during this period, and this new activity absorbs the energies rather fully. During this period, the child's peer interactions are almost exclusively with members of the same sex. The identification with the same-sexed parent at the end of the phallic stage is followed by a long period during which the identification and interaction extends to others of the same sex.

Notice that this period corresponds to Piaget's period of concrete operations, a period during which an enormous growth in cognitive

BOX 22
The Effects of Father Absence on the Child

Partly because of Freud's great emphasis on the importance of the child's successful weathering of the Oedipal crisis and on the need to have both parents present if that period is to be successfully resolved, there has been a good deal of research on the effects of the absent father on the child's development. If Freud is correct then having no father during the crucial Oedipal period should have a major impact, especially on the boy. The boy presumably develops the same love attachment to his mother, but has no father to fear and therefore does not identify with the male or the male role. To the extent that the mother can and does evoke some anxiety or fear in the boy, he will identify with her or will simply maintain his earlier, dependency-based identification with her. If these supposi-

tions are correct, then the boy with no father should be less "masculine" in a number of ways, and the effect should be particularly strong if his father is absent during the Oedipal period, from around 2 to 5 years of age.

The empirical evidence relating to this hypothesis is decidedly mixed, with some studies showing that fatherless boys are less masculine and others showing no difference. It is worth noting, however, that there is no research showing fatherless boys to be *more* masculine, so the weight of the evidence seems to be consistent with the conclusion that there is *some* effect of the father's absence. The most likely effect seems to be a less "masculine" set of behaviors and attitudes on the part of the boy. There is also some, but not unanimous, evi-

skills occurs, suggesting the possibility of a trade-off between interpersonal and emotional development on the one hand and cognitive development on the other. When one is in a period of rapid transition, the other may be somewhat dormant.

THE GENITAL STAGE: AGES 12 TO 18 AND OLDER

The further changes in the genital organs (and the hormonal changes that trigger them) that take place during puberty reawaken the sexual energy of the child, and during this period a more mature form of sexual attachment occurs. From the beginning of this period the child's sexual objects are people of the opposite sex—perhaps teachers or older idols to begin with, and later peers. Freud placed some emphasis on the fact that not everyone works through this period to a point of mature heterosexual love. Some have not successfully completed the Oedipal period, so they have confused identifications, which affects their ability to cope with rearoused sexual energies in adolescence. Some have not had a satisfactory oral period, and thus do not have a foundation of basic love relationships; this too will interfere with full resolution of the conflicts of puberty. So, although the sequence itself is fixed, each individual's experiences at various points in the sequence will make a major difference in overall adjustment.

Freudian theory has several attractions. First, it is a *sequential* theory, and there is now increasing evidence that there are sequences built into many of the child's developing interpersonal skills. Second, it focuses our attention on the importance of the relationship of the

dence suggesting that the effect of the father's absence is greater if he was absent before the child was 5 than if he was absent when the child was older.

Obviously those favoring a psychoanalytic perspective take such findings as support for their position, and particularly as support for Freud's conception of the Oedipal period. But there are other equally plausible explanations of these results. For example, Herzog and Sudia have suggested that the father-absent boy may be showing a brief developmental lag, so that his behavior during childhood may be in some respects less mature than that of the father-present boys. The degree of disorganization of the family after the father leaves is also of importance, as is the mother's attitude toward the absent father and toward men in general. There is considerable family disorganization immediately following a divorce (the most common current reason for father absence in our society), with more erratic discipline and less time spent by the mother with the child. Such changes in family interaction patterns are going to have a significant impact on the child.

Finally, it is possible to suggest that the absence of a father does alter the identification process, but without involving an Oedipal crisis. Boys raised without an adult male are more likely to identify with or imitate the mother, and to the extent that she exhibits or encourages less stereotypically masculine behavior, the son may adopt behaviors and attitudes that are more "feminine."

child to the caregivers, although Freud was *not* very specific about the sort of nurturing behavior on the part of the parents or other caregivers that would be optimal. Still, the emphasis is on the *interaction* between the child's qualities and preoccupations and the responses of the caregivers, and that seems to me to be an appropriate emphasis.

Third, Freudian theory offers several useful additional concepts, which are missing from the nonpsychoanalytic views, such as the concepts of regression and fixation. Freud suggested that a child who has not successfully resolved the problems at any one stage may become "fixated" at that stage and may continue to interact with others and with the environment from the perspective of that early stage. Rappoport refers to these fixations as the "unfinished developmental business of childhood" (Rappoport, 1972, p. 289) and emphasizes that such leftover problems will inevitably affect the way the child or adolescent is able to handle later emerging problems. The twin concept is that of regression. Faced with some severe stress or threat, the child or adult may return to some earlier, more successful, level of functioning. Under threat, for example, some apparently mature and well-functioning adults will show a regression to the oral stage and will quite literally cry for their mothers. In concentration camp situations many prisoners show a return or regression to the pattern of "identification with the aggressor," which was typical of the phallic stage. Less severe forms of both cognitive and emotional regression undoubtedly occur under less marked stresses. This concept of regression is, I think, a particularly useful one, and does not occur in other nonpsychoanalytic views of interpersonal development.

Despite these attractions, however, most developmental psychologists today do not place a great deal of emphasis on the psychosexual stages as Freud described them, although many would agree on the importance of the sequence of maturation that underlies them. Still, many of the concepts that Freud developed have had wide currency and appear to have some validity. Something akin to identification does seem to occur at about age 4 or 5, although it is by no means clear that the Oedipal conflict, as Freud described it, lies behind the process of identification. There is a kind of latency—a long period of consistency—in interpersonal relationships during the elementary school years, and there are shifts in patterns of attachment during adolescence. So Freud was correct in many aspects of his description of the broad outline of the development of attachment, although the dynamics of the process may not be as he suggested.

Erikson

An alternative theory, still within the psychoanalytic framework, which *has* had considerable impact on the thinking of many current psychologists is Erik Erikson's. Erikson has devoted his attention to an explanation of the development of the *ego*—the planful, organizing, rational part of personality in Freudian theory. Erikson has been concerned with the development of these skills and with the sense of identity that develops. He outlined eight stages over the life span, and in each stage he suggested that there was a particular ego quality that has to develop if the individual is to have a fully developed, healthy identity.

But in each stage, or at each *crisis,* as Erikson often referred to the stages, either a healthy or an unhealthy, normal or abnormal, quality could be developed. The early stages Erikson proposes parallel the psychosexual stages proposed by Freud. They are, in some sense, an expansion of Freud's view to include the changes in ego, in identity. The eight stages, again very briefly, are as follows:

BASIC TRUST VERSUS BASIC MISTRUST

The first crisis Erikson sees occurs during the oral period, or the first year of life. What is at issue is whether the child will develop a sense of basic trust in the predictability of the world and in her ability to affect the happenings around her. Erikson believes that the behavior of the major caregiver (usually the mother) is critical to the child's successful or unsuccessful resolution of this crisis. Children who emerge from the first year with a firm sense of trust are those with parents who are loving and who respond predictably and reliably to the child. (Note, by the way, the similarity of this description to the distinction between "securely" and "insecurely" attached infants, given by Ainsworth.) A child who has developed a sense of trust will go on to other relationships carrying this sense with her; but those infants whose early care

310

has been erratic or harsh may develop *mis*trust, and they, too, carry this sense with them into their later relationships. So the resolution of this first crisis has major repercussions for all those that follow.

AUTONOMY VERSUS SHAME AND DOUBT

This second stage corresponds to the anal period and occurs during the second and third years of life. Erikson sees the child's greater mobility as the major change at this time. She can now move around in the world, and this gives her a far wider range of choices, and forms the basis for the sense of independence or autonomy. But if the child's efforts at independence are not carefully guided by the parents and she experiences repeated failures or ridicule, then the results of all the new opportunities for mobility and exploration may be shame and doubt instead of a basic sense of self-control and self-worth. The fact that toilet training occurs during this period as well may create additional difficulties for the parents, since this is an area in which there are more taboos and more occasions when ridicule or failure may occur for the child. Obviously, Erikson believes that a child who enters this crisis with a firm sense of basic trust is more likely to weather the second crisis successfully and emerge with a firm sense of autonomy.

INITIATIVE VERSUS GUILT

This phase corresponds to Freud's phallic stage and occurs some time around age 4 or 5. Again, Erikson is less concerned with the sort of "sexual" development that preoccupied Freud, and is more interested in the impact of the child's new skills and abilities. At this age the child is not just able to move about successfully; she is also able to plan a bit, to take initiative in reaching particular goals. Important cognitive changes lie behind this new level of ability, but having achieved these new organizational skills, the child tries them out, tries to conquer or attack goals of various kinds, and may come up against environmental restrictions as a result. This is a time of vigor of action and of behaviors that parents may see as aggressive. The risk here, as Erikson sees it, is that the child may go too far in her forcefulness. She may break a favorite toy or strike out at her mother or father. When this happens the child may be overwhelmed by guilt.

Erikson acknowledges that the Oedipal crisis, occuring during this same period, has an impact on the child's developing sense of guilt. The identification process results in a kind of internalization of all of the rules and regulations—all the taboos of the parents—and when the child in her new forcefulness exceeds the bounds of acceptable behavior (as she perceives them), then she will experience guilt.

What the parents need to do, at this stage, is help to focus the child on what *is* permissible—to direct all that energy and initiative toward acceptable activities so that the guilt may be kept to a minimum.

INDUSTRY VERSUS INFERIORITY

This crisis or dilemma occurs during the latency period, between the ages of 6 and 12. Again, Erikson focuses on the changes in the child's

skills and life experiences and the impact those changes have on her developing identity. In this case the beginning of schooling is a major force. The child is now faced with the need to win approval through productivity—through learning to read, write, do sums, and other specific skills. The task of this period is thus simply to develop the repertoire of specific skills society demands of the child. The obvious danger is that for one reason or another the child may be unable to develop the expected skills and will develop instead a basic sense of inferiority.

IDENTITY VERSUS ROLE CONFUSION

The crisis occuring during puberty—the genital stage in Freudian language—is a major one in which the adolescent reexamines her identity and the roles she must occupy. Erickson suggests that two "identities" are involved—a "sexual identity" and an "occupational identity." What should emerge for the adolescent from this period is a reintegrated sense of self, of what one wants to do and be, and of one's appropriate sexual role. The risk is that of confusion, arising from the profusion of roles opening to the child at this age.

INTIMACY VERSUS ISOLATION

This is the first of three adult stages Erikson proposes, which do not correspond to any of Freud's psychosexual stages. This crisis occurs during young adulthood, some time around 19 to 25, and is centered around the need for intimacy—for merging one's identity with that of another. This sort of intimacy is really only possible for someone who has successfully dealt with the earlier phases, since only a person with a strong, well-developed identity can enter into this kind of merger. If the individual's sense of identity is not strong enough to deal with this sort of intimacy, then a sense of isolation may result.

GENERATIVITY VERSUS STAGNATION

This phase occurs during the major period of adulthood, from the mid-20s to about 40. Erikson felt that during this period the focus of genital love shifted from the sexual experience itself to the pleasures of conceiving and raising children. This ability to focus one's energies on the raising of children is again an outgrowth of successful resolution of earlier dilemmas. If this is not achieved then a sense of stagnation or purposelessness may arise.

EGO INTEGRITY VERSUS DESPAIR

Finally, Erikson saw a last stage during the mature period from age 40 through old age. For the individual to face and deal with the problems of aging and death, she must have developed a pervasive quality he called *ego integrity*, which includes dignity, practical wisdom, and acceptance of one's own life pattern. Lacking this final integration of ego qualities, the mature person may experience a sense of despair.

Erikson's theory has been quite widely influential, not because everyone agrees that his descriptions of individual stages or crises are absolutely accurate, but because his theory offers one of the few real syntheses between cognitive development and personality development. The transitions from one stage to the next come about not exclusively because of maturational changes, but because of changes in the child's cognitive abilities and changes in the social structure around the child. The crises Erikson sees are the outgrowth of all those forces operating at the same time—the child's psychosexual development, her mental development, her physical abilities, and the new demands made by her society. Erikson's theory also can provide a framework for dealing with individual differences in children's ways of relating to others. Children who have resolved early crises in different ways will approach new tasks differently. *Precise* hypotheses about the long-term effects of differential early rearing experiences have not emerged from Erikson's theory, but the theory can be and has been used as a general guide by many researchers.

SOCIAL-LEARNING THEORIES

The fundamental tenet of social-learning theories is that the child's mode of interacting with others—her attachment or dependency, her aggression, her behavior with peers—are *learned*. All the several kinds of learning are presumed to be involved: classical conditioning, operant conditioning, and observational learning.

For example, in the development of attachment social-learning theorists do not assume that there are any instinctive patterns of interaction between infant and parent. Rather, they suggest that the child's attachment to her mother is based on the mother's nurturance of the child. The mother satisfies the child's needs over and over again. Having been associated so many times with good things—clean diapers, the bath, and food—the mother herself gradually becomes a "good thing" as well, so just being near her mother comes to be reinforcing for the child. Once the child has begun to show the various kinds of behaviors associated with attachment or dependency, such as smiling, clinging, seeking to be held, asking for attention or help, the mother may reinforce them directly, thus helping to maintain the behaviors.

The strength of the child's dependency presumably depends on the frequency of reinforcement for it, although, as I have pointed out before, the relationship is not a simple one. A schedule of partial reinforcement, in which the child makes several bids for help or attention before her mother responds, should result in even stronger dependent behavior than would immediate responses. The baby who makes repeated bids for attention by crying but who is responded to only after several cries may be more clinging and more dependent than the child who gets a response right away (see Box 20 page 278).

Social-learning theories can also account for differences in specific patterns of attachment or dependency relationships. According to this view, children not only learn whom to be attached to or dependent on but also just how to evoke nurturing responses from the other person. Some parents respond to crying, some to requests for help, some to clinging, and so forth, and the child will learn which behaviors are reinforced. A good example of this is the 4-year-old child of a friend of mine who has a beautiful, learned routine. He begins by saying "Mommy" several times. If nothing happens he ups his demand to "Mommy, I want you." If there is still no reaction he pleads "Mommy, I need you!" At this statement his mother's resolve melts and she goes to him. In doing so she has not only established exactly the kind of partial reinforcement schedule that will tend to maintain his dependent responses over a long period of time but she has also reinforced her child's particular pattern of requests for help.

The development of aggression and individual differences in levels of aggressiveness have also been accounted for by social-learning theorists. As I pointed out in the last chapter there is abundant evidence that aggressive responses are affected by reinforcement schedules in predictable ways. Children who are reinforced regularly for hitting the now-famous Bobo doll are significantly more aggressive with playmates in later tests. And the effect of different schedules of reinforcement is also easily demonstrable. For example, Cowan and Walters gave some boys marbles each time they hit the clown. Other groups of boys were rewarded for only every third or every sixth punch. When all rewards for hitting were ceased, the boys who had been rewarded for every sixth time initially persisted longer in hitting the clown than did the other groups. So once again there is evidence that intermittent or partial reinforcement produces behavior that is more resistant to extinction (recall Box 2 page 18).

These effects are not confined to children. Adults can be induced to increase the intensity of shocks given to others when they are praised for giving such severe punishments. Nor are these effects valid only for experimental situations, either. Studies in natural settings show the same general relationships. Bandura and Walters have shown, for example, that families with highly aggressive (delinquent) adolescent sons are much more likely to reward their sons' aggression than are families from similar environments who have nonaggressive sons. Clearly, the reinforcement or nonreinforcement of aggression has some effect.

But how are the aggressive responses learned in the first place? Bandura has emphasized that most of them are learned through modeling. As I have already pointed out in several places in this book, aggressive models are not difficult to find. Parents, teachers, and peers all serve as aggressive models on occasion, as do TV characters. The evidence is clear: Watching someone else behave aggressively not only helps you to learn the specific form of aggression the model shows, but it also serves to "disinhibit" your own aggressive impulses so that you are more likely to behave aggressively. Social-learning theorists, such as Bandura, are thus suggesting that the level and type of aggression shown by an individual child (or adult) is a joint function of the aggressive models she has encountered and the reinforcement contingencies in her typical environment.

I am sure it is clear to you from this very brief description that social learning theories are not really *developmental* theories. Most theorists in this tradition, including Bandura, Sears, Bijou, Baer, and many others, have not been very interested in changes with age in the *type* or quality of dependency or aggression or peer behavior. The primary concern has been to account for differences in *quantity*—individual differences in the strength or vigor of the behavior. It is possible to include some developmental notions within the framework of a social-learning theory, however, and some efforts in this direction have been attempted. Bandura, for example, has begun to talk about the influence that a child's cognitive processes have on her *understanding* of or memory for modeled aggression or reinforcements of aggression. And when the child's cognitive skills are entered into the equation, some developmental changes in what the child learns or the way she responds may be predicted. Some social-learning theorists have also suggested that developmental sequences in such things as attachment patterns may occur because mothers, as a group, tend to shift their patterns of reinforcement at particular ages. So the child's shift in attachment may result not from any process internal to the child, but from a common change in the way in which mothers respond to children's overtures. It seems to me entirely possible—even likely—that parents do shift their expectations, and thus their reinforcement contingencies, as the child gets older. Clinging behavior is far less acceptable to most parents in a 4-year-old than it is in a 1-year-old. But how much of this shift in the parents' expectations results from changes in the child? Do we find clinging in the 4-year-old less tolerable because we know she is *able* to be more independent? So, it may be the more fundamental changes in the child's skills—cognitive and motor skills particularly—that trigger changes in the parents reinforcement patterns, and not entirely the other way around.

Despite such difficulties in handling developmental shifts in the quality of the child's behavior, social-learning theory has been the single most influential view in the United States on the study of the development of personality and interpersonal relationships. Obviously, the child's pattern of response to others *is* influenced by their responses to her. Children *do* learn to behave in ways that will please adults, and they do learn new behaviors from observing models. These forces, in general, seem to be far more potent in the domain of interpersonal behavior than in the area of cognitive or motor development.

| COGNITIVE-DEVELOPMENTAL THEORY | Cognitive-developmental theorists, such as Piaget, Bruner, and Werner, have had little to say about the development of interpersonal relationships in children. Recently, however, several investigators, of whom Lawrence Kohlberg is probably the most prominent, have begun to attempt the more general application of cognitive-developmental theory to the development of interpersonal behaviors. The essential tenet of this approach is that "any behavior of a child is a function of the level of cognitive development he has achieved. An illustrative derivation of this principle applied to attachment is that: a child cannot develop a specific attachment until he can both discriminate and recognize an individual person." (Maccoby & Masters, 1970, p. 91) |

The emphasis here is on the primacy of the child's cognitive development. Changes in the child's cognitive skills may bring about or make possible changes in the child's relationships with others. The child cannot show attachment until she can discriminate her mother from others and until she has some kind of object concept. In fact, of course, the first signs of single attachments do appear at about the point at which the child has acquired the apparently necessary cognitive skills.

In the area of aggression the underlying or necessary cognitive skills are harder to identify, but there do seem to be some possible linkages. I have already pointed out in Chapter 11 that there is an increase in aggression during the 3 to 5 year period when there is a shift from parallel to cooperative play. And the shift in style of play, in turn, may reflect the gradual reduction in egocentrism in the child's thinking.

No cognitive-developmental theorist has attempted anything resembling a complete account of the development of attachment or aggression or any other interpersonal behavior. But it seems clear to me that the child's cognitive skills do inevitably enter into the equation in some way. Bandura and other social-learning theorists have begun to introduce some cognitive concepts into their theories, and some cognitive-developmental theorists have begun to be interested in personality development, so perhaps over the next decades there will be a fruitful blending of the two approaches. What is needed is some understanding of the ways in which the child's cognitive level affects the ways in which she perceives and responds to others around her.

OVERVIEW   As I pointed out initially, no one of these four theoretical approaches accounts satisfactorily for all aspects of interpersonal development. But I see no reason why we should have to choose one or the other of these viewpoints as being totally "right." Each may offer some advantage, and combinations are clearly possible. The ethological view of attachment, for example, may tell us important things about the nature of the earliest patterns of interaction between parent and child, while the social-learning concepts may help us to understand what happens to those earliest patterns over the years of childhood. The cognitive-developmental theorists point our attention to the critical cognitive underpinnings of all the interpersonal relationships. *All* of these forces seem to me to be involved. Erikson's theory perhaps comes the closest to combining these several threads. Certainly his suggestion of a series of discrete stages or crises can be used as a basis for more detailed syntheses of the several theoretical views.

SUMMARY

1. No one theory of the development of interpersonal relationships is completely adequate; no one accounts well for both developmental patterns and individual differences.
2. Ethological theory emphasizes the baby's inborn, instinctive patterns of interaction. She provokes caretaking by crying or movement, then prolongs it by cuddling, smiling, or other responses. With development these instinctive patterns shift and become more volitional.
3. Freud's psychoanalytic approach emphasizes a maturationally based developmental sequence of psychosexual stage. In each stage a particular erogenous zone is dominant. Of particular importance is the phallic stage, beginning at about age 4, when the Oedipal

crisis is met and mastered through the process of identification.
4. Erikson's modification of Freudian theory focuses more on changes in the child's motor and cognitive skills, and the impact of those changes on the child's interactions with those around her. Erikson describes a series of eight stages, over the entire life span, in each of which there is a central crisis or dilemma to be solved.
5. Social learning theorists assume that patterns of interpersonal relationships are learned, through classical and operant conditioning and observational learning. The strength and form of the child's attachments, or her level of aggression, are determined by models available to her and by the response

of those around her to her attachment or aggressive behavior.
6. Cognitive-developmental theory emphasizes
the links between cognitive development and
interpersonal behaviors. For example,
changes in the child's pattern of attachment

may be due to underlying shifts in her cognitive abilities.
7. The several theories should not be viewed as
mutually exclusive; each offers particular
strengths, and combinations of them are
both possible and reasonable.

REFERENCES

Suggested Additional Readings

Baldwin, A. L. *Theories of child development.*
New York: Wiley, 1967.
Contains a good discussion of Freudian
theory; If you are interested in Freud it
might be a good source before you tackle his
writings directly.
Bandura, A. *Aggression, A social learning analysis.* Englewood Cliffs, N. J.: Prentice-Hall,
1973.
The best single source for an understanding
of the social learning approach to personality. Very detailed, but fairly easy to understand.
Bowlby, J. *Attachment and loss* (Vol. 1). *Attachment.* New York: Basic Books, 1969.
The most extensive available statement of
the "ethological" theory of the development
of attachment.
Erikson, E. H. *Childhood and society.* New
York: Norton, 1963.
Erikson's major book and his major theoreti-
cal statement; see particularly Chapter 7,
"The Eight Ages of Man."
Freud, S. *A general introduction to psycho-
analysis.* New York: Washington Square
Press, 1960.
A useful introduction to the flavor of Freud's
thought, though only one of a number of his
major publications.
Herzog, E. & Sudia, C. E. Children in fatherless
families. In B. M. Caldwell & H. N. Ricciuti
(Eds.), *Review of child development research*
(Vol. 3). Chicago: University of Chicago
Press, 1973.
A lengthy and more detailed discussion of

this topic than is contained in Hetherington
and Deur's review. If you have a particular
interest in this topic I would suggest beginning with Hetherington and Deur and then
looking at this paper.
Hetherington, M., & Deur, J. The effects of
father absence on child development. In W.
W. Hartup (Ed.), *The young child: reviews of
research* (Vol. 2). Washington, D. C.: National Association for the Education of
Young Children, 1972.
Kohlberg, L. A cognitive-developmental analysis
of children's sex-role concepts and attitudes.
In E. E. Maccoby (Ed.), *The development of
sex differences.* Stanford, Calif.: Stanford
University Press, 1966.
Does not deal directly with the development
of attachment but does present the cognitive-
developmental approach better than it is
described elsewhere.
Maccoby, E. E., & Masters, J. C. Attachment
and dependency. In P. H. Mussen (Ed.), *Carmichael's manual of child psychology.* (Vol.
2, 3rd ed.). New York: Wiley, 1970.
Particularly good on theories of attachment
and on developmental changes related to the
theoretical alternatives as well, although
written in sophisticated language.
Rappoport, L. *Personality development: The
chronology of experience.* Glenview, Ill.:
Scott, Foresman, 1972.
An excellent introduction to personality
development, including a very good and
simple description of both Freudian and Erik-
sonian stages.

Other Sources Cited

Bandura, A., & Walters, R. H. *Adolescent aggression.* New York: Ronald Press, 1959.

Cowan, P. A., & Walters, R. H. Studies of reinforcement of aggression: I. Effects of scheduling. *Child Development*, 1963, *34*, 543–551.

Fraiberg, S. Blind infants and their mothers: An examination of the sign system. In M. Lewis & L. A. Rosenblum (Eds.), *The effect of the infant on its caregiver.* New York: Wiley, 1974.

13

Development of the Self-Concept and Sex-Role Identity

Child:	Help me tie my shoes. I can't do it by myself.
Mother:	Yes you can. I know you can do it.
Child (with a wail):	Nooooo I can't! I just know I can't do it myself. You have to help me.

What is going on in this interchange between mother and child? Probably many messages are being communicated from child to mother and back again. The child is very likely asking for attention as well as for help, and her mother's insistence that the child can do the job herself is an important part of training in independence. But at another level this child is making a statement about her own image of herself and her skills. She is saying, "I can't do this." In other conversations she may say, "Let me try—I think I can do that," or the equivalent. Obviously, her sense of dependence or independence is intimately tied in with her statements about her own abilities. The other element in such conversations and in the child's own feelings about herself is her developing self-concept.

She comes to know who she is, what is her body and what is someone else's body, what her body can and cannot do, where the parts of her body are located, and whether she is a girl or a boy. At the same time she begins to make some judgments about her own abilities and capacities. She may think highly of herself—have high self-esteem—or she may think of herself as having few skills or abilities valued by others. She may think she is stupid, incapable, and clumsy or able, efficient, and coordinated; or she may have a combination of positive and negative feelings.

The body image and self-esteem develop partly from the child's experiences with her own body and what she finds she is able to do with it. But a great deal of her self-concept, the degree of her self-esteem, is based on her perception of what other people think of her. A child may, for example, think of herself as clumsy because she has been called clumsy or because her occasional lack of coordination has been inordinately emphasized. Let me risk one more personal example: I recall very vividly that when something got broken in our family, no one asked, "Who broke the dish?" Rather, the question seemed (at least to me) to be always, "Helen, when did you break the dish?" I have no way of knowing whether in fact I broke more things than do other children. I do know that I *believed* I did, and that my self image then, and still, includes a sense of physical clumsiness.

Clearly, the development of the self-concept is an important continuing event. What a child knows and believes about herself will affect all her interactions with others, and by influencing the kinds of things that the child will attempt, the self-concept may have very broad effects on her development of new skills. In exploring the development of the self-concept I will use the same procedure as in Chapter 11, beginning with a brief look at the developmental pattern, then at the individual differences, then at the factors that influence the self-

concept. Because the development of sex-role identity is of special importance, I will treat it separately.

THE SELF-CONCEPT
Developmental Patterns

Two cognitive accomplishments lie behind the first stages in the child's developing self-concept. First, she must come to recognize that she is separate from others, that her mother's or caregiver's body is not an extension of her own. Freud talked about the child's early *symbiotic* relationship with her mother, in which she appears to consider the two of them as a single unit. Piaget, too, emphasizes that the very young child has not yet understood the separation of self from not-self. During the first six or eight months, as the child develops the object concept, she also develops the notion of separation of the self from the rest of the world. But once she has done so, another necessary cognitive accomplishment must be acquired. She must figure out that the self is a constant event. In a sense this understanding is merely an extension of her developing notions of object constancy, except that in this instance she and her body are the objects. The child must come to consider her body and herself as a single, continuous event before a stable concept of self can be developed. She usually does so during the first several years, so that by 2 or 3 years of age she appears to have a quite stable, unitary view of herself.

Although children younger than age 2 will respond to their own names when someone else speaks to them, it is not until about 2 years of age that they begin to use their own name to refer to themselves.

The use of the child's own name is an important event in the development of her self-concept, just as the development of other concepts is aided by her coming to have a single label to attach to them. (2-and 3-year-olds, in fact, often call themselves by their own name rather than using pronouns like *I* and *me*.) By age 3 or so the child also shows considerable independence and insistence on autonomy. Of course, this behavior can be seen merely as part of the desire for mastery, but Erik Erikson and others have pointed out that this very powerful push for independence may also be part of the child's developing notion of self. She is asserting herself, showing pride in her own abilities to do things herself, and trying out the boundaries of her skills.

By age 4, as Gordon Allport has pointed out, a new phase, a sort of extension of the self, begins. The child begins to show enormous possessiveness: "That's my dollie!"; "That's my daddy!"; "Don't you play with my blocks." Although this possessiveness may result from her increasing participation in cooperative, rather than parallel, play and thus from more encounters with other children in which there can be some competition for toys, it may also be that the child is extending the self to include "things that belong to me."[1]

During these early years the child no doubt absorbs all the judgments by others about her abilities and behavior, and these early inputs help her to form her overall self-image. But it is not until perhaps age 5 or 6 that the child begins to verbalize her feelings about herself. We know that a 5-year-old has an adult-like image of herself, complete with positive and negative judgments. But because younger children do not express their self-concepts so readily, it is difficult to tell how early these impressions are formed.

In arriving at a self-concept the child is influenced not only by her own conclusions about her skills and abilities but also very heavily by the judgments of others about her and by their actions toward her. She takes in all the statements made to her by others: "Oh, what a clumsy child you are!"; "Can't you ever finish anything you start?" "Sometimes I think you just don't have any brain at all"; "My, you certainly are a good little helper!"; "That was very smart of you to be able to do that yourself." The accumulation of all these messages, along with her own experiences of competence and failure, begin to shape the child's knowledge and belief about herself.

Individual Differences and Factors Influencing Them

By early elementary school age, if not before, children seem to have quite stable images of themselves and to have made value judgments

---

[1] It is interestint to speculate on the connection between the child's early possesiveness and the "territoriality" seen in adult humans and other kinds of animals. Many animals have clear attachments to specific territories; the individual animal is defined partly by the territory that belongs to it. The child's possessiveness about toys and "things that belong to me" may be a sign of the development of some territorial aspects of the self.

about their own characteristics. At this age we can select both children who have generally high self-esteem and those with low self-esteem, and these designations seem to be fairly stable over time. Furthermore, whether a child likes herself or not is predictive of a whole variety of other behavior. Children low in self-esteem are usually more anxious, particularly about doing well in school, in sports, or in any other arena. Among adults, and no doubt among children as well, people who have poor self-esteem tend to be less effective in groups than are those with high self-esteem. Those who feel adequate are likely to take leadership roles, to contribute good ideas, and generally to provide stimulation and guidance to the group. Children with poor self-concepts do less well in school.

Obviously, there is a severe chicken-egg problem here. Does the child do poorly in school and have high anxiety because she has a poor self-concept, or does she have little self-esteem because she does poorly in school? In fact, probably neither of these fairly simple causal notions is correct. There is some evidence that the child does bring a self-concept to the school situation with her and that it does have an impact on all her interactions there. For example, in several studies done with boys, researchers have found that the apparently capable boy (with a high IQ) who does not do well in school is likely to have a low estimate of himself and to see himself as restricted and unable to function independently. In this case it looks as if the child's self-image is among the important causal factors in school failure.

But it is not so simple. Stanley Coopersmith, in a whole series of studies, has found that at least some children who are considered effective and competent by their teachers and who are well liked by their peers are low in self-esteem. These children are successful, but they are very self-critical. They take their mistakes out on themselves, yet their self-criticism apparently does not incapacitate them. They are able to perform well in school and in groups of peers.

For most children the self-concept appears to work as a kind of self-fulfilling prophesy: The child has an idea of how well she can do, so she behaves in ways that tend to confirm her idea. For example, if she believes that she cannot do math problems, she may try a problem once, fail, and conclude, "See, I knew I couldn't do it!" But some children appear to have more complex self-images. Instead of making an overall judgment about their own capacities, they approach new tasks and problems by setting extremely high standards for their own accomplishments. They make a serious effort to meet those standards, and when they do not, they castigate themselves for failure in such internal soliloquies as, "You did it again. You can't ever do anything right!" In the process of making the attempt, however, such children may in fact perform well by objective standards. Other people think the child is doing beautifully; it is only the child who believes she is not good enough.

The child's self-esteem appears to be heavily rooted in her family experiences. Coopersmith's research is again helpful. He found that school-age children with high self-esteem came from families in which the parents also had high self-esteem and in which the children were treated as responsible individuals. Mothers of children with high self-esteem were more accepting and positive toward their children, more affectionate, and more likely to praise the children for their accomplishments. They were interested in their children and showed it. They expected the children to have opinions and wanted them to share those opinions with others. But the parents of the children with high self-esteem also set fairly strict and clear limits for their children's behavior and applied those limits consistently. So such parents provide quite a lot of consistent guidance and discipline and are loving at the same time.

This combination of firm but reasoned control, positive encouragement of independence, and a warm and loving atmosphere shows up again in a particularly interesting study by Diana Baumrind, although she was interested in a broader group of child characteristics than self-esteem, and she studied preschool-age, rather than school-age, children. She selected children who were self-reliant, self-controlled, and explorative, as well as content with themselves, and compared them with children who had poor self-esteem, little curiosity and exploratory behavior, and little self-reliance. The children with the highest self-esteem, self-reliance, and explorative tendencies had parents with the same combination of traits that Coopersmith found in parents of children with high self-esteem. Baumrind calls this combination of parental characteristics *authoritative* parental behavior, in contrast to either *authoritarian* behavior (detached, controlling, and less warm) or *permissive* behavior (noncontrolling and undemanding but quite warm and affectionate). In her study the least self-reliant and effective children were likely to have permissive parents; the most positive and competent children were likely to have authori*tative* parents, and the children of authoritarian parents fell in between.

Bronson has explored the development of a sense of competence in the child as well, but has focused her attention on the period from age 1 to age 2. She argues that the seeds of the child's sense of competence and effectiveness are sown then, so that we should study the relationship of the child to the parent during this period if we want to understand why later some children are more confident and competent than others. Some of the children she first observed at ages 1 and 2 she later observed in nursery school and in other settings, so she is able to look back at the early mother-child interaction patterns of children who later differed in competence. The differences can be made sharply by comparing two particular children, whom Bronson calls Dan and Roy.

Dan at age $3\frac{1}{2}$ was outgoing, confident, at ease with himself, and purposive in his pursuit of goals. Roy, by contrast, was equally outgoing, but seemed discontent, edgy, and in Bronson's words, was "unable to discover the joys of self-actualization." (Bronson, 1974, p. 292) When these two case histories were traced backwards, clear differences in early patterns of interactions were found. Dan's mother let him initiate and pace most of their interactions. Over the period from age 1 to age 2, as Dan's signals and messages became clearer, his mother gradually increased the complexity of her responses, so that by age 2 she was giving rather lengthy explanations and expansions of Dan's language or behavior. Roy's early interactions were very different. His mother seemed far less well adapted to the child's activities. The mother dominated the interaction, paced it, and determined the level of complexity of what went on. She showed little of the gradual increase in complexity that Dan's mother had shown. It seems to me that Bronson's findings are generally consistent with what both Baumrind and Coopersmith have found. The authoritative parent, in Baumrind's study, sets firm limits but also encourages the child's activities and involvement. She is responsive to the child. The authoritarian parent, by contrast, sets the rules herself, more or less without regard for the child's specific needs or interests. This distinction seems to be paralleled by Bronson's observations.

What both of these studies, as well as Coopersmith's, underline is the importance of family experiences in which the child's individual interests, needs, and concerns are encouraged and responded to and respected. In addition, firm limits set and *explained* by the parents appear to contribute to a developing positive self-image on the part of the child.

Social Class and Sex Differences in Self-Concept

It has been common to find in textbooks and other psychological writing statements to the effect that poor children and females generally have lower self-esteem. Such negative self-concepts among poor children are thought by many to be an important factor contributing to the poorer school performance of such children. We know that children with lower self-esteem generally do less well in school. If children from poverty backgrounds have lower self-esteem, perhaps this is why they do less well in school.

Self-esteem among females is also widely thought generally to be lower because so many of the qualities of "femininity" in our culture are less highly valued than are the qualities of "masculinity."

But neither of these generalizations is entirely or consistently true. There are many studies in which poor children have been found to have lower self-esteem or more negative self-concepts, but such a finding is *not* invariable. For example, in one recent study of nearly 4000 children aged 8 to 14, Trowbridge found that children from lower social class families had consistently *more favorable* self-concepts than did children from middle-class families. On the other hand many earlier studies reported consistent differences in the opposite direction. I am not at all sure how to explain such inconsistency in results. It is possible that our culture has changed over the past several decades, so that lower social class status in many communities no longer carries with it the seeds of poor self-concept. But whatever the explanation, there does *not* seem to be any consistent tendency for poor children to have lower self-esteem. At the same time it is still true that children with lower self-esteem—whatever social strata they come from—are likely to do less well in school.

Sex differences in self-esteem are equally inconsistent. There is just no evidence that girls, or women, generally value themselves or their qualities less highly than do males. However, teenage and adult women appear to be *less confident* about their ability to succeed at some upcoming task. Males seem to have greater confidence and a greater sense of potency and control over what happens to them, while women (and teenage girls) seem to feel that they are somewhat less in control of their lives. Other evidence suggests that while the two sexes are about equal in overall self-concept, the particular positive qualities they see in themselves differ somewhat. Men are more likely to see themselves as having such qualities as ambition, energy, optimism, or practicality, while women are more likely to see themselves as having such qualities as attractiveness, cooperation, frankness, sympathy, and ability to be leaders. The qualities men see in themselves are primarily *personal* qualities, while those women see in themselves seem to be more *social* qualities—skills and abilities that involve others.

I find these results puzzling, since among children there is no tendency for girls to be more "affiliative," or more involved with or concerned about social encounters. In fact young boys seem to be *more* concerned with peers in many cases. Why, then, among adults should we find women *defining themselves* in terms of social skills, rather than personal competencies?

I don't have a good answer to this question, but I can suggest one source of influence. Our cultural stereotypes about masculine and feminine characteristics provide a picture of males as being fundamentally *competent*, while females are seen as having primarily *expressive* or social skills. The skills and qualities the stereotypes suggest males ought to have are also the skills and qualities likely to be highly valued by our society.

There is very good evidence that such stereotypes dominate in books, television, and other media. Children's reading books present males as being more competent, more in control of events, and more able to bring about good results. Although this is now changing, females, when they are presented at all in readers, are shown to be ineffective, subservient, and dependent on chance or actions of others for good results. (This is well illustrated in Figure 34.) Television portrayals of males and females are similarly stereotypic. So children are bombarded with information about the "expected" or "standard" male and female

"She can not skate," said Mark, "I can help her.
I want to help her. Look at her, Mother.
Just look at her. She is just like a girl. She gives up."

FIGURE 34

An example of sextyping in a children's reading book. Most books with this type of sexual bias have been revised in recent years. (Source: O'Donnell, M. *Around the corner.* New York: Harper & Row, 1966.)

roles throughout childhood, and such exposure *may* have something to do with the adoption of somewhat different definitions of self among adolescents and adults. But again, let me emphasize that despite the more positive portrayals of males in so many areas, the overall self-esteem of males and females does *not* seem to differ.

SEX-ROLE DEVELOPMENT

This discussion of sex differences in self-esteem leads me naturally to the question of sex-role development in general. Obviously, an important part of the self-concept is the knowledge that "I am a girl" or "I am a boy," and such knowledge carries with it certain implications for behavior as well. How does the child come to understand her own gender? And how does she come to adopt the behavior "appropriate" for her sex?

Developmental Patterns and Correlates

Just as the child's understanding of her own body and its limits changes with age, so does her conception of her own sex. The progression appears to be as follows.

328

By age 3 the child knows the label *boy* and *girl* and can apply the correct label to him- or herself. A majority of 3-year-olds can correctly answer the question, "Are you a little girl or a little boy?" whereas most 2½-year-olds cannot. But knowledge of the correct label does *not* imply that the child has understood or generalized it as would an adult. The 3-year-old does not understand yet that gender is constant—that you can't change gender by changing your clothes or by wishing you were different—nor has she understood the relationship between genital differences and gender. Her classifications of others into categories of "boy" and "girl" are not entirely consistent even at this age, but seem to be based generally on such external characteristics as dress or hairstyle.

By age 4 there is still no complete understanding of gender *constancy,* but the child does categorize others consistently correctly and

FIGURE 35
Imitation of same-sex parent by a child of about 5. This is about the age that most theorists emphasize the importance of this sort of imitation in the development of sex-role identity.

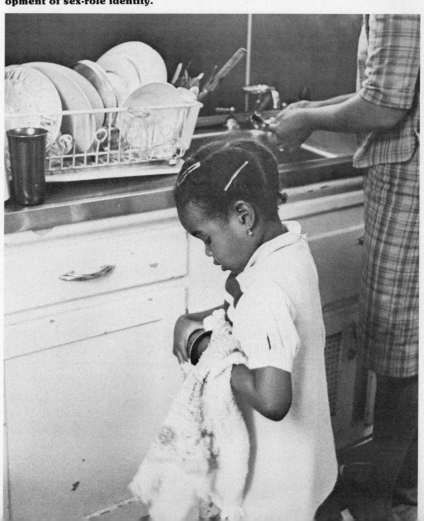

uses appropriate pronouns most of the time (*he, she, him, her*). Understanding of gender constancy does not seem to occur until about 5 or 6. At this age the child understands that she cannot change herself into a boy, and she has grasped the relationship between gender and genital differences. At about this same age, the child begins to show consistent imitation of the same-sexed parent or other adults.

Contrary to what we might expect, this developmental progression is not particularly influenced by the attitudes toward sex that are prevalent in the family. Families that permit or encourage nudity or open discussion of anatomical differences do not have children who grasp the relationship between genital differences and gender any sooner than do children in families that are more modest about nudity and less open in their discussion of sexual differences.

One factor that is related to the child's rate of progression through the developmental sequence, however, is IQ. Brighter children, as measured by standard IQ tests, proceed somewhat more rapidly through the sequence than do children of average intelligence.

By the time they enter elementary school children have a clear notion of their own sex and a clear idea of the stereotypical "female" and "male" role and characteristics. They have normally adopted behaviors consistent with the sex designation and imitate adults of the same sex more than those of the opposite sex. An example of such imitation is given in Figure 35. (All these statements, however, seem to be more true of boys than of girls. Boys show very strong preferences for toys associated with maleness and for adult male activities, whereas girls show weaker preferences for their own sex's stereotypic roles and activities.) The sex-role identity adopted at this early age persists (except in rare individuals who later go through sex-change operations) through childhood and into adulthood. The problem for theorists is to explain how this very fixed identity is established in the young child.

Theoretical Alternatives

The theoretical alternatives are particularly sharply defined. Three major theories have been offered to account for the acquisition of sex-role identity: psychoanalytic theory, social-learning theory, and cognitive-developmental theory. As all three have been discussed at some length at various other points in this book, I need only sketch their approaches to this particular problem.

PSYCHOANALYTIC THEORY

The basic concept that Freud offered to account for the child's acquisition of appropriate sex-role identity and behavior was identification: As a consequence of the Oedipal conflict (described in Chapter 12), the child identifies with the parent of the same sex and presumably adopts all the qualities of that parent, including sex-role behaviors and attitudes. The process of identification, according to Freud, is different for the boy and the girl. The girl's identification with her mother grows out of her primary loving attachment to the mother. But as the boy ordinarily does not have such a loving, dependent relationship with his father, some other mechanism is required. Freud suggested as an alternative "identification with the aggressor." The child, in this view, identifies with the person whom he sees as most powerful. More specifically, it is the power to castrate that is apparently at the heart of the matter as Freud saw it.

One of the difficulties with this theory is that it presumes that the boy of 4 years has some idea of the genital differences between boys and girls. The fear of castration presumably arises partly because the boy sees that girls and women do not have penises and assumes that they have already been castrated. But the available data suggest that knowledge and understanding of genital differences are not present until somewhat later than Freud supposed. Children apparently begin to prefer toys and activities associated with their own sex before they have figured out the anatomical differences.

Nonetheless, there does appear to be some process that might be described as identification, and it takes place at about the time that Freud emphasized. The child does begin to imitate adults of the same sex at about age 4 or 5. But the explanation does not require that we accept Freudian notions of Oedipal conflict and identification with the aggressor. Social-learning theorists have proposed an alternative view of the same facts.

SOCIAL-LEARNING THEORY

Walter Mischel has made the most complete attempt to apply social learning theory to the acquisition of sex role and sex-role behavior. The fundamental tenets of his position can best be stated in Mischel's own words:

In social-learning theory, sex-typed behaviors may be defined as behaviors that typically elicit different rewards for one sex than for the other. . . . According to social-learning theory, the acquisition and performance of sex-typed behaviors can be described by the same learning principles used to analyze any other aspect of an individual's behavior. . . . Sex-typing is the process by which the individual acquires sex-typed behavior patterns: first he learns to discriminate between sex-typed behavior patterns, then to generalize from these specific learning experiences to new situations, and finally to perform sex-typed behavior. (Mischel, 1966, pp. 56–57)

The initial process of discrimination presumably takes several years; the child has to determine that she is a girl (or that he is a boy). Frequent use of the labels *girl, she,* and so on by her parents and others and approval for her correct labeling of herself help her to do so. Beyond this early point, Mischel has suggested, the child is systematically reinforced for sex-appropriate behaviors and for imitating the parent of the same sex. One of the fundamental concepts of this theory, then, is that the child is systematically rewarded for behavior consistent with her sex, for choosing sex-appropriate toys, and so forth.

A second major concept in this theory is that of imitation. When Freud spoke of identification he meant a process by which the child takes in (incorporates) all the qualities of the individual with whom she identifies. Mischel does not want to make assumptions about such internal processes; rather, he emphasizes that what we see is the child copying the behaviors and attitudes of the adult. He suggests that the word imitation is a better description of that process. Bandura and Walters use the phrase observational learning or *modeling* for the same kind of event.

Research by the social-learning theorists has suggested that there are some rules governing the process of imitation. It has been shown, for example, that children will model themselves after the adult who has power over such resources as rewards. When the male is more powerful than the female in an experimental situation, both boys and girls will imitate him; when the female is more powerful, both boys and girls will imitate her. Cross-sex imitation thus can and does occur as a function of the power relationships among members of the group. Mischel assumes that the same is true in a family and that, for example, a child whose mother is more powerful than her father will tend to imitate the mother. But beyond this basic tendency to imitate the one who has power, the child has to cope with the direct consequences of her imitation. If she imitates a more powerful father, she may be rebuked for showing too much "boyish" behavior, whereas her imitations of her mother may be rewarded. So, gradually, she is shaped into adopting the female role.

One of the strengths of this theory is that it can explain very easily the typically low correlations among sex-typed behaviors. A boy may be aggressive in one situation and not in another, even though assertiveness and aggression are considered generally desirable characteristics for boys. A girl may show docile dependence in one situation and assertive independence in another. If Freud were correct about a single, powerful, all-encompassing identification process then we might expect to see greater consistency of behavior traits in all situations and clearer clusters of behavior traits in a given individual. Mischel's point is that if the acquisition of the sex role and sex-typed behavior is governed primarily by imitation and reinforcement, then inconsistency is precisely what we should expect, for the child will likely be rewarded for a particular behavior in one situation and not in another.

But there are several difficulties even here. First, Mischel has not taken the developmental sequence into account. Changes in the child's concept of gender are not woven into the social-learning explanation. Mischel assumes that the child is reinforced differentially for sex-appropriate modeling and behavior, and that she will try to repeat actions that bring pleasurable results; therefore, it isn't necessary for her to have figured out that she's a girl and that she's being rewarded for doing feminine things. Such a cognitive generalization may help, but it's not needed. But an equally important concept in Mischel's theory is that the child is systematically reinforced for imitating same-sexed adults. And here the child's ability to make a consistent discrimination between male and female adults does seem to have some relevance.

A second, more troublesome problem for the social-learning view is that for Mischel to be correct, parents must show systematic reinforcement of "appropriate" behavior in boys and girls starting from the very earliest months and years of life. But there is not a great deal of evidence to suggest that they do. Maccoby and Jacklin, in their extensive review of research on parental treatment of young boys and girls, conclude that during the preschool years there are very few differences. Boys are handled somewhat more roughly and are more likely to be physically punished, and girls are more often protected from physical harm than are boys, but otherwise there are few of the expected differences. Boys do not appear to be systematically rewarded for aggression, and girls are not systematically rewarded for any of the stereotypically female characteristics such as nurturance or dependence.

Thus, although the social-learning view makes considerable intuitive sense, it is not well supported by the currently available facts. There is no good evidence that children under the age of 4 or 5 are differentially rewarded for sex-appropriate behavior and no good evidence that they show any preference for imitating models of the same sex—both of which should be happening if Mischel is right about the origins of sex-role development. Yet, the fact remains that by about age 6 the child has identified her own sex, has begun to show strong preference for toys and activities associated with her own sex, and does model herself on the parent or adult of the same sex. Of course, it may be that early differential reinforcement is more subtle than any of the currently available research has been able to pick up, and that as research progresses, we will discover ways in which early sex-role learning is taking place. But another alternative is offered by cognitive-developmental theory.

COGNITIVE-DEVELOPMENTAL THEORY

Social-learning explanations of sex-role development have a quality of intuitive sense; cognitive-developmental explanations of the same phenomenon, on the contrary, make very little intuitive sense but very good cognitive sense.

Kohlberg, who has been the most thorough and frequent exponent of a cognitive-developmental explanation of sex-role development, begins by describing the developmental sequence I outlined earlier and points out the important cognitive underpinnings of the sequence. The concept of sex identity is, after all, a concept and presumably has a cognitive component like any other concept. The child first learns the label *girl*, just as she learns labels for chairs, toys, and the like. But, like other early labels, sex labels are not used consistently. The child first uses a label to apply only to a few objects. She may use the word *cat* correctly to apply to the family tabby yet still not apply it correctly to other cats in the neighborhood. So she may say that she is a girl but not be able to apply the same label correctly to other girls and women whom she sees.

Later, as is true of other concepts, she learns the dimensions of the concepts of girl and boy and learns some cues that will tell her whether a new person is a girl or a boy, although at this stage, apparently, she does not use genital differences as cues in this discrimination. Then at about age 5 or 6, at the same time that other constancies, such as conservation, are being learned, she also figures out that being a girl is permanent. Just as the clay does not change its weight when its shape has changed, so a girl doesn't turn into a boy by putting on boy's clothing or by getting bigger. Kohlberg thus emphasizes that the development of the concept of sex identity follows the same basic cognitive progression as does any other concept. Only when the child has arrived at the concrete operational stage and has developed a notion of sexual constancy is there any opportunity for development of real sex-role preference. Until she recognizes that she is of a given sex permanently, there can be no question of adopting a role consistent with her sex.

Kohlberg assumes that the child, having figured out that she is permanently a girl, begins to place value on feminine things and to imitate the behavior of women and other girls. What is added here is the notion that people always place positive value on what is consistent with their own self-image; we think that what we are is good, and having figured out our sex, we value all things associated with that sex and begin to imitate others who share it.

The contrast between the cognitive view and the social-learning view of this process, stated in a somewhat oversimplified way, is quite sharp. Mischel sees the child's concept of sex-roles as growing out of her reinforced imitation of same-sexed adults; Kohlberg sees the imitation of same-sexed adults as growing out of the child's concept of gender and sex-roles. The psychoanalytic position is in some sense a mixture of the two, since Freud assumed that the child had some notion of the anatomical differences between male and female—and thus some concept of gender—before the Oedipal crisis occurs; but the major acquisition of sex-role comes about after identification in the Freudian system.

Kohlberg's theory has a number of attractions. First, it offers an important link between cognitive and social development. Psychologists have a tendency to look at the child in pieces, to adopt one theory that covers only cognitive development or only personality development and to assume that separate processes are involved. Kohlberg has suggested that they are linked and that cognitive development is an underlying thread. Second, Kohlberg's formulation fits the developmental facts more closely than do the other alternatives. Finally, his theory does not require systematic differential reinforcement for boyish or girlish behaviors before about age 5 or 6. It is necessary that the child's sex be labeled for her, and such labeling certainly does occur, but he needn't assume other systematic differential treatment.

But again, there are some drawbacks. First of all, children do show *some* understanding of the gender concept as early as age 2 or 3. And this early concept, albeit incomplete and imperfect, should affect behavior in some ways. In fact children of ages 2 to 3 do show some preference for "appropriate" toys. Boys are somewhat more likely to choose guns, trucks, or fire engines, while girls choose to play house, sew, or string beads. So, although there is no consistent tendency for children this young to show more direct imitation of same-sex adults, their behavior does match the stereotypes in some ways. A second difficulty with Kohlberg's formulation is the fact that most 6-year-old girls do not seem to place as strong a value on their own sex-appropriate behavior as do boys. More girls, for example, choose stereotypically boys' toys than the reverse, and more girls say that they would rather be boys than the reverse. Kohlberg suggests that this difference arises because in our society the male role is more valued in general. Also, the female role is more flexible in that it can include some masculine traits, whereas the male role is less likely to include female traits. The girl can compete in a man's world, but it is much less likely that a man will compete in a woman's world. Perhaps girls' greater valuation of the male role comes about because the models she copies have such an attitude.

Notice that Kohlberg does not reject the notion of imitation or the role of reinforcement. He agrees that they occur and that they are important in the development of the sex role, but he argues that they do not play an important role until *after* the child has developed a sense of constant sex identity.

Strong support for this expectation comes from a recent study by Slaby and Frey. They studied a group of children ranging in age from 2 to about 5½. Each child's gender concept was tested with a series of questions designed to determine if the child understood gender identity ("Are you a boy or a girl?" "Is this doll a boy or a girl?"), gender stability ("When you were a little baby, were you a little girl or a little boy?" "When you grow up will you be a mommy or a daddy?"), and gender consistency ("If you wore boy's clothes would you be a boy?" "If you played boy's games would you be a boy?"). This part of the study is obviously just an assessment of developmental changes in gender concept. But Slaby and Frey also tried to determine whether their subjects were more likely to imitate a male or a female model. Each child watched a film that showed an adult male and female doing various activities. The experimental setting was arranged so that an observer could watch the child's eyes during the film to see whether each subject was watching the male or the female adult in the film.

What Slaby and Frey found was that the extent to which the child watched the same-sexed adult was related to the level of her gender concept. Children with more advanced gender concepts—regardless of age—spent more time watching same-sex models than did children with less mature gender concepts. If we assume that watching the same-sexed model in a film is in some way a measure of "imitation," then it looks as if Kohlberg is right; at the very least it appears that the child's imitation of the same-sex adult is affected by her gender concept.

No doubt the process of adapting oneself to the appropriate sex-role begins before age 4 or 5. As Maccoby and Jacklin point out,

Children as young as 3, we suggest, have begun to develop a rudimentary understanding of their own sex identity, even though their ability to group others according to sex is imperfect and their notion about the permanence of their own sex identity incomplete. As soon as a boy knows that he is a boy in any sense, he is likely to begin to prefer to do what he conceives to be boylike things. Of course, he will not selectively imitate male models if he does not yet know which other people around him are in the same sex category as himself. But he will nevertheless try to match his own behavior to his limited concept of what attributes are sex-appropriate. (Maccoby & Jacklin, 1974, p. 365)

With increasing age, as the child's gender concept becomes more complex and sophisticated, so do her concepts of her own sex and of the behaviors that are appropriate for her. She is influenced not only by the behavior of same-sex models around her, but also by information in books, by television, and by the behavior of teachers and other adults. We would expect that boys' and girls' actual *behavior* would thus show greater and greater divergence as the impact of sex-role stereotypes become more prevalent during school and later years.

In part, that is what is found, although as I have pointed out in earlier chapters the major sex differences in both cognitive skills and in social behavior do not emerge clearly until adolescence or adulthood. Quite obviously there is still a *great* deal to be understood about the whole process. If fairly mature concepts of gender identity are present in a 6-year-old, why is it only in adolescence that clear sex differences in behavior in so many areas are found? Does it take that long for the effects of cultural stereotypes to be felt? Or is there some major shift in the social reinforcement systems at adolescence that may account for the changes at this age?

There are many questions still to be answered. But I want to emphasize once again that the self-concept, and more specifically the sex-role identity, are important mediating concepts for the child. Her beliefs about herself and her knowledge of the constancy of her sex affect all her interactions with other people and with objects. The child who believes that she can't play baseball behaves differently from the child who believes that she can. Such a child is likely to avoid baseballs, bats, playing fields, and other children who play baseball. If forced to play she may make self-depreciating remarks like, "You know I can't play," or she may play a self-defeating game, refusing to watch the ball when she swings at it or not running after the ball in center field because she knows she couldn't catch it even if she did get there in time. Similarly, a child who believes that she can't do school work will behave in a way quite different from a child who has confidence in her academic skills. She may try to draw attention by cutting up and being noisy, or she may become silent and withdrawn. She may not try to accomplish the tasks given her on the theory that if you don't try, you can't fail. Or such a self-critical child may try much harder, paying the price in anxiety about failure.

The point is that these beliefs are pervasive, that they affect virtually all the child's behavior, and that they develop early and are not easily changed. We need to know much more about the origins of the child's feelings of self-worth or worthlessness, if only so that we can learn to counteract the latter.

SUMMARY

1. The self-concept includes both the child's view of herself and her abilities, and her degree of self-esteem.
2. The earliest stage in the development of the self-concept is the twin discovery by the child that (a) she is separate from others, and (b) that her body and herself are continuous, constant events.
3. By about age 2 the child has learned her name; by age 3 autonomy is notable, as she asserts her own identity. At about age 4 she shows a kind of territorial possessiveness. By age 5 or 6 she has developed (and verbalizes) a full adult-like image of herself and seems to have made positive and negative judgments about herself.
4. Children who are low in self-esteem are usually more anxious and usually have more difficulty in school than do children with higher self-esteem.
5. Children with high self-esteem most often come from families in which their independent achievements are valued and praised, in which there is a warm, affectionate relationship between parents and children, and in which clear limits are set on the children's behavior.
6. Neither sex differences nor social class dif-

ferences in self-esteem are consistently found, although teenage girls and adult women are somewhat less confident of their ability to succeed at new tasks.
7. Sex-role development follows a similar developmental course. By age 3 the child has the labels boy and girl; by age 4 she uses these labels correctly to classify other people as well as herself and shows some preference for toys and activities associated with her own sex. By age 5 or 6 she has figured out that her gender is fixed and that there is some relationship between gender and genital appearance.
8. Freud's explanation of the development of sex-role identity emphasizes the importance of identification: The child is said to identify with the parent of the same sex as a result of the Oedipal conflict and to adopt the sex-role behaviors and attitudes of that parent.
9. Social-learning theorists emphasize that sex-role identity and behaviors are both taught through differential reinforcement of appropriate label use and through imitation of the behavior of adults of the same sex.
10. Cognitive-developmental theory emphasizes the importance of the child's first discov-

ering that gender is a permanent characteristic. Before that cognitive accomplishment is achieved, the child has no clear sex role; after it, the child imitates adults of the same sex and adopts behaviors and attitudes appropriate to her sex.

11. Research evidence is generally consistent with the cognitive-developmental view, although the development of the gender concept begins earlier than Kohlberg and others have emphasized.

12. Past age 5 or 6, when gender constancy is established, the child's concept of her appropriate sex role is affected by the behavior of the adults around her and by information from books, films, television, and other media. Portrayals of males and females in the media are *heavily* stereotypic and may contribute to the sex differences in behavior observed at adolescence and in adults.

REFERENCES

Suggested Additional Readings

Baumrind, D. Socialization and instrumental competence in young children. In W. W. Hartup (Ed.), *The young child: Reviews of research.* (Vol. 2). Washington, D. C.: National Association for the Education of Young Children, 1972.
An excellent, not very difficult, paper describing Baumrind's very interesting research on the development of "competence" in young children.

Broverman, I. K., Vogel, S. R., Boverman, D. M., Clarkson, F. E., & Rosenkrantz, P. S. Sex-role stereotypes: A current appraisal. *Journal of Social Issues,* 1972, 28, 59–78.
If you are interested in existing sex-role stereotypes in our culture, this is the best review and general discussion I know of.

Kohlberg, L. A cognitive-developmental analysis of children's sex-role concepts and attitudes. In E. E. Maccoby (Ed.), *The development of sex differences.* Stanford, Calif.: Stanford University Press, 1966.
The major theoretical paper by Kohlberg, in a writing style that is not always easy but is generally readable.

Maccoby, E. E., & Jacklin, C. N. *The psychology of sex differences.* Stanford, Calif.: Stanford University Press, 1974.
If you are interested in any aspect of this topic, this is an absolute must. Research literature is covered in detail, but I think the writing style is extremely readable. See particularly the final chapter.

Mischel, W. A social-learning view of sex differences in behavior. In E. E. Maccoby (Ed.), *The development of sex differences.* Stanford, Calif.: Stanford University Press, 1966.
The twin of Kohlberg's 1966 paper. Mischel's first and most easily read statement of his social-learning explanation of the development of sex differences and sex roles. Try this one first before you tackle the next reference.

Mischel, W. Sex-typing and socialization. In P. H. Mussen (Ed.), *Carmichael's manual of child psychology.* (Vol. 2, 3rd ed.). New York: Wiley, 1970.
Broader than Mischel's 1966 paper, describes sex differences and emphasizes a social-learning explanation; dense and difficult to read. Maccoby and Jacklin is a better and more recent general source, but this is a good companion piece if you are particularly interested in the field.

Saario, T. N., Jacklin, C. N., & Tittle, C. K. Sex role stereotyping in the public schools. *Harvard Educational Review,* 1973, 43, 386–416.
The best current review of the presentation of sex-roles in children's reading books and other sources in the schools.

Other Sources Cited

Allport, G. W. *Pattern and growth in personality* . New York: Holt, Rinehart and Winston, 1961.

Bronson, W. C. Mother-toddler interaction: A perspective on studying the development of competence. *Merrill-Palmer Quarterly,* 1974, *20,* 275–302.

Coopersmith, S. *The antecedents of self-esteem.* San Francisco: Freeman, 1967.

Slaby, R. G., & Frey, K. S. Development of gender constancy and selective attention to same-sex models. *Child Development,* 1975, *46,* 849–856.

Trowbridge, N. Self-concept and socio-economic status in elementary school children. *American Education Research Journal,* 1972, *9,* 525–537.

14

**Moral
Development**

For most parents, and certainly for society, the development of "morality" in children is of great importance. Parents want their children to adopt the rules of the society in which they live, to avoid breaking rules or giving offense, and to behave "properly" when they are away from home or not being observed, and not just when their parents are standing over them. Parents want their children to develop good internalized rules and to be able to follow them in many situations; they also want children to make moral judgments about others that are consistent with those rules.

Note that I am suggesting at least three separate (or separable) facets of the problem.

First, the child must adopt some kind of internalized rules. This is what we usually call *conscience*, and it includes an emotional part as well as the set of rules. Presumably, if the child disobeys the dictates of her conscience (disobeys the set of rules), she will feel guilty about it.

Second, the child must be able to match her behavior to the rules. It's not sufficient merely to have a nice, neat set of rules in your head. It's also necessary that you have the ability to inhibit whatever contrary impulses may come up. Suppose I were to give you a final examination and put you in a separate room to take the test. You discover some books in the room that would help on the test. No one is looking, so the chances of your being discovered if you cheat are very low. What do you do? Presumably you have an internalized rule that tells you that cheating is "bad." But having the rule is not the only thing that's important here; you also have to have some way of controlling your impulse to look in those books to find the answers to the questions.

Third, the child must learn to make judgments about moral behavior. This is, in a sense, an intellectual process, presumably the sort of process that a jury goes through in deciding whether someone is guilty or innocent, whether or not the crime was justified, and how bad a crime it was. The development of such judgment seems to follow many of the same laws that govern other aspects of cognitive development.

The more traditional theory and research on morality in children has focused almost exclusively on the development of internalized rules and the development of the ability to inhibit. Cognitive-developmental theorists, such as Piaget and Kohlberg, have focused on the third issue, the development of moral judgments.

TRADITIONAL VIEWS

A major impetus for the study of morality in children has been Freud's theory and the theoretical work of his many followers. In Freudian theory the crucial event in the development of morality is the process of identification, which occurs as a result of the Oedipal crisis. I've discussed this process at some length in Chapters 12 and 13, so I needn't repeat the details here. What should be emphasized is that the process of identification itself, as Freud saw it, is the process of taking in, in their entirety, the rules by which the parent operates. The child not only adopts the parent's behavior but also adopts the parent's attitudes and morality as well. This parent-within-you functions as a kind of internal monitor, which tells you whether your behavior is good or bad, right or wrong, and "punishes" you when you transgress. Freud called the internalized parent the *superego*, which is roughly analogous to the common meaning of the word "conscience." The self-punishment that occurs when the child (or adult) transgresses is called *guilt*.

Although Freud placed considerable emphasis on the fact that the boy, at least, identifies with his father out of fear of the father's power to hurt him, later psychoanalytic theorists have emphasized that in both boys and girls identification (and thus conscience) arises out of fears of loss of the parent's love. The identification process is a sort of protection for the child: "If I make myself completely like my parent, then she will have to love me."

Note, however, that even in psychoanalytic interpretations of the development of morality not all the weight is placed on the development of a set of internalized rules. Such internalized rules are the province of the superego, but the *ego* also plays a role in the development of moral behavior. As I have already pointed out it is not enough to have specified rules of conduct if you do not also have the ability to inhibit "bad" behavior, and this ability to inhibit is one of the functions of the ego rather than of the superego. In psychoanalytic theory the ego is the seat of the organizing, controlling, and planning part of the personality. The ability to make a plan and stick to it, to pay attention selectively to certain important aspects of the world, and to inhibit contrary impulses are all ego functions, and they may be more fully developed in some children (or adults) than in others. Moral behavior, then, is a result of both the internalized rules of the superego and the various ego functions that make it possible for the person to follow those rules.

An alternative view of the development of morality has been offered by a number of learning theorists. Learning explanations have two aspects. First, many theorists, such as Mowrer, propose that after the child is repeatedly punished for some act—for hitting her brother, for example—the whole set of circumstances around that act come to signal pain or discomfort. The child becomes anxious at the very thought of hitting her brother. The internalized rules may thus be viewed as a set of learned avoidance reactions. Second, social-learning theorists, such as Bandura and Walters, have emphasized the important role of imitation. As I have pointed out before, there is an enormous amount of evidence that children do imitate models around them—their parents, other children, people on television, and so on—and that they do learn new behaviors from such imitation. Specifically, the child can learn a variety of moral behaviors through modeling herself after adults; she may see the parent (or others) confess after they have done something wrong, and she can learn to set high standards for her own behavior by watching the parent do the same. (See, for example, Bandura & Kupers or Bandura & MacDonald.) She can learn considerate behavior through imitation (saying "Thank you," deferring to someone older, and so forth). If the child systematically imitates the parent's behavior then gradually she will come to have a repertoire of behaviors that will operate *as if* she had a set of rules about what is right and wrong. The learning theorists, by and large, prefer not to use notions like conscience or to assume the existence of internalized rules. Rather, they have attempted to account for the acquisition of a pattern of moral *behavior* and have assumed that moral behavior is acquired by the same rules as is any other behavior.

Learning research on the development of morality has focused almost entirely on the study of moral behavior and its antecedents. For example, there have been quite a number of studies on the child's developing abilities to resist temptation or to express guilt after some kind of transgression. Other reseachers have looked at individual differences in moral behavior and have attempted to determine whether or not any family interaction patterns are consistently associated with more or less "moral" behavior. In all this research the emphasis is necessarily on behavior, for only behavior—and not internalized rules—can be observed directly. But we can draw some inferences about internalized rules from observing behavior. If a child does resist some temptation, at least we know that some internalized prohibition must have been involved. If the child does not resist temptation, then we don't know if there was no appropriate internalized rule or if the child did have some kind of "No" rule but was unable to control her behavior. Thus, though research on moral behavior is of interest for its own sake, it may also give some hints about the development of internalized rules as well.

CHILD-REARING ANTECEDENTS OF "MORAL BEHAVIOR"

The traditional measures of the strength of the child's conscience are measures of her behavior in tempting situations. The most common procedure is to put the child in a situation in which she will be tempted to do something "wrong" but thinks she won't be found out if she does, and then by some devious means (like a one-way mirror) to watch what the child does. Sears, Rau, and Alpert, in their extensive study of the antecedents of conscience, used a particularly ingenious device.

They put the child in a small room full of extravagantly marvelous toys. Also in the room was a box with a live hamster in it. The experimenter explained that, unless the hamster was watched, he might get out of the box and run away; the child was given a rolled-up newspaper and asked to use it to keep the hamster in the box. The experimenter explained that the hamster was his pet and that he'd be very sad if any-

thing happened to it. The experimenter also said it would be a special favor to him if the child would watch the hamster for him. Of course, the child agreed to do so, meanwhile looking longingly at all the fantastic toys.

The experimenter then left the child in the room with the hamster and the toys. At this point the child thought she was unobserved and was tempted to stop watching the wretched hamster and to start playing with the toys. Some children gave up on the hamster rather quickly; others watched faithfully for long minutes (up to half an hour!). But all the children did eventually falter, and when they did, the experimenter, who was watching in another room, pulled open a trap-door on the bottom of the hamster's box, and the animal disappeared down a chute. When the child went back to check the hamster, it was gone. Shortly afterward, the experimenter came back and exclaimed about his missing hamster.

We can derive several measures of the presumed strength of the child's conscience from this procedure. First, how long does the child resist the temptation to go and play with the toys? Second, after the experimenter has come back into the room and noticed the missing hamster, does the child confess? Third, does the child indicate that she feels guilty about having given in to her impulse to play with the toys? And, fourth, does she offer some reparation to the experimenter for the loss of the hamster?

These four facets of conscience—resistance to temptation, guilt, confession after transgression, and restitution—are the most frequently measured, either by observing the child's behavior in real situations (as in Figure 36) or by asking her to describe what she would do in hypothetical circumstances.

Such measures have been used in a large number of studies, along with various assessments of the kind of child-rearing techniques used by parents. Investigators (including Sears, Rau, & Alpert; and Hoffman) have attempted to explore a series of hypotheses, loosely derived from psychoanalytic theory, about the origins of "strong" or "weak" conscience. For example, because identification is thought to be partly a consequence of the child's fear of loss of love, those parents who use

FIGURE 36
This seems to show the external signs of "guilt after transgression."

threats of loss of love as disciplinary measures may have children who identify most strongly and who will therefore show all the signs of having a "strong" conscience. Similarly, because identification is also presumed to be influenced by the child's fear of the parent's threat of punishment, parents who use strongly power-oriented punishment (spanking, removing privileges, and so on) will also have children who identify strongly and thus abide by rules.

Although both these semipsychoanalytic hypotheses make a certain amount of intuitive sense, they are not well supported by the research data. Martin Hoffman has done the most recent and thorough review of all the literature on the child-rearing antecedents of measures of conscience, and he concludes that power-oriented discipline has exactly the opposite effect. Children whose parents use a lot of physical punishment and other kinds of power assertion are *less* likely to resist temptation, less likely to confess, less likely to express guilt after they have transgressed. Withdrawal-of-love techniques apparently have little effect one way or the other. The one parental disciplinary technique that does commonly seem to be related to more strongly conscience-directed behavior is what Hoffman calls *induction*, by which he means attempts to persuade or convince the child by reason that she should change her behavior. Particularly important, Hoffman suggests, are explanations emphasizing the consequences to other people of the child's actions: "When you hit me, it hurts me"; "It hurts your brother's feelings when you call him names"; "If you make a big mess on the kitchen floor, your mother will just have to go to a lot of extra work to clean it up"; "Don't yell at him. He was only trying to help." Hoffman's analysis of the research literature suggests that parents who use such reasoning techniques to control their children's behavior have children who are more resistant to temptation.

Experimental studies offer further support for Hoffman's conclusions. In the short run strong verbal or physical punishment may inhibit a behavior, but in the long run children who have received milder punishment are more likely to persist in avoiding a particular transgression.

There is also evidence from both experimental studies and from correlational research that a nurturant relationship between the adult and the child gives greater weight to whatever punitive techniques the adult uses. In his review of the correlational research, Hoffman finds that parents who are both warm and affectionate *and* who use inductive discipline have children who are most resistant to temptation.

Frequent use of physical punishment or material deprivation as disciplinary techniques does have *some* effect on the child's moral behavior, however. Hoffman concludes from his review that children who experience this type of discipline are likely to adopt a moral attitude based on fear of detection or punishment. So such children will be "good" if they think they will be caught, but not if they think they won't. In contrast, the children who have experienced inductive techniques are more likely to resist temptation whether they think they will be caught or not. Both groups have understood the rule, but one is better able to match behavior to the rule across varying situations.

In sum, the literature on child-rearing antecedents of "moral behavior" offers little support for somewhat oversimplified psychoanalytic hypotheses advanced by early researchers. Neither physically punitive parents nor those who use withdrawal-of-love techniques have children who are markedly able to resist temptation or who show guilt after transgression. But parental behavior does seem to matter. Parents who use explanations, particularly explanations related to feelings and people, tend to have more "moral" children. This is particularly so for parents who are also warm and nurturant.

CONSISTENCY OF MORAL BEHAVIOR

A separate question involves the consistency of moral behavior over time or in different situations. Is a child who resists temptation in one situation going to show the same resistance in other situations as well? If the set of internal rules is the dominant factor then we might expect that children with clear and well-established sets of internalized standards would show "moral behavior" in a wide variety of situations. But the ability to control behavior enters in as well, and it may be more difficult in some situations than in others to control behavior and to inhibit the impulse to transgress.

The research results suggest that although we make global judgments about other people's honesty or morality ("John is basically not an ethical person"; "You can really trust John"; "John is a good boy"), in fact moral behavior is not highly consistent from one situation to another. In studies in which children have been given a whole series of tests (including such tests as the hamster procedure, pencil-and-paper tests, and others in which the child can apparently cheat without detection) there is usually some correlation among the scores on the various measures, but the correlations are not high. If the situations involved are very similar then there is fairly good consistency on different measures, but as the measurement procedures and situations become more and more different, individual consistency becomes less and less obvious.

In children, at least, situational factors are very powerful. And while it is true that some children (those who have experienced inductive discipline, for example) are likely to resist temptation in a wider variety of situations, the likelihood of getting caught is still a powerful factor in children's moral behavior. If the situation seems foolproof, as if there is no way to get caught, nearly all children will cheat. If detection seems more likely, most will not, and those who do may be those who are more prone to take risks rather than those who are fundamentally more dishonest.

The relative lack of generality and the importance of situational factors provide considerable support for the social-learning view that what we normally think of as "morality" is really just a collection of individually learned behaviors. The child learns not to cheat when there is some likelihood of getting caught, but when there is no possibility of punishment, her feelings of anxiety are not as strongly aroused and she goes ahead.

The lack of generality or consistency among situations also underlines the importance of separating our analysis of the acquisition of standards from the study of the ability to inhibit "bad" behavior. A set of standards may develop through identification or some related process of imitation. But the ability to resist the impulse to transgress appears not to develop as a result of imitation or identification. The child can learn through imitation what behavior she ought to control but not how to control her behavior.

Kohlberg, in his analysis of moral development, has emphasized that the ability to control, to inhibit, develops with age and is related in some ways to the child's cognitive development. The ability to control her own behavior requires some ability to anticipate what will happen in the future; the child must be able to connect what she's doing now with what is likely to happen to her an hour from now, a day from now, or even weeks or months from now. The ability to focus attention for periods of time may also enter in. For example, the child may have to be able to keep her mind on the hamster and off the toys if she is to maintain her watchfulness. This ability to focus attention increases with age, as does the ability to understand causal relationships and to anticipate future events. If we take an IQ test score as a global measure of the child's cognitive development, we may expect to find that among children of a given age those with higher IQs (higher mental ages) are more likely to show resistance to temptation. In fact, that is the case.

As an aside, the ability to control behavior may also be related to such physical characteristics as brain damage. Many children with little impulse control and who show a lot of unacceptable behavior like stealing, cheating, and lying have been found to have some kind of brain damage or dysfunction. When these children are treated for the organic difficulty, their "bad" behavior often drops markedly as well. So we must be careful not to assume that all children who have difficulty in controlling impulses are necessarily either slow intellectually or lacking in internalized standards.

In sum, then, identification may result in internalization of rules, but identification probably has little to do with the child's ability to follow those rules. The ability to follow rules seems to be a function of the kind of discipline the child typically encounters at home, her developing cognitive skills, and the specific situation in which temptation arises.

The contrast between Piaget and Kohlberg's views of moral development and those of psychoanalytic and learning theorists is similar to the contrast between Piaget's view of intelligence and the view underlying IQ tests. Just as for Piaget the question is not "How intelligent are you?" but "What kind of intelligence do you have?" so for Piaget and Kohlberg the question is not "How moral are you?" but "What kind of morality do you operate with?" The cognitive-developmental theorists are not fundamentally interested in the child's moral *behavior*. Rather, they are concerned with her moral *judgments*. On what basis does the child decide whether something is right or wrong? And does that basis change according to some developmental sequence?

Piaget's studies of the development of moral judgment led him to suggest that there are two very broad stages in that development. In the first, which he called the period of moral realism or of "heteronomous morality," the child is limited by the general constraints of her level of cognitive development. Between the ages of roughly 3 and 10 the child is discovering physical laws (such as the laws of conservation) and drawing the erroneous conclusion that moral laws have the same immutability as physical laws. So the child believes that moral rules are fixed, unchangeable, and eternal. She has no understanding at this age of the relativity of moral rules. The child in this stage applies the same sort of logic to rules of games as well as to moral rules. Piaget found that children believe, for example, that the rules of the game of marbles are absolute and unchangeable and have been the same forever.

The child's moral realism also has other facets beside belief in the absolute fixity of rules. Piaget found that the child during this period judges the badness of some action on the basis of consequences, not on the basis of intent. When Piaget asked a child of 5 or 6 questions like, "Which is worse, a child who broke five cups when she was helping her mother set the table or a child who broke one cup while she was stealing some jam?" The child usually said that the child who broke five cups was worse, because more cups were broken. The accidental quality of that damage was not taken into account.

At this same age, according to Piaget's observations, children think a given action is either completely right or completely wrong. Because of their persisting egocentrism, they cannot grasp the possibility that a given action might be seen as right by some people and wrong by others. There is also a tendency, particularly in the very youngest children in this stage, to decide the rightness or wrongness of something by whether or not the person gets punished. In one of his studies Kohlberg asked young children to judge a story in which a child had been asked by her mother to watch her baby brother while her mother went to the store. The child did watch her brother carefully the entire time that her mother was away, but when her mother returned she spanked the child. Kohlberg found that 4-year-olds judged the watching child's

behavior to be bad simply because she was punished. Older children (age 5 or 6) often tried to invent other reasons. They seemed to be reasoning that if the child was punished, she must have done something wrong. As she didn't do anything wrong in watching her baby brother, she must have done something else wrong that we don't know about. Still older children—7- or 8-year-olds—did not assume that punishment means bad behavior. They were able to say that the watching child was good, even though she was punished.

All three of these aspects of moral judgment—judgment by consequences, the absolutism of judgments, and the assumption of an absolute connection between wrongdoing and punishment—decline steadily with age and seem to be related to the child's overall cognitive development.

The second stage of morality, as Piaget has outlined it, characterizes children age 9 or 10 and older. Piaget called it the morality of cooperation or the "morality of reciprocity." By this time the child understands that rules are established and maintained through social agreements and that they can be changed. The child's egocentrism has declined to the point at which she can understand that there may be several points of view on a given issue and that punishment or reward for a given action does not automatically signal the badness or goodness of that action. She makes moral judgments about other people's actions mainly on the basis of the actors' intentions rather than the consequences.

Although the sequence of moral development Piaget described has been found among children in a number of different Western countries, other aspects of Piaget's formulation have been questioned. Recent researchers have found, for example, that children as young as 4 or 5 *notice* the intentions of people, but may not make their moral judgments based on intentions. Bearison and Isaacs, for example, have suggested that what happens in this case may be something like what Flavell and others have noted in the case of the development of memory. You may recall that in Chapter 9 (page 217) I talked about a phase in which a child can use rehearsal or other memory strategies if they are suggested to her, but she doesn't do so spontaneously. This has been called a *production deficiency*—that is, the child fails to produce a helpful mnemonic device on her own, but can use one when it is suggested. Bearison and Isaacs think that something like this may be at work in the early stages of moral development. The 6-year-old child can pay attention to people's intentions in judging actions when those intentions are made very obvious. But when the cues are more subtle, the child reverts to judgments based on the amount of damage. Other recent studies also point to the ability of the 5- or 6-year-old to judge on intentions if the task is simplified. If the child is asked to judge accidents versus intentional wrongdoing, or large verses small amount of damage, but not both simultaneously, she can take intention into account. (See the study by Berg-Cross.)

What this sort of research points to again, as it did in the case of the research on egocentrism in the preoperational stage I discussed in Chapter 9 (page 205), is that the stages Piaget has described are not either/or events. The child does not consistently judge only on the basis of outcomes, and never on the basis of intentions, and then one day suddenly begin taking intention into account. The shift is far more gradual and far more linked to the child's developing cognitive skills. As the child is able to notice more subtle cues for intention, intention may be more regularly taken into account. If we make the task simpler, then younger children are found to include the intention of the wrongdoer in their judgments. It is still true, though, that 5- to 6-year-old children are *more* affected by the size or quantity of the damage than are older children, and that older children more consistently judge on the basis of intention. So the broad sequence is still largely correct, but the process is more complex and more gradual than Piaget at first suggested.

Another sort of argument against Piaget's conception of moral development has been raised by social-learning theorists such as Bandura and his associates. They have shown that children's moral judgments may be heavily influenced by imitation as well as cognitive level. Bandura and MacDonald, for example, had children observe an adult being rewarded for making a moral judgment based on intentions rather than on consequences. After seeing the model each child was then asked to make a judgment about a similar moral dilemma. In this situation children were likely to copy the type of judgment used by the model even if it was at a "higher" level of judgment than the child would ordinarily use. Does this occur because the child learns a kind of verbal formula for moral judgments from the model? Or does observing the model help to alter the child's basic cognitive approach to moral problems? A third alternative is that the model focuses the child's attention on the intentions of the actor, and that this fills the "production deficiency" gap of the younger child. In any case research of this kind raises some perplexing questions for Piagetian theory.

Kohlberg, like some social-learning theorists, was dissatisfied with Piaget's initial formulations of moral development, but for different reasons. Kohlberg noted that on a number of points Piaget has not been supported by later research. For example, Piaget suggested that there is a general trend from an authoritarian to a democratic ethic; later research does not support that generalization. Similarly, Piaget suggested that moral judgments change largely because of the child's interactions with the peer group, and this generalization too has not been consistently supported. Kohlberg found that the most solid and replicable part of Piaget's work on moral development is the suggestion of a connection between the child's moral judgments and her overall cognitive development, so he set out to extend that part of the theory.

Kohlberg's studies of moral development have dealt primarily with children from age 10 through young adulthood. He devised a set of "moral dilemmas" about which he asked each child. Some of the dilemmas, described briefly, are as follows:

A man's wife is dying. There is one drug that will save her, but it's very expensive, and the druggist who invented it won't sell it at a low enough price so the man can afford it. Should the man steal it in order to save her life?

Should a doctor commit a mercy killing of a fatally ill woman who is begging for death because of her pain?

The captain of a group of men calls for a retreat in the face of heavy enemy action in battle. A bridge behind them should be blown up, but the man sent to do that would have little chance of coming back alive. The captain also knows that he is the best person to lead the retreat. What should he do?

Kohlberg has suggested that there are some 32 aspects of morality—32 separate moral issues if you will, such as the value of human life and the reasons for moral action. Each dilemma was designed to explore

352

one or more of these issues. On the basis of children's answers to the dilemmas and the kinds of reasons given for their answers, Kohlberg concluded that there are three main levels of morality, with two substages within each level. The levels and stages, as Kohlberg describes them, are as follows:

LEVEL 1: THE PRECONVENTIONAL (OR PREMORAL) LEVEL

At this level the child's moral judgments are based on such external criteria as whether the person is punished or not. The standards of right and wrong are absolute and laid down by authority, such as parents.

Stage 1: Punishment and Obedience Orientation. The physical consequences of an action determine its goodness or badness. The child's own actions are governed by a desire to avoid punishment. She obeys because adults have superior power, not because they are "right" in some abstract sense.

Stage 2: Instrumental-Relativist Orientation. This is a kind of "naive hedonism"; things that bring pleasant results are good, and those that bring unpleasant results are bad. There is some sign that the child is attentive to other people's needs, but that attention seems to be of a kind of "pork-barrel" variety. The child will help someone else if that person will help her in turn.

LEVEL 2: THE CONVENTIONAL LEVEL

At level 2 the consequences of actions—punishment or reward, pleasure or displeasure—begin to be less important. The child's judgments are instead based on the norms and expectations of the group. What the group (family, society, nation) says is right is right.

Stage 3: The Good Boy-Nice Girl Orientation. The focus in stage 3 is on the smaller group to which the child belongs: family, school, peers. Good behavior is behavior that pleases others. In addition, the child begins for the first time to make judgments consistently based on intentions. If someone "didn't mean to do it" or "means well," that is taken as a mitigating circumstance. The emphasis overall, though, is on conformity to group norms.

Stage 4: The Law-and-Order Orientation. In stage 4 the focus has shifted away from personal and local groups to the larger society. What is right is what the law says is right, and the law is seen as fixed. Doing one's duty, respecting authority, and maintaining the social order as it already exists are all seen as "good." There is no recognition of the arbitrariness of the laws of a particular society or of the changeability of those laws.

LEVEL 3: THE POSTCONVENTIONAL, AUTONOMOUS, OR PRINCIPLED LEVEL

At this level the child (actually a young adult at this point) recognizes the arbitrariness of social and legal conventions. Laws are arbitrary and can be changed. The child attempts to define moral values that are separate from the group norms.

Stage 5: The Social Contract or Legalistic Orientation. In stage 5

TABLE 9
Stages of Moral Development Reflected in Two Aspects of Moral Judgment

Stage	Basic description of stage	Motivation for rule obedience or moral action	Attitude toward the value of human life
1	Punishment and obedience orientation	Obey rules to avoid punishment	The value of human life is confused with the value of physical objects and is based on the social status or physical attributes of its possessor.
2	Naive instrumental hedonism	Conform to obtain rewards, have favors returned	The value of human life is seen as instrumental to the satisfaction of the needs of its possessor or other persons.
3	Good-boy, nice-girl orientation; maintaining good relations, approval of others	Conform to avoid disapproval or dislike by others	The value of human life is based on the empathy and affection of family members and others towards its possessor.
4	Authority-maintaining morality: the law-and-order orientation	Conform to avoid censure by legitimate authorities and resultant guilt	Life is conceived as sacred in terms of its place in a categorical, moral, or religious order of rights and duties.
5	Morality of contract, of individual rights, or democratically accepted law	Conform to maintain the respect of impartial spectators judging in terms of community welfare	Life is valued both in terms of its relation to community welfare and in terms of life being a universal human right.
6	Morality of individual principles or conscience	Conform to avoid self-condemnation	There is belief in the sacredness of human life as representing a universal human value of respect for the individual.

Source: Kohlberg, L. Development of moral character and moral ideology. In M. L. Hoffman & L. W. Hoffman (Eds.), *Review of child development research* (Vol. 1). New York: Russell Sage Foundation, 1964.

the child recognizes that the laws of a given society are arbitrary and changeable, but at the same time there is an emphasis on the need for orderly change, for working within the system. For aspects of behavior not governed by laws, right and wrong are personal decisions, but emphasis is placed on the importance and binding quality of personal agreements and contracts.

Stage 6: The Universal Ethical Principle Orientation. What is right in stage 6 is a question of the individual conscience: Judgments are based on fundamental and universal principles. Each action to be judged is analyzed in terms of the network of basic principles.

To make all of this a bit more concrete I have listed in Table 9 the six stages as they are reflected in two of the 32 aspects Kohlberg discusses. The two moral issues described here are the question of why one obeys rules at all and how one views the value of human life. Some specific answers given by children and young adults to several of the moral dilemmas that relate to the value of human life are given in Table 10.

Bear in mind that Kohlberg, in outlining the sequence of the developmental stages, is not saying that one stage is "better" than another, but merely that one may be more "mature" than another in the sense that it occurs later in a developmental sequence.

Kohlberg's own research has demonstrated that these six stages do develop sequentially. However, Kohlberg emphasizes that at any one time a given child may give answers at several stages. The majority of the child's answers, for example, may be at stage 3, but there will still be a few answers at stage 2 and some at stage 4. The fact that there is a spread of answers across several stages does not mean that there is no order, however. The same child some years later gives the majority of her answers at stage 4, a few still at stage 3, and some at stage 5; the whole system has moved up one notch.

There is also evidence from a number of Kohlberg's cross-cultural studies that the sequence occurs in widely different cultures as well. He has studied children in Taiwan, in Mexico, and in rural villages in Turkey and in the Yucatan; in all cases, the sequence seems to be the same. However, the specific cultural experience does make a difference in both the rate at which the child goes through the stages and the final end stage that is reached. In the two rural villages studied (in Turkey and Yucatan) stage 4 is as high a level as any of the 16-year-olds had reached; there was no subject at stage 5 or 6. But in the United States sample 8 to 10 percent of 16-year-olds were in stage 5 or 6. The cultural context clearly does make a difference, but apparently it does not affect the *order* of the developmental stages.

Kohlberg has also found that the level of moral judgments correlates moderately with the child's measured IQ. Children with high IQs tend to be more advanced in the sequence than are children of the same age with lower IQs. Such a correlation underlines the relationship between

TABLE 10
Examples of Moral Judgments Relating to the Issue of the Value of Human Life

Stage	Age of child making judgment	Judgment made by child
1	10	(Why should the druggist give the drug to the dying woman when her husband couldn't pay for it?) "If someone important is in a plane and is allergic to heights and the stewardess won't give him medicine because she's only got enough for one and she's got a sick one, a friend, in back, they'd probably put the stewardess in a lady's jail because she didn't help the important one."
2	13	(Should the doctor "mercy-kill" a fatally ill woman requesting death because of her pain?) "Maybe it would be good to put her out of her pain, she'd be better off that way. But the husband wouldn't want it, it's not like an animal. If a pet dies you can get along without it—it isn't something you really need. Well, you can get a new wife, but it's not really the same thing."
3	16	(Should the doctor "mercy-kill" a fatally ill woman?) "It might be best for her, but her husband—it's a human life —not like an animal, it just doesn't have the same relationship that a human being does to a family. You can become attached to a dog, but nothing like a human you know."
4	16	(Should the doctor "mercy-kill" the woman?) "The doctor wouldn't have the right to take a life, no human has the right, He can't create life, he shouldn't destroy it."
5	20	(Should the doctor "mercy-kill" the woman?) "Given the ethics of the doctor who has taken on responsibility to save human life—from that point of view he probably shouldn't, but there is another side, there are more and more people in the medical profession who are thinking it is a hardship on everyone, the person, the family, when you know they are going to die. When the person is kept alive by an artificial lung or kidney it's more like being a vegetable than being a human who is alive. If it's her own choice, I think there are certain rights and privileges that go along with being a human being. I am a human being and have certain desires for life and I think everybody else does, too. You have a world of which you are the center, and everybody else does, too, and in that sense we're all equal."
6	16	(Should the husband steal the expensive drug to save his wife?) "By the law of society he was wrong but by the law of nature or of God the druggist was wrong and the husband was justified. Human life is above financial gain. Regardless of who was dying, if it was a total stranger, man has a duty to save him from dying."

Source: Kohlberg, L. Development of moral character and moral ideology. In M. L. Hoffman & L. W. Hoffman (Eds.) *Review of child development research* (Vol. 1). New York: Russell Sage Foundation, 1964; and Kohlberg, L. *Developmental Psychology Today.* Del Mar, Calif.: CRM Books, a division of Random House, Inc., 1971.

the child's overall cognitive development and the development of moral judgment. In order for the child to be able to shift from level 1 to level 2, for example, some loss of egocentrism is required. The child must step back one notch farther from a self-centered to a family- or society-centered view. Such a loss of egocentrism is at least partly a cognitive accomplishment. But the correlation between IQ and level of judgment is by no means perfect, so though some basic cognitive development is necessary, it is apparently not sufficient. Not all children who have the necessary cognitive skills will shift to stage 6 morality.

Kohlberg has offered an exciting new way to look at the growth of moral judgment and has collected a considerable amount of evidence consistent with his theory. As usual, however, we need more information before we can make our own judgments about his theoretical approach. We need more longitudinal studies to determine whether or not the order of stages is universal, as Kohlberg has claimed. We need a great deal more information about the kinds of environmental factors that may foster rapid or complete movement through the stages. Finally, we need to know something about the relationship between moral judgments, as assessed by Kohlberg's dilemmas, and moral behavior. Does a young person who makes moral judgments at stage 6 behave at stage 6? Where there is a disparity between moral judgment and behavior, why does it occur?

The results of studies of the link between moral judgment and moral behavior are somewhat mixed, but there does seem to be some connection. Kohlberg has reported, for example, that college students who are at stage 5 or 6 are less likely to be persuaded to administer stronger and stronger shocks to another student than are those at stage 3 or 4. In experiments of this kind, made famous by Milgram, the experimenter exerts a great deal of psychological pressure on the subject to give severe electric shocks to another student (who is, in fact, a stooge, and does not actually receive the shocks). Many subjects in this setting will continue increasing the severity of the shocks, under urging from the experimenter, until a nearly lethal level of shock has been reached. But subjects at stages 5 and 6 in the moral development sequence are more resistant to this pressure, possibly because of the value they place on individual human life.

There are also fragmentary data that point to some connection between stages of moral development and political behavior. A number of investigators (for example, Haan, Smith, & Block; and Keniston) also found that political activists—often protesters—were more likely to be functioning at Kohlberg's stage 6. Keniston went one step further and divided the protesters (college students in the late 1960s—see Figure 37) into those who took a nonviolent, ideological position versus those who were more radical and violent. The latter group—the physically violent protesters—were likely to be func-

FIGURE 37
**Student protesters in 1970. Some research suggests that students active in this
sort of nonviolent protest were more likely to be functioning at level 5 or 6 on
Kohlberg's development scale.**

tioning at a premoral level (stage 2). The nonviolent, ideological protesters were likely to make moral judgments at stage 6. These findings
seem to be telling us that there is some link between political preferences or behavior and the level or type of moral judgment we typically
use.

Results of research on younger children are more ambiguous. Kohlberg reports that teachers' ratings of children's fairness to their classmates and their adherence to rules in the absence of adults are both related to the children's levels of moral judgment. But other researchers
have had mixed results. There is some indication that children at the
higher stages of moral judgment may be more resistant to temptation,
but that result is not found in every study.

I would like to see a good deal more research on the relationship of
moral judgment and behavior for several reasons. First of all, such research might help to bridge the gap between work arising from psychoanalytic or learning-theory perspectives and the research arising out of
the cognitive-developmental approach. Given that a child or adult
makes judgments at a particular level, what are the "ego factors" or
situational factors that affect her ability to behave at the same level?
Secondly, I find the potential connection between moral judgment and
political behavior fascinating. For example, I would like to know if
there is any connection between more ordinary political choices on
election day and moral judgment. Do political candidates attract sup-

port primarily from voters who share their basic level of moral judgment? I know of no research on questions of this kind, but I find the questions intriguing. At the very least such questions suggest the range of issues that might be addressed using Kohlberg's framework.

SUMMARY

1. I have emphasized throughout this chapter that there are at least three separate questions in the study of moral development: How does the child develop a set of internalized standards of right and wrong, how does the child develop the skills in self-control necessary to follow those internalized standards, and how does the child develop moral judgment?
2. Psychoanalytic theorists have focused primarily on the first of these questions and on the development of ego strength that allows for the second.
3. Social-learning theorists have focused on both the first and second questions, emphasizing the role of imitation (modeling oneself after others) in the development of both self-control and standards.
4. Cognitive-developmental theorists have focused almost entirely on the third question. Piaget and Kohlberg have been particularly interested not in the content of the child's moral judgments, but in their form and logic. They don't care which set of rules the child has adopted. Rather, they are interested in the kinds of rules, how they change, and how application of them changes.
5. Because the three main questions have been addressed separately, it is difficult at this point to consolidate the findings into any unitary theory of moral development. What seems most plausible at this point, however, is that the child acquires her first basic moral standards through some process of imitation or identification and that this process is largely complete by the age of 5 or 6. From this point onward the major changes are in the way the child uses those standards, in the form of the child's judgments, as in, for example, whether or not the standard is seen as absolute or only relative to a particular society. The stages that Piaget and Kohlberg have described may thus be seen as a kind of overlay on the internalized standards already present by age 5.
6. In the development of moral behavior parental styles of discipline make some difference. Parents who use inductive styles of control, emphasizing reasoning and explanation, have children who are more likely to resist temptation or to report feeling guilty after a transgression than are children whose parents use either love-oriented or power-oriented styles of discipline.
7. Some consistency between moral judgments and moral behavior has been found, but the consistency is not perfect. Political behavior, in some instances, seems to be correlated with moral judgment, and under some circumstances, the ability to resist temptation is correlated with moral judgment level. But situational factors still have a powerful impact on moral behavior. In situations in which detection of wrongdoing is very unlikely most children will cheat, whereas in situations in which detection is likely, few children will do so.

REFERENCES

Suggested Additional Readings

Hartshorne, H., & May, M. S. *Studies in the nature of character* (3 vols.). New York: Macmillan, 1928–1930.
A classic series of studies, the first to attempt to discover whether or not there is some unitary trait of "honesty" or "morality."

Hoffman, M. L. Moral development. In P. H.

Mussen (Ed.), *Carmichael's manual of child psychology*. (Vol. 2, 3rd ed.). New York: Wiley, 1970.

A long, dense paper that includes detailed discussions of many issues raised in this chapter; a superb resource for students particularly interested in problems of moral development.

Kohlberg, L. Development of moral character and moral ideology. In M. L. Hoffman & L. W. Hoffman (Eds.), *Review of child development research* (Vol. 1). New York: Russell Sage Foundation, 1964.

One of the earliest presentations by Kohlberg of his view of cognitive development, along with a review of other theoretical approaches. I find Kohlberg's writing style fairly difficult, but I think this is a good first source.

Piaget, J. *The moral judgment of the child.* New York: Collier, 1962.

This is one of Piaget's earliest books, originally published in English in 1932, so it doesn't fit into the full theoretical network Piaget later developed; but it's full of marvelous examples of children's moral logic. Difficult but interesting.

Other Sources Cited

Bandura, A., & Kupers, C. J. Transmission of patterns of self-reinforcement through modeling. *Journal of Abnormal and Social Psychology*, 1964, 69, 1–9.

Bandura, A., & MacDonald, F. H. Influence of social reinforcement and the behavior of models in shaping children's moral judgments. *Journal of Abnormal and Social Psychology*, 1963, 67, 274–281.

Bearison, D. J., & Isaacs, L. Production deficiency in children's moral judgments. *Developmental Psychology*, 1975, 11, 732–737.

Berg-Cross, L. G. Intentionality, degree of damage, and moral judgment. *Child Development*, 1975, 46, 970–974.

Haan, N., Smith, M. B., & Block, J. Moral reasoning of young adults: Political-social behavior, family background, and personality correlates. *Journal of Personal and Social Psychology*, 1968, 10, 183–201.

Keniston, K. Student activism, moral development, and morality. *American Journal of Orthopsychiatry*, 1970, 40, 577–592.

Sears, R. R., Rau, L., & Alpert, R. *Identification and child rearing.* Stanford, Calif.: Stanford University Press, 1965.

PROJECT 8
MORAL JUDGMENTS

Locate at least two teenage subjects, preferably at least three or four years apart in age. If you can manage to test more than two teenagers or young adults, that would be preferable. Try to space your subjects out on the age continuum so that you can maximize your chances of getting differences in level of moral judgment.

Present the following dilemma to each subject:

In Europe a woman was near death from a very bad form of cancer. There was one drug that the doctors thought might save her. It was a type of radium for which a druggist was charging ten times what the drug cost him to make. He paid $200 for the radium and charged $2000 for a small dose of the drug. The sick woman's husband, Heinz, went to everyone he knew to borrow the money, but he could only get together about $1000, which is half of what it cost. He told the druggist that his wife was dying and asked him to sell it cheaper or let him pay later. But the druggist said, "No, I discovered the drug, and I'm going to make money from it." So Heinz became desperate and broke into the man's store to steal the drug for his wife. Should the husband have done that? Why?

Analyze the answer of each of your subjects in terms of Kohlberg's six stages of moral development. In thinking or writing about your results consider the following: Did you have difficulty classifying the subjects' answers, or was each answer clearly in one particular stage? Did the subjects' level of moral judgment and age correlate? That is, did the older subjects give higher levels of answers than the younger subjects? If they did not would that prove that Kohlberg is wrong? Or would you have to do a longitudinal study (see Box 4, page 42) to tell whether or not Kohlberg is right about the order of the developmental stages?

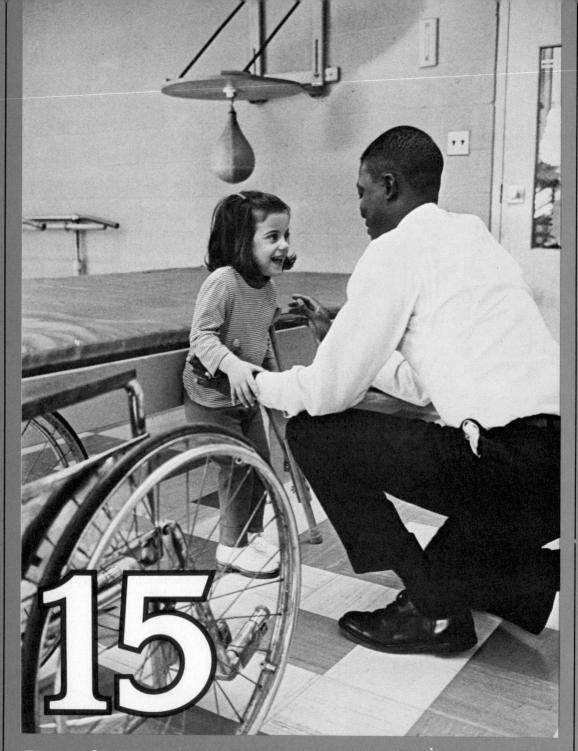

15

Atypical
Development

Even to open the subject of atypical development is to open a can of very wriggly worms. To begin with not all therapists and researchers agree on what exactly should be included in such a discussion or even on what label to use in describing it. The very first course I taught at the university level was entitled, "The Exceptional Child," and that title was intended to cover not just the gifted but also all other groups of children who are not ordinary, including the blind, the deaf, the physically handicapped, the retarded, and the emotionally disturbed. For some years the most common descriptive phrase was "deviant development" instead of "exceptional child," and recently the phrase "atypical development" has come into use. I prefer the latter because it seems less pejorative, although the word *atypical* assumes that we can specify what typical is. We do understand quite well what the expectable sequences of development are, especially during the early years, but as I have pointed out repeatedly, there are wide individual variations in rate of development as well as in specific characteristics like aggression or dependency. In many cases it is difficult to decide when a child's development is sufficiently far from the norm to deserve the label atypical.

A second, equally sticky problem is how to get some kind of handle on the whole range of ways in which a child can be atypical. What kind of taxonomy of developmental problems makes sense? Finally, of course, there is the very complex problem of describing each kind of atypical child and attempting to determine some of the possible causes and cures. Clearly an adequate treatment of this vast subject would require at least an entire book. But lacking that amount of space, I still think it is essential for you to have some grasp of the many ways in which development can go off course. What I offer here is a very brief categorization of difficulties, with some highlighting of the current theoretical and social issues surrounding each group of problems.

INCIDENCE

Let me begin by giving you some initial facts and figures about the incidence of various kinds of difficulties and disorders. Figure 38 gives some recent guesses on the rate of occurrence of various problems. As you can imagine, obtaining very precise estimates of the incidence of some of these disorders is extremely difficult. How is one to define "emotional disturbance," or "learning disabilities"? Depending on your definition, whether it is very strict or quite broad, the incidence figures may vary enormously. The category of "learning disability" is particularly difficult in this respect. The estimate I have given in Figure 38 comes from the Bureau of Education for the Handicapped and includes only children with quite severe problems in reading or other learning. Researchers and school personnel who use broader definitions of learning disability have suggested that as many as 15 percent of all school children should be classified in this category. The esti-

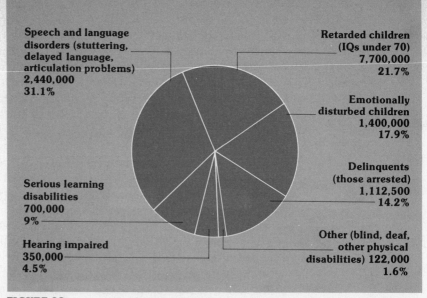

Speech and language
disorders (stuttering,
delayed language,
articulation problems)
2,440,000
31.1%

Retarded children
(IQs under 70)
7,700,000
21.7%

Emotionally
disturbed children
1,400,000
17.9%

Delinquents
(those arrested)
1,112,500
14.2%

Serious learning
disabilities
700,000
9%

Hearing impaired
350,000
4.5%

Other (blind, deaf,
other physical
disabilities) 122,000
1.6%

FIGURE 38
**Incidence of various types of atypical development. (Source: Based on Hobbs,
N. *The futures of children.* San Francisco: Jossey-Bass, 1975.)**

mate made for the 1970 White House Conference on Children (see *Profiles of Children* in the References) was that one out of every seven elementary school children and one out of every four 11-year-olds had
reading problems.

Defining and counting delinquency poses another sort of problem.
What is represented in the figure are those children who were *caught.*
There is simply no way to know the rate of delinquency generally.

But if we take the somewhat conservative figures in Figure 38 as a
starting point and compare them to the total number of children under
age 18 in the population (about 63 million), we arrive at the conclusion
that at a minimum, about 12 percent of the children in this country are
"atypical" in some respect. Using broader criteria we could easily conclude that one out of every five children (20 percent) will require some
kind of special help or attention for a specific problem. When you
think of these figures in terms of the demands made on schools and
other social agencies, the prospect is somewhat staggering.

Of course, not all of the children represented in Figure 38 have
problems serious enough to require special schooling or other intensive programs. Many can be handled in regular classrooms or with periodic counseling. But many of the children listed require intensive interventions, and not all of them receive it. For example, of the 70,000
children with significant visual impairment, only 24,000 are in special
programs in schools or other centers; of the nearly 2.5 million children

with speech and language disorders, only about 1.4 million are receiving help through special programs in schools.

For society as a whole and for the several helping professions in particular, there are several tasks. First, we need to understand the nature and origin of each of these several problems. Second, we need to develop effective treatment programs. And third, we need to focus our attention on prevention whenever possible. There is not enough space in this brief chapter to deal much with the problem of prevention. I have touched in Chapter 3 on some of the preventive measures that seem reasonable during pregnancy, but other sorts of prevention, or very early intervention, need to be explored. All I can do here is touch briefly on some of the questions of origin and treatment of the several disorders so that you will have some feeling for the kinds of problems that exist and our success (or lack of it) in treating them.

For convenience I have divided up the world of atypical development into three clusters: mentally atypical development, emotionally atypical development, and physically atypical development. The three groups blend together in many instances because many children with physically or emotional problems also have mental disorders. But the division may help to make some kind of order out of chaos.

MENTALLY ATYPICAL DEVELOPMENT
The Mentally Retarded

By far the largest, most studied, and most discussed group of children with atypical development is the group we call mentally retarded. Not too many decades ago, when mental ability was thought of as a unitary trait fixed at birth, mental subnormality was considered a kind of incurable disease. More recently psychologists and other professionals working with mentally subnormal children have come to understand that retardation is relative both to the child's situation and the point at which the measurement is taken. Mental retardation is properly viewed as a symptom, not as a disease. The symptom may change, either because the child's circumstances have changed or because of some improvement in her physical status. It is important that this distinction be kept in mind, for too often mental retardation is understood, especially by nonprofessionals, as a permanent label rather than as a description of a current state of affairs.

Obviously, the most common way to assess mental performance is with a standard IQ test, and most definitions of the subvarieties of mental retardation are tied to ranges of scores on such tests. But most professionals do not base judgments on test scores only; they are concerned also with the child's actual adaptation to the demands of her situation, including home and school. Is she able to learn the early self-help skills, like dressing herself, going to the bathroom alone, and so on? When the child reaches school age, is she able to adapt to the demands of school, including the teacher's expectations that she remain quiet for periods of time, pay attention for periods of time, begin to learn to read, and so forth? Whether or not a child is considered by parents, teachers, or psychologists as retarded will be a joint function of the child's test score and her level of adaptation to her life's demands. A child with a low test score who is nonetheless coping well with home and school may be placed in regular classes and may never be labeled retarded. Another child with a higher test score who is not adapting as successfully may be placed in a special class for the retarded.

The severity of mental retardation may vary from a very mild deficit—in which the child's functioning is only slightly impaired—to a very severe retardation in which the child (or adult) is completely unable to care for herself or to learn simple skills. For convenience, the several subdivisions of retardation are usually defined by scores on a standard IQ test, as follows (but bear in mind again that the score will not be the only guiding factor for a diagnostician):

Borderline mental retardation	IQ scores from 68 to 83
Mild mental retardation	IQ scores from 52 to 67
Moderate mental retardation	IQ scores from 36 to 51
Severe mental retardation	IQ scores from 20 to 35
Profound mental retardation	IQ scores below 20

The borderline mentally retarded are quite commonly found in regular classrooms and are often not labeled retarded by teachers or parents at all. The mildly retarded child is quite often found in classes for the educably retarded in public school systems (as shown in Figure 39), whereas the moderately retarded are most often found in classes for trainable retardates. Severely retarded children are usually placed in residential institutions.

As you can see from Figure 38, the number of retarded children with IQs below 70—roughly mildly retarded and below—is quite large. Something in the neighborhood of $2\frac{1}{2}$ to 3 percent of all children are functioning at this low a level, and approximately 100,000 additional retarded children are born each year. Of these, about 75 percent are mildly retarded, about 23 percent are moderately or severely retarded, and 2 percent are profoundly retarded. The problem posed for our society by the presence of such large numbers of retarded individuals is enormous, particularly as automation and industrialization increase. The number of occupations open to even the borderline or mildly retarded individual is steadily shrinking. Obviously, an important effort must be made to isolate more sharply the several causes of retardation and to provide prevention and remediation programs when possible.

CAUSES OF RETARDATION

This is an enormously complex and controversial subject, but the causes of retardation are conventionally divided into two broad categories: physical causes and cultural-familial causes.

Included in the category of physical causes is a very large group of

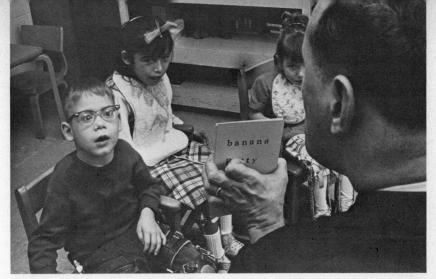

FIGURE 39
Retarded children in a special classroom.

genetic anomalies that seem to be related to retardation in many cases. In Chapter 3 I have described some of these anomalies, such as Down's syndrome (mongolism), which is the best-known and most common of the chromosomal anomalies. There is also a whole series of disease patterns that can be inherited through recessive genes and that result in metabolic deficiencies of one sort or another, with mental retardation as a common side effect.

Another physical cause of retardation is brain damage either *in utero* or after birth. The brain damage itself may result from a whole series of causes, including diseases like rubella, nutritional deficiency in the mother or the child, anoxia before or after birth, and even emotional shock to the mother. As I pointed out in Chapter 3 the timing of these events during the prenatal phase is probably as important as whether or not they occur at all. Whether or not the child suffers some irreparable damage and resulting mental subnormality depends on what part of the nervous system is developing at the time the physical or chemical insult occurs.

Most severely and profoundly retarded children have some kind of brain injury or genetic anomaly. Many also have other sorts of physical defects as well, such as deafness (common among rubella children), cerebral palsy, or heart defects. Such multiple disorders are precisely what we would expect if there were some substantial insult or disorder during the prenatal period.

The cultural-familial group of retarded individuals generally includes all those for whom no known or obvious abnormal genetic cause and no obvious brain damage can be found. That is, nothing is obviously wrong with the child except that she tests and functions in the mildly or moderately retarded range. Usually she comes from a family in which the parents have low IQs, where there is serious family disorganization, mental illness in the parents, emotional or cognitive deprivation, or any combination of these factors. The child's retarded level of functioning in a cultural-familial case is thus presumed to be a joint function of two factors: the impoverished or disorganized home environment and the inheritance of a nonoptimal combination of genes.

As I pointed out in Chapter 10 there is a significant genetic influence on IQ test scores. As there are apparently many genes that contribute to intellectual performance, by chance some people will get "good" combinations, others will get "poor" combinations, and the vast majority will get "average" combinations. Since the child inherits these genes from the parents, if they are themselves retarded, the chances of receiving a less than optimal combination of genes is greater. Simultaneously, of course, the child's physical and emotional environment in a family in which the parents are retarded or borderline is also likely to be less than optimal, and this combination appears to produce what are usually called cultural-familial retardates. Genetic endowment is not the only factor, for the same children reared in more stable or more stimulating environments may function at least adequately. (Recall the studies by Skeels & Heber discussed in Chapter 10.) Of course, many children labeled cultural-familial retardates may also have some kind of nutritional deficiency or minimal brain damage caused by other factors, for such incidents are more common among the children of less bright and less well-educated mothers. So the etiology of these children's retardation may be very complex indeed.

The prognosis for most retarded individuals is mixed. It is clear from research like Heber's or Levenstein's, which I discussed in Chapter 10, that interventions during infancy or early childhood may significantly alleviate some cultural-familial retardation. Many children with a high likelihood of functioning at the mildly retarded level probably could be brought up to normal or below average functioning with substantial interventions in the family, with the child, or both. But there are at least three cautions about this conclusion.

First, as I have pointed out repeatedly, we know far less than we need to about the nature of the intervention that will, or can have, such desirable effects, and we know next to nothing about the *long-range* outcomes of massive early interventions.

Second, while "enrichment" interventions may be helpful for the cultural-familial retardate, they are far less likely to have the same substantial effect on children whose retardation originates from some brain damage. This is not to say that environmental enrichment for brain damaged youngsters would not improve the early lives of such children. No doubt it would. But we should not expect that even massive early interventions will make most brain damaged children intellectually normal.

368

Third, interventions of the sort Heber has used are *expensive*. Other programs, including the home intervention program devised by Levenstein, are less expensive and less massive, but the initial cost per child is still very great. In the long run I think that such an investment would pay off handsomely, since the cost to society over the lifetime of the individual would be far less if the child grew up to be a functioning, capable adult than if she emerged as a borderline retardate requiring public assistance all her adult life. But even if we were sure that early interventions could have large and persisting effects (which we are not), it is not at all clear to me that as a society we are yet prepared to pay the very high initial cost of intervention programs.

Lacking substantial early intervention, the long-term outlook for most retarded individuals is not terribly promising. As I have indicated, many borderline retardates function adequately in school, but their functioning is nevertheless marginal, and the options open to them as adults are few. The mildly retarded individuals may have still less optimistic futures. Some of them are institutionalized, some remain with their families for most of their lives, and still others manage a marginal existence on their own. The moderately and severely retarded are almost all living either in institutions or with families. Many schools have attempted to develop special programs for the mildly and moderately retarded, with some small success. One of the difficulties is that children assigned to special classes are generally those with the worst adjustment problems as well as the lowest test scores. Partly because of this assignment procedure, the focus in many classes for educable and trainable retarded children is on assisting them in emotional and social adjustment rather than on intellectual progress. There is good evidence that participation in such special classes does help the retarded child to achieve better social and emotional adjustment, but on the whole children in such classes do not make as much intellectual progress as do equally retarded children who remain in regular classes. In part, this difference may result from the assignment of the "worst" children to the special classes, but it may also be that teachers of special classes have lower expectations for the intellectual progress of their pupils than do teachers in regular classrooms; therefore, little emphasis is placed on cognitive growth. There is reason to believe that if emphasis were placed on the development of skills like reading and arithmetic, many retarded children in special classes could make more adequate progress in these areas.

Partly because of the mixed results of special classes and because of the concern of parents and educators over the undesireable effects of the label "retarded" that goes with placement in a special class, there has lately been a move toward "mainstreaming." Retarded children and other atypical children are being placed in regular classrooms whenever this is possible. Special classes for the more severely retarded still exist, of course, but the move now is toward including these special classes in regular school buildings rather than isolating the retarded and other atypical children in separate buildings. It will be several years before the verdict is in on the effects of mainstreaming. I have a suspicion, however, that too much emphasis has been placed on *where* the child will be taught, and too little on *what* or *how* she is to be taught. It will do little good to place retarded children in regular classrooms if the teachers are not helped to develop the special skills needed to teach them.

Reading and Other School Problems

Regular classroom teachers face other sorts of problems with atypical development as well. As nearly any teacher can attest, there are many children with apparently normal intelligence who seem to have serious problems with the basic skills taught in school. Problems in learning to read are by far the most common of these difficulties. As I have already pointed out, estimates of the incidence of reading problems vary enormously, depending on the severity of the deficit you "count" as being a problem. The estimate given in Figure 38 includes only children with severe learning problems. But if you count as atypical any early elementary school child whose reading achievement is a year behind the norm and any older child who is at least a year and a half behind the normal rate, then 15 to 20 percent of all school children in this country have reading problems. Most of these children have no obvious mental retardation, no obvious emotional disturbance, and no obvious brain damage. So how are we to account for their reading difficulties?

Several approaches to this question are evident in the research literature and in the writings of educators. Physicians and others with a primarily physiological bias have suggested that many children with reading problems suffer from *minimal brain damage.* Even though the child may not show any signs of gross brain damage, there may be some smaller damage, undetected until the child is faced with the complex task of learning to read. It is entirely possible, even likely, that this is a reasonable explanation in some cases. But you should understand clearly that this is a *hypothesis.* On all the standard tests of brain damage, most poor readers look quite normal. But many physicians and educators have suggested that more subtle tests would reveal some damage.

Another approach, suggested by Kirk, is simply to call children with significant reading (or other academic) problems *learning disabled* without trying to specify the origin of the disability. The phrase "learning disability" has come into quite common usage within the schools and has a very broad definition. The category includes children with difficulties with either spoken or written language; the difficulty may be manifested in problems in listening, thinking, talking, reading, writing, spelling, or arithmetic. What this labeling strategy gives us is a kind of grab bag of problems, lumped into a single category of learning disability. When Kirk first suggested the phrase in 1962 he did not mean to imply any necessary neurological impairment as the basis for the disability. He was simply searching for some general term to cover a variety of specific problems associated particularly with reading. But many professionals and parents have come to use the phrase to suggest not only behavioral disabilities, but neurological deficit. So "learning disability" has come to be almost a synonym for "minimal brain damage" for many people. Hobbs, in his recent book on the problems of categorization and classification of children, comments on this usage:

> The term *learning disability* has appeal because it implies a specific neurological condition for which no one can be held particularly responsible, and yet it escapes the stigma of mental retardation. There is no implication of neglect, emotional disturbance, or improper training or education, nor does it imply a lack of motivation on the part of the child. For these cosmetic reasons, it is a rather nice term to have around. However, no one has ever been able to find evidence of the implied neurological impairment. Furthermore, children with known neurological impairments often do not manifest the kinds of behavior associated with the learning-disability concept. . . . Many critics of the term regard the learning-disability classification as a middle-class nicety. Low-socioeconomic-level children exhibiting the same behavior are likely to be labeled mentally retarded. (Hobbs, 1975, p. 81)

So where does this leave us? Obviously, calling a child learning disabled or minimally brain damaged is not terribly helpful to a teacher or other professional who must design programs to help the child with reading. What would be much more useful would be specific information about those particular learning difficulties common to children with reading problems. But even this is difficult to provide.

Torgesen, in his recent review of the extensive literature on children with reading problems, suggests that there are a *few* common threads: (1) Poor readers are usually found to have greater difficulty with short-term memory tasks than do better readers; for example, they have a harder time remembering and repeating lists of numbers or words. There are other bits of evidence that difficulties with remembering sequences of sounds may be particularly typical of poor readers. (2) Poor readers are usually found to learn various standard learning problems more slowly than do better readers. What evidence is available points to the conclusion that poor readers are not going at learning tasks in a different manner; rather, they seem merely to be slower, or less efficient, in their learning. (3) Poor readers are frequently found to be generally inattentive and distractible compared to good readers— which is perhaps why they have greater difficulty with standard learning tasks.

Note that these findings do *not* tell us whether the origin of the difficulty is neurological or not. All they tell us is that poor readers have some characteristics in common. But the category of learning disability is a very mixed bag, which contains children with widely different problems. Brain damage may be the primary source of the difficulty for some children, but not for others.

Clinicians and educators, faced with this very confusing picture, have focused their attention recently on much more detailed assessments of each individual child. What can the child do? What specific tasks does she have trouble with? Does the problem appear to be primarily one of inattention? Or does the child seem to have difficulties with discriminations among letters or configurations of letters? Once detailed diagnosis has been done, then it is more possible to design a remediation program for the individual child.

EMOTIONALLY ATYPICAL DEVELOPMENT

It is becoming common to differentiate between two levels of severity when talking about emotionally atypical development. The most severe kinds of difficulty are usually called childhood psychoses. Young children who are labeled psychotic ordinarily suffer what amounts to a total breakdown in communication with others and show a lack of emotional contact with adults and other children. Their physical behavior may be bizarre—head banging or whirling, for example—and not well related to the circumstances. They may in fact score at a level of mental retardation on standard tests.

The milder level of emotionally atypical development most commonly consists of a cluster of behavior disorders. Children with one or more behavior disorders do not show the massive, pervasive dysfunctioning that the psychotic child demonstrates. They may function extremely well in many areas, but they have a few areas of excessive behavior (an excessively aggressive child), or in which they show great fear (the child who is afraid of school), or inability to inhibit activity (the hyperactive child), or an overinhibition of activity (the withdrawn or very shy child). In very general terms a behavior disorder is any pattern of behavior that exceeds the norm to some marked degree or is sufficiently bizarre to create management or control problems for parents or for schools.

Severe Emotional Disturbance

The group of children with apparently severe emotional disturbance is now ordinarily subdivided further into two groups—*autistic* children and *schizophrenic* children. One distinction between the two is in time of onset. Autism is present at birth or shortly thereafter, while schizophrenia develops later, often at preschool or school age.

AUTISM

Research and analysis over the past five years has made the definition of autism a great deal clearer. Rutter reports that the three symptoms consistently found among autistic children are "A profound and general failure to develop social relationships; language retardation with impaired comprehension . . . ; and ritualistic or compulsive phenomena." (Rutter, 1975, p. 329) Such children frequently talk little, if at all, are not affectionate or even apparently very interested in relating to adults or other children, and are frequently retarded as well. The children usually have strict routines—things must be done in a certain order or at certain times—and many also have peculiar finger or hand mannerisms or other repetitive body movements.

Where might such a combination of characteristics come from? Many clinicians were initially struck by the autistic child's failure to relate to other people. As infants, such children show far less mutual gaze than do normal children, and parents of autistic children often report that the child somehow does not respond in a usual way to being held. The child does not *withdraw* from people, but she does not relate in a normal way. Could this result from some breakdown in the early parent-child interaction? Could it arise from parental rejection or from lack of warmth on the part of parents? Studies of families of autistic children do not support any of these environmental hypotheses. Aside from the somewhat unexpected (and unexplained) fact that the average education of the parents of autistic children is unusually high, there have been no common denominators found among families of autistic children.

It is beginning to seem more likely that the primary problem for autistic children lies in their very great difficulty with *language*. From infancy they seem to have little or no ability to analyze or make sense of sounds, particularly strings of sounds like language. Other research also indicates that such children have difficulty understanding and using gestures as well, so there may be some very general impairment in the child's ability to use linguistic cues, whether they be verbal or gestural.

But if language impairment is somehow at the core of the problem, how are autistic children different from ordinary language-delayed children? Why is this a special syndrome? Rutter has analyzed the several studies comparing autistic and language-delayed children and concludes that they are quite distinct groups. Language *comprehension* and the understanding of gestures are considerably worse among autistic children than among other language-delayed children. Among autistic children with some language the consistent observation is that they do not use language in social contexts—they do not "chat" with others—while language-delayed children do. Rutter says, "In spite of important similarities between the groups, the deficit seemed different as well as more profound in the autistic children. In autism there seemed to be an impairment in the *use* of language over and above the language incapacity." (Rutter, 1975, p. 341)

These are extremely interesting findings, I think, because they link up with the possibility of a "language acquisition device," which I discussed in Chapter 8 (page 186). If there is some portion of the brain involved in the analysis and comprehension of language—in sound or gesture—then damage to that section (or sections) may be at the heart of the syndrome we call autism.

But then how do we explain the autistic child's failure in social relationships? Obviously, there is still a great deal to understand about the process, but it *may* be that the child's initial and continuing difficulty in understanding sounds and sequences may alter the way in which she responds to the people around her. The failure in social relationships may thus be a *result* of the cognitive deficit, and not the other way around. The repetitive movements common among autistic children may be an attempt on the child's part to create order and system out of a set of experiences that seem to the child to be disordered.

I am not sure that I am yet completely convinced that the central problem for the autistic child lies in a general language disorder, and that the other symptoms are outgrowths of this. It is not clear to me that lack of mutual gaze is a necessary *result* of the kind of language disorder found in autistic children, yet just such a lack is found among autistic infants. So there may be other kinds of primary disorders involved. But I am convinced that the syndrome we call autism has a neurological origin of some kind. The problem is aggravated by the child's inability to form or encourage normal attachments, but the initial difficulty appears to be physiological.

I should emphasize at this point that despite the accumulating evidence suggesting neurological origins for autism, which I find so persuasive, many theorists and therapists remain unconvinced. Researchers who argue from a social-learning perspective, for example, see the reliance on physiological explanations as a kind of cop-out. It is too easy to say that such problems are the result of "the brain" and let it go at that. The phrase "minimal brain damage," which I discussed earlier in this chapter, seems to me to represent just such an empty reliance on physiological "explanations." Researchers and therapists who adopt a psychoanalytic perspective are also unhappy with physiological explanations of autism, which seem to them to leave out the important child-environment interactions after birth. Whatever the status of the child's neurological system at birth, the child *does* relate to the others around her and to the inanimate world. The interactions between her initial status and the responses of the environment are sure to have some effect on the severity of the disorder. Nonetheless, while both of these arguments are true, in part, they do not (in my opinion) reduce the potency of the evidence for a neurological impairment as the *original* disorder in the case of autistic children.

The long-range prognosis for autistic children depends very heavily on whether the child is also retarded. Autistic children of normal intelligence who are able to develop some language may be able to attend regular schools and may function with reasonably normality as adults. Several longitudinal follow-up studies have found that about one-sixth of children diagnosed autistic were employed as adults, and another one-sixth had made a moderately good social adjustment. The remaining two-thirds remained severely handicapped, and most were in institutions of one kind or another.

<table>
<tr><td>

CHILDHOOD
SCHIZOPHRENIA

</td><td>

A second, somewhat different, pattern of disturbance seems to develop later in childhood, at about age 3 or 4, and is often called *childhood schizophrenia*. Most such children develop normally during the early years; they have apparently normal language development and generally normal development of attachments. But for reasons that are not at all well understood, some children show a rather sharp regression to earlier patterns. They may loose speech, become incontinent and overactive, or show bizarre behaviors of one kind or another. The symptoms may be quite similar to those seen in the autistic child, although the age of onset is different and the early development is more normal in the schizophrenic child.

</td></tr>
</table>

Many clinicians would argue with the contention that the early development of the schizophrenic child is normal. They see the seeds of later disturbance in the child's earliest relationships with the mother or other adults. The full breakdown in the child's behavior may occur later, often after some severe stress, such as the birth of a sibling or an illness, but some argue that the origin of the disorder is in the earliest interactions.

Interventions for severely disturbed children of this type have not been markedly successful. Some children show improvement without any kind of intervention, while others show no improvement at all, even with quite intensive therapeutic efforts. Some therapists, utilizing behavior modification techniques based on learning theory, have shown that it is possible to eliminate particular distressing symptoms by rewarding the child for other behavior or, in extreme cases, by punishing her severely each time she performs the undesirable behavior. Ivar Lovaas, at the University of California at Los Angeles, has used such techniques to eliminate self-destructive behavior (like head banging and chewing on fingers) in severely disturbed autistic children. Behavior modification techniques offer some promise of better management of the child's behavior, but it has not yet been shown that the child's interpersonal relationships can be altered significantly by the same procedures. Overall, although a great deal of diligent and sometimes promising work is being done on therapeutic interventions for severely disturbed children, the outlook for such children is discouraging.

<table>
<tr><td>

**Behavior
Disorders**

</td><td>

Much more hopeful is the long-term outlook for children with less severe disorders. Many generally normal children, at one time or another in their lives, have some kind of difficulty that might fairly be described as a behavior disorder (see Figure 40). A child may develop

</td></tr>
</table>

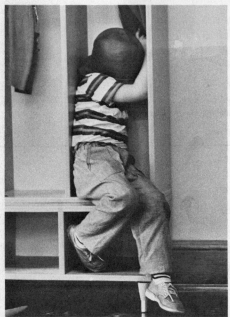

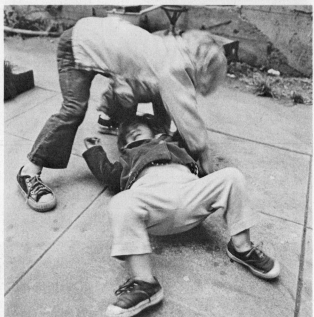

FIGURE 40
Some examples of young people showing behavior disorders.

severe fears, nightmares, or phobias about going to school or may regress to bed wetting or show signs of strain or nervousness, such as nail biting. In adolescence there may be brief periods of fairly severe depression. Such symptoms may result in the child visiting a psychologist, either in school or in some kind of clinic, but the duration of the problem is in most cases quite brief. Most children get over or cope with their problem either spontaneously or after short-term therapy.

The probability that a child will display some significant behavior problem increases at particular times during childhood. Nine- and 10-year-olds are more likely to have problems than are younger children, and there is another peak at about age 14 or 15, during the height of adolescence. In part, the lower probability of behavior problems in very young children comes from the fact that school itself poses problems of adjustment for children and may provoke difficulties that had not been apparent before. In addition, teachers and other school personnel may recognize potentially problematic symptoms when the parents do not, and they may recommend some kind of short-term therapy for a child who would not otherwise have been seen in a clinic or other therapeutic setting. In any case most of the symptoms are short-lived or respond well to short-term treatment.

Because the term "behavior disorder" covers such an assortment of problems, it is difficult to say anything very sensible about the causes or origins of the problem. Without doubt, the origins are different for the several types of symptoms and for different children. Perhaps the most useful framework is one suggested by James Anthony, who describes the causes of behavior disorders as a series of sources of risk. Some children may be "at risk" genetically or because of some physical disorder. And some children are living under conditions of greater environmental risk, because of poverty, lack of warmth and affection within the family, or whatever. Anthony suggests that when a child shows some kind of behavior disorder it is because the cumulative risk has reached a critical point; when the level of stress has receded, the child's symptoms may go away as well. There is very good evidence that among adults an accumulation of stress caused by life changes (such as changing jobs, getting married, moving, and so on) can bring about physical and mental illness. In children, accumulations of stress, combined perhaps with physical or genetic risk to start with, may produce brief or long-lasting episodes of behavior disorders.

One of the forms of family stress that is fairly common in the background of children with behavior disorders, particularly aggressive and delinquent disorders, is chronic physical illness in one or both parents. The illness itself may be stressful to the child, but it may also be accompanied by family upheaval and parental irritability, which add to the child's risk. Parental psychological illness also greatly increases the risk of behavior disorders in children. In some studies as many as 40 percent of children who showed behavior disorders were found to have families in which one parent (usually the mother) had enduring emotional difficulties. The relationship between parents and child, whether the parents show any form of illness or not, also clearly contributes to the child's risk of behavior disorder. In particular, rejecting or uncaring parents seem more likely to have children with aggressive or delinquent patterns (see Chapter 11).

Conceptualizing behavior disorder as a response to an accumulation of risk seems a useful way to look at the problem, for clearly no single cause is at work in most instances. The transient nature of the disorder can then be understood as an excess of stress at one particular time. It is to be hoped that as we come to be able to evaluate children and their families for degrees of risk, we will be able to help alleviate the stresses and provide assistance before stress becomes critical.

Juvenile Delinquency

A special subgroup of children with behavior disorders includes those who have criminal records of some kind. These are young people whose behavior society considers unacceptable: stealing, lying, breaking and entering, assault, and so forth (see Figure 41). Most commonly the crimes associated with juvenile delinquency are crimes involving aggression (although that is more often true for boys than for girls). The proportion of young people under the age of 18 who have been in juvenile court has risen steadily over the past 15 years. In 1968 about 2.5 percent of all children between the ages of 10 and 17 had appeared in court at least once, but the rate has been increasing and, if current trends continue, it is estimated that one of every nine youngsters will appear in a juvenile court before the age of 18.

The rate of juvenile delinquency is about four times as high among boys as among girls and about three times as high in urban areas as in rural areas. The largest percentage of delinquency is found in central-city areas among children from poverty-level families (although the rate of delinquency among more well-to-do suburban children has been increasing lately).

There have been numerous studies of delinquent children, many involving matched-pair designs in which for each delinquent child a nondelinquent child of the same age, sex, and similar family background is studied. The two groups are then compared on a variety of measures, such as early school histories and parent-child interactions (see Conger, Miller, & Walsmith, and Glueck & Glueck). The conclusions to be drawn from such research are that delinquents do come from families with importantly different characteristics, and that signs of difficulties in most cases begin to show up as early as the first years in school.

Sheldon and Eleanor Glueck and a number of other researchers have found that in the families of delinquents discipline is usually either lax or very erratic. Often the father resorts to quite severe physical punishment, but he does so inconsistently. Probably more important, in many families of delinquents there is no basic underpinning of affection for and acceptance of the child; the parents are rejecting toward the child from quite early. Not surprisingly, given such histories, children who later become delinquents show signs of disturbance early in life. In elementary school they are likely to have problems with school work, particularly with focusing their attention for very long periods of time, and their teachers often find them overly aggressive. By ninth

378

FIGURE 41
Delinquents under arrest. The rate of juvenile delinquency is higher among boys and the poor, but is rising for the middle class and for girls.

grade prospective delinquents are markedly different from their peers in a number of respects, including less consideration for the rights of others, greater antagonism toward authority, less friendliness toward classmates, and poorer school and work habits. Future delinquents may also have little self-confidence and self-respect—at least they are perceived that way by others.

One important conclusion to be drawn from such research is that delinquency is not the inevitable result of growing up in impoverished circumstances. Many children from poor families do not become delinquents, and many children from more well-to-do families do. What appears more important is the nature of the child's relationship with the parents from the earliest years. Disorganized family life, accompanied by erratic discipline and rejection of the child, may simply be more likely among poverty-level families—perhaps because parents feel helpless about their own lives—but the same pattern is found among middle-class families as well and is likely to lead to delinquency in either case.

PHYSICALLY ATYPICAL DEVELOPMENT

The group of physically atypical children is enormously diverse. The category makes sense only because all the children I am going to talk about here have some kind of physical dysfunction or damage. In sheer numbers atypical physical development is probably the least frequent (although if we included all brain-damaged and minimally brain-damaged children the number would go up very markedly). However, although the numbers may be small, the degree of difficulty encountered by the physically atypical child may be very great indeed. Many of the children in the several categories I'm discussing here need special schooling and training over very long periods of time, so the costs to society for their care can be and usually are very high (emotionally, as well as financially).

Deaf and Hearing Impaired Children

Most school-age children with hearing loss can function adequately in school with the help of a hearing aid or after some kind of medical intervention to correct the loss. Far more difficult is the situation of the profoundly deaf.

The deaf child suffers from a whole constellation of difficulties: Her experiences may be severely restricted, not only because the whole range of auditory sensations is unavailable, but also because she may be physically limited as well. Her ability to communicate with the other human beings around her is cut off, or at least the usual avenue of communications is blocked. For the profoundly deaf normal speech is almost impossible; unless you can hear your own sounds, it is nearly impossible to tell if you are making the same sound as the model. Some clues can be obtained from the feel of the mouth and throat when various sounds are made, but these clues are generally inadequate to help the deaf child develop a completely intelligible spoken language. Lipreading helps to understand the language of others, but the ability of the congenitally deaf child to acquire this skill has been exaggerated in the popular press; even the very best lip-readers (nearly always people who learned to talk before they became deaf) follow no more than about 80 percent of what is said, and the average deaf individual follows far less. For most deaf children, especially the congenitally deaf, regular schooling is out of the question, for they can neither understand nor be understood by the normal vocal means of communication. Some kind of special school is required, and even then there are major problems.

Until quite recently the common form of training and schooling for the deaf involved heavy emphasis on oral language. The argument was that the deaf child would have to live in a speaking world and would have to learn to understand and make herself understood. Sign language (see Figure 42) was discouraged, and parents of deaf children were often told not to permit signing. This type of treatment, however logical its intent, did not have the desired effect. Deaf children had great difficulty learning to lipread, and their speech was typically bizarre, despite extended efforts. In the past few years the preferred method of training has been "total communication," which involves signing while speaking, and trains the deaf child in both sign language and oral language to the extent possible. Parents are now encouraged to use sign language with their deaf child from the earliest months of life, so that the child is exposed to a language of some kind.

Research by Schlesinger and Meadow on deaf children born to deaf parents suggests that such children, who do learn sign language as their "native" language, are better off both emotionally and cognitively than are deaf children born to hearing parents. Schlesinger is convinced that the child needs *some* form of communication in the early months and years, both to form the basic sense of trust Erikson talks of, and to help in relating to and learning about the world. If this is denied—if the deaf child is not given an early language she can use—then there may be permanent difficulties. "Total communication" is a strategy that seems to meet the several needs of the deaf child, since she is encouraged to use signing, especially during her early years, but is also exposed as much as possible to oral language.

FIGURE 42
Sign language among the deaf. (Gallaudet College Photo)

Nonetheless, the long-term prognosis for profoundly deaf individuals, even with excellent training, is not very good. To be sure, some deaf individuals have made excellent adjustment to adult society, and maintain full jobs and family lives. But many deaf adults have considerable difficulty. The average reading level for deaf adults is only fourth grade, and writing skills are equally poor. This alone would severely limit occupational choices, but when combined with communication difficulties, the problems may be immense. There is reason to believe, though, that the total communication training method may result in deaf adults of the next generation who are better adapted. What little research is available suggests that deaf children who have learned sign language initially have an easier time learning to read and write. They achieve higher levels in nearly all language skills than those trained in the purely oral tradition, so there is some reason to be hopeful.

Blind Children

Blindness may be produced by prenatal insult of some kind or by injury or disease after birth. In either case, although there are severe consequences for the child, the educational implications are not as complex as for the deaf child. To be sure, the range of experiences available to a blind child is restricted, just as it is for the deaf, but the management problem is not so great for the parents. The child can be allowed to explore more freely, for warnings of danger can always be given orally. Wider explorations, as in the neighborhood, are more problematic, but on the whole there is probably not as great a restriction of experience as is common for the deaf.

Blind children are more often found in regular school classrooms than are the deaf, although there are special schools and special classrooms for the blind as well. Typically, there is some initial scholastic retardation among the blind, but this does not seem to be a permanent effect. If a blind child learns Braille and has access to special help and services in school, ordinarily she can make a reasonable adjustment to the academic environment. Adult occupational prospects are better for the blind than for the deaf as well.

SEX AND SOCIAL CLASS DIFFERENCES

Sex differences in the rate of abnormality are quite consistent, with girls consistently less deviant. As you can see from Table 11, except for visual problems, which are slightly more prevalent in girls, boys are more frequently found in nearly every category of atypical development.

Mental retardation is also more commonly found among males, at the rate of about 2 males to every female in special classes for the retarded. Reading problems are at least three times as common among males, as is stuttering. Juvenile delinquency is also more common among boys than among girls, although this difference is narrowing.

There are at least two possible explanations for these persistent

TABLE 11
Sex Difference in Incidence of Atypical Development

	Males	Females
School problems		
Children testing *below* grade level in basic subjects	21.1%	14.1%
Physical handicaps		
Visual problems—Percentage of children aged 6–11 with mild to severe problems	10.3%	11.9%
Hearing problems—Percentage of children aged 6–11 with mild to severe problems	0.5%	0.4%
Speech defects—Percentage of children aged 6–11 with mild to severe problems	9.9%	6.8%
Emotional problems		
Estimated percentage of children seen in psychiatric clinics, aged 10–17	4.5%	2.9%

Source: *Profiles of Children. 1970 White House Conference on Children.* Washington, D. C.: U. S. Government Printing Office, 1970.

findings. First, as Hobbs has argued, it may be that deviance among males is simply less acceptable. Boys are more likely to be sent or taken to physicians or psychologists for evaluation *sooner* than are girls with equivalent problems. So parents, and possibly doctors, may worry more about deviance in a boy, and this may affect the incidence rates we see in Table 11. Hobbs is saying in essence that the actual rates of deviance for males and females may be much more similar than the usual incidence rates suggest, but that in girls, moderate mental subnormality or mild behavior problems are simply better tolerated, so the child may remain in a regular classroom.

There may be some validity to this argument, but there is some counterevidence that points to an alternative hypothesis, namely, that males are simply more vulnerable to a variety of physical stresses than are girls. Singer and his associates, in a study involving 15,000 infants from 13 different hospitals around the country, found that males had significantly more problems during the first year of life. Assessments by physicians uncovered significantly more neurological, mental, and motor problems among the males than among the females. Girls were more likely, at 8 months, to show "abnormal" social and emotional development, but this was the only area assessed in which girls had a higher incidence of deviance. If the only factor producing sex differences in rates of retardation or reading problems at school age were the labeling tendencies of the adults, then why would we find, in objective examinations, that there are parallel sex differences among infants?

It seems much more likely that the male infant is more vulnerable to stress, both *in utero* and after birth. But how are we to account for such differences in vulnerability? Singer et al. suggests that the origin of the difference must, somehow, be contained in the genetic code. Perhaps the Y chromosome (which only males have) contains different, less beneficial "information." Perhaps the girls' faster rate of development through gestation and in the early years of life makes them, in comparison to same-age boys, better able to handle any kind of physical stress that comes along. Or perhaps some intial genetic differences are magnified by differences in rearing practices for boys and girls—although this possibility seems less likely, since as I have already pointed out, there appear to be relatively few systematic differences in the rearing of boys and girls. Whatever the origin of the difference, however, it does appear that the female is, in at least one sense, the "stronger" sex.

Social class differences in deviance rates are also found quite consistently. Children from poor backgrounds are more likely to suffer prenatal and postnatal malnutrition, and their mothers are less likely to have adequate prenatal care. As I pointed out in Chapter 3 the rate of most kinds of birth complications is far higher among the poor. The rate of mental retardation and school problems is also higher among the poor than among the middle class, which may result from differences in prenatal or birth stress, from differences in early environmental stimulation, or from some combination of the two.

OVERVIEW

Obviously, I have only scratched the surface. I have not discussed at all the significant number of children with such physical disorders as cerebral palsy or epilepsy, and I have barely mentioned those children with speech problems. The issues I have raised are obviously complex; I have scarcely touched on the theoretical and factual arguments. Those of you interested in atypical development will need to search elsewhere for detail.

Two points deserve final emphasis, however. First, I want to repeat the information with which I opened this chapter. At least one out of every ten, and probably as many as one out of every five or six, children in our society will need some kind of corrective intervention at some time during childhood or adolescence. Something between 6 and 12 *million* children require help, and many of them need substantial and continuing help. Obviously, if we are going to provide the help they need, we need to know a great deal more about the several disorders and problems and about how to prevent, remedy, or ameliorate them. But we also need to know a great deal more about the *normal* process of development. I am convinced that many of the keys to understanding *a*typical development lie in a better understanding of typical, or normal, development.

Second, there is now a very encouraging trend toward very early diagnosis and treatment for atypical children. A federal law requiring each state to devise means of screening all young children for disorders or developmental delays now exists. As screening becomes better, we should be able to do a far more thorough job of identifying early those children who already have problems and those who are *likely* to have problems later. More effective early intervention may then be possible. But once again we have to remember that intervention is expensive, and there is a real question about our willingness to commit the money and the energy to the problems of atypical children or children at risk.

SUMMARY

1. The largest group of children with atypical development are those with some form of mental retardation. Approximately 1.7 million children are retarded, with perhaps 100,000 retarded children born each year.

2. Mental retardation should be understood as a symptom, not as a disease. The child is retarded in functioning at a given time and under particular circumstances, but the level of functioning may change for a variety of reasons.

3. Mental retardation is customarily divided into several subclasses, including mild retardation (IQ from 52 to 67), moderate retardation (IQ from 36 to 51), and severe retardation (IQ from 20 to 35).

4. The causes of retardation are ordinarily divided into two categories: physical and cultural-familial causes. Included among physical causes are genetic anomalies and brain damage. Cultural-familial retardation is presumed to be a joint product of genetically low intellectual ability and impoverished or nonstimulating environments. Very early, extensive intervention with children at risk for cultural-familial retardation *may* result in significant increases in intellectual performance. Intervention with children with physically caused retardation has been less successful, although intervention does make some difference in the child's intellectual skills.

5. Emotionally atypical development is also usually subdivided into childhood psychoses and behavior disorders. Psychoses include extremely severe forms of emotional dislocation in which the child's relationship with others is impaired; often there is also bizarre behavior and mental subnormality. The prognosis for such children is poor, especially for those who show onset of symptoms very early.

6. Behavior disorders are deviant, usually short-term, patterns of extreme behaviors such as excessive aggressiveness and withdrawl. Short-term psychiatric treatment is very often successful in alleviating the problem.

7. Behavior disorders may be the child's response to an excess of stress or "risk" in her environment, caused either by physical illness, emotional disturbance in the parents, or short-term family dislocation.

8. Deaf children, although not numerous, pose special problems for their families, for schools, and for society as a whole. There are serious management and training problems, including providing the child with some viable language. Recent methods of training in both sign language and oral language seem to offer the most hope.

9. Blind children, although they may require special classes and special assistance, often do well in ordinary classrooms and have

fewer problems with intellectual and scholastic progress than do deaf children.

10. There are consistent sex differences in rates of atypical development, with males being more likely to show virtually every kind of deviance.

11. The total number of children whose development is atypical and who require assistance of some kind is very large. At least one-tenth and probably as many as one-fifth of all children will require some intervention, special education, or help.

REFERENCES

Suggested Additional Readings

Anthony, E. J. The behavior disorders of childhood. In P. H. Mussen (Ed.), *Carmichael's manual of child psychology.* (Vol. 2, 3rd ed.). New York: Wiley, 1970.
An enormously detailed discussion, probably containing more information than you need but full of good data and theory, especially on longitudinal studies of children with behavior disorders.

Conger, J. J., Miller, W. C., & Walsmith, C. R. Antecedents of delinquency, personality, social class and intelligence. In P. H. Mussen, J. J. Conger, & J. Kagan (Eds.), *Readings in child development and personality* (2nd ed.). New York: Harper & Row, 1970.
An unusually good and detailed study of the early history of delinquent youngsters, including a comparatively rare analysis of female delinquents.

Goldfarb, W. Childhood psychosis. In P. H. Mussen (Ed.), *Carmichael's manual of child psychology.* (Vol. 2, 3rd ed.). New York: Wiley, 1970.
Covers some of the same ground as Rutter's paper but more broadly and in greater detail.

Hobbs, N. *The futures of children.* San Francisco: Jossey-Bass, 1975.
An absolutely first-rate discussion of the whole problem of categorization and labeling of children; clear and easy to read.

Kaufman, B. N. *Son/Rise.* New York: Harper & Row, 1976.
If you are interested in autism, this book is a must. It is written by the father of an autistic boy and describes the therapy devised by the parents—an astoundingly successful therapy. While I personally find the style of writing rather flowery, the message is fascinating and impressive.

Meadow, K. P. The development of deaf children. In E. M. Hetherington (Ed.), *Review of child development research* (Vol. 5). Chicago: University of Chicago Press, 1975.
If you are interested in the deaf, this would be an excellent general source, although the Schlesinger and Meadow book is also an excellent first step.

Robinson, H. B., & Robinson, N. Mental retardation. In P. H. Mussen (Ed.), *Carmichael's manual of child psychology.* (Vol. 2, 3rd ed.). New York: Wiley, 1970.
A very good short paper on the many faceted problem of mental retardation.

Rutter, M. The development of infantile autism. In S. Chess & A. Thomas (Eds.), *Annual progress in child psychiatry and child development, 1975.* New York: Brunner/Mazel, 1975.
Although not everyone agrees with Rutter's view on autism, I think this is an excellent first source; the paper is usually clear and easy to read.

Schlesinger, H. S., & Meadow, K. P. *Sound and sign.* Berkeley: University of California Press, 1972.
A marvelous book on the deaf, including data on a group of deaf children of deaf parents.

Torgesen, J. Problems and prospects in the study of learning disabilities. In E. M. Hetherington (Ed.), *Review of child development research* (Vol. 5). Chicago: University of Chicago Press, 1975.
A good although somewhat dense discussion of learning disability and an excellent source of additional references.

Other Sources Cited

Glueck, S., & Glueck, E. T. *Unraveling juvenile delinquency.* New York: Commonwealth Fund, 1950.

Profiles of Children. 1970 White House Conference on Children. Washington, D.C.: U. S. Government Printing Office, 1970.

Rosen, B. M., Bahn, A. K., & Kramer, M. Demographic and diagnostic characteristics of psychiatric clinic outpatients in the U. S. A., 1961. *American Journal of Orthopsychiatry,* 1964, *24,* 455–467.

Singer, J. E., Westphal, M., & Niswander, K. R. Sex differences in the incidence of neonatal abnormalities and abnormal performance in early childhood. *Child Development,* 1968, *39,* 103–112.

16

Age
Overview

In nearly all the chapters so far I have talked about only one aspect of the child at a time: her language, her body, her thinking, her feelings, and so on. I have tried all along to emphasize the interconnectedness of all facets of development, but I suspect that inevitably I have left you with the feeling that the child is a set of disconnected pieces. It's a bit like the dilemma facing a teacher of European history. Do you teach students all about the kings of England and then all about the kings of France, hoping that they will figure out who was king at the same time in the two countries? Or do you teach the two together and run the risk that the student will never learn all the kings of either country in the right order? My own feeling about studying child development is that it is most important to grasp the sequential nature of most facets of development, and I have been willing to sacrifice some sense of wholeness to achieve that goal. But now let me, at least briefly, try to put the child back together for you.

I have begun to think of the overall sweep of development as a series of episodes of rapid growth that we might think of as a time of *disequilibrium,* followed by periods of consolidation or equilibrium. Piaget's and others' theories have led us to think of the child's development in terms of a series of stages, and until recently I think most psychologists had expected that there would be some sort of internal coherence at each stage—that a child who was advanced in the object concept, for example, at 1 year would also be advanced in other ways. But it turns out that the process is much more complex than that. Increasingly it looks to me as if there are times when the several threads of development are proceeding somewhat independently, but that there are times when these threads all come together into a major integration, or "equilibration," to use Piaget's word.

Let me try to make this concept clearer with a specific example. During the preschool years the child seems to work out an excellent set of skills and procedures for handling her normal environment. Over the time from age 2 to age 5 there are many changes in almost every domain, and the several changes aren't clearly connected to each other. This is the time when Erikson's second and third stages—autonomy versus shame and doubt, and initiative versus guilt—occur. The child is developing important new skills in language and motor areas and is trying out her new skills, pushing for more independence. In the early part of this period there is often a great deal of conflict with parents over toilet training, over the child's demands for independence, and over increased aggressiveness. But by about age 5, toward the end of the preoperational period, the child—and the family—seem to have reached an accommodation of sorts—to "have it all together" in some sense. Cognitively, the child has reached a sort of plateau; she has gone about as far as she can go *without* the "operations" such as addition and subtraction, multiple classification, or seriation. Linguistically, the child has mastered the basics of her language and can com-

TABLE 12
Summary of Development: Birth to 2 months

Physical growth	Perceptual development	Language
Rapid increase in physical size	"Nonprimary" system, including attention focused on edges and contours, and on movement	Only vocalization is crying sounds
Growth in brain cells and in density of cells	No systematic scanning of whole figures	
Myelinization of nerves continues	Some basic perceptual skills present from birth, however, including some sound discrimination, and ability to focus eyes and track moving objects	
Probably most activity governed by "primitive" portions of the brain		

municate freely with those around her. Her major motor skills—walking, running, stair climbing, and so on—are present, and the parents and child have reached some sort of adaptive system—a new "dance" if you will, in which the child is allowed to lead more often than before.

What happens to this tidy world is that the child is sent off to school at age 5 or 6, which seems to provoke major changes in both cognitive functioning and in relationships with peers. And as the demands on the child change, so she also must change, which will require new adjustments between parents and child as well. So a new period of change, disequilibrium, and perhaps turmoil begins. What I am suggesting is that the whole developmental process is made up of a series of episodes of such consolidations followed by change, conflict, and new growth along several fronts.

Uzgiris has suggested something like this on the basis of her study of the consistency of cognitive development in infancy. She found that while the order of the child's development of the concept of object permanence, or of means-ends relationship, was constant, the rate with which a child moved from one stop to the next varied quite widely. Uzgiris says

This suggests that it may not be profitable to think of development in stepladder fashion, attainment of one rung in the ladder making it possible to reach the next higher rung. While the attainment of the lower rung may be necessary for moving to the next higher rung, other factors seem to intervene to influence the rate of progression. It is tempting to think that some of these factors may be achievements in other sequences, so that further progression is impeded until other achievements in the constellation are attained. (Uzgiris, 1973, p. 189)

390

Cognition	Interpersonal relationships	Self-concept and morality
Piaget's stage 1 of sensori-motor operations Primarily reflexive action	Basic "signals" to caregiver include crying, cuddling, and looking alert Some smiling, but not reliably to caregiver or to faces Little mutual gaze No evidence of specific attachment	None

Thus the periods of consolidation I am suggesting may be times when the several lines or areas of development have each reached some plateau or interim level. Only when the full collection of skills is present can the child go on to the next stage or phase, but within each stage the separate skills may develop at quite different rates.

The single theory of development that is most similar to what I am suggesting here is Erikson's, although he focuses primarily on the child's sense of identity. Erikson views development in terms of a series of crises or dilemmas, each involving some conflict, but each resolved in some ways. I am not sure I am ready to think of the whole process of development as a series of crises; "crisis" seems too strong a word for much of what I have in mind. But I do think that there are times of integration, followed by periods in which both the child's physical and mental development and her relationship with others are in greater flux.

Let me attempt to apply this notion to the developmental progression by discussing 5 periods, each of which may be thought of as ending with some sort of consolidation.

BIRTH TO 2 MONTHS

For this and each of the other age periods discussed in this chapter I have summarized the several lines of development in a chart. Table 12 gives the summary for the birth-to-2-month period.

I am somewhat hesitant to talk about the first two months of life as a separate "stage," but increasingly there is evidence of substantial neurological change taking place at about 6 weeks or 2 months. Karmel and Maisel, who have studied the perceptual preferences of infants, suggest that there is a shift at about 2 months from a "nonprimary"

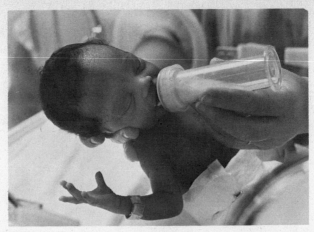

system, which is mainly governed by the *reticular formation* (a very primitive portion of the brain in the brain stem, which governs such body regulation as sleep and breathing), to a "primary" system, which seems to be largely influenced by the cerebral cortex. The infant is born with strategies for scanning the world around her, but these seem largely to be on a kind of "automatic pilot."

Piaget has also suggested that there is a major shift at about 1 month or 6 weeks from activities governed by the initial reflexes the child is born with to activities that begin to have elements of intention. It is at this age, in Piaget's theory, that the child makes the transition from stage 1 to stage 2 of sensorimotor operations (See Chapter 9, page 200).

Interpersonally the first two months are also somewhat distinct. Smiling is not regularly present in the very young infant, and mutual gaze also does not occur reliably much earlier than 2 months of age. Both smiling and mutual gaze are powerful influences on the parent's attachment for the infant, so their absence during the first months of life may affect the quality of the relationship.

The first two months are thus a period of rapid growth in several areas, particularly neurologically. But they are also a time when the parent and the child work out a first set of interlocking signals and responses. By about 6 weeks or 2 months the infant and parent have a fairly good system going, and the infant has the early reflexes well rehearsed and smooth. What breaks up this early integration, I think, is the further neurological development of the child, which brings the cerebral cortex more fully into play, and which now makes possible a whole new range of behaviors on the part of the child.

2 MONTHS TO 18 MONTHS

As you can see in Table 13, I think this broad period is probably subdivided into two phases. Again I think that it may be useful to think of

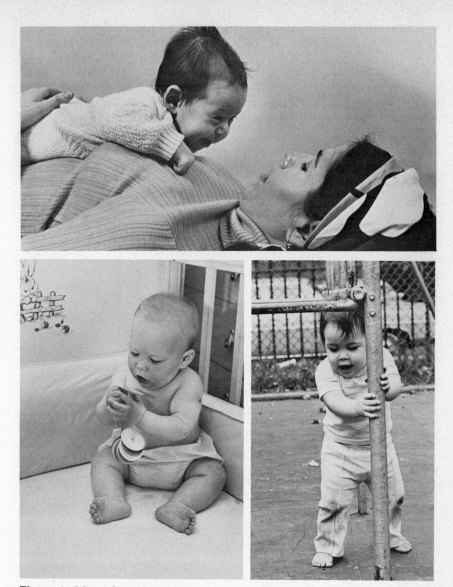

The period from 2 to 18 months.

each of these phases as beginning with some new development within the child or some major change in her environment. Those changes in turn require new adaptations and new adjustments in the child's relationships with others and in her mode of interacting with the things around her.

The period from 2 months to about 8 months is marked at the beginning by the neurological changes I have just talked about. The 2-month-old child is a quite different person to relate to. She smiles to the sound of the human voice and at the sight of a human face; she will

TABLE 13
Summary of Development: 2 months to 18 months

Physical growth	Perceptual development	Language
2 months–8 months Neurological development continues At about 18 months most new brain cells present Improving motor skills through this period, but no standing or crawling	Development of remaining perceptual constancies "Discrepancy principle" present Early stages of development of object concept Visual acuity improves	Cooing and babbling during this stage No words
8 months–18 months Neurological growth completed largely by 18 months Crawling and walking	Object concept is completely understood	First words at about 1 year Perhaps 10-word vocabulary by 18 months

meet your gaze, and she begins to make some sounds other than crying. These are all major changes from the point of view of the parent; the infant is now a much more social creature. At the same time her cognitive development goes into high gear, and she begins to explore and understand the objects around her. The parents must re-adapt to this more social infant, who has more skills and is more often alert and awake.

So a new period of adaptation occurs. The child adapts in new ways to her environment, and the parents must adapt to this new child. By six months the parents and infant have their "act" together fairly well, but again some changes in the child usher in a new phase.

First, there is some indication that another fairly major neurological shift takes place at about 6 to 7 months. Some of the "primitive" reflexes, such as the Babinsky, which I discussed in Chapter 4 (page 84), drop out at about this time, which suggests that the cortex has become still more dominant. Brain development is not complete at this age, but relatively few new cells are added after this point. Later changes appear to be primarily increases in the interconnecting links among cells and in myelinization of the nerve fibers. Some further evidence for the possible importance of a neurological shift at 6 to 8 months comes from studies of atypical children, many of whom show fairly normal development for the first six months, then begin to show

Cognition	Interpersonal relationships	Self-concept and morality
Piaget's stages 2 and 3 of sensorimotor period By the end of this period infant seems to explore and examine things more systematically and repeats interesting things.	Smiling and mutual gaze usher in a new phase of parent-infant relationships, with greater intricacy and "play" in their interactions Infant still has "diffuse" attachments during early part of this period Specific attachment begins about 6 months	None
Piaget's stages 4 and 5 of sensorimotor period Experimentation and intentional exploration	Strong single attachment shifting somewhat toward the end of this period to multiple attachments	Beginning of self concept toward the end of this period

divergence. This is a pattern that has been found among Downs' syndrome children, for example.

A second big change that takes place at around 6 to 8 months is the change in the child's attachment patterns. At about this age (or a little before) the child develops a clear, strong, single attachment, usually to the mother or major caregiver. This shift in the child's behavior inevitably alters the relationships of the adults with the infant, as well as the reverse.

Finally, at about 8 months most children begin some form of independent locomotion—usually crawling. This new skill, based on maturational changes, profoundly alters the child's experiences and her relationships with adults. Erikson suggests that the phase of "autonomy versus shame and doubt" begins only in the second year of life, but one could argue that the first push for autonomy is seen when the child is first able to move around her world more freely—and this happens at about 8 months.

So, once more the well-organized system of interactions with people and objects that the child has developed shifts rather sharply, partly because of maturational changes that make crawling possible, and partly because of cognitive advances that make specific attachments possible.

From 8 months through about 18 months the child and parents

TABLE 14
Summary of Development: 18 months to 6 years

Physical growth	Perceptual development	Language
Major brain growth complete by age 2, although some refinements after this time Motor skills become more refined Better coordination	Not much new happens during this period	Enormous changes in language: first word at about 1 year; about ten words by 18 months; 50 or more by 2 years 2-word sentences begin at about 18 months to 2 years; By age 6 nearly adult level of language usage

work out a new system, a new organization or integration. The parents must come to terms with the child's new physical independence, and the child must deal with the enormously enriched experience that her independent movement makes possible. There is rapid growth in cognitive skills and a state of flux in the relationship with the parents. Parents may begin, during this period, to set more limits on the child's behavior and may say "no" with far greater frequency than before. The problem for the parents is exacerbated at 1 year or so, when most children begin to walk, so the range of movement for the child is increased, as is the speed with which she can get into trouble.

Cognitively, the child of this period is still in the sensorimotor stage. She still operates on, explores, and "understands" her environment through the actions she can perform on it. By about 18 months she has gone about as far as this cognitive strategy will take her. So there is a kind of sensorimotor synthesis or plateau at this age, accompanied by some level of accommodation or synthesis in the relationship with the parents.

But once again this equilibrium is upset, and again by changes in the child's skills.

18 MONTHS TO 6 YEARS

At about 18 months or 2 years there is a "great leap forward" on two fronts—cognition and language. The child makes the enormous transition from sensorimotor functioning to internal representation, sum-

Cognition	Interpersonal relationships	Self-concept and morality
Major change is shift from sensorimotor to pre-operational thought in Piaget's view Child able to represent things internally, using words or images to represent By age 6, has developed basic classification skills, but lacks "operations" of multiple classification, addition, subtraction, seriation, etc. Social class differences in cognitive skill are found consistently during this period	Gradual shift during this period from focus on adults to focus on peers Shift with adults from touching and being near to more "distal" forms of attachment, such as asking for attention or approval Peer groups shift from parallel to cooperative play Only consistent sex difference is that boys are more aggressive	Near adult-like self-concept and gender concept develop during this period

marized in Table 14. She can now think about things independent of her actions on them. She can represent things to herself and make one object "stand for" another object in her play. At the same time there is a kind of explosion in her language, both in the number of words she knows and in her use of those words in sentences. As I pointed out in Box 14, (page 202), there is little agreement among linguists or psychologists about the relationship between these two changes. Does language expand so rapidly at age 2 or so *because* the child's cognitive

The child 2 to 5: Independence at last!

development has proceeded to the level of internal representation? Or is it the other way around? Or is the development of language governed by some process of neurological maturation, as I suggested in Chapter 8? Whatever the causal relationship between the two, it is clear that both language and cognition enter enormously important new phases at about 18 months or 2 years.

In the meantime the child's motor skill is improving; her coordination is better and better, so that she is able to do more things for herself. The powerful combination of greater physical coordination and the ability to express her desires in language manifests itself in more and more demands for independence. And this same combination undoubtedly also contributes to the shift in the form of the child's attachments. When language is rudimentary or nonexistent, and the child's locomotion is poor, then clinging, touching and holding, crying, and standing near are just about the only stress-related attachment behaviors available to the child. But as language becomes more skillful, she becomes able to stay in touch with the adults and peers around her in new ways. She can call to her mother, "Mommy are you still there?" or she can ask for attention: "Hey Dad, come and see my picture." The attachment may be no less strong, but it can be maintained in a greater variety of ways and at greater physical distances. So the child's world broadens both because she can move around so much better and because her language and cognitive skills make it possible for her to move around and still stay in contact.

The new language and cognitive skills, and the increased encounters with the world that go with them, also clearly have some impact on the child's developing self-concept and sex-role identity. The child now understands that there is a "self," a continuing physical entity. And she can now understand the things that other people say about her, the gender labels that are used, and the comments others make about her skills and difficulties. This information, along with her own explorations and conclusions about herself, all enter into the developing self-concept.

All of these changes make significant new demands on the relationship with the parents. The parents must adjust to a child who is demanding far greater independence and who may *appear* to be far less attached to or interested in being near the parents. Aggression among peers increases, and the child may begin to express her displeasure toward the parent with aggression. I am reluctant to mention the "terrible twos," but this phrase—passed on from one generation of parents to the next—has some basis in fact. Children of this age may be significantly more difficult to handle or relate to than is an 8-month-old or even an 18-month-old. So, new adjustments must be worked out between parent and child.

As I mentioned earlier, this set of problems, or "crises" to use Erikson's terms, is ordinarily faced and surmounted by about age 5 or

6. Freud, too, thought that this phase of development, the phallic period with its Oedipal crisis, was completed or partially resolved by age 5 or 6. So once again a new equilibrium in the child's relationship with the parents is achieved. A new cognitive equilibrium is achieved at about this point as well. The child has pushed the preoperational skills about as far as they can take her. She has a good working system, but has still to develop the next and more powerful set of cognitive skills, the concrete operations.

With the emergence of "operations" and the beginning of school, there is yet another shift.

6 YEARS TO 12 YEARS

The summary information about this period is in Table 15. There is a good deal of argument among psychologists about whether major cognitive advances occur at about age 6 or 7 because the child starts school, or whether children all over the world start school at about this age because they are then cognitively "ready" for the experience of school. But regardless of the direction of the causality, the two events coincide in our culture, and there is a new surge of development of important cognitive skills and a parallel major change in the child's social and interpersonal patterns. Again, these changes have profound effects on both the cognitive and familial equilibrium achieved during the previous phase.

In the cognitive domain the changes are really massive. There is very good evidence now that there is a kind of "marriage" of language and thought at this age. The child is now able to *use* language effec-

The school-age child.

TABLE 15
Summary of Development: 6 to 12 years

Physical growth	Perceptual development	Language
Rate of physical growth slowed down No major neurological changes	Not much happening in perceptual development at this age Constancies all present	Some improvement in language, but no major changes Language now used in cognition

tively in her thought. She uses language to help her remember things and to solve new problems. In addition to this new role of language in the child's thought, there are the very substantial changes in the level of abstraction of which the child is now capable. With the development of concrete operations, the child is able to analyze, compare, sort, put into order, add, subtract, multiply, and divide experiences, objects, or events. The availability of these *mental operations* makes possible not only specific learning, such as mathematics, but changes the way in which the child relates to the world around her.

Schooling seems to accelerate this process by focusing the child's attention on abstractions, particularly through reading. Before school age and outside school the child talks mostly about things that are right in front of her. But in school the emphasis is heavily on telling rather than on showing, on describing in abstract rather than concrete terms. And as the child learns to read, whole new worlds of experience are opened to her. She can come to "know" things she has never directly experienced.

As I have mentioned before, children who do not attend school appear to develop some features of concrete operations, although their development seems to be somewhat slower than is typical of children attending school. But school seems to be necessary for the development of the ability to *generalize* from one experience to the next.

The beginning of schooling disrupts the parent-child equilibrium as well. Not only does the child now spend far less time with the parents than before, but she also may begin to make new demands for independence. Our society considers the beginning of schooling as a mark of maturity; the 6-year-old is usually thought to be entitled to certain

Cognition	Interpersonal relationships	Self-concept and morality
Major shift in cognitive skill: beginning of concrete operations	Schooling begins, which means a major change in the relationship with parents	Self-image already nearly fully formed at age 6
Child now able to deal with abstractions, can use inductive logic	New demands made on child by parents, and new demands on parents made by child	Moral development has reached about stage 2 of Kohlberg's system by age 12: child takes intention of person into account in judging morality
No consistent sex differences at this age	Same-sex peer groups dominate peer relationships	
	Role of peers paramount	
	Boys still more aggressive	
	No other consistent sex differences	

additional privileges. At the same time the parents begin to have new expectations for their child. They want her to do well in school, to learn to read and to acquire other specific skills, and there are frequently expectations that the school-age child will help around the home more than before. So there are new demands on both sides—for greater independence on the part of the child and for more responsibility on the part of the parents. This is the period Erikson refers to as the "industry versus inferiority" crisis; the child must face and master the whole new range of skills demanded by society and by the parents.

Having recently gone through this "crisis" with my youngest child, I can attest to the renewed levels of stress that develop between parent and child. The 5-year-old is often an extremely easy child to have around because the parent and child have developed a good working system. But the beginning of school disrupts that, and a whole new system must now be worked out. Over the period of the elementary school school years, another equilibrium is developed between parent and child, so that by age 11 or 12, again, there is likely to be a fairly decent working system. During this time the child is achieving another cognitive equilibrium with the development of the full range of concrete operations.

AGE 12 AND OVER

As you can see from Table 16, two major changes usher in this new phase of disequilibrium: the physical changes of puberty and the cognitive changes of formal operations. There is no obvious link between these two changes. No psychologist that I know has suggested that formal operations occurs *because* of the hormonal changes associated

TABLE 16
Summary of Development: 12 years and over

Physical development	Perceptual development	Language
Puberty is the major physical change Secondary sex characteristics develop, and there is a sharp spurt in physical growth generally Sexual maturity achieved	Nothing very interesting is happening at this time	A few new refinements in language but nothing very interesting here either

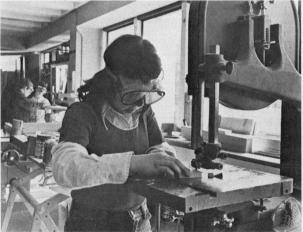

Adolescence.
The child is preparing for both new occupational and interpersonal roles.

Cognition	Interpersonal relationships	Self-concept and morality
A major new cognitive level is achieved by *some* children Not all children achieve formal operations Formal operations includes deductive logic, systematic exploration and experimentation and advanced classification skills Boys now consistently better at spatial skills and somewhat better at math reasoning Girls somewhat more verbal	Hormonal changes of puberty help shift focus away from same-sex groups to opposite-sex groups and then opposite-sex pairs This is Erikson's stage of "identity versus role confusion" Wide ranging new personal demands on the child within the peer group from parents and from society Few sex differences even now Girls somewhat less confident of success Boys still more aggressive and dominant	Self-image may undergo special stress at this age, particularly for late-maturing children In Kohlberg's system stages 3 to 6 of moral judgment may be achieved during adolescence and young adulthood

with puberty. That all of us go through puberty without all of us achieving full formal operations suggests that there can be no very intimate connection between the two events. But the fact that the two occur together in many cases has the effect of creating disequilibrium for the child on two fronts simultaneously, and this in turn creates new difficulties not only for the child in relating to her peers, but also within the family.

The most noticeable changes at this age are the changes associated with puberty. Since I have described these in Chapter 5, I needn't go into them here in detail. But there are marked changes in body size and in secondary sex characteristics. The child achieves the outward signs of physical maturity, and with apparent maturity go new demands. Parents expect more responsible behavior, better judgment, and more planning. The child faces occupational choices toward the end of high school, and perhaps most importantly, the child faces enormous changes in relationships with peers. There is a gradual shift away from same-sex peer groups toward heterosexual pairings. This shift is accompanied by anxiety and distress for many teenagers.

The cognitive advances occurring at the same time for most teenagers make it possible for the child to bring new logical skill to bear on problems, but may also produce new stresses within the family. The 14-year-old no longer accepts the parents' justification for rules and regulations; she wants the rules explained and wants a say in family decisions—particularly decisions that affect her. The emerging sexual interests of teenagers may also arouse anxiety in the parents, so new rules or restrictions may be imposed just at the time when the child is expecting greater independence. Once again, the old parent-child equilibrium is disrupted and a new relationship must be established over the next years.

<table>
<tr><td>OVERVIEW</td><td>

One difficulty in trying to tie together the myriad threads of development, as I am sure you have already found, is that there is no single adequate theory of development. Freud and Erikson described some aspects of interpersonal development; Piaget has described cognitive development in great detail. The three men have observed similar critical periods, but the fact that important things seem to happen in different developmental domains at approximately the same time doesn't tell us *why*. How does neurological maturation fit into the picture? Are all the big changes really triggered by some kind of neurological change? At 2 months, at 6 months, and perhaps even at 18 months we might buy such a hypothesis, but what about the very large set of changes between ages 5 and 7? There is no important physical change at that time that I know of, so why is there a major cognitive change? At puberty there are obvious hormonal and physical changes, but do they trigger the cognitive changes that occur at the same time?

</td></tr>
</table>

The framework I have suggested for making sense of some of what happens does not deal with this sort of question either. I have argued that we can think of development in terms of surges or periods of disequilibrium, followed by periods of equilibrium. Descriptively, this makes fairly good sense for cognitive and physical development. The concepts of disequilibrium and equilibrium, I think, also help to make sense of the relationships between parent and child over the developmental period. But notice that the specific event or series of events that triggers the next phase of disequilibrium changes over time. In the early years it seems to be primarily physical changes (neurological changes and accompanying motor maturity) that trigger new relationships with adults and with the world around. But physical changes are not invariably the trigger; some social changes, such as schooling, and some internal changes in the child's cognition seem also to make shifts from an equilibrium to a disequilibrium state. So the framework I have suggested does not tell you how the several threads of development are causally related to one another any more precisely than do theories such as Piaget's or Erikson's. We are left with the obvious (but not very helpful) conclusion that developmental changes have multiple causes, and that physical growth, cognitive growth based on experience, and changes in interpersonal relationships influence visible shifts and changes. But we are a long way from charting the complex interactions among them.

404

Another way to approach the problem of synthesizing all facets of development is to search for general principles or trends that may at least describe the development process more coherently.

Heinz Werner, for example, has defined development as a process of increasing differentiation and hierarchic integration. If the growth of the individual child—physically, cognitively, emotionally—is a development process, we should see signs of such increasing differentiation or hierarchic organization. And we do. The child's language development shows both: She has more new words for more precise things and at the same time she has new superordinate words, which describe the hierarchic relationship among things. So a child may acquire the words *collie, poodle,* and *beagle*—a differentiation process—and also learn that the words *dog* or *animal* apply to all of them, which is a hierarchical concept. The development of classification skills shows the same two aspects.

Piaget emphasizes another important dimension of development, the gradual decentering of the child. I discussed the concept of egocentrism in Chapter 9 in connection with the preoperational child. But egocentrism is not the exclusive property of the child from 2 to 5 years; younger infants are still more egocentric, and egocentrism is only gradually lost over the entire span of development. The child gradually comes to be able to look at the world from perspectives other than her own, to step away from the center of herself, and to consider the views and feelings of others. This a slow process, beginning with the newborn infant's complete confusion of self and other, and ending in the formal operational child's ability to empathize with others, to put herself in someone else's emotional shoes.

Still a third theme that runs through development is the shift from dependence to independence. Obviously, there is a marked shift in the child's interpersonal relationships, from reliance on others toward more independence and more autonomy of movement. We often think of this shift as taking place mostly during the early years, when the child begins to insist on doing things for herself, but a similar shift can be seen again in adolescence, when she may demand a new level of autonomy. In cognitive development, too, a shift toward autonomy can be seen perhaps most vividly in the change from concrete to formal operations. Roughly between ages 7 and 12 the child shifts from reliance on the concrete, the physically present, to the ability to think about thinking. The formal operational child becomes much more independent of specific experiences and is able to function deductively.

Although unitary concepts like the three I have described do not explain development in any final sense, they do help us to describe it more systematically and to maintain some sense of the wholeness of the process.

Two final points are worth emphasizing. First, I find it intriguing to note that the *length* of each of the periods or phases of equilibrium and disequilibrium increases with each period. It is possible that this is merely the result of my selection of periods to discuss, but I don't think that is the explanation. I suspect that each new phase involves more and more complex processes, and each time it takes the child longer to arrive at a new level of synthesis or equilibrium. It may take the family longer in each case, too, to arrive at an interpersonal equilibrium. The period of family stress may get longer each time; certainly many families report that the stress associated with adolescence lasts for several years, while the earlier problems associated with the beginning of school may last 6 months or a year. What I am suggesting is that at each new level, the complexity of the relationships—both the cognitive and the personal relationships—increases, so the time to work them out increases as well.

Second, while the sequence of phases or stages I have described is the same for most children, the *rate* of development may vary widely. Mentally retarded children, for example, go through all the changes more slowly. They are slower to change in their personal relationships as well as in cognitive development. The assignment of age levels to the various shifts and changes is intended to indicate only the *most typical* ages; clustered around the typical age there is a whole range of possible ages in a group of normal children. As we move up the developmental sequence, the range of ages within which normal development occurs becomes broader. The shift from preoperational to concrete operational thought may occur anywhere from age 4 to about age 8; but the range of normal variation for the emergence of formal operations may be from perhaps age 10 to age 16 or 18. So the rate of development varies widely even while the developmental sequence appears to remain largely the same.

REFERENCES

Suggested Additional Readings

As most of the material discussed in this chapter has been covered in greater detail elsewhere with references provided, there is little to add here. There are only a few books and articles that attempt to deal with the full range of changes in any integrated way.

Dragastin, S. E., & Elder, G. H., Jr. (Eds.). *Adolescence in the life cycle.* New York: Halstead Press (Wiley), 1975.
This collection of readings may be useful to those of you interested in the period of adolescence. It contains some good overviews, which help to synthesize the information about the adolescent years.

Rappoport, L. *Personality development: The chronology of experience.* Glenview, Ill.: Scott, Foresman & Co., 1972.
If you are looking for a good text organized around specific ages rather than discussing topics as I have in this book, Rappoport's book is an excellent place to start. Although he does not *integrate* the different aspects of development at any one age as well as one might hope (but then who does?), he covers each age range thoroughly. Well written, easy to read.

White, S. H. Evidence for a hierarchical arrangement of learning processes. In L. P. Lipsitt & C. C. Spiker (Eds.), *Advances in child devel-*

opment and behavior (Vol. 2). New York: Academic Press, 1965.

Now somewhat out-of-date, this paper may nonetheless give you some feeling for the complexities of attempting to integrate several aspects of development at the same time period. White focuses on the period from 5 to 7 and analyzes the several types of changes, particularly in cognition and perception. Difficult reading, but excellent.

Other Sources Cited

Karmel, B. Z., & Maisel, E. B. A neuronal activity model for infant visual attention. In L. B. Cohen & P. Salapatek (Eds.), *Infant perception: From sensation to cognition. Vol. II. Basic Visual Processes.* New York: Academic Press, 1975.

Uzgiris, I. C. Patterns of cognitive development in infancy. *Merrill-Palmer Quarterly*, 1973, *19*, 181–204.

Name Index

Italic numbers refer to end-of-chapter reference section entries.

MacFarlane, J. W., 42, *49*, 254, 260, *264*
McGraw, M. C., 115, *131*
McIntire, R. W., 159, *176*
McNeill, D., 167, *176*
McReynolds, P., *49*
Madden, J., *264*
Maisel, E. B., 391, *407*
Maratsos, M. P., 171, *176*
Marolla, F., 67, 77
Masters, J. C., 297, 316, *318*
May, M. S., *359*
Meadow, K. P., 189, *191*, 381, *386*
Milgram, S., 357
Miller, N. E., 297
Miller, W. C., 378, *386*
Miranda, S. B., 144–145, *153*
Mischel, W., 26, 331, 332, 333, 334, *338*
Moerk, E. L., 184, *191*
Moore, M. K., 137, *153*
Moore, T., 159, *176*
Morgan, G. A., *231*
Mosher, F. A., 220–221, *231*
Moss, A., *230*, *264*
Moss, H. A., 19, *29*, 35, 42, *49*, 94, *105*, 275–276, 285, *298*
Mowrer, O. H., 297, 342
Moyle, W. J., *78*
Mundy-Castle, A. C., 140–141
Mussen, P. H., 5, *49*, 54, *103*, 128, *130*, *152*, 167, *176*, 297, *318*, *338*, *360*, *386*
Muzio, J. N., 90, *105*

Neimark, E. D., *229*
Nelson, K., 159–161, 170, *175*, 183, *191*, 208–209, *231*
Niswander, K. R., *387*

Oden, M. H., 42, *49*
O'Donnell, M., 328
O'Leary, S., 294, *298*
Olver, R. R., 215, 219, *229*, *230*, *231*
Opper, S., *29*, *229*
Osser, H., 180, *191*
Ottinger, D. R., 64, *78*

Palermo, D. S., 171, *176*
Pallus, J., *78*
Parke, R., 294, *298*
Patterson, G. R., *49*

Pavlov, I. P., 12
Pawsat, R., 81, *104*
Pederson, F. A., 99, *105*, *231*
Phillips, J. R., 184, *191*
Phillips, W., 147, *153*
Piaget, J., 20, 22–23, 25, 26, 27, 28, *29*, 36–38, 88, 143, 195, 196, 197–198, 199, 201, 202, 204, 205, 206, 208, 209, 213, 214, 216, 220, 221, 222, 223, 224–225, 226, 228, *229*, *230*, 239, 242–243, 244, 302, 307, 316, 341, 349–352, *359*, *360*, 392, 404, 405
Pick, A. D., *152*
Pick, H. L., *152*
Potter, E. L., 54

Ragozin, A., 279, *298*
Ramey, C. T., 64, *78*
Rappoport, L., 306, 309, *318*, 406
Rau, L., 343, 345, *360*
Reed, V., 77
Reese, H. W., *230*
Reid, J. B., *49*
Rheingold, H. L., *105*
Ribble, M. A., 98, *104*
Ricciuti, H. N., 65, *78*, 296, *318*
Richardson, S. A., 65, *78*
Ripple, R., *29*, *229*
Robey, J. S., 117, *131*
Robinson, H. B., *386*
Robinson, N. M., *386*
Rockcastle, V., *29*, *229*
Roe, K. V., 158, *176*
Roffwarg, H. P., 90, *105*
Rosen, B. M., *387*
Rosenblum, L. A., 297, *298*, *319*
Rosenkrantz, P. S., *338*
Rosman, B. L., *153*
Ross, D., 286
Ross, S. A., 286
Rubenstein, J., 99, *105*, *231*
Rugh, R., 77
Ruppenthal, G. C., 37, *49*
Rutter, M., 372–373, *386*

Saario, T. N., *338*
Sackett, C. P., 37, *49*
Sacks, E., 258, *264*

Saenger, G., 67, *71*
Salapatek, P. H., 87, *103*, 143, 149, *152*, *153*, *407*
Sameroff, A. J., 77
Scarr-Salapatek, S., 247, *264*
Schaffer, H. R., 93, *105*, 270, 271, 272, 274, 277, 279, 280, *298*, 302
Schantz, C. V., *230*
Scheinfeld, A., 151, *153*
Schlesinger, H. S., 189, *191*, 381, *386*
Schribner, S., *230*
Scott, R. B., 117, *131*
Sears, R. R., 24, 34, 281, 287, 297, *298*, 315, 343, 345, 360
Seitz, V., 265
Sheldon, W. H., 126, *131*
Sheridan, M. D., 61, *78*
Shettles, L., 77
Simon, T., 239, 240, 242, *264*
Simonian, K., *78*
Singer, J. E., 383, 384, *387*
Skeels, H. M., 253–255, *264*, 368
Skinner, B. F., 181, *191*
Slaby, R. G., 335–336, *338*
Slobin, D. I., 169, 180, 183, *191*
Smith, H. T., *103*
Smith, M. B., 357, *360*
Smith, M. E., 162, *176*
Spiker, C. C., 48, *153*, *406*
Starr, R. H., *78*
Stayton, D. J., 277, 278–279, 297
Stein, A. H., 290, 297
Stein, Z., 66, 67, 68, 77
Stendler, F., *29*
Stephenson, E., 37, *49*
Steritt, G. M., *231*
Stern, D. N., 269, *298*
Stevenson, H. W., *105*, *153*, *230*
Stodolsky, E., 173, *176*
Stone, L. J., *103*
Streissguth, A. P., *104*
Sudia, C. E., 309, *318*
Susser, M., 67, 77

Takaishi, M., 109
Tanner, J. M., 109, 121, 122, 123, *131*
Terman, L., 42, *49*

Subject Index

Reinforcement
   of aggression on TV, 288–290
   and crying in babies, 278–279
   schedules of, 16–17, 281, 287
   theory of language development, 181–184
Rejection from parents, and aggression, 287
Research methods, 31–49
   clinical method, 36–39
   correlational techniques, 44–45, 62, 64
   in developmental psychology, special
      problems of, 41–42
   experimental procedures, 39–41, 45–46
   good and bad, 46–48
   interpretation of data from, 43–46
   laboratory vs. real life, 45–46, 289
   normative, 26
   observational techniques, 32–37, 50–51
Reversibility, development of concept of,
      206–207
Rooting reflex, 84
Rubella, 60–61

Schema
   Kagan's concept of, 145
   Piaget's concept of, 198
Schizophrenia. *See* Emotional disturbance
School
   effect on cognitive development, 223, 400
   impact of beginning of, 399–400
   performance, and self-esteem, 324
   for physically handicapped children, 380–382
   for retarded children, 369–370
   sex-role stereotyping in, 327
School-age child, overview of, 399–401. *See also*
      Concrete operations period; Latency stage
Self-concept, 321–328
   developmental patterns of, 322–323
   individual differences in, 323–326
   and rate of physical maturing, 127–128
   sex differences in, 326–328
   social class differences in, 326–327
Semantic development, 169–172
Sensorimotor stage of development, 199–204.
      See also Infancy, overview of
Sequences of development
   author's bias toward, 27
   in cognitive development, 204–224
   in development of attachment, 270–273
   in development of sex-roles, 328–330
   Erikson's stages, 313–319
   importance during prenatal period, 58–59
   in moral development, 349–357
   psychosexual stages, Freud's view of, 305–310
Sex differences
   at adolescence, 108, 109

in aggression, 285, 294–295
in attachment and dependency, 276, 294
in atypical development, 383–384
in cognitive development, 228
in infancy, 94, 100–101
on IQ test scores, 262
in language development, 172–173
in perceptual development, 150–151
in physical growth, 108–109, 128–129
in prenatal development, 73–74
in self-esteem, 326–328
Sex-role, development of, 328–330
   theories of, 330–336
Sexual differentiation during prenatal develop-
      ment, 58
Sleeping, patterns of, in infancy, 90–91, 92
Smell, sense of, at birth, 82–84
Smile, and attachment in infants, 270–271,
      303–304
Social class differences
   in atypical development, 384
   and cognitive development, 226
   in infants, 101–102
   in interpersonal relationships, 295
   in IQ test scores, 245, 246, 247–248
   in language development, 173–175
   in perceptual development, 151
   in physical development, 129
   and prenatal complications, 74–75
Socialization. *See* Parent-child interaction
Social learning theory, 24–25, 181–184,
      313–316, 331–333, 342–343
Specimen description, 32, 50–51. *See also* Ob-
      servation
Sperm cells, 4
Stanford-Binet Test of Intelligence, 239–241
Sucking reflex, 85
Superego and moral development, 352
Swallowing reflex, 85
Symbols, development of, 204
Syphilis, effect of on prenatal development, 61

Taste, sense of, in infants, 84
Television
   effects on aggression, 288–290
   and sex-role sterotypes, 327–328
Temperament
   effects on attachment patterns, 278
   individual differences in, in infants, 91–94
   and parent-infant relationships, 94
Thalidomide, effect on prenatal development,
      63
Theories of development, 20–26
   cognitive-developmental theory, 22–24,
      196–198, 316–317, 333–336, 349–357

77 78 79 80 9 8 7 6 5 4 3 2 1